MW00785233

Teaching About Social Justice Issues in Physical Education

A Volume in:
Social Issues in Education Series

Series Editor

Todd S. Hawley

Social Issues in Education Series

Series Editor

Todd S. Hawley
Kent State University

Teaching About Social Justice Issues in Physical Education (2019)
Jennifer L. Walton-Fisette, Sue Sutherland, & Joanne Hill

Teaching About Social Justice Issues in Physical Education

Edited by

Jennifer L. Walton-Fisette
Sue Sutherland
Joanne Hill

INFORMATION AGE PUBLISHING, INC.
Charlotte, NC • www.infoagepub.com

Library of Congress Cataloging-In-Publication Data

The CIP data for this book can be found on the Library of Congress website (loc.gov).

Paperback: 978-1-64113-719-5
Hardcover: 978-1-64113-720-1
E-Book: 978-1-64113-721-8

Copyright © 2019 Information Age Publishing Inc.

All rights reserved. No part of this publication may be reproduced, stored in a retrieval system, or transmitted, in any form or by any means, electronic, mechanical, photocopying, microfilming, recording or otherwise, without written permission from the publisher.

Printed in the United States of America

CONTENTS

PART III

CURRICULUM DEVELOPMENT: WHAT ARE THE POSSIBILITIES?

DEDICATION

To Theresa: For questioning and challenging me to be socially just in all aspects of my life.

—Jen

To Aiden: Keep fighting for what you believe; you will make a difference.

—Sue

To Beatrix: Keep asking "but why?"

—Joanne

To all those doing social justice work who have paved the way and for those of you who are about to take part in the journey.

INTRODUCTION

Physical Education Is a Social Justice Issue

Jennifer L. Walton-Fisette

We strongly believe that physical education is a social justice issue. This has been supported and argued by scholars in physical education, such as Bain (1975, 1990), Dodds (1985), Kirk (1986), Evans (1993), Fernandez-Balboa (1993, 1997) and Tinning (2002). More recently, Robinson and Randall (2016) compiled a theoretically-rich book that centered on social justice issues in physical education; Azzarito and colleagues (2017) called attention to revitalizing the social justice agenda—an agenda that may have remained hidden, dormant or ignored for decades, and a special issue in the journal of *Physical Education and Sport Pedagogy* (Walton-Fisette & Sutherland, 2018) focused on social justice issues in Physical Education Teacher Education. Consistent across all of this scholarship, was the consideration of the historical, political and social contexts, along with the social identities and lived experiences of future physical education teachers and primary and secondary students. Furthermore, the dominant message was that we, physical educators, must explicitly address and educate our students about and for social justice, at the primary, secondary and higher education levels.

The realities accompanied by the shifting demographic landscape in schools throughout our global society, lead to numerous questions that the physical education community may need to consider as we attempt to teach for and about social

Teaching About Social Justice Issues in Physical Education, pages ix–xii.
Copyright © 2019 by Information Age Publishing
All rights of reproduction in any form reserved.

justice: How are we, physical educators, addressing these changing demographics in our society? How do these demographic changes inform our curriculum, instruction and assessment practices? The standards and grade-level outcomes that we employ? Policies that are being enacted at the national, province and/or state level? What steps are we taking to make our programs more socially just and to educate our students about social identities, social inequalities and social justice? We do not have the answers to all of these questions; however, the purpose of this book is an attempt to respond to the last question—to provide Physical Education Teacher Educators (PETEs) and primary and secondary physical education (PE) teachers with content knowledge and pedagogical practices that specifically address social justice issues in a physical education setting.

BOOK ORGANIZATION

The purpose of this book is to provide PETEs and PE teachers with tangible lessons and activities that can be implemented into your classes. The chapters are connected to research and sometimes theory; however, practical application of social justice content is emphasized in each of the chapters. The book is divided into three parts:

- Part I—Knowledge Construction of Social Justice Issues
- Part II—Social Justice Issues: Strategies and Lessons in Physical Education
- Part III—Curriculum Development: What are the Possibilities?

Before describing each of these sections, it is important to inform you that the use of the English language is not consistent across the chapters. We believe it is important to retain the author(s) usage of the English language in their country of origin. Furthermore, the chapters are short in nature with the hope to guide you with the most salient content and methods needed to employ these activities and lessons. Another point to note, is that these chapters do not address all social justice issues, nor do the chapters in Part II provide an exhaustive list of strategies and lessons on the identified social issue. Our hope is that we have provided a valuable resource to PETEs and PE teachers on how to begin or continue your work on teaching about and for social justice.

Part I—Knowledge Construction of Social Justice Issues is comprised of two chapters, which focus on transformative pedagogy and action research. Transformative pedagogy frames the pedagogical practices that are emphasized in the strategies and lessons chapters in Part II. The action research chapter provides a process that will allow us, teachers, to explore our own beliefs, experiences and current teaching practices as we consider engaging in different or new pedagogies in our attempt to address social justice issues.

Part II—Social Justice Issues: Strategies and Lessons in Physical Education comprises the majority of the chapters in this book. The social justice issues addressed in this chapter are: Self-identity, Body, (Dis)ability, English Language Learners (ELL), Gender, Indigenous, Race, Religion, Sexual Identity, Social Class and Bullying. There are two chapters included for each social issue (except for bullying and indigenous); one chapter is specific to PETE and the other focuses on primary/secondary PE. It is in this section that we cannot and did not provide all of the possibilities that could be explored, taught and addressed at each level for each social issue. We acknowledge that collectively, it may provide a limiting perspective on each of the issues, but we believe we will have the opportunity to build upon and expand on the valuable chapters that are included in this book. Unlike Parts I and III, a template was utilized in the development of these chapters to offer some consistency. The sections include:

- Action Research and Reflection
- Context
- Unit/Lesson Set Up
- Strategy/Activity/Lesson
- Intersectionalities (if applicable)
- Challenges and Possibilities
- References/Resources

When engaging in social justice work, it is important to participate in reflective practice and to consider the context in which the experience—in this instance, teaching lesson, occurs. Both the action research and reflection and context sections relate to Chapter 2. Often times, when attending a conference or obtaining a lesson idea from the internet or textbook, we are left to figure out how the lesson is set up or designed before implementation can occur. We know that planning and preparing are both critical in the execution and outcome of a lesson. The strategy/activity/lesson is the central component of each of the chapters in this section. Figures and appendices are included to provide additional content and resources. Quite often, social justice issues are not addressed in isolation, rather, they often intersect with other social justice issues (e.g., gender and sexuality). We have asked authors to include how the specified social issue may intersect with other social justice issues if applicable. We acknowledge that educating others about social justice issues can be challenging, uncomfortable or expose more questions than answers. That is why we asked the authors to include the challenges that they have encountered and those that you may experience, as well as the possibilities that may result from teaching this particular social justice lesson. The chapters conclude with a list of references and resources.

Part III—Curriculum Development: What are the Possibilities? focuses on how we may address social justice issues across the curriculum, beyond the individual lesson plan. The first chapter provides an overview of considerations and possibilities. The last two chapters emphasize a particular curriculum model that can and has been implemented to teach about social issues. The authors explore the process of how this can be done.

Collectively, we hope that this book is a valuable resource for you as you teach for social justice in physical education. We acknowledge and understand that you may only be interested in certain chapters, because they align with your beliefs, experiences, standards or curriculum. Each chapter has been written to stand on its own even though we attempted to have consistency across the chapters in Part II. Throughout this process, we have learned from the chapter authors and hope you enhance your knowledge and pedagogical practices as well. We also hope that we continue to engage in social justice work and intentionally seek to educate our students about and for social justice.

CONTRIBUTING AUTHORS

Alan Ovens	University of Auckland, NZ	a.ovens@auckland.ac.nz
Alexandra Baird	University of Bedfordshire, UK	alexandra.baird@beds.ac.uk
Ali Brian	University of South Carolina, USA	brianali@mailbox.sc.edu
Brian Culp	Kennesaw State University, USA	bculp1@kennesaw.edu
Carla Luguetti	University of Victoria, AUS	Carla.NascimentoLuguetti@vu.edu.au
Charlotte Shipley	Positive Space Consulting, CAN	charlar47@gmail.com
Daniel B. Robinson	St. Francis Xavier University, CAN	drobinso@stfx.ca
Eimear Enright	University of Queensland, AUS	e.enright@uq.edu.au
Jason Arday	University of Roehampton, UK	Jason.Arday@roehampton.ac.uk
Jennifer L. Walton-Fisette	Kent State University, USA	jfisette@kent.edu
Joanna Sweeney	Hounslow Heath Infant and Nursery School, UK	Joanna.Sweeney@HHIN.org
Joanne Hill	University of Bedfordshire, UK	Joanne.Hill.beds.ac.uk
Julie Fimusanmi	Leeds Beckett University, UK	J.Fimusanmi@leedsbeckett.ac.uk
Karen Shelley	University of Queensland, AUS	k.shelley@uq.edu.au
Kate Jadis	St. Francis Xavier University, CAN	jadis_kate@hotmail.com
Kimberly L. Oliver	University of New Mexico, USA	koliver@nmsu.edu
Leanne Coll	Deakin University, AUS	leanne.coll@deakin.edu.au
Leigh Sperka	University of Queensland, AUS	l.sperka@uq.edu.au
Louise McCuaig	University of Queensland, AUS	l.mccuaig@uq.edu.au

Lynn Randall	University of New Brunswick, CAN	lrandall@unb.ca
Mara Simon	Springfield College, USA	msimon3@springfield.edu
Michelle Flemons	Lincroft Academy, UK	mflemons@lincroft.beds.sch.uk
Rachael Harrison	The Get REAL Movement, CAN	rc220118@dal.ca
Rachel O'Brien	University of Sydney, AUS	rsch4284@uni.sydney.edu.au
Rod Philpot	University of Auckland, NZ	r.philpot@auckland.ac.nz
Sally Taunton Miedema	University of South Carolina, USA	staunton@email.sc.edu
Samantha Zanini	St. Francis Xavier University, CAN	x2009ije@stfx.ca
Sara B. Flory	University of South Florida, USA	sbflory@usf.edu
Sarah Hill	Hounslow Heath Infant and Nursery School, UK	
Shrehan Lynch	University of East London, UK	s.lynch@uel.ac.uk
Sue Sutherland	Ohio State University, USA	sutherland.43@osu.edu

PART I

KNOWLEDGE CONSTRUCTION
OF SOCIAL JUSTICE ISSUES

CHAPTER 1

FIVE PRINCIPLES OF TRANSFORMATIVE PEDAGOGIES IN PETE

Rod Philpot and Alan Ovens

Enacting a transformative pedagogy in physical education teacher education (PETE) requires teacher educators to simultaneously and flexibly juggle institutional policies, professional accreditation standards, program expectations, resource limitations and student receptivity. Theoretically, it involves accommodating the relational, distributive and participative aspects of social justice in respect to advocacy for equitable distribution of access to educational services and to outcomes, recognizing social and cultural difference, acknowledging and valuing the diversity of students we teach (Cochran-Smith, 2009). Transformative pedagogy should enable students to actively participate in decision making as a form of embodied action (North, 2008). Enacting a transformative pedagogy is by no means an easy task.

In this chapter we propose five principles that may help teacher educators manage this complexity and guide them with their own efforts towards enacting a transformative pedagogy. We propose that transformative pedagogies require embodied awareness, a focus on diversity, the enactment of democratic principles including student voice, active questioning of your own practice, and a critique of the mechanisms of oppression. Although individual teaching practices may

Teaching About Social Justice Issues in Physical Education, pages 3–11.
Copyright © 2019 by Information Age Publishing
All rights of reproduction in any form reserved.

3

align more strongly with individual principles, we stress that the ability to enact a transformative pedagogy lies in the consideration of, and complex multi-layered relationship (Ovens, 2017a) between all principles. In the following discussion we firstly examine the concept of transformative pedagogies before outlining the five principles that underpin this concept.

TRANSFORMATIVE PEDAGOGY

Ukpokodu (2009) suggests that transformative learning occurs when a person develops an awareness of their habits of mind, develops new viewpoints and perspectives, and comes to see some aspect of the world in a different way. The process of transformational learning relies on pedagogies that move away from knowledge transmission and toward communicative learning where a learner searches for meaning through reflecting on values, social norms, and assumptions through which a truth claim is made (Mezirow, 2009). Mezirow calls for transformative learning opportunities (pedagogies) that challenge taken-for-granted frames of reference and open these frames for possible change.

When we apply this to the context of PETE, transformative pedagogies enact teaching approaches that enable PETE students to examine the educational, moral, and political influences that guide their work as professional teachers, encourage reflective thinking, and foster dispositions for social justice (Ukpokodu, 2009). Transformative pedagogy must cater for both personal and social change (Tinning, 2019). While personal change does not guarantee social change, it is difficult to envision any social change in PE without personal change in teachers.

It is important here to stress that transformative pedagogies are not generic and enacted by using some pre-set strategies. Referring specifically to the context of PE/PETE, Tinning (2017) described transformative pedagogy as an "educational perspective" that concerns itself with questions of justice, democracy and ethics (Tinning, 2017). The important point here is Tinning's use of the word 'perspective'. Rather than a teaching strategy, a perspective is a particular attitude that guides professional decision making and actions. In other words, the practice of transformative pedagogy embodies and is guided by principles designed to promote equity and social justice rather than enact some teaching strategies that have proven successful in some educational context. There is no single transformative pedagogy or model waiting to be discovered (Walton-Fisette, et al, 2018).

In the following section we outline a small but powerful set of principles that can guide teacher educators through the complexity of their individual contexts. Transformative practices will always be woven around the context of the practice, the learners and the breadth and scope of a PETE program (Ovens, 2017a, Philpot, 2016). While implementing these principles requires a commitment in time and effort, they also cannot be reduced to a teaching method that is learned through transmission and then enacted with no consideration of the teacher, learner, and context (Friere, 1970; Ovens, 2017b). Rather, the principles help teacher educators to be adaptive and willing to challenge the status quo in the quest to find those novel and innovative solutions that are effective in their own settings.

PRINCIPLE 1: PROVOKE UNDERSTANDING THROUGH AN EMBODIED AWARENESS

This principle is based on the fundamental point that we are bodies and that we experience the world through an embodied consciousness. Experiences of discrimination, oppression and social injustice are not only evidenced by visible divisions of resources or opportunities, but are embodied by the individual as emotions, memories, feelings and bodily restrictions. In fact, our bodies are deeply implicated in all aspects of human experience since they are the means for making sense of and making connections with a world in which they co-participate in creating (Macintyre, Latta, & Buck, 2008). The implication is that teachers need to be sensitive to the corporeal and sensual nature of how people know and learn, so they can actively provide meaningful, real and profound learning experiences that shape the embodied learner in an ethical way.

Provoking an embodied awareness involves learning activities that provide sensual experiences. In other words, it is how the learner *feels* the experience that is crucial. Transformative teaching should enable each student to feel empowered, feel emancipated, feel heard, feel respected, feel expressive, and feel creative (Ovens & Powell, 2011). It is through sensual experiences that learners feel attached and connected—to friends, to community, to teachers, to learning, to body and to self. It is also through such experiences that the desire to act, to advocate, and to seek justice is created. However, it is not only important how this is achieved, but also vital to reflect on how current practice may create the opposite feelings of being disempowered, restricted, controlled and disembodied. Included in this is becoming conscious of how our desires and need to consume are commercialized, manipulated and normalized.

Provoking an embodied awareness is enhanced through an immersion with, and meaningful connection to an authentic situation, problem or experience. We suggest teachers must be more deliberate in creating teachable moments and activities that evoke feelings, rather than them being a 'lucky', unplanned byproduct or teachable moment. We include in this the need for critical reflection and discussion on the aesthetic, pleasurable 'bodily' experiences, suggested by the likes of Booth (2009), Pringle (2010) and Ross (2008). Overall, we believe that an embodied awareness emerges through meaningful, authentic, relevant and embodied teaching and learning activities and teaching contexts.

PRINCIPLE 2: RECOGNIZE AND WORK WITH DIVERSITY

This principle is based on the belief that awareness of the diversity in communities is critical to fostering social justice. As a concept, diversity rejects the notion of a 'normal' group and 'others' and instead constitutes diversity and difference as central to the mixture of students in each lesson. Recognizing diversity extends beyond awareness to valuing diversity as a key pedagogical resource. Working with diversity includes introspectively recognizing that one's own values and beliefs define how we frame our world and the possible implications of acting on these perspectives. A lack of understanding of diversity is a barrier to teaching for social justice (Walton-Fisette et al, 2018) and PETE students need to understand diversity before they embark on developing the agency to address injustice (Ukpoduku, 2016).

Diversity encompasses many characteristics including ethnicity, socio-economic background, home language, gender, sexuality, special needs, disability, and giftedness. Teaching needs to be responsive to diversity within ethnic groups, for example, diversity within first nation's people and immigrant populations. Evidence shows teaching that is responsive to student diversity can have very positive impacts on low and high achievers at the same time. By seeing and respecting the similarities and differences among persons and cultures, the teacher can use diversity to enhance the learning within the lesson. Acknowledging other cultures and worldviews and recognizing that factors such as race, class, and culture frame how people interpret, understand, and explain others' words and actions can transform silences into productive discussions.

Social justice issues of diversity related to physical education featured in literature highlight issues of body shape (Tinning, 1985), disability (Fitzgerald, 2012), gendered bodies (Gerdin, 2016), discrimination based on sexuality (Sykes, 2011) and obesity (Burrows, 2016). Recent literature further examines how the intersectionality (see chapters in Section II) of these identities serves to privilege and oppress groups in society. The transformative pedagogical work that examines diversity such as examinations of media photographs to develop an awareness of and to challenge to dominant portrayals of gender and race (Oliver, 2001; Oliver & Kirk, 2017) and ethnicity (Legge, 2010) are explicit attempts to disrupt frames of reference and enable students to notice and name concepts they are unfamiliar with. To build on this, inclusion of diversity can come through greater inclusion of cultural activities and games (e.g., Indigenous games) and disability games (e.g., boccia, goalball), and greater critique of dominant forms of PE in schools. In addition to recognizing diversity and how it may oppress students, further work is required to provide PETE students with the pedagogical skills to address injustice.

PRINCIPLE 3: INVOLVE STUDENTS AS CO-CONTRIBUTORS TO COURSE DESIGN

This principle is based on two key notions. The first is that transformative pedagogy should employ practices that interrupt and call into question the logic underpinning existing or prevailing ways of thinking, seeing and saying. Involving students in course design in PETE disrupts the logic that they do not have a right and a responsibility for their own learning. It also respects that students should get some say given they are the recipients/users/direct beneficiaries of the course they are enrolled in. The second notion is the deliberate repositioning of the student as a subject of pedagogy. Rather than being passive consumers of course content, students are expected to harness their own capacities and engage their potentiality for developing professional skills, broadening their perspectives on teaching, considering the rationales underlying pedagogy, and assess their own developing perspectives toward teaching. By requiring students to co-contribute to course design, the students are involved in the educational process of producing a course that is meaningful, inclusive, challenging and professionally worthwhile.

This principle leads to four implications for PETE pedagogy. Firstly, it means that emancipation is the starting point and not the outcome of the course pedagogy. PETE students begin as equal participants in the pedagogical process and share the responsibility for the production of the course. Secondly, it sets up the possibility for novelty and creativity to frame course content and activities. New roles and new responsibilities allow new ways of knowing and being to emerge. Thirdly, this principle challenges the intentionality inherent in pedagogy as a vehicle for incorporating stock knowledge and particular values about teaching. Fourthly, it makes transparent the decision making central to the power and production of a course. Students can be invited to contribute to decisions such as what assignment tasks will be undertaken, how will achievement be assessed, when will work be due, and how will final grades be determined.

PRINCIPLE 4: QUESTION YOUR OWN PRACTICE

This principle is based on the notion that we (PETEs) should pay more attention to how the instructional practices and structures we use embody social justice theory. PETEs must concurrently teach about and enact social justice and social theory. The distinction between 'teaching about' and 'enacting' is subtle, but important. When the pedagogy in a course has a singular focus on teaching about social justice, the core ideas and concepts become knowledge to be learnt or absorbed by student teachers and applied in school contexts. In other words, we often see teacher educators teaching about social justice in ways where the concept becomes reduced to theory taught through a transmission pedagogy and the teaching is either telling (the lecture), modelling (the demonstration lesson or microteaching), or apprenticeship (the practicum) (Ovens, 2013). In contrast, we suggest that theory should be put into practice so that the focus shifts to examining how the core ideas and concepts central to social justice become enacted within and lived through the instructional practices and structures of the course. PETEs should consider the coherence between their advocacy for social justice pedagogies and their own pedagogical practices.

The central point of this principle is that while PETE students may be encouraged to ask critical questions *in* their teacher education courses, they are often not encouraged to ask the same question *of* their teacher education courses (Segall, 2002). A common example is the way teacher educators highlight the importance of questioning how teachers meet the individual needs of their students, but rarely do they turn this critique on themselves and ask how their own teacher education lessons meet the individual needs of their student teachers. If theory is not reflexively applied to understanding one's lived practice, the pedagogy involved becomes an exercise in separating theory from practice, while effectively disguising the process of doing so (Segall, 2002). By teaching a detached theory of social justice, power, oppression, and privilege, students are anesthetized from challenging their own education and the methods used to ensure that theory is disconnected from everyday practice because it becomes content to be learnt rather than lived (Segall, 2002).

PRINCIPLE 5: ADDRESS THE MECHANISMS AND CONSEQUENCES OF OPPRESSION.

This principle is based on the need to understand those attitudes and behaviors (e.g., racism, sexism, ageism, heterosexism) that perpetuate oppression and acknowledge the real social and economic disadvantages that oppressed people face in society. When discussing social justice in lessons or staff meetings, it is important to dismantle structures that sustain oppression and not simply focus on the psychological harm of oppression. This requires a careful examination of systems of power in conjunction with an emphasis on social change and student agency both inside and outside of the classrooms (Hackman, 2005)

The context of PE offers many examples such as oppressive language and images about body size, shape and health; oppressive teaching practices that favor able bodies or create gendered classrooms; and oppressive facilities that privilege sport over other forms of movement. A transformative pedagogy has the dual aim of drawing attention to some of these taken for granted structures (consciousness raising) and educating to enable prospective PE teachers to challenge these structures (taking action). A transformative pedagogy in PETE can illuminate examples of how PE teachers have recognized oppressive structures and worked to facilitate changes in their schools. This can be seen in the attempts of physical education to change discourses around healthism, 'healthy' bodies, the position of sport in PE or sport-as-PE, and gender.

In countries such as Australia and New Zealand where PE curricula have been replaced by a new curriculum area called Health and Physical Education (HPE), new possibilities for transformative practice emerge as the field of HPE is less bound by history and is unencumbered with sedimented teaching practices (McIntyre, Philpot, & Smith, 2016). At a policy level, HPE introduces new ways to orientate school practice (Bowes & Ovens, 2014) and endorses examinations of how bodies are socially constructed and oppressed or privileged (Tinning, 2012). The transformative potential of this curriculum is catalyzed (or not) upon enactment in both (H)PETE and school HPE, where the dispositions and practices of individual teacher educators and teachers intersect with curricula to endorse or challenge the mechanisms of oppression relevant to PE.

PRACTICING THE PRINCIPLES

More than 15 years ago, Gard and Wright (2001) suggested that rather than transforming society, PE was deeply implicated in the reproduction of society. More recently Tinning (in press) cautions that PE educators are more likely to get swept up in the wake of social change rather than creating the social change.

Transformative pedagogies are not workshops or one-off activities whereby initial teacher education programs can 'tick off' that they have addressed cultural, gender or religious differences. The transformative potential of transformative pedagogy is exponentially more powerful when a social justice perspective is infused as a normal taken-for-granted practice through a PETE program, across many courses and educators (Nieto, 2000) and ultimately within schools' PE programs (Philpot, 2017). Real empowerment of PE teachers that can lead to the transformation of the subject area paradoxically requires the field of school PE to be disrupted sufficiently to be ready for change. The work of transformative pedagogues plants seeds for change that may require many years to germinate (Gerdin, Philpot, & Smith, 2018). Transformative teaching should be conceptualized as a process that strives for greater democracy and social justice rather than an outcome. Given the broader social forces in the world beyond education, a truly equal and democratic world is more aspirational than probable.

We are cognizant that this chapter is largely descriptive of the broader principles of transformative pedagogy and, as such, fails to provide pragmatic teaching strategies. In our own roles as physical education teacher educators we are acutely aware of structural constraints around enacting these principles, yet we reflexively recognize that, in many instances, we choose to constrain ourselves and fail to exercise the agency we have when we work with PETE students. Ultimately, we hope that these principles provide a framework through which the examples of practices that follow can be read and critiqued.

REFERENCES

Booth, D. (2009). Politics and pleasure: The philosophy of physical education revisited. *Quest, 61,* 133–153.

Bowes, M., & Ovens, A. P. (2014). Curriculum rhythm and HPE practice: Making sense of a complex relationship. *Teachers and Curriculum, 14,* 21–28.

Burrows, L. (2016). Obesity warriors in the tertiary classroom. In E. Cameron & C. Russell, (Eds.) *The fat pedagogy reader: Challenging weight based oppression through critical education* (pp. 101–121). New York, NY: Peter Lang,

Cochran-Smith, M. (2009). Toward a theory of teacher education for social justice. Part 2. In A. Hargreaves, A. Lieberman, M. Fullan, & D. Hopkins (Eds.), *Springer International handbooks of education: Vol. 23. Second international handbook of educational change* (pp. 445–467). New York, NY: Springer.

Fitzgerald, H. (2012). 'Drawing on disabled students' Experiences of physical education and stakeholder responses. *Sport, Education and Society, 17*(4), 443–462. DOI:10.1080/13573322.2011.609290

Freire, P. (1970). *Pedagogy of the oppressed.* New York, NY: Seabury Press.

Gard, M., & Wright, J. (2001) Managing uncertainty: Obesity discourses and physical education in a risk society, *Studies in Philosophy and Education, 20*(6), 535–549.

Gerdin, G. (2016). The disciplinary and pleasurable spaces of boys' PE—The art of distributions. *European Physical Education Review, 22*(2), 315–335.

Gerdin, G., Philpot, R., & Smith, W. (2018). It's only an intervention but it can sow fertile seeds: Graduate physical education teachers' interpretations of critical pedagogy. *Sport, Education and Society, 23*(3), 203–215.

Hackman, H. (2005). Five components for social justice education. *Education, Equity & Excellence in Education, 38*(2), 103–109.

Legge, M. (2010). E noho marae—Transforming learning through direct Māori cultural experience. In C. J. Jesson, V. M. Carpenter, M. McLean, M. Stephenson, & R. D. Airini (Eds.), *University teaching reconsidered: Justice, practice, equity* (pp. 139–149). Wellington, New Zealand: Dunmore Publishing Ltd.

Macintyre Latta, M., & Buck, G. (2008). Enfleshing embodiment: falling into trust with the body's role in teaching and learning. *Educational Philosophy & Theory, 40*(2), 315–329.

McIntyre, J., Philpot, R., & Smith, W. (2016). PE teachers' understanding and implementation of the New Zealand Health and Physical Education Curriculum. *Journal of Physical Education New Zealand: Te Ao Kori Aotearoa, 49*(2), 5–9.

Mezirow, J. (2009). Transformative learning theory. In J. Mezirow, E. W. Taylor & Associates (Eds.), *Transformative learning in practice: Insights from community, workplace and higher education* (pp. 18–32) San Francisco, CA: Jossey Bass.

Nieto, S. (2000). Placing equity front and center: Some thoughts on transforming teacher education for a new century. *Journal of Teacher Education, 51*(3), 180–187.

North, C. (2008). What's all this talk about "Social Justice"? Mapping the terrain of education's latest catch phrase. *Teachers College Record, 110*(6), 1182–1206.

Oliver, K. (2001). Images of the body from popular culture: Engaging adolescent girls in critical inquiry, *Sport, Education and Society,* 6(2), 143–164.

Oliver, K., & Kirk, D. (2017). Challenging body culture in physical education. In C. Ennis (ed.) *The Routledge handbook of physical education pedagogies.* (pp. 307–318). New York, NY: Taylor and Francis.

Ovens, A. (2013). Criticality in HPE: Think Piece 6: Disturbing practice in teacher education. *New Zealand Physical Educator, 46*(2), 20–21.

Ovens, A. (2017a). Putting complexity to work to think differently about transformative pedagogies in teacher education. *Issues in Teacher Education, 26*(3), 38–50.

Ovens, A. (2017b). Transformative aspirations and realities in physical education teacher education (PETE). In C. Ennis (Ed.) *The Routledge handbook of physical education pedagogies* (pp. 295–306). New York, NY: Taylor and Francis.

Ovens, A., & Powell, D. (2011). Minding the body in physical education. In S. Brown (Ed.) *Issues and controversies in physical education: policy, power and pedagogy* (pp. 150–159). Auckland: Pearson.

Philpot, R. (2016). Shaking student's cages: A Freirean pedagogy that influenced PETE students' beliefs about physical education. *International Journal of Critical Pedagogy, 7*(1), 143–164.

Philpot, R. (2017). Critical pedagogies in PETE: In search of a socially critical program. *European Physical Education Review, 25*(1), 48–64.

Pringle, R. (2010). Finding pleasure in physical education: A critical examination of the educative value of positive movement affects. *Quest, 62*(2), 119–135.

Ross, B. (2008). Faking physical education. *Journal of Physical Education New Zealand, 41*(3), 62–66.

Segall, A. (2002). *Disturbing practice: Reading teacher education as text.* New York, NY: Peter Lang.

Sykes, H. (2011). *Queer bodies: Sexualities, genders, & fatness in physical education.* New York, NY: Peter Lang.

Tinning, R. (1985). Physical education and the cult of slenderness: A critique. *ACHPER National Journal, 107*(Autumn), 10–14.

Tinning, R. (2012). A socially critical HPE (aka physical education) and the challenge for teacher education. In B. Down & J. Smythe (Eds.), *Critical voices in teacher education: Teaching for social justice in conservative times* (pp. 223–238). Dordrecht, The Netherlands: Springer.

Tinning, R. (2017). Transformative pedagogies and physical education. In C. Ennis (Ed.) *The Routledge handbook of physical education pedagogies* (pp. 281–294), New York, NY: Taylor and Francis.

Tinning, R. (2019). Critical pedagogy in physical education as advocacy and action: A reflective account. In H. Larsson, R. Pringle, & G. Gerdin (Eds.), *Critical research in sport, health and physical education: How to make a difference.* New York, NY: Routledge.

Ukpokodu, O. (2009). Pedagogies that foster transformative learning in a multicultural education course: A reflection. *Journal of Praxis in Multicultural Education, 4*(1), Article 4.

Ukpokodu, O. (2016). Realizing transformative learning and social justice education: Unpacking teacher education practice. In S. Tomlinson-Clarke & D. Clarke (Eds.) *Social justice and transformative learning: Culture and identity in the United States and South Africa.* (pp. 113–143). New York, NY: Routledge.

Walton-Fisette, J., Philpot, R., Phillips, S., Flory, S., Hill, J., Sutherland, S., & Flemons, M. (2018). Implicit and explicit pedagogical practices related to sociocultural issues and social justice in physical education teacher education programs. *Physical Education and Sport Pedagogy, 23*(5), 497–509.

CHAPTER 2

TAKING ACTION FOR CHANGE

(Participatory) Action Research and Social Justice Education

Joanne Hill

Only action research which aspires to be emancipatory warrants the term action research.

—*Tinning (1992, p. 205)*

Action research (AR) is a methodology for inquiring into and making change in one's own practice. It has a cyclical and structured process involving reflection, planning, action and observation, that has the possibility of producing sustainable reflection and change in an educator's practice (Kemmis & Wilkinson, 1998). All education is about change, but especially for social justice education (SJE) as 'the hope is it transforms or broadens attitudes, beliefs, and behaviours' (Goodman, 2011, p. 32). Action research provides the tools for educators to create opportunities to take action against oppression and marginalization, a key element of SJE. Action Research has been written about frequently in physical education (PE) and education more broadly; this chapter's purpose is not to outline what AR is or can do in itself, but to consider connections between teaching for/about social justice (SJ) and changing practice through research. I first explore how reflection on practice is valuable in SJE, then address how AR and social justice align, and

Teaching About Social Justice Issues in Physical Education, pages 13–20.
Copyright © 2019 by Information Age Publishing
All rights of reproduction in any form reserved.
13

conclude with ways that AR can be instigated for SJE and in using the strategies in this book.

SOCIAL JUSTICE EDUCATION AND REFLECTIVE PRACTICE

SJE and critical pedagogy have been conceptually aligned with the ideas of critical theory, and with democracy, emancipation, and uncovering or taking action against oppression (Hill et al., 2018; Rivzi, 1998). Bell, Goodman and Varghese (2016) have argued that self-knowledge and critical exploration of identity by educators is necessary for SJE. We should reflect on our positions in systems or institutions of inequality in order to fully develop SJE in our teaching. Teaching—from early years to higher education contexts—is a reflective profession. However, not all reflection is critical. Brookfield (2017, p. 9) distinguishes between technical and critical reflection. Technical reflection involves such decisions as a policy on handheld devices in the classroom or setting assessment deadline dates, but 'these technical decisions become critical when we start to see them in their social or political context'. Decisions with a social justice implication are embedded all throughout a department, not just in the curriculum (Cochran-Smith, et al., 1999). This concerns the power dynamics in education. We are expected to conform—and have our students conform—to norms of behaviour (for instance, students will sit quietly and listen). This, Brookfield (2017) points out, is a dominant ideology in education, one that we can critically reflect upon. Critical reflection is focused on illuminating power: understanding 'how educational processes and interactions are framed by wider structures of power and dominant ideology'; and uncovering hegemony: finding out 'assumptions and practices that seem to make their teaching lives easier, but that actually end up working against their own best interests'—that is, exploitation (Brookfield, 2017, p. 9). We are often constrained by official curriculum and timetabling decisions that happen without our input; have little control over the classroom space we are given; struggle to follow our own interests in our courses, let alone give our students a say in what they study.

To fully align with the principles of SJE, 'the improvement of practice should be linked to an understanding of the material and ideological conditions, which constrain practice and the way it is informed' (Tinning, 1992, p. 206). Although not all key texts on SJE (Bell et al., 2016; Goodman, 2011) mention AR, the emphasis in SJE literature on reflection and context-driven change suits the framework of AR. Reflective processes for educators through other means (aside from AR) have been or are encouraged by those researching SJE. For instance, narrative and self-study are promoted as powerful ways for educators to uncover assumptions and biases, and to open up dialogue (Ovens & Fletcher, 2014). Self-study is an opportunity to question your practice, ideas and actions in your pedagogy and curriculum. Social justice demands more of educators, and self-study is no different; Ovens and Fletcher's (2014, p. 7) encouragement 'to be more, to improve, to better understand', although written about self-study, would also apply to SJE.

ALIGNING ACTION RESEARCH AND SOCIAL JUSTICE

Kemmis and Wilkinson (1998, p. 21) express AR as 'a spiral of self-reflective cycles of:

* Planning a change
* Acting and observing the process and consequences of the change
* Reflecting on these processes and consequences, and then
* Re-planning, and so forth'

AR is carried out, not by outsider researchers, but by practitioners themselves. As a research methodology, it encourages teachers and other practitioners to pose and solve problems about their own practice (Tinning, 1992). AR implies learning for ourselves and leading social transformation—key goals of SJE—and therefore can provide educators with a way of doing social justice (Bristol & Ponte, 2013; Greenwood & Levin, 1998).

Advocates of AR also encourage teachers/researchers to keep control (not re-linquish it to an 'expert' outsider researcher). However, sometimes it is useful for outsiders to help, because it can be difficult for teachers to adopt a critical stance on their work and practice—if they believe they are already equitable, 'what fresh evidence might cause them to question this belief?' (Brooker et al., 1998, p. 191), or they will find evidence that supports what they already believe. So, collabora-tion with outsiders can also help the reflection and observation processes. For instance, Petrie, Devcich, and Fitzgerald (2018) outline how a teacher created reflective journals, which were then shared with two co-researchers outside his school to prompt discussion about his practice. Personal experience is privileged in action research, and as Bristol and Ponte reflect, can make social justice a chal-lenge if teacher/researchers may stop being critical of their own experience. Per-haps 'we need an external dissenting voice' in order to fully focus on what we can do better, and not how we can get other people to do better (Bristol & Ponte, 2013, p. 521). Similarly, social justice and AR remind us to avoid making assumptions about the problems that learners have, as this perspective 'works to disadvantage further those who start off at a disadvantage' (Lumby & Coleman, 2016, p. 183). That external dissenting voice could come from students themselves. Our culture supports authority and simple thinking; students are not used to thinking that they can create knowledge or their own sense of truth (Brookfield, 2017). If AR is done *with* students or other stakeholders, not *for* them, and collaborative problem analysis is centered, we might get closer to questioning authority (Greenwood & Levin, 2007).

Participatory action research (PAR) is a specific AR methodology that may align particularly well with social justice. PAR is useful for two reasons: listening to other voices, and helping students manage the emotional reactions they might have if they are new to dealing with SJE and knowledge of oppression (Goodman, 2011), because it includes them in the enquiry, decision making and reflection.

PAR is a specific form of action research that focuses on collaborative elements, to engage young people in their own inquiry, reflection and action, and harness this inquiry to 'speaking back and challenging conditions of injustice' (Cammarota & Fine, 2008, p. 3). Frameworks such as this in educational or youth settings promote using research 'for resistance' and hence PAR with youth 'represents not only a formal pedagogy of resistance, but also the means by which young people engage in transformational resistance' (Cammarota & Fine, 2008, p. 4).

The typical action research cycle of plan-act-observe-reflect is taken up by PAR practitioners, but they go further to emphasize:

- The social process (a collective and individual undertaking)
- Participatory examination (done on oneself or one's group, not on others)
- Collaboration (working together)
- Emancipation (freeing ourselves from unjust structures limiting development)
- Criticality (to contest unproductive and unjust processes)
- Reflection (cycles of action)

—(from Kemmis & Wilkinson, 1998)

Each of these elements can help practitioners to enhance knowledge of practice. Many of these elements explicitly mention social justice or aspects of change to structures and practice that recall SJE tenets. So practitioners of PAR are doing social justice, and learning how to better teach *for* social justice, in the process of learning to better teach *about* social justice. 'For' and 'about' are inseparable to some degree.

DEVELOPING AN ACTION RESEARCH
CYCLE FOR SOCIAL JUSTICE CHANGE

So how does an educator start AR in order to teach for/about SJ? How does (s)he start that process? Before you start, you might ask questions about the context and the learners you are addressing. Sellars (2017, drawing from Gore and Zeichner, 1991) suggests ways to reflect on political and social issues in schooling, which could draw out some useful places to start:

- What do I believe to be the purpose of education, the philosophy, values, function?
- Who sets the curriculum and does it support the needs of learners from different social and cultural groups?
- How can I minimize disadvantage to particular individuals or groups?
- Have I identified bias or prejudice and moved to diminish these? and
- Have I identified my own assumptions, perceptions and values?

Educators studying their own practice and their students' experiences are encouraged to generate their own knowledge of their students' needs and real

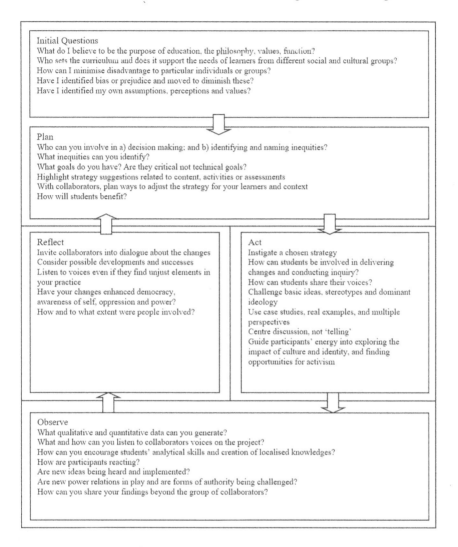

Initial Questions
What do I believe to be the purpose of education, the philosophy, values, function?
Who sets the curriculum and does it support the needs of learners from different social and cultural groups?
How can I minimise disadvantage to particular individuals or groups?
Have I identified bias or prejudice and moved to diminish these?
Have I identified my own assumptions, perceptions and values?

Plan
Who can you involve in a) decision making; and b) identifying and naming inequities?
What inequities can you identify?
What goals do you have? Are they critical not technical goals?
Highlight strategy suggestions related to content, activities or assessments
With collaborators, plan ways to adjust the strategy for your learners and context
How will students benefit?

Reflect
Invite collaborators into dialogue about the changes
Consider possible developments and successes
Listen to voices even if they find unjust elements in your practice
Have your changes enhanced democracy, awareness of self, oppression and power?
How and to what extent were people involved?

Act
Instigate a chosen strategy
How can students be involved in delivering changes and conducting inquiry?
How can students share their voices?
Challenge basic ideas, stereotypes and dominant ideology
Use case studies, real examples, and multiple perspectives
Centre discussion, not 'telling'
Guide participants' energy into exploring the impact of culture and identity, and finding opportunities for activism

Observe
What qualitative and quantitative data can you generate?
What and how can you listen to collaborators voices on the project?
How can you encourage students' analytical skills and creation of localised knowledges?
How are participants reacting?
Are new ideas being heard and implemented?
Are new power relations in play and are forms of authority being challenged?
How can you share your findings beyond the group of collaborators?

FIGURE 2.1.   Prompts for Setting Up (Participatory) Action Research for Social Justice

problems, through participatory work; this insider perspective does not presume authority over others, but involves a critical analysis of power and privilege, including considering who you are doing research for (senior management or the students?); honoring people's values and needs; and challenging dominant views about who can be a researcher and who benefits from research, emphasizing trust and respect for students and their own research skills (Atweh, Christensen, & Dornan, 1998). If (P)AR is about doing research or changing practice with people, then a way in which educators could use this book is in reflecting on their own context to find ways to adapt or amend the suggestions made here to their own students, engaging those students in understanding their situations, barriers, and strengths, to create critical pedagogies or teaching for/about SJ that works for them. Educators looking to pay (more) attention to social justice should focus on their own students' needs, paying attention to where they are and what their experiences are, and making that a part of the action research cycle. Building in dialogue with colleagues and students; inviting them to take part in decision making and enquiry. In this you can draw from the chapter authors' own reflections of what has worked for them, consider if it would work in your situation, and if so, find ways to implement it. The grid above (Figure 2.1) sets out the four stages of AR and adds Sellars' (2017) initial questions for reflective change of equity, to offer some prompts (drawing from Goodman, 2011; Kemmis & Wilkinson, 1998; Rovegno & Kirk, 1995) concerning the stages of a (participatory) action research project for educators looking to initiate critical enquiry into their own practice and context.

CONCLUSION

The process of education is not imitation, but the creative application of all we know brought into creative dialogue with the historical moment. (Bergmark, Ghaye & Alerby, 2007, p. 463)

AR may enable educators to examine where their practice could become more aligned with social justice, what social justice means in their local context, and subsequently reflect upon creating pedagogies, curricula and environments for change. Both AR and SJE are never completed in the sense of reaching the end of a project. They are journeys of continually listening and contributing to extended conversations. As an educator examining your own practice, from defining what social justice means to yourself, your learners and your context, through to investigating how it is implicated throughout all decisions, curriculum designs, and educational materials (Cochran-Smith et al, 1999), you are on a journey that could frame your practice for the years to come. There is no quick fix for 'adding' social justice to your teaching, as Ovens and Philpot stated in Chapter 3. For genuine social justice, structural and cultural change in education is needed. AR could provide the evidence and reflective practice to succeed.

REFERENCES

Atweh, B., Christensen, C., & Dornan, L. (1998). Students as action researchers: Partnerships for social justice. In B. Atweh, S. Kemmis, & P. Weeks (Eds.), *Action research in practice: Partnership for social justice in education* (pp. 114–138). London, UK: Routledge.

Bell, L. A., Goodman, D., & Varghese, R. (2016). Critical self-knowledge for social justice educators. In M. Adams, L. A. Bell, D. Goodman, & K. Y. Joshi (Eds.), *Teaching for diversity and social justice* (3rd ed.). New York, NY: Routledge

Bergmark, U., Ghaye, T., & Alerby, E. (2007). Reflective and appreciative actions that support the building of ethical places and spaces. *Reflective Practice, 8*(4), 447–466.

Brooker, R., Smeal, G., Ehrich, L., Daws, L., & Brannock, J. (1998). Action research for professional development in gender issues. In B. Atweh, S. Kemmis, & P. Weeks (Eds.) *Action research in practice: Partnership for social justice in education.* London, UK: Routledge.

Brookfield, S. D. (2017). *Becoming a critically reflective teacher.* San Francisco, CA: Jossey-Bass

Bristol, L., & Ponte, P. (2013). "Muddying the space": Social justice, action research and professional learning. *Professional Development in Education, 39*(4), 513–530.

Cammarota, J., & Fine, M. (2008). Youth participatory action research: A pedagogy for transformational resistance. In J. Cammarota & M. Fine (Eds.), *Revolutionizing education: Youth Participatory Action Research in motion* (pp. 1–11). New York, NY: Routledge.

Cochran-Smith, M., Albert, L., Dimattia, P., Freedman, S., Jackson, R., Mooney, J., Neisler, O., Peck, A., & Zollers, N. (1999). Seeking social justice: A teacher education faculty's self-study. *International Journal of Leadership in Education, 2*(3), 229–253.

Goodman, D. (2011). *Promoting diversity and social justice* (2nd ed.). New York, NY: Routledge.

Gore, J., & Zeichner, K. (1991). Action research and reflective teaching in preservice teacher education: A case study from the United States. *Teaching and Teacher Education, 7*(2), 119–136.

Greenwood, D. J., & Levin, M. (1998). *Introduction to action research: Social research for social change.* London, UK: Sage.

Greenwood, D., & Levin, M. (2007). *Introduction to action research: Social research for social change* (2nd ed.). Thousand Oaks, CA: Sage.

Hill, J., Philpot, R., Walton-Fisette, J. L., Sutherland, S., Ovens, A., Phillips, S., Flemons, M., & Flory, S. (2018). Conceptualising social justice and sociocultural issues within physical education teacher education : international perspectives. *Physical Education and Sport Pedagogy, 25*(3), 469–483.

Kemmis, S., & Wilkinson, M. (1998). Participatory action research and the study of practice. In B. Atweh, S. Kemmis, & P. Weeks (Eds.), *Action research in practice: Partnership for social justice in education* (pp. 21–36). London, UK: Routledge.

Lumby, J., & Coleman. (2016). *Leading for equality: Making schools fairer.* London, UK: Sage.

Ovens, A., & Fletcher, T. (2014). Doing self-study: The art of turning inquiry on yourself. In A. Ovens & T. Fletcher (Eds.). *Self-study in teacher education: Exploring the interplay of practice and scholarship.* London, UK: Springer

Ovens, A., & Philpot, R. (this volume). *Five principles of transformative pedagogies in PETE.* Chapell Hill, NC: IAP.

Petrie, K. Devcich, J., & Fitzgerald, H. (2018). Working towards inclusive physical education in a primary school: 'Some days I just don't get it right'. *Physical Education and Sport Pedagogy*, [iFirst] 1–13. http://doi.org/10.1080/17408989.2018.1441391

Rivzi, F. (1998). Some thoughts on contemporary theories of social justice. In B. Atweh, S. Kemmis, & P. Weeks (Eds.) *Action research in practice: Partnership for social justice in education* (pp. 47–56). London, UK: Routledge.

Rovegno, I., & Kirk, D. (1995). Articulations and silences in socially critical work on physical education: Toward a broader agenda. *Quest, 47*, 447–475.

Sellars, M. (2017). *Reflective practice for teachers*. London, UK: Sage.

Tinning, R. (1992). Action research as epistemology and practice: Towards transformative educational practice in physical education. In A. C. Sparkes (Ed.), *Research in physical education and sport: Exploring alternative visions* (pp. 188–209). London, UK: Routledge Falmer.

PART II

SOCIAL JUSTICE ISSUES: STRATEGIES AND LESSONS IN
PHYSICAL EDUCATION

CHAPTER 3

ACCESSING PRE-SERVICE TEACHERS' SELF-IDENTITY THROUGH CRITICAL REFLECTION

Jennifer L. Walton-Fisette and Sue Sutherland

ACTION RESEARCH & REFLECTION

During our doctoral programs, we came to learn the importance and relevance of addressing sociocultural and social justice issues. At the time, it was more from a theoretical perspective, in reading the likes of Freire (1970), Ladson-Billings (2001), and Cochran-Smith (1995) in education more broadly and Bain (1975, 1990), Dodds (1985), Kirk (1986), Evans (1993), Fernandez-Balboa (1993, 1997) and Tinning (2002) in physical education. The work of these scholars, among others, certainly influenced our critical conscious and social justice perspective; however, we did not necessarily have the pedagogical knowledge to educate our own students about issues related to social justice and inequity. Throughout our careers, we have researched various resources to inform our planning about and for social justice issues and have engaged in 'trial and error' in teaching about such challenging and personal issues with our pre-service teachers. One of the many lessons we have learned along the way is the importance of students explor-

Teaching About Social Justice Issues in Physical Education, pages 23–32.
Copyright © 2019 by Information Age Publishing
All rights of reproduction in any form reserved.

ing and reflecting upon their own self-identities. For many of our students (and probably true for pre-service teachers globally), in order to be open to learning about social justice issues, they first need to have a sense of who they are and the factors that have influenced their own identities.

UNIVERSITY AND PROGRAM CONTEXT

Jennifer teaches in the Physical Education Professional program at Kent State University in Ohio, USA. There are two tracks that lead to licensure: physical education and health and physical education. We also offer a non-licensure program, Physical Activity and Sport Performance (PASP). The licensure program consists of content-based courses (e.g., Target and Field Games, Fundamental Movement, Gymnastics and Dance, Outdoor Pursuits), kinesiology courses (e.g., Anatomy and Physiology, Motor Skill Analysis), education-based courses (e.g., Education in a Democratic Society, Introduction to Exceptionalities) and pedagogical courses specific to physical education (e.g., Teaching in PE, Secondary Content and Methods, Adapted Physical Education, Student Teaching). The PASP program includes many of the same content and kinesiology courses, with the addition of courses that are specific to a minor, with Athletic Coaching being the most popular. There is no sociocultural/social justice course in the physical education program. Approximately 60% of our students are first generation students; many of whom have to work simultaneous to working on their bachelor's degree.

Sue teaches in the Physical Education program at Ohio State University in Ohio, USA. The Physical Education, Sport, and Physical Activity undergraduate degree offers two tracks: physical education teacher education (licensure) and physical activity and coaching specialist (non-licensure). We also offer a health education licensure endorsement for students in the physical education track. The physical education teacher education (PETE) program is comprised of content-based courses (Concepts of Fitness and Wellness, Adventure-based Learning, Teaching Invasion Games, Teaching Court Games, Teaching Racquet Sports, Lower Elementary Content, Upper Elementary Content), Lifespan Motor Development, Qualitative Skill Analysis, Sociocultural Issues), general education courses (Teaching Reading Across the Curriculum, Psychological Perspectives on Education), and pedagogical courses (Teaching Physical Education, Leisure, and Exercise, Introduction to Adapted Physical Activity, Elementary Methods, Secondary Methods, and Student Teaching). The physical activity and coaching specialist program is comprised of many of the courses from the PETE program, but also add courses from social work, youth development, programming, and leadership among others.

ASSIGNMENT SET-UP AND IMPLEMENTATION

To access students' self-identity, quite often, it is important for students to engage in activities and assignments that get them to participate in a reflective process through writing. Thus, the assignments that will be shared are not particular to a specific lesson, rather, an assignment that creates the opportunities for discussion in class. The following two assignments are implemented in two different courses (both assignments are included below). The first, *Physical Activity Autobiography*, is an assignment in an Introduction to Physical Education, Fitness and Sport course, which is taken by all of our students at the beginning of the physical education program. This assignment is completed during the first week of the semester. The second assignment, *Social Identity Paper*, is completed in a Secondary Methods course taken in their senior year, also during the first week of the semester. The following provides a step-by-step process on how to implement these assignments into your PETE courses.

Physical Activity Autobiography

Step 1: Before you implement this assignment (or a modified version of it), it is important for you to reflect upon the students in your program and more specifically, the student body of the course. The importance of engaging in this process is to utilize verbiage and a frame of reference that the students will be able to understand, especially since these assignments are completed during the first week of the course. For example, we express how privilege, marginalization and social inequalities can be challenging to discuss and understand and may make them feel uncomfortable. In this course, current sporting events are utilized to highlight examples of privilege, marginalization and/or social inequalities, such as NFL players taking a knee during the national anthem and the local professional baseball team's (i.e., Cleveland Indians) discriminatory logo of Chief Wahoo. Using such examples allows for elaborate discussion and debate, which is often predicated on the students' personal feelings and beliefs about the issue, without ever considering the social and political ramifications of these sporting contexts. We learned that the terminology and frame of reference with the student body at one institution may not be the same at another institution.

Step 2: Based on your knowledge of the students, develop questions that get the students to reflect upon their experiences as physical movers. In this course, we have students who want to become teachers, coaches, personal trainers, and other human movement professionals. Thus, we ask them to reflect upon their physical activity, physical education, and sporting experiences. The intent of the question is first to get them to talk about their overall experiences in these contexts, but then to challenge them to explore the factors that influenced their own lived experiences and to consider how their peers may have experienced the same activity. For our students, this is the first time that someone has asked them questions beyond, 'tell us about your sporting experiences', 'tell us about your physical education classes in school'. Although those questions are certainly important, the hope is to get them to reflect upon their experiences at a deeper level.

Step 3: Establishing how you will evaluate the students' needs some thought and consideration. For example, will you assess the students based on content, written structure, promptness, and/or all of the above? For us, the focus is primarily on the content of the assignment so the criteria reflect that. However, the structure and submission of the assignment is of value for students' overall development as a future professional, so we include criteria for those as well, but to a lesser degree.

Step 4: At this time, you will need to determine how you will review the assignment in class. Do you hand out a hard copy and tell them the due date? Refer them to the online learning system that your institution uses? Read over it and ask if there are any questions? Or, lead up to this assignment by using examples that may tie into to their own lived experiences related to physical activity, physical education, and sport? In knowing our students here in Ohio, using sporting examples draws the students into the discussion. On the first day of class, we pose questions to students related to current issues in sport (e.g., Colin Kaepernick kneeling during the national anthem, NCAA violations, Cleveland Indians name and logo) to open the door for discussion related to privilege, marginalization, and inequity. For example, do you support/not support NFL players taking a knee and why? What is your understanding of Colin Kaepernick and other NFL players taking a knee? For those of you playing or coaching a sport, what will you do when the national anthem is played? Regarding the Cleveland Indians logo, what does the logo depict? Is it a mockery of Native Americans? Should the logo be changed to something else? What are the reasons for not changing the logo? The students begin to understand on the first day of class that they will be expected to delve into discussions of issues at a deeper level than their opinion or only based on what they experienced in the past (which, of course, is important). These discussions segue into explaining how important it is for us to get to know them for who they are and for *them* to have an understanding of who they are and where they came from.

Step 5: Upon submission, provide detailed feedback and comments to the students based on the criteria established. We suggest that you provide posing questions to them to challenge their current thinking and understanding of certain issues related to social justice and inequity. This provides a private forum to get them to reflect upon their past experiences and their beliefs related to such issues.

Step 6: Over the course of the semester, as you teach about social justice issues, continuously ask the students to reflect back to their physical activity autobiography and their lived experiences in an attempt to deconstruct biases and beliefs and develop a critical consciousness.

Social Identity Paper

Step 1: As previously stated, we believe having students explore their own self-identities is valuable and important for them to have an understanding about social justice issues. In the Secondary Methods course, it is critical for the preservice teachers to come to understand who they are, what they believe and value first, because they will then need to learn how their identities and beliefs influence the decisions and actions they make as teachers, which may positively or negatively affect students' learning experiences in physical education. With that being said, prior to the first day of class, we suggest that you create an assignment that gets students to explore their own identities. Establishing how you will evaluate the students, needs some thought and consideration. For example, will you assess the students based on content, written structure, promptness, and/or all of the above? For us, the focus is primarily on the content of the assignment so the criteria reflect that. However, the structure and submission of the assignment is of value for their overall development as a future professional, so we include criteria for those as well, but to a lesser degree. Furthermore, you will need to decide how you want the assignments submitted. We have them submit to a discussion board on our online learning system to allow their peers to read one another's identity papers and comment/pose questions if so desired.

Step 2: In the first class of the semester, we participate in some initiatives (e.g., different handshakes, Chicken Baseball, Have You Ever (described in Chapter 5) to get students up and moving, learn more about each other (most of the students in the class have already taken numerous courses with each other prior to this one), and set the stage for how frequent and detailed social justice issues will be addressed throughout the course. When we return to the classroom, they begin to reflect upon and discuss their experiences in physical education at the secondary level (this is done through a think/pair/share), which opens the door to identifying and discussing many social justice issues that can occur in a physical education setting.

Step 3: At the end of the first class, we go over their first two assignments of the course: teaching philosophy (due the next evening) and social identity paper. The students follow the assignment criteria and assigned readings for considerations for the teaching philosophy, but tend to get nervous with the social identity paper. Although the assignment is not due until the end of the week, we prepare them in advance so they have time to think about it. We explain to the students that this assignment may be challenging to them—for a variety of reasons—e.g., do not know what social identities or issues are, do not feel comfortable sharing personal information with others, and/or do not even know where to begin. We also inform the students that their social identity papers will be shared with the class, so they need to decide how personal and vulnerable that they are willing to make themselves. Furthermore, we explain that although it is acceptable to not share all of who they are, it is important for them to reflect upon why they are not willing to share certain aspects of who they are with others. The assignment is due by the end of the first week and uploaded to our online learning system in a discussion board.

Simultaneous to explaining about the social identity paper, we also inform the students that there is a part two to the assignment. After they submit their papers, they are expected to a) read each other's paper (if you have a larger class, ask them to read X number of papers in the class) and comment if they so choose on the discussion board, and b) write a reflection paper that may include how they felt writing their social identity paper, explaining the process that they took in writing it, how they felt after reading their classmates' identity papers, etc. The reflection paper is due two days after the social identity paper. These assignments occur between our second and third meeting times of the course (over a weekend).

Step 4: We believe that if you want your students to make themselves vulnerable and share who they are, then it is important for us as teacher educators to do the same. Once all of the social identity papers have been uploaded, we upload our own for students to read. We choose not to upload them beforehand, because we do not want the students to feel that they need to model our identity papers; rather, we want them to interpret and share accordingly to what is suitable to them.

Step 5: Read their social identity papers and reflections before the next class meeting. If you feel it is appropriate, comment on the discussion board, along with the students. Prepare to have a conversation in class about their social identity and reflection papers.

Step 6: Create an opportunity to discuss the identity papers in class. In our experience, some classes are open to discussing their identities in person, whereas other classes are not. Students tend to focus more on how they felt writing the papers and learning about one another. We make a point to inform them that we will be connecting to their social identities frequently throughout the class as we address social justice issues in the physical education setting.

Step 7: Provide opportunities for discussion and reflection on social justice issues that may/do arise in physical education and provide pedagogical strategies on how to address them when they are teaching. *Note: In the Kent State University PETE setting, our pre-service teachers have the opportunity to teach 10 lessons at the middle school level and four lessons at the high school level in the secondary methods course. After each teaching day, we come back to campus to have a debrief about what transpired in the field. Often times, our discussions focus on social justice issues that they encountered (they keep a social justice journal to reflect upon these experiences). In the Ohio State University PETE setting, our pre-service teachers teach two, 10-day units at the middle school level. After each teaching day, the students engage in a critical friends discussion relative to what happened during the lessons. Within these discussion, issues of social justice certainly arise and all students and the university supervisor brainstorm solutions to the issues that can be implemented during the next lesson(s). Often times, within these discussions, we connect the social justice issues that they observed or experienced in the schools to their own self identities. Sometimes, the students are able to understand how their own identities and beliefs will influence their teaching as well as their responses to students; however, many students need guidance through questioning and deconstructing the incidents that occur for them to understand the connection between their self-identity and issues related to social justice.

INTERSECTIONALITIES

Due to the nature of these assignments, the *Physical Activity Autobiography* and *Social Identity Paper*, afford students the opportunity to identify and reflect upon a wide variety of social justice issues. However, the likelihood is that the students will not have the knowledge and understanding of how their social identities intersect with one another; rather, they will look at them as separate identities. It will be important for you, as the physical educator, to inform students about what is meant by intersectionalities and to challenge them to reflect upon their own identities and how theirs intersects with one another.

CHALLENGES AND POSSIBILITIES

Addressing social justice issues is challenging and complex. Asking students to reflect upon who they are and their own social identities can be daunting for many students. For these reasons, we believe having them reflect through writing is an important first step in getting students to learn about their own self-identities. We believe that engaging in this process creates opportunities for students to be more open about discussing social justice issues, becoming more aware of social inequities and can relate to their own self-identities, lived experiences and ways they were privileged and marginalized to those they encounter in the primary and secondary schools. Students tend to have a difficult time talking about these assignments directly in class. We suggest having them discuss in pairs and small groups instead of sharing with the entire class. Although these assignments stand alone, the intent is to get them to reflect upon their lived experiences and identities early on in the courses to pave the way for other learning opportunities that address social justice issues in physical education.

INTRODUCTION TO PHYSICAL
EDUCATION, FITNESS & SPORT

Assignment #1—Physical Activity Autobiography

1. Write a response to the following questions:
   - What physical activity, sport, and physical education opportunities and experiences did you have growing up? Were they positive or negative? What contributed to this?
   - How did you feel as a physical mover as a child, a high school student and now? Do you believe these experiences/opportunities were similar/different for other people? Why? Explain.
   - Describe experiences that you have had where you were privileged, discriminated against, or stereotyped in sport, physical activity, and

physical education (e.g., based on your gender, race, sexuality, age, religion, ability, etc.). How did you feel? What did you learn from it?

2. Criteria for the written response:
    - Page Length—minimum of 2.5 pages
    - 1 inch margins
    - Double-spaced
    - 10 or 12 point font
    - Be sure to spell/grammar check!!!
    - **Staple or paper clip pages together**

3. Assignment #1 is due, in class, on…

Category	Unacceptable Level (0–33)	Acceptable Level (34–43)	Target Level (44–50)
PA / Sport Experiences	You describe less than 3 physical activity/sport experiences that you had growing up and/or do not describe how you felt when you engaged in those activities.	You generally describe 3 physical activity/sport experiences that you had growing up and how you felt when you engaged in those activities.	You describe, in detail, more than 3 physical activity/sport experiences that you had growing up and how you felt when you engaged in those activities.
	0–13.9	**14–16.9**	**17–20**
Influence of Social Identity	You do not reflect upon how other individuals might/might not have had similar/different experiences than you. You do not describe how your experiences in physical activity/sport were influenced by your social identity.	You reflect upon how other individuals might/might not have similar/different experiences than you. You describe how your experiences in physical activity were influenced by your social identity.	You reflect upon and describe how other individuals might/might not have similar/different experiences than you. You describe how your experiences in physical activity/sport were influenced by your social identity and reflect upon how you felt and what you learned from those experiences.
	0–13.9	**14–16.9**	**17–20**
Structure of Paper	Your reflection is less than 2.5 pages, is not double-spaced, and has more than 3 spelling/grammar errors.	Your reflection is a minimum of 2.5 pages, double-spaced, and has no more than 3 spelling/grammar errors.	Your reflection is a minimum of 2.5 pages, double-spaced, and has no more than 2 spelling/grammar errors.
	0–2.9	**3–4.9**	**5**
Submission	You submit your assignment late.	You submit your assignment on time.	You submit your assignment on time.
	0–2.9	**3–4.9**	**5**

SECONDARY PHYSICAL EDUCATION CONTENT & METHODS

Social Identity Paper

Who you are and how you identify will impact who you are as a teacher. Write a reflective paper that explores your own sense of social identity. You MUST include social identities such as gender, social class, race, sexual orientation and (dis)ability (select influences in which you most identify and describe why—you do not need to select all possible social identities). In addition, include how your family, school, work, and/or social and religious experiences have contributed to the development of that identity (again, do not need to include all, only the most pertinent). Describe how your identity has developed/changed over time. Your paper will be viewed by your classmates, thus, take this into consideration as you write your paper. That is, share to the level of your comfort, be thoughtful, and allow others to learn more about who you are.

Submit your paper on BLACKBOARD by 10 pm on Saturday, Jan. 20th. **You will be asked to read everyone's paper and post a reflection on BLACKBOARD by 8 pm on Monday, Jan. 22nd.** The reflection should include how you felt about writing your own social identity paper—what was your process, how did you feel during/after, what did you think and/or how did you feel when you read your classmates' papers, etc. **Thus, there are TWO written assignments you will be completing.** I highly recommend that you post comments on one another's submissions on the discussion board. Your paper should be typed and a minimum of 2.5 pages. Be sure to spell/grammar check before submitting your papers, as points will be taken off for misspelled words. School systems do not hire teachers who cannot communicate in a professional manner.

Limited (0–12)	Proficient (13–16)	Advanced (17–20)
• You describe 1 or less social influences that comprise your social identity. • You do not provide a description of how your family, school, work, social, and/or religious experiences have contributed to the development of your identity. • You do not provide a description of how your identity has developed/changed over time. • More than 3 spelling/grammar errors.	• You describe 2 social influences that comprise your social identity. • You provide a description of how your family, school, work, social, and/or religious experiences have contributed to the development of your identity. • You describe how your identity has developed/changed over time. • 2–3 spelling/grammar errors.	• You describe 3 or more social influences that comprise your social identity. • You provide a detailed description of how your family, school, work, social, and/or religious experiences have contributed to the development of your identity. • You describe how and why your identity has developed/changed over time. • You describe how your social identity might impact who you are as a teacher (i.e., your teacher identity). • 0–2 spelling/grammar errors.

REFERENCES

Bain, L. (1975). The hidden curriculum in physical education. *Quest,* 24(1), 92–101.

Bain, L. (1990). A critical analysis of the hidden curriculum. In D. Kirk and R. Tinning (Eds.), *Physical education curriculum and culture: Critical issues in the contemporary crisis* (pp. 23–42). New York, NY: Falmer Press.

Cochran-Smith, M. (1995). Color blindness and basket making are not the answers: Confronting the dilemmas of race, culture, and language diversity in teacher education. *American Educational Research Journal, 32*(3), 493–522.

Dodds, P. (1985). Are hunters of the functional curriculum seeking quarks or snarks? *Journal of Teaching in Physical Education, 4,* 91–99.

Evans, J. (Ed.) (1993). *Equality, education and physical education.* London, UK: Falmer.

Fernandez-Balboa, J. M. (1993). Sociocultural characteristics of the hidden curriculum in physical education. *Quest, 45*(2), 230–254.

Fernández-Balboa, J. M. (1997). Physical education teacher preparation in the postmodern era: Toward a critical pedagogy. In J. M. Fernández-Balboa (Ed.), *Critical postmodernism in human movement, physical education, and sport* (pp. 121–138). Albany, NY: State University of New York Press.

Freire, P. (1970). *Pedagogy of the oppressed.* New York, NY: Herder and Herder.

Kirk, D. (1986). A critical pedagogy for teacher education: Toward an inquiry-oriented approach. *Journal of Teaching in Physical Education, 5,* 230–246.

Ladson-Billings, G. (2001). *Crossing over to Canaan: The journey of new teachers in diverse classrooms. The Jossey-Bass Education Series.* San Francisco, CA: Jossey-Bass.

Tinning, R. (2002). Toward a 'modest pedagogy': Reflections on the problematics of critical pedagogy. *Quest, 54,* 224–240.

CHAPTER 4

LAYING THE FOUNDATION FOR SOCIAL JUSTICE IN PHYSICAL EDUCATION

Exploring Self-Identity

Sue Sutherland, Jennifer L. Walton-Fisette, and Carli Alfriend

ACTION RESEARCH AND REFLECTION

Although we are at vastly different points in our teaching journey, there are certain experiences and beliefs that bind us together. We have all taught at the secondary school level; Sue in the UK at both a large state school and a school for "students with moderate learning difficulties", Jennifer at a suburban middle and high school in New England, USA, and Carli at a Title I school in an urban school district in Ohio, USA. In addition, we all have a strong belief in social justice within our classrooms and have recently worked together to promote social justice education (SJE) at the local, state, national, and international levels. Each of us came to understand our belief in SJE during our undergraduate program and early teaching career. Carli, who is just finishing her second year of teaching, is fully immersed in this reflective endeavor on a daily basis. Sue and Jennifer have since moved on to faculty roles in Physical Education Teacher Education

Teaching About Social Justice Issues in Physical Education, pages 33–42.
Copyright © 2019 by Information Age Publishing
All rights of reproduction in any form reserved.

programs, but their early teaching experiences set the foundation for a continued interest in SJE. Within their respective doctoral programs, both Sue and Jennifer gained more theoretical knowledge about SJE both in general education (e.g., Cochran-Smith, 1995; Freire, 1970; Ladson-Billings, 2001) and physical education (e.g., Bain, 1975, 1990; Dodds, 1985; Evans, 1993; Fernandez-Balboa, 1993, 1997; Kirk, 1986; and Tinning, 2002). Transforming this theoretical knowledge into their own teaching through trial and error and ongoing reflective practice has resulted in both Sue and Jennifer embedding SJE within their courses and programs. Guided by our own practice and experiences, we all feel that exploring and understanding self-identity is the foundation for effectively engaging in SJE.

CONTEXT

Our own positionality is important to disclose as it is the foundation we draw from as we engage in SJE. We are all white, educated, affluent, athletic, women, ranging in age from mid-twenties to mid-fifties, two of us identify as LGBTQ and one as heterosexual, and currently live in the Midwestern USA. Sue and Jennifer began working together to promote SJE four years ago and have presented and published in various contexts during that time. Carli graduated from Ohio State University and has taken courses from Sue and has presented with Sue and Jennifer at the state and national level. While clearly different in relation to number of years in the profession, we are all strong advocates for SJE in our professional contexts and indeed, our personal lives.

Sue is a faculty member in the Physical Education program at Ohio State University, USA. She teaches a variety of courses in the undergraduate program including Adventure-based Learning, Elementary Content, Elementary Methods and Field Experience, Sport and Disability, and Sociocultural Issues in Physical Education, Sport and Physical Activity. Sue has been interested in issues of equity since beginning her teaching career in the late 1980s. Her work and research interest has shifted from inclusive physical education and outdoor adventure education for individuals with disabilities, to focusing on creating community and developing interpersonal and intrapersonal skills in physical education through student centered pedagogy, to engaging with SJE and critical pedagogy in both her teaching and research.

Jennifer is a faculty member in the Physical Education Teacher Education program at Kent State University, USA. She teaches a wide range of courses in the undergraduate and graduate programs, such as Introduction to Physical Education, Fitness and Sport, Game Performance of Target and Field Games, Motor Skill Analysis, Secondary Content and Methods, Inquiry into Professional Practice (taken during student teaching) and Curriculum Development. Although the program does not have a stand-alone course, Jennifer integrates social justice issues across all of the courses that she teaches. Her research interest focused on adolescent girls' embodied identities and co-constructed activist research with girls and has now evolved to more broadly focus on SJE and critical pedagogy across her research, teaching and service engagements.

Carli graduated from the Physical Education program at Ohio State University and has just completed her second year teaching physical education. She teaches in a Title I middle school in a large metropolitan area in Ohio. Carli's school has over 600 students from a variety of different countries around the world. As a physical educator for seventh and eighth grade students, Carli feels it is vital to support each of them in becoming not only comfortable, but confident with who they are as an individual. Her students face a number of challenges in their home lives from poverty, gangs, drugs, violence, and murder of family members. To create an environment where students can engage with each other and the teachers in a positive way, Carli uses activities that explore self-identity with her students.

ACTIVITIES TO EXPLORE SELF IDENTITY

The activities discussed in this chapter are ones that we have each used when working with secondary age students in order to explore self-identity. While not necessarily part of a specific unit of instruction, we have used these activities to help create an inclusive class environment where all students feel accepted and respected. An added bonus of these activities is the opportunity for us to understand different aspects of our students more fully. *Comfort Zones* introduces the idea of interpersonal and intrapersonal comfort level and allows students to understand their similarities and differences through answering a series of questions. *Judgment Circle* is an activity that Carli uses with her classes early in the semester when she notices cliques and power differences in the group. *What I Wish My Teacher Knew* allows students the opportunity to share something that is important in their life or a challenge they are facing that helps their teacher to understand them more. *Participation Identification* provides students with an opportunity to consider different aspects of their self-identity specifically within a physical education environment.

Carli's reflection on why she does these activities with her students encapsulates our purpose of engaging in self-identity work in secondary school.

> By exploring self-identity activities students become more comfortable within the classroom and with themselves; creating an enhanced class and school dynamic. I have had students tell me that these activities help them to understand that they are not alone in the way they feel, live, love, or see in the world; therefore, they are more likely to share with others about their experiences. As my students become educated on their own self-identity, their confidence shines as their personalities are expressed. I have seen such a change in my classes since exploring self-identity, for this reason I believe that these in-depth conversations should be a staple in physical education classes at every age.

Comfort Zones

This activity has been adapted from Growth Circles (Frank, 2013) to focus on zones of personal and social comfort.

Step 1: Before the activity begins you will need to set up the comfort zones using polyspots, small dome cones, tape, rope, etc. You can determine the size and shape of the zones based on your specific context and environment. We typically use circles, as the center circle for a basketball court can form the inside circle and you can then create two more concentric circles. Whichever shape you choose, the inside shape is the panic zone, the middle shape is the progress zone, and the outside shape is the comfort zone (see Figure 4.1).

Step 2: Explain to your students that this activity will help them to understand how they feel in different personal and social situations. Point out the different zones you have marked on the floor and describe each zone and what it might look, feel, and/or sound like to be in that zone. In the *Comfort Zone,* students feel safe and secure, they are talking and laughing with friends, and they are fully engaged in the activity. In the *Progress Zone,* students feel a little uncomfortable, but are willing to try the activity, they are talking about what is happening and questioning the situation, they are still engaged, but a little more hesitant. In the *Panic Zone,* students feel threatened and unsafe, there is little sound, and they are frozen and not engaging in the activity. Each of the zones relate to our comfort levels in various situations and where learning may occur. In the comfort zone, learning will occur as we already feel comfortable, but we may not necessarily learn new things about ourselves. The progress zone presents the optimum environment for learning about ourselves to occur, as we feel challenged but secure. Very little productive learning occurs in the panic zone as we feel threatened and often shut down or disengage from the situation.

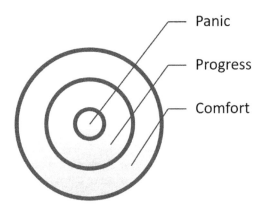

FIGURE 4.1.   Set up for Comfort Zones

Step 3: Everyone starts in the comfort zone and as you read different situations (see examples in Figure 4.2), the students and teacher choose a zone based on how they feel about that particular situation. Once students move to their zone, you can ask for volunteers to share why they chose a particular zone. This allows students to learn about each other's level of comfort within different situations. The situations can be reasonably innocuous to begin with and then move onto more context specific situations. You can also ask your students to name situations for the group to respond to. If you do this, our suggestion is that, unless you have created a safe and respectful learning environment where students understand that what is shared during the activity stays within the group, you remind students that the situations are school appropriate.

Step 4: After the activity has finished it is important to have the students debrief and reflect on the situation by asking them to discuss with a peer and then share with a larger group or whole class. This reflection session could include questions such as:

- What did you learn about yourself and/or others during this activity?

Sample Situations

How do you feel about…
- Flying in a plane
- Heights
- Holding a snake
- Singing a song
- Singing a song right now in front of the class
- Playing basketball
- Camping in a tent
- Running a mile
- Performing a dance
- Taking a math test
- Presenting a project to the class
- Asking for help
- Meeting people you don't know
- Speaking in another language
- Being in a group with someone who is different from you
- Telling someone you love them
- Confronting a friend about something they did or said
- Intervening when you see someone being bullied
- Introducing yourself to someone new
- Saying no to friends

Other situations can be added to the list based on your specific context or environment.

FIGURE 4.2.   Comfort Zones

- What activities put you in your comfort or panic zone?
- Why might we all have different comfort and/or panic zones?
- In which zone do you feel you learn most about yourself? Why might that be?
- How can we help our classmates move from their comfort zone into the progress zone?
- How can we help our classmates if they move into their panic zone?

Judgment Circle

Step 1: This activity can be used to explore what students think and to help them to become more confident and comfortable with themselves. It can also create opportunities for beneficial conversation and foster a positive class atmosphere.

Step 2: Decide upon the issue that you want the students to consider in this activity (see Figure 4.3 for examples). This will be based on your observation of student interactions during your class. You will need a piece of paper and pen or pencil for each student in the class.

Step 3: To begin the activity, have all students sit in a circle in the gym or classroom. Using a circle allows all students to see and acknowledge each other. To set the stage for the activity, you express your concern for what has been occurring in the class and some outcomes you want to see from the activity. It is important to discuss with the students that we each have something going on in our lives that others probably do not know about. You then ask a question pertaining to the issue you are witnessing in the class. Students then write down their answer on the paper, crinkle it up, and throw it into the middle of the circle. Ask the student

Sample Questions

- What makes students at this school popular?
- What is something that someone would not know about you just by looking at you? (This question is typically where student get surprisingly personal)
- What is your most difficult struggle?
- Why do students make fun of others?
- Why do students disrespect their teachers?
- Who do you live with?
- Do you think you have personal or material items or traits that someone else desires?
- What do you take most for granted?
- If you could change one thing about yourself, what would it be?
- Have you ever been bullied? If so, how?
- If you could buy one item what would it be?
- Why do you think students act like the rules don't apply to them?

Other questions can be added to the list based on your specific context or environment.

FIGURE 4.3. Judgment Circles

to remain quiet while all students complete the task. When all students have put their paper in the middle, mix up the papers and YOU read them out loud. Having you read the statements, other students cannot identify who wrote the comment by recognizing their handwriting.

Step 4: As you read the statements, you can discuss what is written and ask if other students have experienced similar things or feel the same way. You have to be willing to probe further and prompt discussion when appropriate as this is where the students will learn about their self-identity and the identity of their classmates. They can also understand some of the factors within their environment that influence their self-identity.

What I Wish My Teacher Knew

Step 1: The purpose of this activity is to provide your students with an opportunity to privately express something they want you to know about them that they might not feel comfortable bringing up in conversation. It allows students to reveal a part of their identity. In order for this activity to be beneficial for the students, there needs to be a level of mutual trust and respect.

Step 2: Each student will need a piece of paper and a pen or pencil. Allow students to spread out in your environment as appropriate so they have some privacy in their writing. Ask your students to write down what they wish you knew about them that would help you to understand them better. Invite them to write what they feel comfortable sharing that you do not already know. Assure them that their classmates will not see what they write. However, you must also ensure that they understand your role as a mandated reporter as there may be implications for some things that they share.

Step 3: Treat what they choose to share with you with the care and respect that it deserves. Use this information to begin conversations with your students that will allow you to support them where possible, encourage them to overcome challenges, and help them to be successful in school.

Participation Identification

Step 1: Quite often, students at the secondary level already self-identify based on their skill ability in a PE setting, may or may not get involved in the lesson activities and tend to either interact with students in the class or keep to themselves. Simultaneous to the students' experiences, teachers tend to make decisions and even judge students without actually learning from them why they engage/do not engage in class, etc. Thus, the purpose of this activity is for students to self-identify their skill ability, level of involvement and social interaction based on the descriptors provided (see Figure 4.4).

Step 2: This activity can be done as a whole class, a station depending on the design and content of a lesson or however you deem fit as the teacher of the class. This activity can certainly be conducted more than once throughout a quarter, se-

Name _____   Date _____

Class _____

Carefully read the descriptions below. In each column, circle the description that best resembles your skill ability, level of involvement, and social interaction in physical education.

Based on the descriptions you circled above, how would you best define your overall engagement in physical education? Be specific and detailed.

Skill Ability	Level of Involvement	Social Interaction
I am high-skilled.	I am highly involved and engaged in PE and am often assertive in games/activities.	I interact with boys and girls in class.
I am average to high-skilled.	I am regularly involved and engaged in PE and am sometimes assertive in games/activities.	I mostly interact with the boys in the class.
I am average skilled.	I am sometimes involved and engaged in PE, other times I hang back from the 'action'.	I mostly interact with the girls in the class.
I am low to average skilled.	I am rarely involved or engaged in PE. I try to keep away from the 'action' of the game/activity (i.e., I try to be invisible).	I am ignored by my classmates.
I am low skilled.	I do not engage or participate in PE. I do not change my clothes, am frequently absent, have a note to be excused, or go down to the nurse.	I do not like to interact with any of my classmates.

FIGURE 4.4. Participation Identification Activity

mester or academic year, as their responses may differ across units of instruction. Writing instruments and a private space will be needed for each student. Students are to circle the description that best resembles them either in the big picture of physical education (if conducted at the start or end of the school year) or in a particular unit of instruction.

Step 3: If you have created a mutually respectful, safe environment, provide students with the opportunity to discuss in pairs and small groups 'why' they selected these descriptions along with what has influenced their feelings about their skill ability, level of involvement and social interaction. As a teacher, this can provide important information concerning how students feel about themselves, which can hopefully inform you as you plan upcoming learning opportunities for your students.

INTERSECTIONALITY

We have found that while students will begin to recognize the different facets of their self-identity through engaging in these activities, there is a tendency to focus on the most important facet(s) based on their particular context. That list may include, gender, appearance, athletic ability, academic ability, religion, socio-economic status, gang affiliation, among others. It is important to understand that what students consider important about their self-identity is fluid relative to age, social relationships, grades in school, etc. Helping students develop a positive self-identity that recognizes and celebrates how different facets of self-intersect is something we can, and should, attend to in our teaching. While we have addressed self-identity in this chapter, the authors of the other chapters of this book provide wonderful suggestions of how to focus on different aspects of social justice. We recommend that you consider how information presented in these chapters can intersect to provide your students with the understanding and tools to fully recognize and appreciate their own self-identity.

CHALLENGES AND POSSIBILITIES

Engaging students in exploring their self-identity and recognizing commonalities and differences with their classmates in a safe and respectful way is vital in building a caring community within your classes. We know firsthand that this work is not without challenge and certainly will not be a smooth journey. However, we firmly believe and can attest that the time spent in this process is beneficial for you, your students, and your physical education community. We recommend that you introduce these activities once you have fostered a mutual level of trust and respect in your classes.

REFERENCES

Bain, L. (1975). The hidden curriculum in physical education. *Quest,* 24(1), 92–101.

Bain, L. (1990). A critical analysis of the hidden curriculum. In D. Kirk and R. Tinning (Eds.), *Physical education curriculum and culture: Critical issues in the contemporary crisis* (pp. 23–42). New York, NY: Falmer Press.

Cochran-Smith, M. (1995). Color blindness and basket making are not the answers: Confronting the dilemmas of race, culture, and language diversity in teacher education. *American Educational Research Journal, 32*(3), 493–522.

Dodds, P. (1985). Are hunters of the functional curriculum seeking quarks or snarks? *Journal of Teaching in Physical Education, 4,* 91–99.

Evans, J. (Ed.) (1993). *Equality, education and physical education.* London, UK: Falmer.

Fernandez-Balboa, J. M. (1993). Sociocultural characteristics of the hidden curriculum in physical education. *Quest, 45*(2), 230–254.

Fernández-Balboa, J. M. (1997). Physical education teacher preparation in the postmodern era: Toward a critical pedagogy. In J. M. Fernández-Balboa (Ed.), *Critical postmodernism in human movement, physical education, and sport* (pp. 121–138). Albany, NY: State University of New York Press.

Frank, L. S. (2013). *Journey toward the caring classroom: Using adventure to create community* (2nd Ed). Oklahoma City, OK. Wood 'N' Barnes.

Freire, P. (1970). *Pedagogy of the oppressed.* New York, NY: Herder and Herder.

Kirk, D. (1986). A critical pedagogy for teacher education: Toward an inquiry-oriented approach. *Journal of Teaching in Physical Education, 5*, 230–246.

Ladson-Billings, G. (2001). *Crossing over to Canaan: The journey of new teachers in diverse classrooms. The Jossey-Bass Education Series.* San Francisco, CA: Jossey-Bass.

Tinning, R. (2002). Toward a 'modest pedagogy': Reflections on the problematics of critical pedagogy. *Quest, 54*, 224–240.

CHAPTER 5

CHALLENGING BULLYING

Lessons from Adventure-Based Learning

Sue Sutherland

ACTION RESEARCH AND REFLECTION

While there is no doubt that bullying has been present in schools for many decades, there has been a dramatic increase in the attention given to bullying both in the media and academia (Hymel & Swearer, 2015). Bullying has been defined as intentional, repetitive, aggressive behaviors where there is an imbalance of power between those involved (Olweus,1993). However, children often discuss the effects of bullying on the person targeted, the use of both verbal and physical aggression, and social exclusion in their definitions of bullying (Hellstrom, Persson, & Hagquist, 2015). In the real life of schools, it is important to pay attention to the ways in which children discuss bullying as it allows us the potential to disrupt the bullying cycle. Recent statistics have revealed the extent to which bullying occurs in US schools:

- Twenty eight percent of middle and high school students reported being bullied (National Center for Education Statistics, 2013)
- Approximately 30% of young people reported bullying others (Bradshaw, Sawyer, & O'Brennan, 2007)

Teaching About Social Justice Issues in Physical Education, pages 43–52.
Copyright © 2019 by Information Age Publishing
All rights of reproduction in any form reserved.

- 70% of both young people and staff indicate that they have seen bullying in school (Bradshaw et al., 2007)
- 20% of middle school students have experienced bullying in physical education (Bradshaw et al., 2007)

I have become more focused on addressing bullying in my work and teaching over the past 20 plus years. The initial impetus in this concern for me was my work with individuals with disabilities both in the education and outdoor adventure settings. Upon moving into the teacher education realm, I become more interested in helping the pre-service teachers (PSTs) understand the prevalence of bullying and the implications for students in a physical education environment. Using a "living the curriculum" approach (Oslin, Collier, & Mitchell, 2001), I introduced my students to adventure-based learning (ABL) as a means of creating an emotionally and physically safe physical education environment. This early attempt at addressing the issue of bullying through ABL was naïve and lacked the depth of understanding that students needed to move beyond a cursory effort. While the students understood how to create an emotionally and physically safe environment in their classes, they were less successful in specifically understanding how to address bullying through their pedagogy. Upon further reflection, I became much more intentional in providing specific knowledge and experiences, coupled with focused reflection, that fostered a deeper understanding of the issue of bullying in physical education, and how ABL can be used to disrupt the cycle of bullying through a strength-based approach. The changes in my approach to teaching about bullying have, along with other courses in our program, resulted in our PSTs feeling more confident in addressing bullying and creating a physical education environment that is welcoming and safe for all students. It is important to understand that this is an ongoing reflective process for me and the activities that are presented in this chapter are part of the current iteration of this process.

CONTEXT

As has been stated in a couple of other chapters in this book, I am a faculty member in the Physical Education program at Ohio State University, USA. At the undergraduate level, I teach within both the Physical Education Teacher Education (PETE) program and the Physical Activity and Coaching Specialist (PACS) program. The courses where I conduct my pedagogical work on challenging bullying are Adventure-based Learning, Elementary Methods, and Sociocultural Issues in Physical Education, Sport, and Physical Activity. Outdoor adventure education (OAE) has been an interest of mine since my undergraduate program in the UK, but it really became a passion when I moved to the USA and realized the power of OAE on a wide variety of individuals and groups. Transferring this passion into the PETE program at Ohio State University resulted in the Adventure-based Learning course, which provides students with the knowledge and skills needed to understand, experience, and facilitate ABL with school aged students. During this course, we also discuss bullying, positive youth development, social and emotional learning, power, and privilege to foster critical reflection regarding the school environment and, more specifically, the physical education or physical activity environment. The ABL course lays the foundation for further discussion on bullying in both the Elementary Methods and Sociocultural Issues in the Physical Education, Sport, and Physical Activity program, where additional critical pedagogies to address bullying and social justice are explored.

ACTIVITIES TO CHALLENGE
BULLYING IN PHYSICAL EDUCATION

The activities presented in this chapter are incorporated into the ABL course in the Ohio State University PETE and PACS programs. Adventure-based Learning is a holistic, student-centered curricular model that fosters personal growth and social development (Dyson & Sutherland, 2014) through a purposeful sequence of activities that focus on interpersonal and intrapersonal development of participants (Cosgriff, 2000). More specifically, ABL "embodies a student-centered approach, encompassing a form of adventure, where the educative purpose of the experience is emphasized, and students reflect on their personal and social development through a debrief process" (Sutherland & Legge, 2016, p. 308). When teaching ABL, there are certain key components that are essential: "experiential learning, sequence and flow of activities, student centered facilitation, processing (brief and debrief), emotional and physical safety (including Challenge by Choice and Full Value Contract), and cultural responsiveness" (Sutherland & Legge, 2016, p. 308). Each of the four activities is incorporated into the ABL course with a specific goal in mind. *The Body* introduces the concept of creating a physically and emotionally safe classroom environment with student input. *Have you Ever?* allows students to understand how members of their class have things in common as well as things that are different in a fun, engaging environment. *Ten Together* is used to highlight that everyone makes mistakes and that is completely acceptable. This activity also focuses on the influence of group reactions to mistakes. *Floating Stick* highlights ways to deal with, and possible solutions for, frustration in a group situation. It is important to remember that these activities are a sample of how ABL can challenge bullying through a strength-based approach that focuses on building community within a classroom and fostering personal and social skills.

The Body

Step 1: Prior to introducing the activity, I ask students to reflect on their own physical education/physical activity experience focusing on the environment that helped or hindered participation. I do this through a think, pair, share format so that students can think about their own experience before discussing with a partner, and then sharing with the whole class. During the whole class discussion, we focus on the aspects of the environment that encouraged or hindered participation.

Step 2: Students are then asked to individually consider what behaviors, words, actions, qualities, and instructional strategies would promote a safe, respectful, welcoming environment for our ABL course. Given time to reflect on this question, I ask students to write or draw everything they believe will create a physically and emotionally safe environment on the inside of the body outline I have provided (see Figure 5.1, note: I try to use gender-neutral body outlines for these activities. I have also used cartoon or seasonal characters in the past).

Step 3: On the outside of the body outline, I ask students to write or draw everything they believe will detract from or hinder a physically and emotionally safe environment in our ABL course.

Step 4: Once students have completed their individual body outline, they share in small groups and complete a new body based on a discussion of their collective outlines. This outline is a consensus of all students in the small group.

Step 5: Each small group presents their body outline to the whole group explaining what they wrote or drew inside and outside of the body. After these presentations, the whole class comes to a consensus of what to include on the inside and outside of the body. The class then creates a final body outline that represents how an emotionally and physically safe learning environment will be created for the ABL course. I give the class the option to either use a larger version (on a large poster size sheet) of the body outline they have been using up to this point, or draw their own outline. All students must be involved in creating the whole class version of the body outline. This final body then becomes the contract that the students sign regarding their continued contribution to a physically and emotionally safe learning environment.

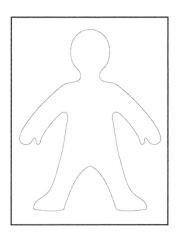

FIGURE 5.1. Gender-neutral Body Outline

Have You Ever?

This activity has been adapted from Childs and Wilson (2014) to appreciate different experiences, strengths, honesty, and empathy.

Step 1: Create Have you Ever question cards or sheets of paper. I use spiral notecard books (2" × 4" cards) as I have found them to be more durable with multiple classes. You will need to create two sets of questions based on your context or situation. See Figure 5.2 for examples of questions.

Round 1 Questions

• Been to the zoo	• Spit out your drink because you were
• Been to the beach	laughing
• Gone swimming	• Stuck your finger in a birthday cake
• Ridden a bike	• Eaten just the inside of an oreo
• Read a book	• Made silly faces in the mirror
• Sung a song	• Made up fake languages with your friends
• Shoveled snow	• Made a prank phone call
• Been on a motorcycle	• Lied about doing your chores
• Been outside of the state	•
• Cut the grass	• Locked yourself out of the house
• Found hair in your food	• Built a fort
• Played video games for more than 4 hours in	• Ate food that fell on the floor
a day	• Eaten so much candy you were sick to your
	stomach

Round 2 Questions

• Been embarrassed about a new haircut	• Hurt someone with your words
• Been unhappy with how you look	• Been told you were ugly
• Judged someone because of how they look	• Apologized for hurting someone
• Heard someone talk behind a friends back	• Lost a friend because of drama
• Talked badly about someone behind their back	• Made fun of someone's clothes
• Made fun of someone's clothes and then	• Taken a joke too far
thought maybe that's all they could afford	• Seen someone bullied on social
• Said something to someone in this class that	• Been called a name you didn't like
you should not have	• Seen someone get bullied and stepped in
• Said something on social media you wouldn't	• Seen someone get bullied and not done
say in person	anything
• Screenshot something you shouldn't have	• Called someone a name you know they didn't
• Screenshot something you shouldn't have,	like
then sent it to other people	• Judged someone by the color of their skin
• Made fun of someone you like just because	
your friends were	
• Made a mistake you wish you could take back	
• Used the words *gay* or *retarded* in a negative	
way	

FIGURE 5.2   Sample Have you Ever Questions

Step 2: Arrange polyspots on the floor in a circle. You will need one polyspot for every student in your class. Place one polyspot in the center of the circle and put the Have you Ever Question cards or sheets on this polyspot.

Step 3: Each student stands on a polyspot (not the one in the center of the circle). I explain that this is a non-contact activity and state the rules of the game as follows:

- If you can answer *yes* to the question you need to move to another polyspot
- You cannot move to the poly spot to the immediate left or right of the one you are currently standing on
- Please walk during the game
- Remember it is a non-contact activity
- If you do not find an unoccupied polyspot in the circle, you move to the polyspot located in the center of the circle
- The person on the polyspot in the center of the circle reads the next question from the cards/sheet and places the cards/sheet on the polyspot before moving to an open polyspot.

I start on the polyspot in the center of the circle and read the first question to begin the game.

Step 4: At the end of round 1, before moving to round 2, I ask the students to ask their own Have you Ever questions when they are on the center polyspot. I remind them that the questions should be school appropriate! I also add the same condition to the end of round 2. It is interesting to see what questions the students ask during both rounds. I often find that they will ask deeper questions than I have written on the cards/sheets, which then leads to wonderful discussions in the debrief.

Step 5: As with any ABL activity, it is of vital importance to debrief this activity to allow the students to process what happened and how they can transfer what they learned in this activity to their lives beyond the ABL course, especially when working with young people.

Ten Together

This activity has been adapted from Toss 10 (Frank, 2013) to increase the challenge level for undergraduate students. *Ten Together* is designed to expose participants to making mistakes and explore the impact of reactions to these mistakes.

Step 1: You will need one foam ball (about the size of a tennis ball) for each student in your class. Explain to the students that they need to complete 10 tasks, performed by all students at the same time, in consecutive order, and without mistakes (e.g., dropping a ball, performing an incorrect task, not performing the task simultaneously, and not performing the tasks in order). If the group breaks any of the rules they start the tasks again from #1.

Step 2: Each student has a foam ball and stands in a circle. Practice the following tasks so that they get used to the sequence of tasks. During the practice rounds, don't worry about mistakes, as you want them to learn the tasks. I suggest practicing the complete sequence of tasks 3 times before starting the activity.

1. Throw the ball in the air, clap once, and catch
2. Throw the ball in the air, clap once, and catch with one hand
3. Throw the ball in the air, touch the ground, and catch
4. Throw the ball in the air, turn around, and catch
5. Throw the ball in the air, do one jumping jack, and catch
6. Pass (throw) the ball one person to the right while catching a ball from the person on the left*
7. Pass (throw) the ball one person to the left while catching a ball from the person on the right*
8. Pass (throw) the ball to a person directly across the circle and catch the ball thrown
9. Throw the ball in the air from behind your back and catch in front
10. Throw the ball in the air, do a celebration dance, and catch

* Increase the challenge level by asking students to catch with one hand.

Step 3: Stand back and let the class begin the activity. I ask that they are honest and own up when they make a mistake, but they are not allowed to call out one of their peers if they make a mistake. If a mistake is made, the groups start the sequence again from the first task.

Step 4: This activity has taken groups anywhere from 20–40 minutes to complete depending on how they work together to overcome mistakes and frustration. It is important to monitor how the group reacts to mistakes and deals with their frustration. While you want the group to make mistakes, you do not want it to get to a level where the group shuts down and does not engage in the activity. In situations where you feel the group, or some individuals, may be engaging in behaviors that are detrimental to individual or group functioning, there are a number of strategies you can employ.

- Stop the activity and ask how many in the group have made one or more mistakes during the activity. Then talk about positive and negative reactions to mistakes, explaining how you would feel if you made a mistake and someone blamed you for the group not being successful, as opposed to the group helping you to get over making the mistake and give suggestions on how to avoid making the same mistake again.
- Allow a group to start from task 4, 5, or 6 once they have successfully reached that task. For example, if a group successfully reaches task 4, then any mistakes from that point forward means that they return to start the sequence at task 4 rather than task 1. Be careful not to introduce this too soon as it can dilute the purpose of the activity.

- Facilitate a discussion about choosing to overcome frustration through positive strategies rather than engaging negative behaviors such as placing blame, checking out, or sabotaging the success of the group. Positive strategies could include encouraging each other, being positive in actions and words, helping others to overcome mistakes, or listening to all viewpoints or solutions to complete the activity.

Step 5: Engage the group in a debrief highlighting what they learned from the experience that will help them in their life beyond the course. It is important to focus on making mistakes and supporting each other during group work. *Together Ten* can only be completed when all group members are involved and feel part of the group. Thus, helping students understand that making mistakes is human nature and how we learn, everyone brings strengths and weaknesses to all tasks, and encouraging rather than blaming someone helps both the individual and group to be successful.

FLOATING STICK

This activity is designed to work on individual and group communication skills, while also highlighting the effect of and solutions for frustration.

Step 1: You will need lightweight tent poles (one pole per 12–16 students), the lighter the better.

Step 2: Students stand in two lines facing each other, 6–8 students per line. Students hold their arms at chest height with their index and middle fingers of both hands outstretched (palms facing down).

Step 3: Lay the tent poles (one per group) on the backs of the students' fingers.

Step 4: Start with the tent pole at the chest height of the shortest person in the group. Explain that the challenge is to lower the pole to the ground while adhering to the following rules:

- The back of each person's fingers must stay in contact with the tent pole at all times
- Pinching or grabbing the tent pole is not allowed
- Fingers must stay parallel to the ground
- Nothing else may be in contact with the tent pole

Breaking any of these rules results in restarting the task

Step 5: This activity can take groups varying lengths of time to complete depending on how well they communicate and work through their frustration. As with the *Ten Together* activity, it is important to monitor the level of frustration within each group during this activity. If you feel the level of frustration is detrimental to group functioning, there are some strategies that you can employ to refocus the group.

- Prompt the group to consider how they are communicating during the activity and how they might improve in their communication.

- Engage in a discussion about making mistakes and supporting each other through these mistakes (see Step 4 in *Ten Together*).
- Facilitate a discussion about dealing with frustration rather than letting it overwhelm an individual or group (see Step 4 in *Ten Together*).

Step 6: As with the other activities highlighted in this chapter, it is vital to engage the group in a debrief after the activity to allow them to reflect on what they learned about their personal and social development in the activity and how it can be transferred to other areas of life. Every time I have facilitated this activity, the debrief invariably focuses on how we deal with frustration and the positive strategies that can be used to move past frustration. Be prepared to engage in this discussion with your students as it is a powerful learning experience that can be transferred beyond the activity.

Debriefing is the most important aspect of facilitating ABL, but is difficult for inexperienced facilitators to execute effectively (Dillon, Tanehill, & O'Sullivan, 2017; Sutherland, Ressler, & Stuhr, 2011; Sutherland, Stuhr, & Ayvazo, 2016). Unfortunately, it is not within the scope of this chapter to expand upon different methods of debriefing. Rather, I suggest referring to the following resources for a more detailed discussion on possible models or frameworks for debriefing (Dyson & Sutherland, 2014; Sutherland, 2012; Sutherland, Stuhr, & Ressler, 2014).

INTERSECTIONALITY

Using a strength-based approach through ABL to challenge bullying highlights the importance of understanding intersectionality. Highlighting commonalities within students' self-identities or experiences, while also celebrating differences, lays the foundation for fostering a community within a physical education classroom. Creating an emotionally and physically safe learning environment allows all students to engage positively in physical education. There is a wealth of information on different sociocultural issues within this book and I urge readers to engage with each of the chapters.

CHALLENGES AND POSSIBILITIES

Bullying in school and beyond is a serious issue facing young people throughout the world. Physical education is an environment where bullying can occur for a wide variety of reasons including skill level, gender, body size, ability/[disability], religion, and heteronormativity. It is incumbent on all school personnel to address bullying when it occurs and to create an environment where bullying is challenged. Providing undergraduate PETE students with the tools to do just that is important for the future of our teaching profession. At Ohio State University, we choose to provide our students with the knowledge and strategies to challenge bullying through the strength-based approach of ABL. While ABL is by no means the only approach to achieve this goal, it is one that has proven successful at Ohio State.

REFERENCES

Bradshaw, C. P., Sawyer, A. L., & O'Brennan, L. M. (2007). Bullying and peer victimization at school: Perceptual differences between students and school staff. *School Psychology Review, 36*(3), 361–382.

Childs, L., & Wilson, M. (2014). *R.A.I.S.E.—Active group lessons for bullying prevention and social skills: A physical education activity guide & resource manual for middle school.* Beverley, MA: Project Adventure Inc

Cosgriff, M. (2000). Walking our talk: Adventure based learning and physical education. *Journal of Physical Education New Zealand, 33,* 89–98.

Dillon, M., Tannehill, D., & O'Sullivan, M. (2017). "I know when I did it, I got frustrated": The influence of 'living' a curriculum for preservice teachers. *Journal of Teaching in Physical Education, 36,* 445–454.

Dyson, B., & Sutherland, S. (2014). Adventure education in your physical education program. In J. Lund & D. Tannehill (Eds.), *Standards-based physical education curriculum development* (5th ed., pp. 229–254). Burlington, MA: Jones and Bartlett Learning.

Frank, L. (2013). *Journey toward the caring classroom: Using adventure to create community in the classroom.* Oklahoma City, OK: Wood 'N' Barnes Publishing.

Hellstrom, L., Persson, L., & Hagquist, C. (2015). Understanding and defining bullying—Adolescents' own views. *Archives of Public Health, 73,* 4.

Hymel, S., & Swearer, S. M. (2015). Four decades of research on school bullying: An introduction. *American Psychologist, 70*(4), 293–299.

National Center for Education Statistics. (2013). *Student Reports of Bullying and Cyber-Bullying: Results from the 2013 School Crime Supplement to the National Crime Victimization Survey.* Retrieved from https://nces.ed.gov/pubsearch/pubsinfo.asp?pubid=2015056

Olweus D. (1993). *Bullying at school: What we know and what we can do.* Malden, MA: Blackwell Publishers.

Oslin, J., Collier, C., & Mitchell, S. (2001). Living the curriculum. *Journal of Physical Education, Recreation & Dance, 72*(5), 47–51. doi:10.1080/07303084.2001.10605753

Sutherland, S. (2012). Borrowing strategies from adventure-based learning to enhance group processing in cooperative learning. In B. Dyson & A. Casey (Eds.), *Cooperative learning in physical education: A research-based approach* (pp. 103–175). Abingdon, Oxon; Routledge.

Sutherland, S., & Legge, M. F. (2016). The possibilities of "doing" outdoor and/or adventure education in physical education/teacher education. *Journal of Teaching in Physical Education, 35,* 299–312. Doi:10.1123/jtpe.2016-0161

Sutherland, S., Ressler, J., & Stuhr, P. T. (2011). Adventure-based learning and reflection: The journey of one cohort of teacher candidates. *International Journal of Human Movement Science, 5*(2), 5–24.

Sutherland, S., Stuhr, P. T., & Ayvazo, S. (2016). Learning to teach: Pedagogical content knowledge in adventure-based learning. *Physical Education and Sport Pedagogy, 21,* 233–248. Doi:10.1080/17408989.2014.931365

Sutherland, S., Stuhr, P. T., & Ressler, J. (2014). Group processing in cooperative learning: Using the Sunday afternoon drive debrief model. *Active + Healthy: Australian Council for Health, Physical Education and Recreation (ACHPER), 21*(2), 12–14.

CHAPTER 6

REAL JOCKS CAN'T DANCE

Aesthetic Pedagogical Disruptions of Body Work in Physical Education

Louise McCuaig and Karen Shelley

ACTION RESEARCH & REFLECTION—BODY WORK IN HEALTH AND PHYSICAL EDUCATION

Some thirty years of teaching Health and Physical Education (HPE) with Australian school and university students resulted in Louise's enthrallment with bodies. During this time she has marshaled disorderly groups of bodies, disciplined unruly bodies, corrected sporting bodies, tended injured bodies, comforted sobbing bodies and provided literally thousands of learning experiences in, through and about bodies. Not surprisingly, the Australian curriculum documents shaping her HPE work reflects the unique and explicit remit of HPE and its teachers to manage, construct, discipline and care for young bodies. Teachers of HPE assist students to study the personal behaviors and actions that influence their health, develop effective interpersonal skills, engage in regular physical activity and facilitate students' recognition of the biological and sociological factors that influence their growth and development (Queensland Schools Curriculum Council, 1997). Whilst HPE teachers are not the only teachers who engage with young people's

Teaching About Social Justice Issues in Physical Education, pages 53–67.
Copyright © 2019 by Information Age Publishing
All rights of reproduction in any form reserved.

bodies in schools, they are primarily engaged in what we term 'body work', work on their own and others' bodies, work about bodies and work through bodies.

Of course, 'body work' is by no means a new phenomenon in Australian or international HPE contexts. Military, sporting and health discourses have shaped programs of PE across the globe and in Australia since the early 1900s (Tinning, 2001). Literature in the PE field would suggest that, to date, PE has figured prominently as a form of bodily control and discipline (Lawson, 1993; Tinning, 2001). According to Kirk (1998), physical activity programs in schools have, throughout the last century, "played an important and highly specialized role in regulating children's bodies to suit the needs of school and society for social order" (p, 14). In the 1990s, HPE researchers drew attention to the field's bodily focus, one that privileges a specific, mesomorph body type. Tinning (1990) identifies how the predominantly 'fat free' muscularity of the mesomorph body shape, has come to signify a range of positive social attributes. Mesomorph children and teachers thus "'naturally' represent success in sport, high peer-group status, embody healthiness, discipline and positive personality traits such as trustworthiness and loyalty" (Evans & Davies cited in Tinning, 1990, p. 24).

A powerful discourse working within this discursive terrain is that of sport. Gendering bodies through sport has been a powerful discursive practice within HPE, as notions of what is and what is not acceptable behaviour in sport, and thus HPE, are tied to traditional roles of femininity and masculinity. As a result of the dominance of sport discourses within HPE contexts, Sparkes and Templin (1992) argue that women physical education teachers experience a double marginality, whilst Sparkes (1994) and Squires and Sparkes (1996) reveal the consequences for those HPE teachers, male or female, who fail to adhere to these heterosexual discourses.

Perhaps ironically then, past and recent Australian HPE curricula explicitly seek to challenge the hegemony of the sporty, fit body of PE. As with their New Zealand colleagues, Australian HPE teachers have been responsible for teaching the most morally contested subject matter within school curricula including sexuality, identity, substance abuse and risk taking behaviors (McCuaig & Tinning, 2010). Moreover, these endeavors are underpinned by an emphasis on the teaching and modelling of social justice principles to provide a "foundation for developing active and informed members of society, capable of managing the interactions between themselves and their social, cultural and physical environments in the pursuit of good health" (Queensland Schools Curriculum Council, 1999, p. 1).

Research would suggest however, that HPE teachers have long felt ill-equipped, both professionally and philosophically, to embrace and construct the kinds of holistic HPE programs advocated within contemporary HPE curriculum documents (Macdonald et al, 2002; Tinning, 2001). Tinning (2004) elaborates further noting how the "PE teacher will do pedagogical work on/for the student's body without saying a word and perhaps even in spite of the activities developed to enact the new curriculum" (p. 224). HPE teachers' construction of their embodied subjectivities, drawing as they do upon the dominant discourses and practices located within HPE institutions may, Tinning (2004) argues, provide a key limitation to the creation of "pedagogical practices that empower young people in terms of bodily knowledge" (p. 230). For example, Yager and O'Dea (2008) argue that "failure to address trainee teachers' body image problems may also lead to the inadvertent modelling or unintentional transfer of poor body image, disordered eating and exercise students to school students" (p. 10). Consequently, in seeking to co-construct HPE teachers whose pedagogical practices are aligned with the sociocritical intent of current HPE curricula, teacher educators have increasingly recognized the need to "unpack" this messy terrain of self-constitution.

CONTEXT—AESTHETIC PEDAGOGICAL DISRUPTIONS

This HPE landscape fueled Louise's desire to undertake doctoral research in the School of Human Movement and Nutrition Sciences at The University of Queensland (UQHMNS), which resulted in an invitation to lecture into the HPETE program. The Bachelor of Health, Sport and Physical Education (BHSPE) is one of five core undergraduate programs currently offered at UQHMNS and provides graduates with a qualification to teach Health and Physical Education (HPE) and Science for grades 7–10. Students undertake a four-year program where they spend their first eighteen months studying foundational knowledge and skills in the bio-physical and psycho-socio-cultural aspects of human movement. The majority of students who enter the BHSPE program are Australian school leavers whose age is approximately 17–18 years.

National and international research would suggest that the profile of HPETE has changed little since Abernethy, Macdonald and Bramich's (1997) study at UQHMNS found they were typically sociable, competitive and mesomorphic. Such a profile may offer opportunities and promise, but it nonetheless poses some challenges. Upon being charged with the task of teaching these HPETE students, Louise was convinced that change could be achieved through approaches that sought to disrupt the very identity and bio-knowledge lenses that teachers employ in their work with young people. One of her primary aims was to co-construct teachers who had an insight into the anxieties and mixed messages that many young people experience in relation to their bodies. Louise was inspired by Maxine Greene, who calls for educators to "cross the empty spaces between ourselves and those we teachers have called "other" over the years" (Greene, 1995, p.3), to explore alternative realities and "break with the taken for granteds" (Greene, 1995, p. 3). Drawing on imagination, Greene (1995) argues, provides the pedagogical means of crossing these boundaries.

Scholars such as Gard (2001, 2006) have argued that aesthetic experiences often serve to contrast and contest the biomedical and psychosocial knowledges of the profession's body work. Teacher education colleagues have likewise argued that an "exploration of dangerous styles of art and aesthetics that relate educational inquiry and practice to life worlds might become sites for transformation of self and pedagogy" (McDermott, 2002, p. 53). Following an engagement with the richness of this scholarship, Louise was inspired to implement a suite of arts-based activities within her HPETE undergraduate courses. For more than a decade this suite of learning experiences has been adapted to meet the specific curriculum or pedagogical aims of various courses, however the core activities and purpose of providing aesthetic provocations of privileged biophysical and moral under-standings of the body has remained consistent.

UNIT SET UP—DEVISING THE
REAL JOCKS CAN'T DANCE UNIT OF WORK

Real Jocks Can't Dance is part of a semester long course within the BHSPE pro-gram called Educating for Better Health. Typically, approximately 40 students enroll in this course, which is offered in the third year of a four year BHSPE program. Slightly more males then females are usually enrolled (55% males and 45% females), with percentages varying slightly from year to year. After the ini-tial two-hour lecture, students engage in a weekly two hour interactive workshop for the remaining 12 weeks of the semester. These workshops focus on unpacking the Australian HPE curriculum—underlying principles, content and pedagogy; major health issues facing young Australians, conducting health education lessons with a focus on Sexuality and Human Relationships Education; health education assessment; school policies pertaining to health and health education and enacting the Health Promoting Schools Framework by enhancing community and school partnerships.

Additionally, students undertake an hour-long experiential unit of work, the *Real Jocks Can't Dance* program, that provides learning experiences inspired by Madonna's "Vogue" dance. Primarily, this aesthetic pedagogical provocation en-gages teams of students in the construction of a contemporary dance routine in accordance with the themes and style of Madonna's popular dance hit—Vogue. In choreographing and performing the steps of this dance, the HPETE students are set the challenge of performing their routine in a gender that is an alternative of their own. Drawing on bell hooks' (2009) critique of Madonna's appropriation of voguing and sociocritical literature how individuals "read" their own and oth-ers' bodies, this experiential unit facilitates students' confrontation with taken-for-granted values and beliefs about bodies, gender and sexuality.

These provocations are situated within an exemplar unit of work entitled *Real jocks can't dance: Exploring the construction of gendered identities through con-temporary dance* [See Appendix 1]. In this inquiry-based unit, HPETE students explore the ways in which the beliefs, stereotypes and norms regarding gender and sexuality shape young people's identities and their relationships with oth-ers. Students explore these practices through their engagement with an aesthetic physical activity. In teams, students create and perform a dance routine for all staff in the School of Human Movement and Nutrition Sciences (HMNS). Participa-tion in this unit:

- Facilitates students' understanding and experience of an inquiry-based teaching and learning process.
- Explores social and cultural understandings of gendered bodies and the processes of normalization that influence individual identities and engagement in physical activities.
- Promotes students' understanding and experience of aesthetic physical activities.
- Engage with content descriptors from the Australian HPE curriculum to identify the tasks that underpin the design of HPE units of work.

One of the first tasks is to establish the assessment challenge. Importantly, this assessment task is not a component of the course's formal assessment practices, which focus on the design, delivery and critique of a socio-critical learning experience on one key socio-critical concept (e.g., normalization, identity construction, gender stereotypes, discrimination, marginalization and power). Instead, the challenge is designed to model authentic, engaging and robust assessment practices in HPE. In the first lecture, students are therefore provided a handout which states:

> Your class is to create and perform a dance performance for the HMNS staff to the music of Vogue by Madonna. The challenge for you and your group is to draw on a theme/narrative that explores the human capacity to "do gender and sexuality". Many of us believe that we can read people and their bodies to identify certain attributes or the 'truth' of them, such as their class, gender, sexuality, ethnicity, etc.

A range of learning experiences are then delivered in 2-hour workshops across a 12-week semester course. In the following section, we provide an overview of the pivotal suite of learning experiences that endeavor to disrupt students' taken-for-granted knowledges, beliefs and values.

STRATEGY/ACTIVITY/LESSON—
A SUITE OF PEDAGOGICAL PROVOCATIONS

Scaffolded delivery of the following three learning experiences is provided to students within the context of the *Real Jocks Can't Dance* unit as follows (see further information in Appendix 1). The key tasks of each learning experience include:

1. **Introductory Stimulus task**: following a brief introduction, students are provided with an overview of the dance challenge. It is important to note here that Madonna's Vogue and voguing has been selected as it has attracted considerable socio-critical critique from scholars such as bell hooks (2009) and is unlikely to be familiar to students. This latter point is significant as the very performance of a physical activity that is unfamiliar (e.g., Contemporary dance) to music that is not contemporary, has been designed to elevate the capacity of HPETE to feel uncomfortable. The steps of this learning experience involved:

a. Watch the 'Vogue' film clip through a number of times.
b. In response to the video, students engage in a preliminary identification of the key themes and discuss the representation of gender.
c. Watch a short excerpt of *Paris is Burning* from YouTube—this footage provides insight into the history of voguing and the lives of the leading figures in the vogue movement.
d. Class discussion follows with students to establish the role that marginalization of the black, Hispanic, gay population of New York, USA, played in the birth of voguing.

2. **Revealing gender stereotypes**: In an attempt to deploy learning experiences that will allow students to see how their 'eyes have been crafted', Louise asks students in gender specific and mixed gender groups, to complete the following tasks.

a. Draw and label the male and female reproductive organs without reference to personal digital devices.
b. Brainstorm responses to two questions; "What is the best and worst things about being a boy?" and, "What is the best and worst things about being a girl?".

The responses Louise recently received from her current group of students provide some interesting indicators of the dominance of gender and body discourses within our field [see Appendix 2]. Each team post their responses at allocated sites in the gym. Teams then take a 'gallery walk', judging the best drawings and collecting data on the attributes of male and female gender stereotypes.

3. **Transforming stereotypes into movement:** building on these foundational themes about gender stereotyping and bodies, in this third lesson students explore the strategies they can employ to translate these ideas into movement. This work involves two phases of activity as follows:

Phase One
a. Introduce lesson challenge: Today we are going to integrate the concepts we have learnt about gender into our own choreography and dance—feminism and masculinity.
b. Introduce first activity—Doing gender: how do young people perform gender on our campus?
c. When instructed, students leave the gym to gather data on the ways in which young people move and use their bodies to signal gender.
d. Students given a set time to return to class (after half an hour).

Phase Two
a. Return to classroom and allocate a reporter
b. Reporter to write points from group observation under headings of attired, external signs, movement.

c.   Teacher to facilitate discussion about how gender is 'shown' through attire, external signals and movement—key differences, ambiguities and aspects such as use of space.

d.   Students allocated one hour to embed these findings into their dance routines and movements.

While Louise has gathered substantial evidence through student feedback that these learning experiences are enjoyable and engaging, the extent to which they were achieving the deeper, critical work was to remain a mystery until Karen commenced her association with Louise to undertake a doctoral study.

CHALLENGES AND POSSIBILITIES

Karen was interested in the pedagogies Louise employed and their influence on students' understanding of sociocultural approaches to health education (see for more information Shelley, 2018; Shelley & McCuaig, 2018). Karen subsequently observed an entire semester of Louise's teaching in an undergraduate health education course that contributed to the HPETE degree discussed above. Six students from the cohort of 44 agreed to be interviewed by Karen at the end of the teaching semester about their opinions on the course and associated pedagogical strategies. Field notes were made by Karen during the teaching semester and student work also contributed to the gathered data set. During this process, the challenges of undertaking this work quickly became evident.

MESSINESS AND CONFUSION

In choreographing and performing the steps of this dance, Louise wanted students to explore how individuals "read" their own and others' bodies. In addition, students participate in the initial dance rehearsals, where they learn the relatively complex vogue steps of the two choruses, in full body lycra. This was a deliberate strategy of Louise's to simulate the sense of ill-ease, exposure and self-consciousness and marginalization the less physically coordinated school students experience in HPE classes. In the interviews when students were explicitly asked "what do you think the lecturer was trying to achieve with this task?", the six HPETE students understood that the task was about trying to place students out of their comfort zones. However, as Michelle admits, her colleagues did not really understand the intent of the course in general, or the Vogue aspect specifically. Michelle stated that:

> … there's a lot of students that just didn't understand why we were doing this course. I don't know if it was that it wasn't properly explained at the beginning or if they just are too young to understand health and haven't had those kinds of situations that I have. I honestly don't know what it is but they just did not understand the course, did not understand Vogue, did not understand the assessment. It was pretty frustrating, seeing that when I understood it (Michelle, 23-year-old).

Interestingly, the seemingly body-confident HPETE students felt more uncomfortable in the dance domain than performing in the body lycra. As Anthony stated in the end-of-semester interview, "… well the dancing thing, I sucked at that … I was terrible, and it felt so uncomfortable" (19-year-old). Dressing as "a gender other than your own" created some initial discomfort for some of the students, but generally the students reported no real discomfort. For example, Erin recalls that: "I was a tomboy when I was younger, so it didn't bother me at all" (27-year-old female). Participants who reported a mild discomfort initially, stated that this feeling dissipated quickly, as the group had fun with the task and enjoyed the dressing and portrayal of an alternative gender. In fact, the cohort did appear to have a lot of fun, so much so that a female student placed a drink bottle down the front of her pants and proceeded to chase other male students around the room attempting to simulate intercourse with them.

Interrogating Gender Stereotypes

Within the context of this unit, Louise also delivers a second activity where groups are given four pieces of different colored paper on which students were to draw and label reproductive systems and list the best and worst things about being a boy or a girl. In Karen's reflective notes, she commented how comfortable the HMS students were with these activities, with students confirming this at the end-of-semester interviews. Erin, for example, recalls that she "really, really liked that task", and Billy reflected that his group were "fairly comfortable with it". Reasons underpinning this level of comfort were attributed to the cohorts increasing cohesion across two and a half years of shared study, and their earlier engagement with a human anatomy course. However, the students did acknowledge that this comfort at university may not translate to comfort when teaching sexuality education in schools. This sentiment was captured by Kaycee who stated that:

> I think once I've gone out and taught one [sexuality] lesson or one unit then I'll be fine, but I don't know. Like I said before, I feel comfortable with all the people in my cohort, but I wouldn't want to stand at the front of the class and talk to them about chlamydia or vaginas. I'd just be embarrassed… I think I'm going to be so embarrassed when I have to teach sex ed. I feel like I'm just going to giggle because I'm immature. (Kaycee, 22-year-old)

With the myriad of competing and conflicting discourses in HPETE, this is a difficult space to teach in. Wright (2003) maintains that some discourses are espoused by those considered more credible or believable. Although most interviewed students considered Louise to be a credible and experienced HPE teacher, broader message systems and biomedical discourses appeared more powerful and persuasive and were largely unchallenged. Scholarship is clear: if the messages given in HPETE are not strong enough, they will not influence students to change their beliefs or their professional practice. While students in this study used humor to diffuse discomfort, this humor prevented them from venturing out of their comfort zones into the potentially uncomfortable "shoes of others" (Maxine Greene). Louise's pedagogical provocations were largely thwarted.

Being aware of the need to push students to a point of discomfort, however, is to walk a paradigmatic and pedagogical minefield. If students are pushed too far they may disavow both the message and the messenger, not pushing far enough results in the acceptance and perpetuation of existing beliefs, that is, "business as usual" (Tinning, 2004). Undertaking this work can "inspire a paralyzing sense of guilt or powerful resistance" (Hytten, 2001, p. 442), so pushing too far can also result in students feeling overwhelmed, impotent and unwilling to address inequity because the challenges seem insurmountable. In the context of the pedagogical strategies designed here by Louise, humor was the gatekeeper to empathy and deeper emotional engagement with concepts that may have posed a threat to their ontological security (Tinning, 2004).

CONCLUDING THOUGHTS AND
IMPLICATIONS FOR PRACTICE

For Karen, Louise's pedagogical work in the domain of producing empathetic fledgling teachers who can meaningfully engage with the young people they themselves will teach, is closely aligned to the scholarship on privilege and social justice pedagogy. Making students aware of their relative privilege and associated existing beliefs and values, and considering the impact of this privilege on their future students is a critical task in prompting a social justice orientation amongst HPETE students. According to Maxwell and Aggleton (2013), the concept of privilege "facilities an immediate connection to social spaces and self-understandings, dispositions and worldviews that see power as natural and unquestioned" (p. 4). As Kimmel (2002), further explains:

> Being white, or male, or heterosexual in this culture is like running with the wind at your back. It feels like just plain running, and we rarely if ever get a chance to see how we are sustained, supported and even propelled by that wind … To be white or straight, or male or middle class is to be simultaneously ubiquitous and invisible. You're everywhere you look; you are the standard against which everyone else is measured (p. 1)

Although Louise made a deliberate attempt in her course to make the 'wind visible', such work did not guarantee smooth or even certain pedagogical journeys. Although remaining committed to pedagogical provocations, Karen's insight provides Louise, and us all, with a recognition of our need to embrace turbulence, sudden updrafts or simply watch our students run on by.

APPENDIX 1

Lesson 1: Setting the Vogue Challenge

Learning Experience What will students do?	Teaching Points, Cues and Questions What will teacher say?
Introductory Task	**Key Reflection Questions**
Students will: 1. Watch the 'Vogue' film clip through a number of times 2. In response to the video, students will critically engage in the subject matter in the video and begin to understand how gender is represented. 3. Watch a short excerpt of *Paris is Burning* from *YouTube* 4. Class discussion about the era in which the film was produced and how we are working gender into the dance routine.	**Q.** Does anyone know where voguing came from or when it originated? A. Arose in 1960s and from America **Q.** What sort of dancing is vogue? A. Voguing is characterized by model-like poses integrated with angular, linear, and rigid arm, leg, and body movements *Students will watch video on voguing and excerpts from Paris is Burning documentary on the culture that surrounds Voguing Q. What is prevalent within this clip? **Q.** What stereotypes do we see being challenged? **Q.** How do we know they are being challenged? **Q.** What do the movements look like? **Q.** Would this type of clip be suitable for a year 9/10 class? *Ensure students are recognizing the gender stereotypes being challenged, the angular, linear and rigid movements, and the characters that accompany vogue style dancing. **Key Teaching Points** • Representation of gender is not simple • Vogue was a representation of society at the time • Recreate gender through your teams dance and costumes

Lesson 2: Interrogating the 'Truths' of Gender Stereotypes

Lesson 2 Learning Experience	Teaching Points, Cues and Questions	Organization
Students will:	BHSPE Students encouraged to consider:	
1. Organize students into dance teams	1. Importance of group work and discussion as a means of engaging with potentially sensitive topics	1. Divide class into dance teams
2. Allocate colored paper		2. Allocate resources
3. Four tasks—Best/worst thing about being a boy, best/worst thing about being a girl, female reproductive system, male reproductive system.	2. Establishing the differences between biophysical and sociocultural determinants	3. Set task
	3. Importance of correct terminology for reproductive systems and developing students' knowledge of these	4. Visit each team to establish progress and on-task levels
		5. Announce available time
4. Students to place their responses on the gym wall		6. Provide Blu-tac for posting responses
5. Gallery walk around six stations		7. Establish 6 stations for students to post responses and visit during gallery walk (being a boy, being a girl, female reproductive system, male reproductive system, 2 discussion stations)
6. Teacher to facilitate discussion of key messages	4. Opportunities posed by mixed and single sex groups/classrooms	
	5. Techniques for managing complex debates	
	6. Understanding next lessons	8. Monitor progress through each station
		9. Facilitate class summary of themes

Lesson 3: Translating Understanding of Stereotypes into Movement

Students will:	Key Teaching Points
1. Sit in front of teacher for instructions 2. Welcome back and introduce lesson 3. Introduce first activity—gender experiment 4. When instructed students will leave the class space to do own research 5. Students encouraged to walk around campus in their dance groups to gather data on gender. 6. Students given a set time to return to class (after half an hour)	• Today we are going to integrate the concepts we have learnt about gender into our own choreography and dance—feminism and masculinity **Gender Experiment** • You will be creating an experiment, similar to a science experiment, to find out what constitutes gender and how the is reflected through movement • You will be required, in your groups, to come up with a hypothesis, aim and methods, as well as discussions on the data you will collect today • You need to fill in the worksheet when observing—look at attire / external signs, and especially movement • Ambiguous = you cannot decide Male or female? **What causes the ambiguity? Why can't we capture gender? It is the attire, external signs or the movement?** • You will need conversation between genders in your group • **What tips can you give people to 'do' their genders?**

Class Discussion	Key Teaching Points

Students will:
1. Return to classroom and allocate a reporter
2. Reporter to write points from group observation under headings on the board
3. Other class member to gather their notes
4. Once all reporters have finished writing on the board, class to sit in from of whiteboard
5. Teacher to facilitate discussion about how gender is 'shown' through attire, external signals and movement
	• There are 2 levels on which we can convey gender
	  – Costuming—subtle costuming works best—costuming and props work well when they do not 'stick out' or are 'obvious'
	  – Movement—men and women move in different ways—assumption that men take up space and women always move out of the way—encouraged in culture
	• Ensure students have a clear understanding of the sections and the work/themes/beats/moves that will be required.
	Key Questions:
	
	• **How can you convey gender, through movement?**

APPENDIX 2

TABLE 6.A1   Fourth Year HMNS Pedagogy Female Students' Responses to Question "What is the Best/Worst Thing about Being a Girl/Boy?"

Best Thing About Being a Boy	Worst Thing About Being a Boy	Best Thing About Being a Girl	Worst Thing About Being a Girl
• Having a penis	• Erections—at inappropriate times	• Having babies	• Big breasts
• Standing up to pee	• Wet dreams	• Wearing skirts/dresses	• Childbirth
• Being born and everybody happy "It's a boy"—carry the family name	• Body Hair e.g. Hairy back	• Jewelry	• Periods
• Standing while urinating	• Hair Loss e.g. going bald	• Getting hair done	• Waxing
• Thinks with penis	• Beer guts	• Being elegant	• Make up
• No hips	• Thinks with penis	• Being in touch with our emotions	• No respect
• Small bum (sometimes!)	• Testosterone (e.g. fighting)	• Childbirth	• Pap smears
• No make-up	• Beer gut/man boobs	• Girl talk	• Gender inequity
• No childbirth	• Snoring	• Slumber parties	• Periods/pain
• No fashion dilemmas	• Hairy	• Reason to have chocolate	• Childbirth
• No menstrual cycle	• Swear a lot Macho image	• Good listeners	• Periods!—cramps
• Not as much responsibility	• Clueless about women	• Manipulation—use body for advantage	• Menopause
• Gender inequality	• Circumcision?	• We can multitask	• Birthing
	• Homophobia	• Good memory—to remember everything they have done wrong	• Emotional
	• No multi 'o's		• Water sports are dangerous
	• Have to wait to get it up		• Hips
	• Communication		• Camping—going to the toilet
	• Impotence		• Keep up with fashion

TABLE 6A.2   Fourth Year HMNS Pedagogy Males' Responses to Question: "What Is the Best/Worst Thing About Being A Girl/Boy?"

Best Thing About Being a Boy	Worst Thing About Being a Boy	Best Thing About Being a Girl	Worst Thing About Being a Girl
• Piss wherever, whenever	• Get in trouble lots for no reason	• Sensitive!!	• Hard to achieve the O
• Easy to achieve the "O"	• Always in trouble for the "superior' sex!	• Can get sex [scrubbed out]	• Have monthly periods—fluctuating hormones
• No stigma with sex were encouraged	• Harder for us to get _ _ _ _ _ .	• Babysitters Club	• Multiple sexual partners = sluts
• No hormonal fluctuations—periods etc.	• We always have to do all the work e.g. asking out, picking restaurants etc.	• The "Gatekeepers"	• Weaker sex means they can be taken advantage of—RAPE
• No barriers to achievement other than your own motivation	• Can't get cranky and blame it on "that time of month"	• Good 'bits'	• Having to give birth
• Don't have to give birth	• Get picked on!	• Having one week a month where they can be cranky and everyone "understands"	• Periods
• Standing and pee; pee anywhere; so easy so convenient	• Having to make the first move	• Giving birth	• Getting preggers
• Always being right	• Copping a blow to the family jewels!!	• Going out with quality gentleman from HMS	• Getting your period once a month
• Pee standing up	• Unwanted movement	• Always being right	• Moods
• Don't get pregnant	• Morning mess	• Not much	• Menopause
• Being able to throw	• Chafing	• Motherhood	• Cellulite
	• Bruising Morton and being hit in Gangulies		• Have to sit down to pee
			• Have to wipe after
			• Greater reliance on toilet paper
			• Pregnancy and childbirth
			• Periods
			• Contraceptive pill

REFERENCES

Abernethy, P., Macdonald, D., & Bramich, K. (1997). Undergraduate subject relevance: A human movement studies case study. *The ACHPER Healthy Lifestyle Journal, 44*(4), 5–9.

bellhookes. (2009). Reel to real: Race, class and sex at the movies. Routledge.

Gard, M. (2001). Dancing around the 'problem' of boys and dance. *Discourse: Studies in the Cultural Politics of Education, 22*(2), 213–225.

Gard, M. (2006). *Men who dance: Aesthetics, athletics & the art of masculinity* (vol. 9). Peter Lang.

Greene, M. (1995). *Releasing the imagination: Essays on education, the arts, and social change*. Jossey-Bass.

Hytten, K. (2001). Thinking though a pedagogy of whiteness. *Educational theory, 51*(4), 433–450. doi:10.1111/j.1741-5446.2001.00433.x

Kimmel, M. (2002). Toward a pedagogy of the oppressor. *Tikkun Magazine*, Nov/Dec.

Kirk, D. (1998). *Schooling bodies: School practice and public discourse, 1880—1950*. London, UK: Leicester University Press.

Lawson, H. (1993). After the regulated life. *Quest, 45*(4), 523–546

Macdonald, D., Hunter, L., Carlson, T., & Penney, D. (2002). Teacher knowledge and the disjunction between school curricula and teacher education. *Asia-Pacific Journal of Teacher Education, 30*(3), 259–275.

Maxwell, C., & Aggleton, P. (2013). *Privilege, agency and affect: Understanding the production and effects of action.* United Kingdom: Palgrave MacMillan.

McCuaig, L., & Tinning, R. (2010). HPE and the moral governance of pleasurable bodies. *Sport, Education and Society, 12*(3), 277–294.

McDermott, M. (2002). Collaging pre-service teacher identity. *Teacher Education Quarterly, 29*(4), 53–68.

Queensland School Curriculum Council. (1997). *Science key learning area Years 1–10 syllabus-in-development May 1997.* Brisbane, Qld: Queensland School Curriculum Council.

Queensland School Curriculum Council. (1999). *Health and physical education, years 1–10 syllabus.* Brisbane: Publication Services, Education Queensland.

Shelley, K. (2018). *Shaken or stirred? Considering the usefulness of critical pedagogy in preparing teachers to implement socio-critical health education.* Unpublished doctoral thesis, The University of Queensland, Brisbane, Australia.

Shelley, K., & McCuaig, L. (2018). Close encounters with critical pedagogy in socio-critically informed health education teacher education. *Physical Education and Sport Pedagogy, 23*(5), 510–523.

Sparkes, A. (1994). Self, silence and invisibility as a beginning teacher: A life history of lesbian experience. *British Journal of Sociology of Education, 15*(1), 93–119.

Sparkes, A. C., & Templin, T. J. (1992). Life histories and physical education teachers: Exploring the meanings of marginality. In A. C. Sparkes (Ed.), *Research in physical education and sport: Exploring alternative visions* (pp. 118–145). London, UK: Falmer.

Squires, E., & Sparkes, A. (1996). Circles of silence: Sexual identity in physical education and sport. *Sport, Education and Society, 1*(1), 77–102.

Tinning, R. (1990) *Ideology and physical education: Opening Pandora's Box.* Geelong, Australia: Deakin University Press.

Tinning, R. (2001). *Physical education and the making of citizens: Considering the pedagogical work of physical education in contemporary times.* Paper presented at AIESEP. Taipei: Taiwan.

Tinning, R. (2004). Rethinking the preparation of health and physical education teachers: Ruminations on knowledge, identity and ways of thinking. *Asia-Pacific Journal of Teacher Education, 32*(3), 241–253.

Wright, J. (2003). Poststructural Methodologies—The body, schooling and health. In J. Evans, B. Davies, & J. Wright (Eds.), *Body knowledge and control—Studies in sociology of physical education and health* (pp. 19–32). New York, NY: Routledge.

Yager, Z., & O'Dea, J. A. (2008). Prevention programs for body image and eating disorders on University campuses: A review of large, controlled interventions. *Health Promotion International, 23*(2), 173–189.

CHAPTER 7

ALL KINDS OF STRONG

Disrupting Dominant Discourses of Fitness within Elementary School Physical Education

Mara Simon and Shrehan Lynch

We are our bodies and only in and through them do we know ourselves.

—*Caddick (1986)*

ACTION RESEARCH AND REFLECTION

This chapter explores how the physical body intersects with the sense of self towards embodied identity through critical pedagogy that aims to disrupt students' understandings of social norms related to fitness, specifically the idea of strength, within school physical education (PE) curricula. Students' bodies, or the physicality of who they are as individuals, are often policed, coded, and constructed in schools towards cultural norms of thinness, whiteness, and hegemonic masculinities (Azzarito, 2009). Given that PE is a discipline with an extraordinary focus on the body, it is vital for educators who work within the spectrum of health, physical activity/fitness, and PE to disrupt these confining discourses which position students' bodies as "right" or "wrong." This chapter thus provides a three-part lesson series on how to create a space within PE for positive body self-representation and

Teaching About Social Justice Issues in Physical Education, pages 69–84.
Copyright © 2019 by Information Age Publishing
All rights of reproduction in any form reserved.

69

how to challenge dominant discourses related to fitness constructs and the notion of a "strong body."

Embodied identity, or the social interactions that "form selves through language and material practices," is enacted in relation to institutional and cultural discourses (Wright, 2000, p. 38). As Caddick (1986) writes, "we are our bodies and only in and through them do we know ourselves" (p. 76). Who we are as physical beings intertwines with who we are as intellectual and emotional beings, all of which together form our identities, or how we place ourselves in the world in which we live (Caddick, 1986). Consequently, outside forces or cultural messages regarding body norms and desirability play a significant role in shaping young people's self-conceptions or the body-self, especially through "mass media of fitness, health, and sport" (Azzarito, 2009, p. 19). The body, the self, and the understanding of the self within specific contexts are socially-constructed and represent the intersection of multiple social identifiers (e.g., race, gender, socioeconomic status, sexuality, ability) and dominant discourses (Garrett, 2004).

Interested in the body as a social construct, we have both examined discourses of the body from various lenses. Within PE, health, and fitness contexts, we have identified that notions of femininities are often constructed in opposition to masculinities. Specifically, from a feminist perspective, oppositional gender binaries serve to reinforce desired hegemonic masculinities as competitive, strong, and muscular while normative femininities represent women as slim objects of desire (Azzarito, 2009; Azzarito & Katzew, 2010). As such, PE typically represents a space where girls are excluded, positioned as problematic in their avoidance of participating, or considered less desirable and weaker contributors to class activities (Azzarito & Solmon, 2009; Oliver, Hamzeh, & McCaughtry, 2009). These "deeply rooted ideas about what is desirable in terms of femininities create powerful normalizing processes" that significantly impact how young people make sense of themselves within a gendered order and hierarchy (Garrett, 2004, p. 140). However, young women are not the only ones negatively impacted by hierarchical gendered norms and representations within PE; instead, traditional hegemonic femininities and masculinities serve to disengage a significant number of students across the gender spectrum, since many students who identify as male are also not represented within the standards of hyper-masculinity often embraced within PE contexts (Gorely, Holyroyd, & Kirk, 2003).

Not only are students' bodies gendered within PE, health, and fitness contexts, but they are also racialized within a space where whiteness is considered ideal, as "pervasive messages of beauty and success...are embedded in discourses of whiteness" (Azzarito, 2009, p. 22). Whiteness has informed educational practices and policies since the inception of our national educational system, and PE is not immune to the often-invisible, yet dominant messages which position whiteness as normal and desired within schools (Gillborn, 2005). Embedded within notions of whiteness in PE and fitness are discourses of neoliberalism, where individuals are held responsible for their body shape and size versus recognition or awareness of how structural and systematic overlapping oppressions might inform an understanding of what is a desirable body and who has the time and resources to work towards the desirable body (Azzarito, Macdonald, Dagkas, & Fisette, 2017). Furthermore, despite well-intentioned research aiming to increase physical activity and decrease obesity, ethnic minorities continue to be singled out for being overweight. Much of this research overlooks and neglects both the impact of structural oppression on body size, shape, and representation as well as how cultural norms and practices inscribe physical activity with meaning and value in ways which orbit around whiteness. In other words, some critical research has illustrated how ethnic minorities might be more physically active than typically constructed within media discourses, but in ways which fit within the meaning-making of their cultural values, norms, and desires (Azzarito, Marttinen, Simon, & Markiewicz, 2014; Oliver & Lalik, 2004).

In an attempt to provide a succinct overview, we have not enaged in an analysis of all of the social identifiers which might impact how young people make sense of their physical and emotional selves. However, the above analysis of race and gender provide evidence towards the idea that PE, with its heavy focus on the body, has a responsibility to enact opportunities for students to explore their own embodied identities through a lens of body positivity with the underlying aim of disrupting socially constructed discourses about desirable bodies. The construction of the body to which young people must often ascribe, typically focused on slenderness, muscularity, and physicality, is considered problematic, because it excludes or marginalizes those who do not fit within normalized or accepted body ideals (Azzarito, 2009). Even within research that has focused on transforming fitness curricula towards body empowerment (Azzarito, Marttinen, Simon, & Markiewicz, 2014), the focus has been high school students. However, elementary school students should not be overlooked as a starting point for deconstructing dominant discourses. Therefore, we have chosen to provide an example of transformative pedagogy specifically aimed at upper elementary school (i.e., third, fourth. and fifth graders; 8—11 year olds). We would encourage physical educators to be particularly conscious of how notions of fitness, health, and the body are presented to young people and to present these lessons with the underlying aim of destabilizing the accompanying hegemonies in order to provide students with PE experiences that lead towards empowerment and body positivity.

CONTEXT

In order to self-reflect on our own biases, values, and experiences, which could affect our interpretations and enactments of discourses of fitness and embodiment, this section presents our positionalities, or the identifiers that inform our own meaning-making. Acknowledging elements of our identities are important, because they inform how we come to understand the world around us and, in particular, how and why we might advocate for disrupting concepts of which we have benefitted from.

MARA

I am a white, female, Jewish, upper-middle-class professor of physical education at a predominantly white institution in the northeast region of the United States. Physically, I am athletically skillful and was even more so when I was in secondary school and university. I played numerous sports successfully during this period and went on to be a competitive distance runner post-college. In many ways, I represent much of what is highly-valued within the majority of PE contexts—a highly-skilled, slim, white student. I do, however, also understand a position of marginality based on my religious identity. Given the recent rise of anti-Semitism in the United States[1], this part of my identity feels particularly salient in terms of how I make sense of social and structural oppressions. I maintain a monumental level of privilege in my whiteness, but want to acknowledge that growing up as a religious minority in rural, small-town America led to first-hand experience of the pain and trauma of prejudice, stereotypes, and fear of an "other." This has, in part, contributed to my desire to engage in social justice work.

SHREHAN

I am half British, half Arab, passably white, able-bodied, and consider myself from a middle-class background. Like Mara, I have been privileged with highly-skilled movement abilities from a young age. Although my sporting abilities meant I was valued in PE, I did face a level of body-shaming from peers who considered my movement skills as anti-feminine. Until recently, I have kept my Palestinian heritage silent, however, after in-depth self-identity work, I have begun to understand the cultural discourses circulating my silence. This was one of the reasons I chose teacher education as a profession. My current role involves educating future teachers in a diverse teaching institution in London, UK. This role provides me with the opportunity to amplify the importance of multiculturalism and sociocultural perspectives with other educators and share my passion for social justice work with them.

In the following sections, we present a three-part lesson sequence that engages with fitness from a critical perspective and from our beliefs that teachers should work towards enacting change (within individual practice or towards larger systemic disruptions). The lessons provided could be integrated within a longer fitness or health unit and are designed for older elementary school students. The lessons are intended to provide a space for all students to think critically about messages regarding the body they have received and how they make sense of their own body in relation to these messages. We have drawn upon images for use in activities, which are purposefully selected to represent a variety of body shapes and sizes.

---

[1] https://www.adl.org/resources/reports/2017-audit-of-anti-semitic-incidents

SET-UP & LESSON

Table 7.1 provides an overview of the critical fitness lesson sequence that can be implemented with upper-elementary students. The focus is on the "strong body," and it provides students with an opportunity to question their previously held assumptions towards strength. Strength in our lesson sequence is considered through multiple ways; an individual can be emotionally, physically, and mentally strong. We designed a number of activities that promote students' thinking towards strength differently and hope that by interrogating stereotypes, they might begin to identify strength beyond physicality and feel empowered regarding their body-self.

Below are some helpful tips that will make the lessons effective and run smoothly:

- *Bigger and high-quality images will create a stronger impact.* The images (see Handout A) will be more effective if presented on a large-scale, either through projection onto a screen or printed onto a poster. Alternatively, the images could be printed off on standard printing paper and provided per individual student.
- *Language is important.* Do not be afraid to name and challenge stereotypes related to strength and obesity, especially based on students' responses. It is important to do this in a supportive and meaningful way. For example, when you wish to challenge a student's statement, it can be received with less defensiveness when couched in the language of "I wonder" (e.g., "I wonder why I am hearing that fat people are lazy, is that true?")
- *Circle-based discussions.* Full group discussions should be done in a circle with the teacher at the same height as the students (versus students sitting in groups with the teacher standing at the front). It is also important to have a visual representation of any questions posed to the group in order to support students of all linguistic abilities (e.g., the verbal question printed out or displayed on a projector).
- *Modify where necessary.* While we have presented elements of a scripted lesson, educators must engage with the content in a way that is meaningful to them. Therefore, educators should feel free to design their own script for enacting lessons while still maintaining the core intention of each scripted interchange. For example, the questions might remain the same, but the teacher might draw from their own experiences or frame the questions differently. It is essential that the purpose, which is to assist students in critiquing discourses on the body while simultaneously developing body positivity for their own bodily capabilities and representations, is not lost with modifications.
- *Self-analysis.* Physical educators should take some time before engaging in these lessons to reflect on their own biases as well as identify any students who embody potentially marginalized social identifiers. We have provided

TABLE 7.1. Three-Part Critical Fitness Lesson Sequence

Lesson	Objective	Materials	Assessment
Lesson 1: What is strong?	Students will be able to identify multiple ways of being strong through self-reflection and group discussion.	Poly dots, images (Handout A), music, paper, pencils/crayons.	Student drawings, reflection journal (Handout B), group discussions.
Starter	**Activities**		**Closure**
Different ways of being strong • Group discussion • Students greeted and sit on a poly dot in a circle. • Teacher asks students to consider: What does strong look like? What does a strong body look like? What are some activities people do to increase their physical strength? **Student Drawings** Students draw a picture of a strong body. Students draw a picture of what their own strong body looks like. Teacher collects the drawings and notes that the class will return to them at the end of the lesson.	**Musical Poly Dots** • Spread poly dots with the images provided in Handout A taped underneath (1 image per dot, include about 1 dot per 3 students). • Students move about the space in the locomotor movement specified by the teacher (walking, skipping, galloping, etc.) while the music plays. When the music stops, each student goes to the closest poly dot, resulting in small groups of 2–3 students at each dot. The group turns the poly dot over to look at the image underneath and discusses whether this person looks strong or not and why. **Discussion:** Ask students to describe some of the images that were under the poly dots. As students answer, hold up the poly dot with the accompanying image and ask the class to come to a consensus on whether the person in the image is strong. **Physical Challenge** • Students engage in a series of challenges for one minute each (or 30 seconds) that highlight their physical strengths. • For example: how many sit-ups can you do in one minute. Could include: pushups, lunges, mountain climbers, high knees, sprints, jumping jacks, etc. **Discussion:** Ask students to identify and describe the strengths of their own body in relation to physical activity/fitness.		**Small Group Discussion** • Students identify many different ways of being strong (emotionally strong, physically strong, mentally strong), identify stereotypes of strong bodies, and about their own physical body strength. • Students asked if they want to change/add anything to their drawings from the beginning of the lesson/ if their view of a strong body has changed. • Students complete the first prompt in their journals ("What does 'strong' look like?" —Handout B)

Lesson	Objective	Materials	Assessment
Lesson 2: Who is strong?	Students will be able to disrupt stereotypes of both strength and obesity.	Images (Handout C), Yoga mats (optional), calming music, yoga poses (10).	Group discussion, pair share, reflection journal.
Starter	**Activities**		**Closure**
• Different ways of being strong-group discussion	**Yoga as Physical Strength**		**Pair Share**
• Students are seated in a circle. Teacher presents images of Lebron James and asks students to consider:	• Each student gets a yoga mat (if possible).		• Ask students to discuss with a partner what has changed about their thinking in the class so far. Ask them to consider why/what made them have previous assumptions. Link back to how the media wants people to think in certain ways.
• Who is this? Describe how he looks?	• Lead the students through deep breathing and mindfulness exercises.		
• Is Lebron James strong? Why or why not? How do we know?	• Teach 10 yoga poses, starting with simple and leading up to more complex.		
• Then show Jessamyn Stanley picture 1. Ask students to consider:	• Ask students to create a sequence with the yoga poses.		• Students complete the second prompt in their journals ("Can a person be strong without having big muscles? Can a person be strong and overweight?"—Handout B)
• Jessamyn Stanley, a woman who is dedicated to her yoga teaching and body positivity. Is she strong? Why/ why not? How do we know?	Stereotyping strength discussion		
• Then show Picture 2 & 3, Jessamyn doing advanced yoga poses. Ask: Do you think she is strong? Is anyone here familiar with yoga? Who does yoga? Do people in your families practice yoga? When we think about media images, who is presented as engaging in yoga?	• Revisit photos after yoga		
	• Was yoga hard or easy? Do we still think Jessamyn is not strong?		
	• Do you have to be slim to be strong?		
	• Black athletes are not physiologically superior to white athletes.		
	• Highlight and disrupt racial and obesity stereotypes related to physical ability, for example, Black athletes as physically superior and the connections between obesity and ethnic minority identity.		

(continues)

TABLE 7.1. Continued

Lesson	Objective	Materials	Assessment
Lesson 3: I am strong	Students will be able to determine their personal strengths beyond physical strength.	Paper, crayons, clipboards, cup stack, stopwatches, Handout B, D, E	Self-representation of strength (Handout D), fitness bingo (Handout E), reflection journal.
Starter	**Activities**		**Closure**

Starter

Timed Cup Stack
- Students take part in teams in a timed cup stacking activity. Add up team's scores and see who was the fastest.
- Then students have a go individually, measuring each other's time.
- Lead into a group discussion on how being timed and competition can change mental and emotional strength into stress. Ask students to consider: What else contributes to mental and emotional stress? What are the differences between mental, emotion, and physical stress? What mental, emotional, and physical strengths do you have to overcome the stresses?

Activities

Fitness Bingo
- Students complete Handout E, where they design a strength bingo board and then complete their designed board.

Self-Strength-Portrait
- After students have gained a number of different ways they can be strong they can complete Handout D, where they will identify ways in which they are strong or not and represent this through a body drawing.

Gallery Walk
- Students will then take part in a gallery walk where they will view each other's portraits in an attempt to understand that everyone is strong is different ways.

Closure

Group Discussion
- Ask students to consider: how being strong relates to the ways we represent ourselves, strong as a verb (we are 'stronging' - engaging in that which makes us strong), and to think about the word "strong" beyond muscles/physicality.
- Students complete the last prompt in their journals ("How are you strong?"—Handout B)

a helpful personal reflection task to complete before beginning this lesson sequence that will support teachers in creating inclusive teaching spaces (see Handout F).

INTERSECTIONALITY

Although not all are represented outwardly, the body itself represents an individual's multiple, interwoven social identifiers. Subsequently, there cannot be a body without intersectionality. Bodies cannot separate themselves from the mind or the self, such as emotional or cognitive identities. Thus, any focus on the body requires acknowledgment of how multiple portions of an individual's identity intersect (Bowleg, 2012). With this in mind, the lesson sequence was designed with intersectionality at its forefront. Although the lessons are focused on disrupting body stereotypes, underlying frameworks of social justice movements, such as feminism and anti-racism, informed their development. For example, the included images specifically represent a wide variety of physical, racial, and gendered identities. Subsequently, a physical educator enacting these lessons is encouraged to identify and discuss any stereotypes that might emerge from students' identity work. The Bingo game asks students to re-construct their body-selves outside of discourses of physicality. This lesson will be most successful if the teacher understands how various intersections of social identifiers such as race, gender, socioeconomic status, sexuality and (dis)ability are present and inform their students' meaning-making within PE class, and how these social identifiers might position students outside the established norms and values of a PE, school, or societal context. Ultimately, teachers have a responsibility to recognize the oppression that comes from the positionality of embodying multiple marginalized social identifiers (Bowleg, 2008). In PE, this means developing teaching environments and social interactions which identify and destabilize the discourses that lead to an "othering" of students via an empowering and valuing lens of social justice.

CHALLENGES AND POSSIBILITIES

We would be remiss if we did not address the challenges that come with the tall order of enacting lessons such as the ones presented. Disrupting dominant discourses within any domain requires an individual to swim upstream, to go against the social forces that keep hegemonies intact and maintain systems of oppression. The teacher must be able to recognize the need for engaging in social justice work within a PE context as well as understand the complicated interweavings of the body-self, identity, and marginalization that are often preserved within a "hidden curriculum" in PE (Prosser, 2007; Rønholt, 2002). School administrations may not understand or value such PE curricula and instead look for the teacher to present more traditional enactments of PE. Similarly, students may resist the pedagogy presented, in favor of that which they are accustomed and may be unwilling to be vulnerable in a way which leads to social development and a greater understanding of stereotypes and discourses of the body.

Despite challenges, there is hope as research indicates that there is the possibility for change within PE and that critical pedagogy can be transformative when implemented effectively. For example, Azzarito and her colleagues described the valuable effects of a critical fitness curricula when implemented within a predominantly ethnic minority high school setting (Azzarito, Simon, & Marttinen, 2016). This research illustrated students' need and desire for more meaningful PE experiences. Based on this research and other transformative pedagogy research (Lynch, 2018), we argue that enacting critical pedagogies with elementary students could be a viable opportunity for engaging students in difficult, but important, topics. Specifically, upper elementary students are generally self-aware enough to begin to engage in critical conversations about stereotypes and how they reinforce systems of oppression. As the epicenter of physicality, the body-self, and embodied identity within a school curriculum, PE has the loaded responsibility of assisting students in making sense of themselves up against dominant discourses which reinforces "us/them" binaries related to various social identifiers (e.g., race, gender, sexuality, socioeconomic status and ability). By destabilizing marginalizing hegemonies, physical educators can create inclusive learning environments, which provide students with the emotional tools to navigate complex hierarchies of bodily constructs in positive and empowering ways.

RESOURCES

Handout A. Images[2]

Handout B. Reflection Journal

Lesson 1

What does "strong" look like?

_____

_____

_____

_____

Lesson 2

Can a person be strong without having big muscles?

_____

_____

_____

Can a person be strong and overweight?

_____

_____

_____

Lesson 3

How are you strong?

_____

_____

_____

_____

Handout C. Image of LeBron James and Jessamyn Stanley

LeBron James

Jessamyn Stanley

Handout D. Self-Strength-Portrait.

Draw yourself. On the inside, draw anything that represents being strong for you and anything that you do not have put it on the outside of the body. For example, I do not have big muscles because I am not a weightlifter and I do not do any strength exercises to give me big muscles for physical strength. However, I do have a big heart that helps with emotional strength, I can help my friends in times of need.

Example:

Handout E. Bingo.

WHO IS STRONG?
BINGO

Task: Design a bingo board that incorporates elements of LOTS of different kinds of strength. When you have written in each of the boxes, find a student who has that type of strength, ask them about that strength and have them write their name in the box. Each box must be completed with a different partner in the room, and you must complete the entire board before turning it in! You may write your name in only one of the boxes on your sheet. The first board to have a different name & prompt in each box has BINGO!

B	I	N	G	O
Example 1: Emotional Strength—Crying in the last month because I was sad about a friendship		Free Pass		
		(write or draw your own in the spaces)		
			Example 2: Mental Strength – In the last month I have had taken tests, which cause me a lot of stress. I was able to overcome this by working hard and doing relaxing activities.	

Handout F. Teacher Reflection

Consider the questions below and answer on a separate sheet of paper.
- How do you identify? Consider race, gender, class, ability, religion, sexual preference, age, and others.
- What part of your identity do you see influencing your teaching?
- What biases might stem from each identifier? (Consider all factors).

As an example consider:
  - Do you think being overweight is caused by laziness, self-indulgent overeating, and/or poor dietary habits?
  - Are your lessons focused on combatting the "obesity epidemic?" If so, how does that make you view students that would be considered overweight?
  - Are your minority students frequently those that are disciplined? If so, why? Do you have a bias toward certain students?
  - What holidays do you celebrate that your students do not? Do you incorporate/ask those students about their holidays? If not, why not? How does this impact how you teach? Why?
- What identities do you need to learn more about and why? How will you make these changes?
- Is there anything in your teaching you feel will change based on this reflection? If so, what?

REFERENCES

Azzarito, L. (2009). The panopticon of physical education: Pretty, active and ideally white. *Physical Education and Sport Pedagogy, 14*(1), 19–39.

Azzarito, L., & Katzew, A. (2010). Performing identities in physical education: (En)gendering fluid selves. *Research Quarterly for Exercise and Sport, 81*(1), 25–37.

Azzarito, L., Macdonald, D., Dagkas, S., & Fisette, J. (2017). Revitalizing the physical education social-justice agenda in the global era: Where do we go from here? *Quest, 69*(2), 205–219.

Azzarito, L., Marttinen, R., Simon, M., & Markiewicz, R. (2014). "I'm beautiful": A case for adoption a sociocultural perspective in physical education teacher education. In S. B. Flory, A. Tischler, & S. Sanders (Eds.), *Sociocultural issues in physical education: Case studies for teachers* (pp. 115–132). New York, NY: Rowman & Littlefield.

Azzarito, L., Simon, M., & Marttinen, R. (2016). "I guess people are more attracted to white people than black people: Shedding light on racial prejudice, misrepresentation, and (in)visibility of ethnic minority bodies. In D. Robinson & L. Randall (Eds.), *Social justice and physical education: Critical reflections and pedagogies for change* (pp. 15–35). Toronto, Canada: Canadian Scholars' Press.

Azzarito, L., & Solmon, M. (2009). An investigation in students' embodied discourses in physical education: A gender project. *Journal of Teaching in Physical Education, 28*(2), 173–191.

Bowleg, L. (2008). When Black + lesbian + woman ≠ Black lesbian woman: The methodological challenges of qualitative and quantitative intersectionality research. *Sex Roles, 59*(5–6), 312–325.

Bowleg, L. (2012). The problem with the phrase women and minorities: Intersectionality: An important theoretical framework for public health. *American Journal of Public Health, 102*(7), 1267–1273.

Caddick, A. (1986). Feminism and the body. *Arena, 74,* 64–88.

Garrett, R. (2004). Negotiating a physical identity: Girls, bodies and physical education. *Sport, Education and Society, 9*(2), 223–237.

Gillborn, D. (2005). Education policy as an act of white supremacy: Whiteness, critical race theory and education reform. *Journal of Education Policy, 20*(4), 485–505.

Gorely, T., Holroyd, R., & Kirk, D. (2003). Muscularity, the habitus, and the social construction of gender: Towards a gender-relevant physical education. *British Journal of Sociology of Education, 24(*4), 429–448.

Lynch, S. (2018). *Transformative pedagogy for community building: A disability focused immersion project in physical education.* Paper presented at the European Congress of Adapted Physical Activity 2018 Conference, Worcester, England.

Oliver, K. L., Hamzeh, M., & McCaughtry, N. (2009). Girly girls can play games/*Las niñas pueden jugar tambien*: Co-creating a curriculum of possibilities with fifth-grade girls. *Journal of Teaching in Physical Education, 28*(1), 90–110.

Oliver, K. L., & Lalik, R. (2004). 'The Beauty Walk, this ain't my topic': Learning about critical inquiry with adolescent girls. *Journal of Curriculum Studies, 36*(5), 555–586.

Prosser, J. (2007). Visual methods and the visual culture of schools. *Visual Studies, 22*(1), 13–30.

Rønholt, H. (2002). "It's only the sissies…": Analysis of teaching and learning processes in physical education: A contribution to hidden curriculum. *Sport, Education and Society, 7*(1), 25–36.

Wright, J. (2000). Bodies, meaning and movement: A comparison of the language of a physical education lesson and a Feldenkrais movement class. *Sport, Education and Society, 5*(1), 35–49.

CHAPTER 8

UNIVERSAL DESIGN FOR LEARNING IN PHYSICAL EDUCATION

Ali Brian and Sally Taunton Miedema

REFLECTION

Section 504 of the Rehabilitation Act signed into law in 1974 and PL 94–142 (now the Individuals with Disabilities Education Improvement Act IDEA-IA, 2004) signed into law in 1975 represented the first pieces of civil rights and educational laws in the United States supporting and protecting the rights of individuals with disabilities (Yell, 1998). Prior to these hallmark pieces of legislation, children with disabilities could be and often were denied a free and appropriate education (Altshuler, & Kopels, 2003). Prior to these laws many people subscribed to a medically-oriented model suggesting that physical, mental, and emotional limitations prevent those with disabilities from completing the same day-to-day activities that most children without disabilities perform (Tate & Pledger, 2003). As a result, most children with disabilities either attended specialized schools, were left at home without education, or potentially placed into hospital settings.

After 1975, more and more children with disabilities were being placed in self-contained classrooms but within public schools. However, after 1997, in addition to self-contained classrooms, students with disabilities had the right to be

Teaching About Social Justice Issues in Physical Education, pages 85–98.
Copyright © 2019 by Information Age Publishing
All rights of reproduction in any form reserved.

educated within their least restrictive environment (LRE) (IDEA, 1997). The LRE should be the placement where the student can achieve the greatest amount of success with the least amount of restrictions/supports/services needed (Winnick & Porretta, 2016). As a result, children with disabilities were and continue to be placed within general classrooms (including general physical education) with or without appropriate educational support services (WHO, 2011).

In most cases children with disabilities can achieve as much success in all facets of education as peers without disabilities when teachers create an appropriate learning environment (Liberman & Houston-Wilson, 2009). However, a paradigm shift was needed away from what children with disabilities cannot do (medical model) to a strengths-based approach (Brisenden, 1986; Triano, 2000). The social model of disability represents a strengths-based approach (Barnes & Mercer, 2004). Within an educational setting, per the social model, what are deemed the primary rules of any activity are decided by the teacher and reinforced socially by both the teacher and the students. The teacher can decide the rules and create activities that meet the needs of all learners ahead of time. Setting up appropriate learning environments that meet the needs of all learners requires both the knowledge and skills, as well as the disposition to care to do so (Winnick & Porretta, 2016). Yet, the general physical education teachers may not receive extensive coursework or have prior knowledge to include students with disabilities into their general physical education classrooms (Martin, Kwon, & Healy, 2016). Although most teachers believe all students can learn, many pre-service and in-service physical education teachers (collectively referred to as physical education teachers) feel ill-prepared to teach students with disabilities (Martin et al,, 2016; Morly, Bailey, Tan, & Cooke, 2005).

Not only do physical education teachers feel ill-prepared to teach students with disabilities in general physical education (referred to here as an inclusion placement), but they also report difficulties with teaching classes that enroll only students with disabilities (referred to here as self-contained) as well as providing adapted physical education services in small groups or one-on-one (Ammah & Hodge, 2005; Block & Obrusnikova, 2007). Lack of preparedness to teach children with disabilities is often attributed to pre-service teachers only receiving one adapted physical course in their physical education teacher education (PETE) program combined with receiving little to no support as a practicing physical education teacher (Block & Obrusnikova, 2007; Rizzo, 2013; Vickerman & Coates, 2009). Thus, more courses during PETE training is greatly needed.

In ideal circumstances, offering several adapted physical education courses above and beyond the usual "Introduction to Adapted Physical Education" (which students typically receive and mainly learn about the etiology of disability rather than pedagogical content knowledge to support the unique attributes of all learners), such as one focusing on teaching children in self-contained classrooms, another on becoming an itinerant adapted physical educator or servicing small-groups/one-on-one placements, and a separate course focusing upon teaching physical education to achieve inclusion (more on the word "inclusion" later as that term possesses its own set of challenges). Given the daunting nature inherent with modifying existing PETE curricula, the purpose of this chapter will be to provide recommendations for maximizing learning in a PETE program where only one adapted physical education course exists in order to combat feelings of ill-preparedness.

CONTEXT

Presently, I, Dr. Ali Brian, am an Assistant Professor and Dr. Sally Taunton Miedema is a post-doctoral research fellow in an undergraduate, masters, and doctoral granting Department of Physical Education that is situated within a College of Education at the University of South Carolina. The University of South Carolina is a large, public, land-grant university, with a research-intensive focus, located in Columbia, South Carolina, within the southern region of the United States. Although The University of South Carolina is situated within Columbia (an urban, capital city), once one leaves campus, one is almost instantly placed in a rural, sometimes low-income, environment. Our program presently only offers one adapted physical education course to undergraduate and master's students. Our master's program is a Master's of Arts in Teaching that has the sole purpose of obtaining a physical education teaching license. Prior to my arrival, the adapted physical education course did not include any service-based learning or practicum experiences where pre-service teachers would have interactions teaching students with disabilities. Rather, the course included 50 minutes of classroom instruction three days per week.

We decided to start a program for children with disabilities and their parents to come to our university where my students volunteer to work in the program (this serves as a volunteer practicum for our pre-service physical education teachers). In addition, our pre-service teachers, teaching assistants, and we provide adapted physical education programming to students with disabilities at local schools during our regularly scheduled 50-minutes of class time. The volunteer program did not come at a cost to content; but, the school-based practicum needed to occur during class time. Thus, there was a small trade-off between content and experience, but the adapted physical education literature consistently supports the use of practicum experiences as a best practice (Taliaferro, Hammond, & Wyant, 2015). Thus, we felt the trade-off was necessary.

Assuming we are able to get the pre-service teachers to "buy-in", the next challenge is what content do we have our students focus on? Physical education teachers in South Carolina are required to teach students with disabilities in inclusion, self-contained, and in small-group or one-on-one adapted physical education settings. How does one prepare pre-service teachers to handle multiple contexts through one adapted physical education course?

There is no panacea, but our suggestion is to focus upon Universal Design for Learning (UDL). UDL is a common, curricular framework within Special Education (see Universal Design for Learning) but much less common in Physical Education. In the following sections, we shift towards a practical focus. In lesson set-up, we illustrate the necessary tools needed to prepare PETE students to teach physical education via UDL. In strategy/activity/lesson, we provide a sample lesson plan and in Universal Design for Learning, we situate how you get your students to buy-in and also define UDL.

LESSON SET-UP

Before we teach UDL and the steps towards learning to implement UDL, we first teach our students about high-quality physical education. Claudine Sherrill, the emeritus Adapted Physical Education professor from Texas Women's University, often stated that high quality physical education is adapted physical education and vice-versa. Pre-service physical education majors need to understand what high quality physical education is before they can learn UDL. Delving into what is (e.g., LET US play principles, Teaching Physical Education for Learning, etc.) and what is not good physical education (e.g., Busy, happy, good; roll out the ball, etc.) is beyond the scope of this chapter. However, physical education teachers need to understand how to maximize student learning (globally; see resources) first before learning UDL. Assuming, pre-service teachers understand the basics regarding what is and what is not high quality physical education for learning we now offer the following steps, which may be helpful towards adopting a UDL curricular framework:

First, assess students' present level of performance (PLOP) in the cognitive, affective, and psychomotor domains. The cornerstone of UDL is creating lesson plans that meet the needs of all learners ahead of time. UDL lesson plans are in stark contrast to creating a lesson plan situated for the "average" student and then creating modifications for students as needed. Please refer to Strategy/Activity/ Lesson for a more detailed description of UDL.

In order to meet the needs of all learners ahead of time, it is paramount to understand each student's PLOP. For the purpose of this chapter, we will focus on psychomotor assessment with the guise that understanding the PLOP for all domains are equally important. There are several gross motor skill assessments readily available that can provide physical education teachers with a baseline of their students' gross motor skill PLOP. For example, the Test of Gross Motor Development (TGMD)—2 or 3 (Ulrich, 2000; Webster & Ulrich, 2017) is a normative-referenced, process-oriented assessment that can not only serve for a PLOP assessment, but can also help with determining placement (e.g., adapted physical education, inclusion, self-contained), as well as provide a measure of your students' growth. The TGMD requires training and the physical education teacher must implement the TGMD following all standardized procedures to determine placements. Thus, the TGMD is hard to use in a large class and rarely occurs in an authentic setting. Functional, alternative, and product-based measures (e.g., distances, times, correct trials, etc.) might be more useful if the physical educator is constrained by space and time. Thus, the TGMD might be more useful for one-on-one or small-group settings, while alternative assessments that can occur in an authentic setting are often more practical for inclusion, general, or larger classes. For more details regarding assessment strategies please refer to the resources list.

Next, assess the needs of each learner including preferences, decisions, and supports. UDL lessons require multiple means of action and expression (CAST, 2011), among other caveats. For some learners, if a physical education teacher offers too many options without understanding each student's needs, then certain students (such as those with Autism Spectrum Disorders) might become overwhelmed by the choices. Assessing each student's preferences beforehand not only assists with UDL planning, but can help to combat the potential for feeling overwhelmed. Examples of preference assessments include: pictures, visual schedules, videos, verbal prompts, teacher demonstrations, peer demonstrations, peer assistance, textures (e.g., yarn ball, rubber, foam), sounds (bells, buzzers, crinkles), visuals (lights, neon taping), least-to-most prompting decisions (e.g., tactile models and maps, hand-over-hand guidance), and others. Please refer to the Resources section for more information on preference assessments.

Determining learner preferences after the PLOP can then lead to a better understanding of the types of supports needed. There is considerable overlap among learner preferences and determining types and levels of supports needed. For example, if a student does not prefer to be touched, then hand-over-hand guidance cannot be a support choice. Similarly, if a student possesses sensory aversion to certain sounds or textures, then providing certain audio prompts (e.g., clapping, a belled-ball) may not be an option. Taking a preference assessment into account, determining levels of support that are needed and appropriate is necessary to create a UDL lesson plan ahead of time that meets the needs of all learners. We prefer to begin with a least-to-most prompting hierarchy although most-to-least can certainly be useful when students present with severe and multiple disabilities. Starting with a least-to-most prompting hierarchy and then reverting back to most-to-least helps combat dependency upon feedback and supports eventual independence. Please see the resources for specifics regarding prompting hierarchies.

Afterwards, determine a reasonable amount of progress that can be made within the timelines given (e.g., lesson, unit, block, year, etc.) so that realistic goals will be aligned with each timeline. A great place to start, if students are uncertain as to what is a "realistic" amount of progress, would be to look at your state's benchmarks or grade-level outcomes (GLO). Assure them that in time, they will have a better gauge of PLOP and adequate yearly progress for individual learners, but GLO's are a good starting place.

Once, physical educators understand each learner's PLOP and outcomes desired, then teach them to create developmental task analyses. Developmental task analyses provide teachers with the knowledge base to both upward and downward extend tasks when student progress moves faster or more slowly than anticipated.

Developmental task analyses also assist teachers with differentiating instruction within a UDL lesson. Of course, while it is the ultimate goal within any UDL lesson plan to meet the needs of all learners at all times, doing so can be a very lofty aspiration. Thus, understanding the range of downward and upward extensions available via developmental task analyses assists with being flexible and offering some differentiation within UDL lesson plans (Davis & Broadhead, 2007; Davis & Burton, 1991; Lieberman & Houston-Wilson, 2009).

After teachers learn to differentiate via task analysis, they can then begin to create UDL lesson plans that meets the needs of all learners ahead of time. Meeting the needs of all learners ahead of time and offering all "multiple means of action and expression, engagement, and representation" to all students at all times are requirements in order for a physical education teacher to provide lesson plans that are universally-designed.

STRATEGY/ACTIVITY/LESSON

Before we demonstrate example lessons that are UDL, we first show examples of what is not UDL. To illustrate UDL and non-UDL lessons, let us take a look at a few sample scenarios from a softball unit.

Non-Example #1: 10 v. 10 (or larger) Softball Games. Here we show how 10 v. 10 softball, which happens often in today's USA physical education curricula is a non-option. After pre-service teachers play 10 v 10, we then debrief. Prompting questions include: how many practice trials did you receive, how much physical activity did you achieve, (from the teaching perspective) were you able to monitor your students and provide quality feedback frequently, etc.? Hopefully, our students will come to a consensus that 'full-sided" and/or adult versions of games are a non-option in physical education for a host of reasons. Reasons can include feelings of exclusion, higher-skilled students dominating over lower-skilled students, very few practice trials, high bouts of sedentary behavior, not developmentally appropriate, and increased likelihood of bullying, and more (Brian & Lehwald, 2018; Brian, Ward, Goodway, & Sutherland, 2014)

Non-Example # 2: Smaller-Sided Games with Modifications. Smaller-side games are a good start (e.g., 1 v 1, 2 v 2, 3 v 3); however, providing modifications after the task starts can potentially place students on "display" and possibly open-up opportunities for bullying. Immediately, one may think that providing modifications leading to bullying is "crazy". For students with mild disabilities, or for a student without a disability, for whom the content is new or somewhat difficult, using the "modification" places them on display to their peers. For example, during a basketball unit, a "modification" for a student with a disability could include a lower basketball hoop with a lighter ball. Perhaps, those modifications could help a student with lower PLOP and without a disability perform the skills correctly during basketball. However, both the student with a disability and lower-skilled student without a disability would then be performing a different task than their peers in the same class. These students would technically not be included alongside their peers. The irony in these scenarios is that the modifications are designed to "include" students in general physical education. However, these modifications, which are solely for students who need "assistance" places them on display and could potentially increase the likelihood for bullying. Thus, often times students for whom content is new or challenging may opt out of choosing the modifications and struggle to successfully complete the task. After debriefing the task, it is our hope that our students come to understand that modifications for an individual student should be a last resort. For students with severe disabilities, offering modifications may be the only option. However, to every extent possible, we teach our pre-service teachers to try to offer all modifications to all learners at all times to mitigate potential for embarrassment or bullying. Please see the UDL example below as a strategy to offer all modifications at all times to as many students as possible.

Universal Design for Learning. The underlying premise of UDL is not to create modifications to remove extant barriers, rather, the purpose is to prevent the barriers from existing in the first place. To create UDL lessons, teachers aim to include all children in the original activities of the lesson by providing multiple means of engagement, representation, and action and expression. Multiple means of engagement provide different options for students to find interest (i.e., choice and autonomy), maintain high levels of effort and persistence (i.e., goals and objectives, mastery-oriented feedback) while allowing for self-regulation (i.e., self-assessment, expectations, personalized strategies) during daily lessons (CAST, 2011). Multiple means of representation includes delivering content to students with various options for perception (i.e., alternative ways content is presented) and comprehension (i.e., provide background and generalization of content knowledge, guides students processing of information (CAST, 2011). Multiple means of action and expression targets delivering content with opportunities to engage with numerous physical actions (i.e., access to technology, engage through multiple responses), ways of expression/communication (i.e., levels of supports, tools to complete tasks, technology), and promotes the use of executive functions (i.e., self-monitoring, goal setting, strategy development) (CAST, 2011).

UDL Example: After pre-service teachers experience examples like #1 and #2, we then transition into UDL. We first provide pre-service teachers with sample classes that include students of varying PLOP, with and without a multitude of disabilities. We try to provide scenarios that include students with either Autism Spectrum Disorders, physical impairments (e.g., visual impairments, hearing impairments, quadriplegia, etc.), or intellectual disabilities. All K–12 physical education classes are different, all students present differently, understanding the list presented in Lesson Setup (e.g., preferences, PLOP, needs assessment) assists with how to approach UDL. Typically, we will demonstrate a UDL lesson for one scenario, then, we ask our pre-service teachers to create UDL lessons that support the needs of the students within their scenarios. Here is an example UDL lesson.

Scenario: A sixth-grade class that includes two girls who play on their school's softball team, three boys on the school's baseball team, one student with a visual impairment, 10 students (boys and girls) of "average skill level" but who do not play on any sport team, and four students of very low skill level and are amotivated to be in physical education.

The UDL Task—1 v 1 Softball Game (see Appendices). First, we show a video of the task being completed by sixth-graders. Then, we breakdown the task into components: batting, fielding, and running. We use pre-service teachers to demonstrate each component (choosing a variety of ethnicities, genders, and PLOP). We place the sequence of components on the wall written up in bulleted form on large posters as reminders. In addition, we have several pictures all around the gymnasium demonstrating correct performances of each component. Next, we show a variety of choices that pre-service teachers can choose within their task. These choices include kicking a ball (stationary), batting a foam ball off a tee with a plastic bat, and two variations of the task such as running to a polyspot after striking or hitting towards targets. We also offer a wide-variety of equipment choices for all pre-service teachers including beep foam balls (small, medium, large), guide wires or beeping bases or both, and different types of bats (foam paddles, plastic small bat, plastic big barreled bat, etc.). We situate the equipment choices as a challenge rather than a way to make the task easier. For example, if a pre-service teacher can score a run using all the different equipment options they get a bonus run. At the end of the task, pre-service teachers are then asked "based upon today's performance, what is one thing you would like to improve when we complete this task again next time? Can you set a goal to measure improvement?" Once all pre-service teachers understand the task and task choices, we pair up pre-service teachers at random hoping to see a mix of pairings by ethnicities, genders, and PLOPs (regardless of disability). Pre-service teacher duos then perform the task followed by a debrief. Within the debrief, pre-service teachers are asked how the task would look for the amotivated student? Being a 1 v 1, would the amotivated student be as "on-display" as he/she would during a 10 v 10 version? What other "challenges" could they think of to help encourage the use of multiple pieces of equipment? Finally, we ask them to report on how the UDL lesson plan met the following components of UDL:

Multiple Means of Engagement: Trying to successfully use each piece of equipment, different versions of the task.

Multiple Means of Representation: Hopefully, the pre-service teachers will recognize the use of video, verbal demonstrations, peer demonstration, lists on the wall, pictures throughout the gymnasium, and more.

Multiple Means of Action and Expression: Setting one's own goals, determining one's own criterion for success, basing the lesson on each student's PLOP, needs, and preferences.

Sometimes items can transcend categories, but regardless when planning UDL lessons, pre-service teachers realize all student needs, PLOP, and preferences are considered ahead of time when constructing the lesson.

Intersectionalities

Guskey's Model of Teacher Change. Guskey's model of teacher change (Guskey, 2002) situates the role of professional development on securing lasting teacher change. For the purposes of this chapter, we situate how we cultivate "buy-in" from our pre-service physical education teachers regarding going above and beyond the basic course and credit hour requirements for my Adapted Physical Education course at the University of South Carolina. According to Guskey, if teachers believe they can affect student learning and that their efforts result in positive student growth, then they are more likely to buy into changing. Seeing students learn as a result of the pre-service physical education teacher's efforts more often results with positive changes in their attitudes and beliefs. Our pre-service teachers work with the same students all semester both in the schools and during our weekly adapted physical education program where our pre-service teachers volunteer their time. Our pre-service teachers assess students, write students' goals, write students' lessons, and watch students improve. In the beginning, our pre-service teachers may be hesitant towards participating in the "extra" volunteer work required for the practicum. However, by the end of the semester their evaluations consistently state how the service-based learning and volunteer components of class are their favorites parts, that practicum experiences are where they learned the most, and that they grateful to see the students improve as a result of their efforts.

CHALLENGES AND POSSIBILITIES

The term inclusion, within the adapted physical education field, often provokes heated debate and controversy. The divide in adapted physical education regarding inclusion is situated within issues surrounding inclusion "as a placement" and inclusion "as a philosophy". Some scholars feel that when students with disabilities are placed into general physical education courses that they are not actually included (Qi & Ha, 2012). Students with disabilities, according to critics of "inclusion as a placement" consider such an environment as one of integration rather than inclusion. Thus, those who feel inclusion is more of an integration placement rarely support "inclusion as a philosophy," do not feel that UDL is feasible, and promote placements within a self-contained classroom. Unfortunately, there is very little empirical support for UDL, as well as, other inclusion strategies in physical education. There is also very little literature to support self-contained classrooms being more effective than inclusion placements. Quickly, UDL became an evidence-based best practice in the field of special education to meet the needs of a wide variety of learners within their least-restrictive environment

(Rose, 2000). However, in physical education, UDL as a best-practice is not a new concept but it is not used very often. Thus, many challenges exist regarding the implementation of UDL both as a placement and as a philosophy warranting further research.

Additional Challenges. In addition to the challenges identified above, ecological validity, feasibly, and limited time and resources often present as barriers towards UDL. In-service and pre-service teachers may view small-sided games and offering multiple means of representation very challenging when they teach larger classes in smaller spaces. However, we recommend using shorter/smaller dimensions with the small-sided games and also offer low-cost recommendations for issues with equipment. Shorter dimension not only ease any spacing constraints but also can provide a developmentally appropriate context for students who are either new to or experienced with the content. For example, for expert students, using shorter dimensions can increase the speed of the ball requiring a challenging pace of play. For those for whom the content is new, smaller dimensions can ensure that students correctly execute the skill. It is easier to kick a soccer ball a shorter distance than a further distance. However, it can be challenging to defend a soccer ball from a shorter distance as the speed of play can be very quick. Thus, we suggest variance in tasks based upon PLOP and teachers have numerous options.

APPENDICES

1 v 1 Game (Rolling or Kicking) Brian and Lehwald (2018)

Two students are placed within an area approximately 60–90 ft. x 20–30 ft. At one end of the area a poly spot is placed to serve as home base while two different colored poly spots are set 30–45 feet in front of the home base poly spot about 3–5 feet apart and another poly spot is placed 25–40 feet further out from the two poly spots. One student is the kicker and stands at home base and the other student is the fielder and stands on the furthest poly spot. The student who is the kicker must kick the ball on the ground within the boundaries and then runs through the middle poly spot on the right. The fielder fields the ball and runs through the poly spot to the left of the kicker's poly spot. Whomever reaches the spot first gets the point. After each turn, players switch roles. Play continues until each student completes a number of turns at the teacher's discretion. If students have trouble kicking the ball then you can have the student roll the ball instead of kicking it. This allows for the running to the base to be worked on. Safety Concern—Both the kicker and fielder must run straight through their assigned poly spot avoiding a collision with the other player. *Extension*, Same as original except the fielder's base poly spot is moved and set 3–5 feet to the side of the kicker's home base poly spot. Now the kicker must run to the poly spot 30–45 ft., turn around and run back to the poly spot at home base. After fielding the ball, the fielder runs all the way to the poly spot next to home base and tries to beat the runner there. If students need motivation, have the defense earn a point each time the ball is not kicked on the ground.

Equipment Options
- Kickball: Beeping kickball, belled ball, playground ball, Suisse ball, and others.
- Softball: Beep baseball, standard softball, indoor softball, beeping handball, handball, belled ball, foam ball, yarn ball, etc.
- Bat: Foam lollypop paddle, plastic whiffle ball bat, plastic wide-barrel bat, etc.
- Can use a batting tee, batting tee with a small funnel on top for a larger ball.
- Bases: polyspots, cones, beep bases. Can use guide wires for running pathways, can have peers assisting as clappers at each base.

Student Arrangement

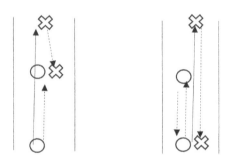

RESOURCES

UDL—Articles

Brian, A., Grenier, M., Lieberman, L. J., Egan, C., & Taunton, S. (2017). 50 million strong for all: Universally designing CSPAPs to align with APE best practices. *Journal of Physical Education, Recreation & Dance, 88*(7), 30–36.

Grenier, M., Miller, N., & Black, K. (2017). Applying universal design for learning and the inclusion spectrum for students with severe disabilities in general physical education. *Journal of Physical Education, Recreation & Dance, 88*(6), 51–56.

Hall, T., Strangman, N., & Meyer, A. (2003). Differentiated instruction and implications for UDL implementation. Wakefield, MA: National center on accessing the general curriculum. *Preventing School Failure, 52*(2), 21–30.

Lieberman, L. J. (2017). The need for universal design for learning. *Journal of Physical Education, Recreation & Dance, 88*(3), 5–7.

Lieberman, L., Lytle, R., & Clarcq, J. A. (2008). Getting it right from the start: Employing the universal design for learning approach to your curriculum. *Journal of Physical Education, Recreation & Dance, 79*(2), 32–39.

Taunton, S., Brian, A., & True, L. (2017). Universally designed motor skill intervention for children with and without disabilities. *Journal of Developmental and Physical Disabilities, 29*(6), 941–954.

UDL—Books
Nelson, L. L., & Rose, D. H. (2014). *Design and deliver: Planning and teaching using universal design for learning.* Baltimore, MD: Brooks.
Rapp, W. (2014). *Universal design for learning in action.* Baltimore, MD: Brooks.

UDL—Websites
http://www.readingrockets.org/article/response-instruction-and-universal-design-learning-how-might-they-intersect-general-0
http://www.cast.org

Instructional Tools
Textbooks

Lieberman, L. J., & Houston-Wilson, C. (2009). *Strategies for inclusion: A handbook for physical educators.* Champaign, IL: Human Kinetics.
Davis, W., & Broadhead, G. (2007). *Ecological task analysis and movement.* Champaign, IL: Human Kinetics.
Rink, J. (2014). *Teaching physical education for learning.* New York, NY: McGraw Hill.
Preference Assessment—https://vkc.mc.vanderbilt.edu/ebip/preference-assessments/
Prompting Hierarchy—http://www.rockybay.org.au/wp-content/uploads/2013/04/6.4-Prompting-Techniques-to-Support-AAC-Use.pdf
Small Sided Games—Brian, A., Ward, P., Goodway, J. D., & Sutherland, S. (2014). Modifying softball for maximizing learning outcomes in physical education. *Journal of Physical Education, Recreation & Dance, 85*(2), 32–37.
LET US Play—Weaver, R. G., Webster, C., & Beets, M. W. (2013). Let us play: maximizing physical activity in physical education. *Strategies, 26*(6), 33–37.
Placek, J. H. (1983). Conceptions of success in teaching: Busy, happy and good? In T. J. Templin & J. K. Olson, (Eds.), *Teaching in physical education* (pp. 46–56). Champaign, IL: Human Kinetics.

Assessments

APEAS Assessment—http://users.rowan.edu/~conet/APE/APEAS.II.Test.Manual.071215.pdf
Brockport Physical Fitness Test—Winnick, J. P., & Short, F. (2014). Champaign, IL: *Human Kinetics.*
Developmental and Adapted Physical Activity Assessment—Horvat, M., Kelly, L., Block, M., & Croce, R. (2018). *Developmental and adapted physical activity assessment, 2E.* Champaign, IL: Human Kinetics.
TGMD-3—Webster, E. K., & Ulrich, D. A. (2017). Evaluation of the psychometric properties of the Test of Gross Motor Development—Third edition. *Journal of Motor Learning and Development, 5*(1), 45–58.
TGMD-2—Ulrich, D. A. (2000). *Test of gross motor development-2.* Austin, TX: Prod-Ed.

REFERENCES

Altshuler, S. J., & Kopels, S. (2003). Advocating in schools for children with disabilities: What's new with IDEA?. *Social Work, 48*(3), 320–329.

Ammah, J. O., & Hodge, S. R. -=Secondary physical education teachers' beliefs and practices in teaching students with severe disabilities: A descriptive analysis. *The High School Journal, 89*(2), 40–54.

Barnes, C., & Mercer, G. (Eds.). (2004). *Implementing the social model of disability: Theory and research.* Leeds, UK: Disability Press.

Block, M. E., & Obrusnikova, I. (2007). Inclusion in physical education: A review of the literature from 1995–2005. *Adapted Physical Activity Quarterly, 24*(2), 103–124.

Brisenden, S. (1986). Independent living and the medical model of disability. *Disability, Handicap & Society, 1*(2), 173–178.

Brian, A., & Lehwald, H. (2018). Softball. In P. Ward & H. Lehwald, (Eds.), *Effective physical education content and instruction: An evidence-based and teacher-tested approach.* Champaign, IL: Human Kinetics.

Brian, A., Ward, P., Goodway, J. D., & Sutherland, S. (2014). Modifying softball for maximizing learning outcomes in physical education. *Journal of Physical Education, Recreation & Dance, 85*(2), 32–37.

Center for Applied Special Technology (CAST). (2011). *Universal design for learning guidelines version 2.0.* Wakefield, MA: National Center on Universal Design for Learning.

Davis, W., & Broadhead, G. (2007). *Ecological task analysis and movement.* Champaign, IL: Human Kinetics.

Davis, W. E., & Burton, A. W. (1991). Ecological task analysis: Translating movement behavior theory into practice. *Adapted Physical Activity Quarterly, 8*(2), 154–177.

Guskey, T. R. (2002). Professional development and teacher change. *Teachers and Teaching, 8*(3), 381–391.

Individuals with Disabilities Education Act. (1997). *Individuals with disabilities education act (IDEA) 1997/Services to parentally placed private school students with disabilities.* United States Department of Education. Retrieved from https://www2.ed.gov/about/offices/list/oii/nonpublic/idea1.html

Individuals with Disabilities Education Improvement Act, H.R. 1350, 108th Cong. (2004).

Lieberman, L. J., & Houston-Wilson, C. (2009). *Strategies for inclusion: A handbook for physical educators.* Champaign, IL: Human Kinetics.

Martin, E., Kwon, E. H., & Healy, S. (2016). Preparing future physical educators for inclusion: Changing the physical education teacher training program. *Revista da Associação Brasileira de Atividade Motora Adaptada, 17*(1), 9–12.

Morley, D., Bailey, R., Tan, J., & Cooke, B. (2005). Inclusive physical education: Teachers' views of including pupils with special educational needs and/or disabilities in physical education. *European Physical Education Review, 11*(1), 84–107.

Qi, J., & Ha, A. S. (2012). Inclusion in physical education: A review of literature. *International Journal of Disability, Development and Education, 59*(3), 257–281.

Rizzo, T. L. (2013). Top 10 issues in adapted physical education: A pilot study: How far have we come?. *Palaestra, 27*(3), 21–27.

Rose, D. H. (2000). Universal design for learning. *Journal of Special Education Technology, 15*(1), 66–67.

Taliaferro, A. R., Hammond, L., & Wyant, K. (2015). Preservice physical educators' self-efficacy beliefs toward inclusion: The impact of coursework and practicum. *Adapted Physical Activity Quarterly*, *32*(1), 49–67.

Tate, D. G., & Pledger, C. (2003). An integrative conceptual framework of disability: New directions for research. *American Psychologist*, *58*(4), 289.

Triano, S. (2000). Categorical eligibility for special education: The enshrinement of the medical model in disability policy. *Disability Studies Quarterly*, *20*(4).

Ulrich, D. A. (2000). *Test of gross motor development.* (2nd Ed). Austin, TX: Pro-Ed.

Vickerman, P., & Coates, J. K. (2009). Trainee and recently qualified physical education teachers' perspectives on including children with special educational needs. *Physical Education and Sport Pedagogy*, *14*(2), 137–153.

Webster, E. K., & Ulrich, D. A. (2017). Evaluation of the psychometric properties of the Test of Gross Motor Development-Third edition. *Journal of Motor Learning and Development*, *5*(1), 45–58.

Winnick, J., & Porretta, D. (Eds.). (2016). *Adapted physical education and sport, 6E.* Champaign, IL: Human Kinetics.

World Health Organization. (2011). *world report on disability*. WHO Library Cataloguing-in-Publication Data.

Yell, M. L. (1998). *The law and special education*. Merrill/Prentice-Hall, Inc., 200 Old Tappan Road, Old Tappan, NJ 07675.

CHAPTER 9

A SOCIALLY JUST (DIFFERENT) ABILITY CURRICULUM IDEA IN PHYSICAL EDUCATION

Shrehan Lynch

TAKING THE 'DIS' OUT OF DISABILITY: IMMERSED IN ABILITY

"Jay[1], Jay, do you have your PE kit for school? Did you remember your calcula-
tor for your math's test? Let's run through some sums just in case on the way to
school." On a recent visit to my hometown in England my mother reminded me
how much I felt the need to look after my older brother growing up. She said,
"You always wanted him to succeed." My brother, five years my elder, struggled
at school in every possible way; socially, academically, and structurally. Observing this and the pain it caused him progressing through school as his younger
and only sister maddened me beyond belief. I could not understand why those at
school, including the teachers, did not appreciate other people's abilities that were
different from their own. On reflection, many years later, after having taught in
the public and private sector of education and now in the position of shifting into
teacher education, I realize that even though Jay did not have the label of differ-

---

[1] Pseudonym used to protect identity

Teaching About Social Justice Issues in Physical Education, pages 99–110.
Copyright © 2019 by Information Age Publishing
All rights of reproduction in any form reserved.

ence when he was at school, it should not have mattered. He should have been equitably treated with love, respect, and equality.

Throughout the years, Jay has been ostracized and faces extreme segregation in our society. Despite "being himself," he has been sectioned under the Mental Health Act, incorrectly arrested, and banned from public spaces for expressing his views. I have observed police sergeants come to the door of my parents' house apologizing for ignorant police behavior, social service workers in tears when the social system has failed, and members of our society complaining about *his* behavior. All of which could have been avoided with all members of society partaking in (dis)ability-awareness education (see Leicester, 2001).

The term (dis)ability draws attention to a deficit and a presumption towards an inability to perform culturally accepted tasks; moreover, people with (dis)abilities are viewed as lesser and perceived as incompetent (Annamma, Connor, & Ferri, 2016). Consequently, I use the term (dis)ability with a parenthesis between "dis" and "abilities," also referred to as dis/ability, to iterate several points. First, the parenthesis (or the dash) acknowledges theoretical, practical, and political work that has taken place in both ability and (dis)ability (Goodley & Runswick-Cole, 2016). Second, as Annamma, Connor, and Ferri (2016) claimed, the separation of the words asks us to consider what type of ability we value and how we value humans. For example, if we constantly focus on the inability, are we recognizing an individual's ability? Lastly, considering that "disability" is a historically situated and socially constructed term (Adams, Reiss, & Serlin, 2015; Charlton, 1998), it is a subjective state and a means to identify in society. Furthermore, it is important to destabilize normative notions on what (dis)ability is and reimagine what we mean by ability to be truly and wholly inclusive of all people in our society.

(Dis)ability is inextricably linked to ableism or the assumption of being able-bodied and a "productive citizen." Our society has normalized ableism through assumptions that tend to discriminate and oppress people with (dis)abilities (Sensoy & Di Angelo, 2017). In education, the term ableism describes discrimination, segregation, and/or exclusion of students with (dis)abilities when they fail to meet the "norms" of the majority. In other words, school settings prefer students that walk rather than roll or talk rather than sign (Hehir, 2002). Ableist assumptions could potentially have severe negative effects on students with (dis)abilities, because difference is regarded as deficit, or in need of remediation or elimination. It is the work of educators in schools who provide *critical* experiences with students in order to conceptualize people with (dis)abilities as people (*differently*)abled rather than (dis)abled. Instead, differences ought to be understood as natural human variances rather than faulty mutations (Connor & Gabel, 2013).

As a result of theoretical knowledge, my life experiences having a brother that was (differently)abled, and personally holding the label of dyslexia, I have been immersed and engaged in socially just work for some years. In short, it has led me to advocate for a reframing on what we mean by ability that is inclusive of all students in education.

CONTEXT

Destabilizing Ableism: 'It Ain't About Us if it is Without Us'

Most recently, I have been teaching courses in a physical education teacher education program in the United States, and I have adopted a sociocultural perspective towards my teaching. There are three principles to it; first "the 'social' elements of a sociocultural perspective are concerned with power and social relations, political and economic factors, and dominant and subordinate groups" (Cliff, Wright, & Clarke, 2009, p. 296). The second, "the 'cultural' aspect refers to shared ways of thinking and acting (ideas, values, beliefs, behaviors), which differ from one culture to another and even within cultures" (Cliff, Wright, & Clarke, 2009, p. 296). Lastly, a sociocultural perspective is encompassed within social justice education as it incorporates investigating systems of power, privilege, and appreciating diversity. Each of my classes attempt to have an underlying sociocultural focus; however, in line with the aims of this chapter, I will discuss an example aimed at destabilizing ableist perspectives within physical culture. Unfortunately, a sociocultural perspective has historically been under-recognized in common practices of physical culture. Instead, a biomedical model reinforcing individualism, competition, heteronormativity, sexism, and ableism has been encouraged (Cliff et al., 2009; Fernandez-Balboa, 1993).

To support curriculum development, I carried a reading with me in (dis)ability studies and am often reminded of Charlton's work (1998, p. 1) "Nothing about us without us." This quote describes the importance of delivering socially just objectives in collaboration with marginalized groups positioned at the forefront of their liberation. Providing a platform for minorities creates a space for human connection, where students can learn that we have more human traits that are similar rather than different. Furthermore, there are an array of (different)abilities, and individuals should be considered experts about their own lives (Keefe, Moore, & Duff, 2006). Therefore, to make curriculum relevant, I found it essential to involve local (differently)abled communities into the teaching space to tell their narratives. While I will review an example used in a higher education setting, the unit outline, and general idea can be used in both primary and secondary teaching spaces.

My local context serves a large varsity wheelchair adapted sports population. As a keen advocate for adapted sports, I was a familiar face within the adapted athletics department. When teaching a basic physical education tennis course, collaboratively with the wheelchair tennis team, I co-created a syllabus that would enable students to have exposure to people with (different)abilities. This experience provided students with the opportunity to question their previously held assumptions related to ability. Unknown to the students, my underlying goal for the course was to raise their consciousness related to ableism in an empowering way. Importantly, the class focused on liberation, not indoctrination. From the research gathered from this immersion experience, I found that the organization of the class disrupted norms of what students were used to in education and this supported students in their journey towards understanding ableism through new experiences, humbling encounters, meaningful relationships, and achieving personal endeavors (Lynch, 2018). As a result, I have continued promoting immersion experiences within physical education as a pathway to include minority groups to share their narratives and to allow students to question previously held assumptions related to ability.

SET-UP & LESSONS

Democracy Means Participation: Organizational Structure of Class

In what follows (see Table 9.1) is a modified curriculum to the one I delivered with undergraduate students that can be used in multiple educational settings. The learning experience outline serves as one idea and should avoid being seen as a 'canned curriculum,' as with any liberatory educational idea they should be shaped to the cultural/contextual educational needs of your students; as a result, learning needs expressed by students or identified by the educator should be forefront when delivering these lessons (Darder, 2012). For this reason, the learning experience plan (see Table 9.1) is not split into days or weeks as it is dependent on the context you teach in, and the amount of time per lesson you have with your students. You may need a whole week on one learning experience, or your students may need one lesson. Also, the activities offered are related to tennis, the chosen example for this scenario; however, activities can be adapted/changed to the activity that you choose (e.g., a striking/fielding unit, or an activity discussed with the community group chosen). Lastly and most integral to the delivery of the learning experiences, the curriculum followed social justice education principles: self-love and knowledge, respect for others, issues of social injustice, social movements and social change, awareness raising, and social action (Picower, 2012).

To make the curriculum possible, I recommend several strategies:

1. **Plan**. This curriculum takes a long time to prepare before classes begin. Ensure you have all the relevant paperwork completed with your administration considering outside community members will be entering school. Learning experience 3 (students explore the feeling of others lived experiences) and 4 (students inquire into societal oppression and injustice while experiencing negotiation, responsibility, and empowerment) include resources such as wheelchairs, cameras, etc. so having prearranged equipment would be advantageous.

2. **Positive Relationships**. Get to know the community members selected before the lessons begin. In the example shown (see Table 9.1) I use a wheelchair tennis team, but in your local context a (different)ability may be more appropriate. It is highly important that you build a strong relationship with the group before they come into the class so that you

TABLE 9.1. (Different)ability Focused Learning Experience Plan

Learning Experience & Underlying Goal	Task	Class Discussion Questions/Prompts Throughout [change per age group]	Social Justice Education Element
1. Students explore self-identity. Stereotypes are deconstructed. *Students learn their history and ability* Students share identities with classmates.	• Individual task: allow students to discover what they can do in the gym (e.g., keep a tennis ball on the racket while moving around the gym, serve into the service box, etc.) • Partner work: discover what each other can do (e.g. keep a rally for 20 shots, return 10 drop shots from a peer, take part in a group task). • Small groups: Student's select own team based on a variety of abilities. Students discover similarities among each other's abilities and what they can all do as a team. • Team building activities to demonstrate team cohesion and the importance of listening to others and drawing on people's strengths.	• What abilities do you have? Why? • What abilities does your partner have? Why? • What abilities does your team have? Why? • What if someone has different abilities? • How do we work together when we have different abilities? • Are there abilities that we value more? • Define what you think the term disability means? • Can people with disabilities play sports?	• Self-love and knowledge • Respect for others
2. Students explore others self-identity. *Community members share knowledge and experiences with students.*	• Session led by wheelchair tennis team [or your chosen community group]. Students can see the team perform at their abilities. Team pre-selects activities based on their strengths/knowledge. • Teacher asks students to get into their mixed ability teams. Wheelchair tennis team play games with students. • After playing students can ask the athlete they have been working with any questions they have.	• What abilities do the athletes have? • Is there anything they could do that you could not? • What are people in wheelchairs referred to in our society? • Do you think that term is fair? Why is it necessary/unnecessary? • What other disabilities do you know about? Are they the same as people who use wheelchairs? Why? What abilities do they have?	• Respect for others • Issues of social injustice

(continues)

TABLE 9.1. Continued

Learning Experience & Underlying Goal	Task	Class Discussion Questions/Prompts Throughout [change per age group]	Social Justice Education Element
3. Students explore the feeling of others lived experiences. *Students empathize with community member's experiences and come to question what normal ability is.*	• Students get the opportunity to try out wheelchairs. Students partake in a range of activities that they did the previous learning experience but in the chair. • Students play wheelchair tennis in pairs. • [If the community team were a goalball team then students could wear blindfolds to be immersed in visually impaired goalball—adapt to your community/the activity/ies appropriate]	• What was it like being in the wheelchair? • Did you have the same abilities as learning experience one and two? • Do you have the same abilities as the athletes? • What can you learn from this experience?	• Self-love and knowledge • Respect for others
4. Students inquire into societal oppression and injustice while experiencing negotiation, responsibility, and empowerment. *Students learn how (dis)abled people are impacted in school and what steps to take to address inequities.*	• School task: In teams or pairs, students are required to go around school buildings, notice boards, cafeteria, etc. and assess what is accessible and what is not. Allow students to take a camera to identify this or provide resources to allow them to consider other (dis)abilities, e.g., blindfolds and crutches. • Discuss hidden disabilities and whether the school is accessible for hidden disabilities. • Group task: Allow students to work together to formulate an action plan to address inaccessible spaces. Ask them to provide resources for other classes, e.g., posters, flyers, letters, etc.	• What is a hidden disability? • How do we ensure we do not judge someone based on a disability? • What are we going to do about areas of our school that are not accessible? • What things outside of school are inaccessible? Is this fair? • Whom should we speak to or what steps should we take to address injustices? • What happens if we do not change our school/structures outside to cater for everyone's needs?	• Issues of social injustice • Social movements and social change

5. Students invent games/activities. *Students demonstrate respect for others by creating fair and inclusive games.*	• Group task: students develop games that are inclusive for the community group. They develop rules, modifications, decide the equipment needed. • Students play their games. • See Butler (2016) for information on student invented games to promote democracy and social justice.	• Where could your game be played? • Is it fair? • What can you change to make your game even more even? • What did you change in your game after playing it?	• Respect for others • Social action
6. Students experience democracy through collaboration. *Students teach peers ability awareness.*	• Group interplay: Students play games with other groups explaining why they are doing the activities/games and gain feedback. Students take it in turns to play/give each other constructive feedback related to their games. • Game enhancement: after students have played a variety of different games they come back as a group and decide if they will change their own game in any way.	• What did you learn from watching the other group's games? • What feedback did you give the group? • How do you receive feedback from other groups? • What ideas can you share amongst the groups? • Were the games fair? What needs to change if they were not fair?	• Awareness raising • Social action
7. Students engage and reflect on action and empowerment. *Students put their learning into practice and are responsible for creating an inclusive festival*	• Festival of learning: students run a festival for the wheelchair tennis team and another class/their class. • Students get feedback on their games from athletes. • Students reflect and create their end of learning experience assessment, e.g., storybook (can use pictures from learning experience 4). • Teacher collects feedback from students and community members on the class to action for next time.	• How well did your team work together? Did you embrace everyone's abilities? • How did you feel gaining feedback from the athletes? Would you implement their suggestions? Why/why not? • Was your game inclusive? Why/why not? • What do you think about the term (dis)ability? • Have your views changed over the course your learning experiences? Why? • What has made you enjoy or not enjoy this semester/class? • What do you want to know more about? • What should I change next semester as your teacher?	• Social action

can collaboratively establish how the class will be delivered and ensure that the group can attend the planned school site classes (learning experiences 2 and 7).

3. **Be flexible**. Plans may change as your term, quarter, semester, etc. goes on, your community members may also have other requirements that come up or your students' identity may necessitate different learning needs. Therefore, remember social justice education is fluid.

4. **Open Communication**. Constant dialogue between you (the teacher), your students, and the community group will allow for a democratic experience where all should feel like they can participate and speak openly. The class discussion questions are set up whereby students could come together in a share circle and discuss freely before or after each activity. For large class numbers, this may work better in small groups. The conversation should go in the direction that the students require. As the educator, ensure you allow students the opportunity to ask each other questions along with providing them time to answer each other's questions. If students do not feel comfortable speaking openly there are several steps you can take (1) incorporate cooperative learning games where students must communicate to complete required tasks, (2) allow students to 'pair share' before a group share circle, (3) use index cards/individual whiteboards throughout the class where students can share their ideas and you can anonymously read them/address points in a group share circle, (4) have an online discussion board out of class where students can discuss ideas.

5. **Inform** parents/guardians, principals, and other staff members in advance of your curriculum plans. If necessary, provide an overview of the plan and your intentions to gain feedback from staff members. Information could include challenging other staff members to ensure their pedagogy is more inclusive and community orientated.

6. **Alternative assessments**. Ditch normative physical education practices and mechanical pedagogies related to high activity levels, waiting times, motor competence progress, ability tracking, standardized tests, and teacher as authoritarian for an effective lesson. Social justice education is not in line with standardized practices and goes against the historically normalized practice's education adopted. A (different)ability curriculum focuses on social and emotional learning for social good/responsibility; standardized practices cannot measure this. Therefore, to assess this class, I recommend allowing student choice of assessments such as journaling through scrapbooking, storybooks, photo books, and video narratives. Such assessments allow students to tell a story of coming to an understanding related to ability and can be done individually, then as a group. Additionally, when assessments are collected, peers could provide feedback on students' assessments. Not only will this demonstrate

group cohesion, but allows students to take responsibility and ownership of their learning.

INTERSECTIONALITY

Identities are Complex: Where Are You in the Social Hierarchy?

While the focus of this chapter and the learning experiences outlined are attentive to ability, many layers make up a person's social identity. Ability is just one. It is important, as educators, we recognize that identity is in constant flux and interdependent on other parts of people's identities (e.g., their context and culture). In this instance, by understanding that ability is something all individuals have in conjunction with race, class, gender, ethnicity, and religion, we can see how complex ability is and how it is perceived depending on other social identities. By looking at ability in this way, it can be considered an intersectionality approach and allows us to be multidimensional in our understandings of social justice (Sensoy & Di Angelo, 2017). Intersectionality helps us understand that all oppression is interconnected and interrelated (hooks, 2015).

The most dominant and normative human identity in our society is one that is white, male, cisgendered, heterosexual, Christian, and able-bodied. When an individual does not have *one* of these dominant characteristics they are seen and positioned as 'less than' in society with such a decision always determined by white counterparts (Artiles, 2011). With this in mind, we can understand the term 'disability' further. One of the reasons that 'dis' is used is because it negates and looks to deprive something/one of power (Goodley & Runswick-Cole, 2016). To demonstrate how power is deduced from individuals we can consider scholarship from Annamma, Connor, and Ferri (2016) who claim that a person of color with a (dis)ability is positioned lower in relation to a white counterpart with a (dis)ability. Said another way, a person of color with a (dis)ability is positioned lower in society and *even more* alien to the norm. Equally, if a female has a (dis)ability they are positioned lower in society as they deviate from the most dominant and normative identity. Social hierarchy is an important consideration when deciding your chosen community group and a significant discussion point with appropriate classes. For example, if you collaborate with a female wheelchair tennis team, then it is worth mentioning that their experiences are going to be different to a men's team and why.

Intersectionality & Ability: Physical Education Class. When considering what does this mean for me? As teachers of a (different)ability curriculum, we must recognize that we need to be advocates of all types of oppression in our classes. It is not enough to focus efforts on ableism and neglect other oppressors. We must consider all sociocultural issues and seek to align our classes with unbiased and new cultural understandings. An intersectionality approach would represent a sustained political commitment to ending all types of oppression (hooks, 2015) and truly be a socially just education.

CHALLENGES AND POSSIBILITIES

Holistic Considerations: If It Were Easy, Everyone Would Do It

When I implemented my (different)ability curriculum, the biggest barrier I faced was language. Within the context I was teaching, terms such as: "retard," "that is retarded," "you are dumb," "you are mental," "disabled person," and "are they handicapped?" were frequently used by students. This inappropriate and inconsiderate language *has* to be addressed and confronted by the educator. Pedagogically, this also means ensuring your language is person-first (person with a dis/ability) and absent from ableist microaggressions (e.g., "Oh you cannot shoot a hoop? You should be able to do that by your age").

Organizationally speaking, a socially just physical education means redesigning programs to align with social justice education principles (Picower, 2012) and allowing students to engage with new experiences. Specifically, a redesign entails reexamining the dominant goal of physical education. The (different)ability curriculum outlined moves away from focusing on skill and fitness to intangibles that we need in our society. Some considerations are discussed.

Physical Education Curriculum: A Democratic Approach. Social justice education espouses a democratic approach that appreciates all abilities and the participation of all students. When delivering my (different)ability curriculum, students were initially shocked by the structure of the class. They were not used to democratic teaching approaches that asked them to engage with their learning environment and the community. Due to the nature of the class being sport specific, students brought their assumptions to the class that it would be competition focused and involve measurement of psychomotor skills. They thought I was looking for (hyper)abled, sensationalized views of the normal body that does exceptional things. Such an approach is not cogent with democratic principles, and I had to ensure I was explicit about this. Consider your answer to these questions:

- Are you over-enthusiastic about individual pursuits?
- Do you constantly praise the winning team?
- Do the winning team get external rewards?
- Is your curriculum focused on the psychomotor aspect of physical education or does it encompass affective and cognitive elements too?
- Do you always use your most skilled student to demonstrate?
- When students get the highest grade for physical education, do you publicly recognize their intelligence/sporting ability?

If the answer is yes to any of the above, then you might be (hyper)ableizing your curriculum and only value those that are considered exceptional. In support of a democratic approach, it is important to review our biases related to our program and the purposes/outcomes we desire for all students.

Physical Education Curriculum: Structural Alignment of Classes. In research by Evans, Bright, and Brown (2015) investigating the experiences of non-disabled students in a wheelchair basketball unit, they found that students began to see similarities between their abilities and those with physically (different) abilities. Meanwhile, rarely did students reference other disabilities. With that being said, the learning experience outlined in this chapter focuses on physical (dis) abilities, and the majority of our (differently)abled population have hidden (dis) abilities. Therefore, it is integral that both are discussed in class. These discussions will come with challenges considering students in your class are likely to have hidden (different)abilities. Consequently, I would recommend covering this topic late in the year when you are aware of each of your student's learning needs, have built a positive classroom community, and built student rapport.

In comparison to a typical K–12 physical education teaching position where you will see the same group of students for an entire year and in some cases consecutively for several years. As a tertiary educator, I was positioned to see the students in my tennis class twice a week for 15 weeks, and unless they took another class in the kinesiology department, it was unlikely I would get the opportunity to teach those students again. With this knowledge in mind, the reality of a stand-alone course challenging perspectives is slim, but sequential courses building on each other mean that students would get the opportunity to learn about social justice issues consistently. Therefore, when considering your curriculum long-term, try positioning each of your courses to allow for an in-depth learning experience in all types of oppression.

SUMMARY

Everything considered, the strategies and learning experiences in this chapter represent the desired state that we could teach in and not necessarily a reality; teaching demands are at an all-time high and with multiple social injustices, it will always be a stretch as to where we must spend our time. Ultimately considering that ability is not something that is static, but one that is interconnected with many other oppressors, being an educator that is willing to constantly learn, be reflective, and attempt socially just work is a worthy task ahead.

REFERENCES

Adams, R., Reiss, B., & Serlin, D. (2015). *Keywords for disability studies*: New York, NY: University Press.

Annamma, S. A., Connor, D. J., & Ferri, B. A. (2016). *DisCrit: Disability studies and critical race theory in education. Disability, culture, and equity series.* New York, NY: Teachers College Press.

Artiles, A. J. (2011). Toward an interdisciplinary understanding of educational equity and difference: The case of the racialization of ability. *Educational Researcher, 40*(9), 431–445.

Butler, J. I. (2016). *Playing fair*. Illinois: Human Kinetics.

Cliff, K. P., Wright, J., & Clarke, D. (2009). What does a 'sociocultural perspective' mean in health and physical education? In M. Dinan-Thompson (Ed.), *Health and physi-*

cal education: Issues for curriculum in Australia and New Zealand (pp. 165–182). Melbourne, AU: Oxford University Press.

Charlton, J. I. (1998). *Nothing about us without us: Disability oppression and empowerment.* Berkeley, CA: University of California Press.

Connor, D. J., & Gabel, S. L. (2013). "Cripping" the curriculum through academic activism: Working toward increasing global exchanges to reframe (dis) ability and education. *Equity & Excellence in Education, 46*(1), 100–118.

Darder, A. (2012). *Culture and power in the classroom.* New York, NY: Routledge.

Evans, A. B., Bright, J. L., & Brown, L. J. (2015). Non-disabled secondary school children's lived experiences of a wheelchair basketball program delivered in the East of England. *Sport, Education & Society, 20*(6), 741–761.

Fernandez-Balboa, J.-M. (1993). Sociocultural characteristics of the hidden curriculum in physical education. *Quest, 45*(2), 230–254.

Goodley, D., & Runswick-Cole, K. (2016). Becoming dishuman: Thinking about the human through dis/ability. *Discourse: Studies in the Cultural Politics of Education, 37*(1), 1–15.

Hehir, T. (2002). Eliminating ableism in education. *Harvard Educational Review, 72*(1), 1–33.

hooks, b. (2015). *Feminist theory: From margin to center* (3rd ed.). New York, NY: Routledge.

Keefe, E. B., Moore, V. M., & Duff, F. R. (2006). *Listening to the experts: Students with disabilities speak out.* Baltimore, MD: Brookes.

Leicester, M. (2001). A moral education in an ethical system. *Journal of moral education, 30*(3), 251–260.

Lynch, S. (2018). *Transformative pedagogy for community building: A disability focused immersion project in physical education.* Paper presented at the European Congress of Adapted Physical Activity 2018 Conference, Worcester, England.

Picower, B. (2012) Using their words: Six elements of social justice curriculum design for the elementary classroom. *International Journal of Multicultural Education. 14*(1), 1–17.

Sensoy, O., & DiAngelo, R. (2017). *Is everyone really equal?: An introduction to key concepts in social justice education.* New York, NY: Teachers College Press.

CHAPTER 10

EMPOWERING ENGLISH LANGUAGE LEARNERS IN PHYSICAL EDUCATION

Using "Sight and Action"

Brian Culp

ACTION RESEARCH & REFLECTION

I clearly remember my first day of student teaching in the elementary school. The lesson was designed to incorporate fitness as an introductory activity before involving learners in station work. After two years of preparation through my PETE program, I was excited about the opportunity to utilize the instructional strategies I had learned. Despite having only a few hours of leading youth in formalized settings up to that point, I felt confident and eager to instruct.

As students arrived, I continued the attendance routine that my cooperating teacher had put into place, watching as students sat in their assigned spots in the gym. It was time to move. I glanced around in an attempt to find my cooperating teacher, who appeared to have left the gym. Voices in the gym were beginning to become louder. Decision time. I decided to begin class. Students were asked to stand up, move to the center of the room, and find personal space for the fitness

Teaching About Social Justice Issues in Physical Education, pages 111–119.
Copyright © 2019 by Information Age Publishing
All rights of reproduction in any form reserved.

activity. However, there was an issue. One of the boys refused to move. I asked again to no avail. This request was made several more times in the next minute or so and I began to notice that our exchange was attracting an audience.

The boy continued to look up at me as I traded glances with him and gestured. Voices in the gym became louder and I could hear laughter. Dumbfounded and embarrassed, I began to think about the cooperating teacher returning to the room and witnessing me not being in control of the class. Panicking, I walked up to the student and put my hand down on his shoulder in a half nudge, reminding myself of the designated area in the gym for students to sit out. The boy grabbed my hand and stood up. With the student in tow, I led him to the designated area in full view of his classmates who were fully enjoying the spectacle. I felt embarrassed and thrown off of my game. In that moment of removing the student, the only thing I could think of is that I would not reward students for insubordination. The rest of the class needed to see that I meant business. I started the lesson. A few minutes later, the cooperating teacher came back into the gym, looked at the boy, then at me, before observing me teach. There was no discussion at that moment of my instruction. As I taught, I noticed that the cooperating teacher was spending some one-on-one time with the student in a movement activity in which I was not familiar.

After class was over, there was a planning period where the events of the previous class were discussed. The first question I received from my cooperating teacher was not about how well the lesson went, it was about why I chose to sit a student out of activity. I presented my opinion that the boy posed a disciplinary problem and was distracting the class. The cooperating teacher mentioned to me that this may have not been necessarily the case. When I inquired as to why, the cooperating teacher told me that the boy had just moved from Honduras and comprehension and proficiency in speaking English were non-existent. By the definition given to me, "Wilmer" was classified as an English language learner (ELL). Since school had only began a few days earlier, I presumed that it was also likely that my class was Wilmer's first structured physical education class in the United States.

Since I taught that first class on a Friday before Labor Day, I had an extended weekend to consider my actions before my next teaching. Doubt began to set in. As I was conscientious of so many other aspects of my teaching, I was frustrated with myself for not accounting for this scenario in my preparation. Upon further reflection, I also concluded that I was not prepared to think or act on a scenario such as this in my teacher education classes and I wanted to know why. I had no other incidents during the rest of that wonderful semester student teaching.

Although I had gotten off to a bad start with Wilmer, I would later learn from my cooperating teacher some strategies for inclusion of ELL students in the classroom. Among these were assessing needs, using a buddy system, learning key words and phrases (in multiple languages) for use in instruction and utilizing short demonstrations and pictures. Even so, I still reflect on that incident often, as it was a critical incident in my life that helped drive much of my efforts in teaching physical education. In today's schools, it is not enough to have content knowledge or the ability to design lessons. We must also have knowledge of our students, their situations, and use that information in creating positive environments for movement that are inclusive for all learners (Fairbain & Jones-Vo, 2010; Tomlinson & Imbeau, 2010).

Current Statistics and Discussion

There is no one concise definition that encompasses the description of "English language learner". As noted by Blackburn, Cornish, and Smith (2016), ELLs do not comprise a homogeneous group, or hold a single description that defines their cultural backgrounds. English dominated countries such as the United States, the United Kingdom, and Australia, have received and continue to receive students from diverse countries and cultures as a response to unique social, historical, and political antecedents, including legal and illegal immigration, slavery, transportation, colonialism, geographical proximity, political persecution and exile, war and invasion, and a host of other push-and-pull factors (Blackburn, Cornish, & Smith, 2016). Other factors that hamper the creation of a uniform definition of English language learner include immigrant status, (i.e., first or subsequent generation arrivals), country of birth origin for the new migrant (whether it is English-speaking or non-English-speaking), and the degree of acculturation of the individual into the dominant culture.

Generally, ELL students are in the process of actively acquiring English whose primary language is one other than English. These students require specialized or modified instruction in classes and are often from non-English speaking homes and backgrounds. Additionally, these students come from cultural backgrounds and communities with different understandings and expectations of education, language and learning (NALDIC, 2018). English language learners are referred to in educational circles by a host of terms, including limited English proficient (LEP) students, non-native English speakers, English learners (or ELs), language-minority students, or bilingual students/emerging bilingual students (Culp & Schmidlein, 2012). In the United States, United Kingdom, Australia, and Canada, the instruction of English language learners may be termed as English as a second language (ESL), English as a foreign language (EFL), English as an additional language (EAL), or English for speakers of other languages (ESOL).

In the United States for example, the majority of states classify ELL learners through their own educational guidelines based off of the federal definition. As of this writing, federal law used the term "limited English Proficient" for English language learner, denoting these students as a student:

- who is aged 3 through 21;
- who is enrolled or preparing to enroll in an elementary school or secondary school;

- who was not born in the United States or whose native language is a language other than English;
- who is a Native American or Alaska Native, or a native resident of the outlying areas; and
- who comes from an environment where a language other than English has had a significant impact on the individual's level of English language proficiency; or
- who is migratory, whose native language is a language other than English, and who comes from an environment where a language other than English is dominant; and
- whose difficulties in speaking, reading, writing, or understanding the English language may be sufficient to deny the individual —
  ○ the ability to meet the State's proficient level of achievement on State assessments;
  ○ the ability to successfully achieve in classrooms where the language of instruction is English; or
  ○ the opportunity to participate fully in society. (Garcia, Kleifgen, & Falchi, 2008)

English language learners are a diverse group and the fastest growing-segment of the school age population in the United States. They face unique challenges including poverty, familial transiency, non-citizenship status, and the burden of serving as the "family hero" (Center for Immigration Studies, 2018). Some English-language learners are recently arrived immigrants and refugees who have encountered war, persecution, and disruption in schooling. Along with feelings of helplessness, frustration, and insecurity, immigrant and refugee youth drop out from school at higher rates than their English-speaking peers. Undoubtedly, this is impactful for future mobility and the attainment of social capital for these students.

In the early 2000s, a handful of scholars in physical education began to advocate for transformative strategies that took into account the health, educational and social needs of ELL students By 2010, more intentional discourse about best practices for empowering ELL learners' language was invoked (Burden, Columna, Hodge, & Martinez de la Vega Mansilla, 2013, Columna & Lieberman, 2011; Santillan, Jacobs & Wright, 2015; Sato & Burge-Hall, 2010). In outlining how to best serve students, these authors acutely identified that 1) education programs routinely fail to prepare teachers for ELL learners, 2) more attention needed to be placed on ensuring success across content areas, 3) and negative attitudes and dispositions regarding ELL learners were in need of being challenged and changed. Burden, et. al (2013), in particular, provided six core strategies to help ELL learners thrive in physical education environments:

- *Vocabulary and language development-* for example, utilizing specific movement terms such as spatial awareness to build on larger concepts

- *Guided interaction*-how teachers structure lessons so that students can work together
- *Metacognition and authentic assessment*-where teachers model and explicitly teach thinking skills
- *Explicit instruction*-direct teaching of concepts, through learning words and phrases in students' native languages
- *Meaning-based context and universal themes*- taking something meaningful from student's everyday lives and using it to interest them
- *Modeling, graphic organizers and visuals*-utilizing visual aids to help ELL students link concepts to supporting ideas.

The instruction of English-language learners has been an issue of considerable debate over the past 40 years. Discussions of citizenship status and national identity has driven policies on how English-language education should be interpreted. In some cases, this has led to states adopting "English as the official language" statutes, and citizen referendums prohibiting dual-language instruction except in special cases (Schildkraut, 2003).

Irrespective of opinion on how to teach ELL students, the inconvenient truth is that topics related to immigration, language, instruction and learning has become politicized and routinely distorted. The scope of this chapter does not allow for a robust discussion of the aforementioned. Therefore, it is suggested that readers review literature by Culp (2017) and Stanec, Bhalla, and Mandigo (2016) to get a sense of how these policies have relevance for current practices related to health and physical education for immigrant populations.

Toward a Shared Language in the PE Classroom

The deficiencies that I had in my early years of teaching were profound. At the time, I had no appreciation for how important language and communication could serve as a "barrier or channel" to effective physical education for ELL students. Additionally, I had little understanding on factors that affect how students learn in the classroom and specifically how this could be modified for use in physical education environments.

There was more that I needed to learn in order to get to a better understanding of the ELL learners in my class. Moving toward a more "shared language" meant that I needed to learn about my students beyond the mere constructs of teaching and learning. In order to better connect with our ELL learners, we need to know about their families, who works with their families, what countries they are from, what languages they speak, and what traditions are emphasized. This is not an inclusive overview of all we should seek to know, but this information is vital in helping to foster equitable education for ELL learners. To assist in this endeavor, I developed an assignment termed "Sight and Action" to get pre-service teachers thinking about the realities ELL learners may face when arriving into our classes.

CONTEXT

I prepare future professionals in PETE at a public coeducational research institution in the southeastern United States. The institution is located in a county that is one of the fastest growing in the United States and is in within a thirty minute drive to a major metropolitan city. Hispanic and Asian populations constitute the largest growing segment of the people in the area, with this increase attributed largely to immigration.

The PETE program is situated in a department that has the mission of preparing highly qualified professionals and opportunities for enhanced wellness for all. As part of their teacher preparation, students participate in practicum experiences and lead comprehensive school activity programs. The "Sight and Action" activity is presented to students in a foundations of physical education course, a course typically taken by prospective PETE majors during their first year in the program.

LESSON SET UP

Over the years, I have found that the "Sight and Action" activity works best when the following steps are followed:

1. After discussing health disparities among underrepresented populations in physical education at the beginning of the course.
2. After a discussion of current statistics related to immigrants, refugees and migrants in the United States, again preferably at the beginning of the course.
3. As will be described fully in the next section, this activity involves observation by the student of environments where English is not necessarily spoken as the primary language. Therefore, the instructor must give some thought to the types of situations where this can be found. Some examples of this are language classes, festivals, religious ceremonies, local classrooms and recreational programs targeting immigrant and refugee populations. It would be immensely helpful for the instructor to visit these sites firsthand. Also, it is suggested that the instructor establish a relationship with persons in these groups who are willing to serve as guides or translators for pre-service teachers who are observing.

STRATEGY/ACTIVITY/LESSON

In "Sight and Action," students are required to observe or immerse themselves in a locale where English is not used as a first/primary language in communication. Optimally, this would be participant observation in a setting where health enhancing physical activity and movement takes place, however this can be modified to an observation of others in the setting. Students are required to observe the setting for a minimum of two hours. I require students to take three pictures (with permission from the locale), which best describe the activity and the people involved in it. Additionally, students are required to bring back an artifact of some sort (i.e., flyer, giveaway).

After they finish their observations, students are required to answer the following questions:

1. Describe in a few sentences the physical environment (i.e., weather, time of day) and type of people (i.e., old vs. young, class perception, local vs. visitors), the type of activity observed or participated in, languages spoken/ways of communication and any other descriptors you feel are of note.

2. Why did you select this particular environment to observe/participate in? What did you think you would witness before you arrived in respect to communication? Did that perception change in your observation? Why or why not?

3. In the setting you observed, what types of movements/actions seemed to be encouraged? What types of movements/actions were not encouraged? What do you think were reasons for this?

4. Were there situations where you felt most comfortable as opposed to least comfortable? Please explain.

5. Discuss what implications you think this has for teaching physical education to ELL learners. After reflection and research, did your impressions match with your initial impressions in question one?

Occasionally, I have added one additional piece to this activity that requires students to create a graphic organizer that explains a sport skill or technique in English contrasted with another language of their choice. I leave room in my course for students to present the results of "Sight and Action" towards the last few weeks of the semester. As you can imagine, the presentations open the door for a host of discussions on issues related to equity, identity, voice power and inclusion.

CHALLENGES AND POSSIBILITIES

Mayes, Cutri, Rogers, and Montero (2016) feel that language, thoughts and actions depend on each other in subtle but profound ways. For English language learners, honoring their language and culture provides opportunities to help these students develop cognitively while nurturing their self-worth. Additionally, it has the bonus effect of fostering in these students a positive view of their culture and provides them reasons to view the experiences of others favorably. The best teachers understand that potential and growth for ELL learners are tied to an appreciation of their native cultures and languages (Lee, 1997).

In the years that I have instituted this activity, the main challenge that I have faced has involved helping students find appropriate sites that force them to think about the questions posed. First year students in PETE programs are in the process of learning professional dispositions. They will make mistakes and often have answers that vary in the level of sophistication. Often, students do not have the critical ability to seek out places where ELL learners can be found. If given a choice, students will likely select places to observe where they have some familiarity (i.e., sporting event, athletic practice). Instructors must keep this in mind and challenge students to get out of their comfort zones as they support their development as future professionals. If the investment is made however, I have found that on the whole, students develop not only an appreciation for the experience of ELL learners, but become architects for successful outcomes in physical education.

REFERENCES

Blackburn, A. M., Cornish, L., & Smith, S. (2016). Gifted English language learners: Global understandings and Australian perspectives. *Journal for the Education of the Gifted, 39*(4), 338–360.

Burden, J. W., Columna, L., Hodge, S. R., & Martínez de la Vega Mansilla, P. (2013). Ethnolinguistically relevant pedagogy: Empowering English language learners in physical education. *Quest, 65*(2), 169.

Center for Immigration Studies. (2018). *Mapping the impact of immigration on public schools.* Accessed 4/20/18 at: https://cis.org/Report/Mapping-Impact-Immigration-Public-Schools

Columna, L., & Lieberman, L. (2011). *Promoting language through physical education: Using sign language and Spanish to engage everyone.* Champaign, IL: Human Kinetics.

Culp, B., & Schmidlein, R. (2012). Preparing PETE students for culturally and linguistically diverse learners. *Strategies, 25* (7), 11–14.

Culp, B. (2017). "Illegitimate" bodies in legitimate times: Life, liberty, and the pursuit of movement. *Quest, 69* (2), 43–156.

Fairbain, S., & Jones-Vo, S. (2010). *Differentiating instruction and assessment for English language learners: A guide for K–12 teachers.* Philadelphia, PA: Caslon.

García, O., Kleifgen, J. A., & Falchi, L. (2008). *From English language learners to emergent bilinguals* (Equity Matters Research Review No. 1). New York, NY: The Campaign for the Educational Equity, Teachers College, Columbia University.

Lee, C. C. (1997). Cultural dynamics: Their importance in culturally responsive counseling. In C. C. Lee (Ed.), *Multicultural issues in counseling: New approaches to diversity* (2nd ed., pp. 15–30). Alexandria, VA: American Counseling Association.

Mayes, C., Cutri, R. M., Rogers, P. C., & Montero, F. (2016). *Holistic multicultural education: Understanding the whole student* (2nd ed.). Lanham, MD: Rowman and Littlefield Education Press.

National Association for Language Development in the Curriculum (2018). *EAL learners in the UK.* Retrieved 7/16/18 from https://naldic.org.uk/the-eal-learner/eal-learners-uk/

Santillan, Y., Jacobs, J. M., & Wright, P. M. (2015). Integrating best practices in ELL classrooms with quality physical education instruction. *JOPERD: The Journal of Physical Education, Recreation & Dance, 86* (3), 51–53.

Sato, T., & Burge-Hall, V. (2010, Fall). Strategies for including English language learners in physical education. *Virginia Alliance of Health, Physical Education, Recreation, and Dance Journal, 31*(2), 8–10.

Schildkraut, D. J. (2003). American identity and attitudes toward official-English policies. *Political Psychology, 3*, 469.

Stanec, A., Bhalla, J., & Mandigo, J. (2016). Exploring the issues faced by immigrant students in physical education. In Robinson, D. B. & Randall. L. (Eds.), *Social justice in physical education: Critical reflections and pedagogies for change* (pp. 248–270). Toronto, CA: Canadian Scholars Press.

Tomlinson, C. A., & Imbeau, M. B. (2010). *Leading and managing a differentiated classroom*. Alexandria, VA: ASCD.

CHAPTER 11

USING CHILDREN'S CULTURAL EXPERIENCES AND TRADITIONS TO ADD MEANING AND RELEVANCE TO PE TEACHING IN THE PRIMARY AGE RANGE

Sarah Hill and Joanna Sweeney

REFLECTION AND CONTEXT

In a school where 98% of pupils have English as an Additional Language (EAL), ensuring social justice in our diverse classrooms came way before our specialism in PE. Indeed, the school is so diverse that it has become second nature to cater for a wide range of ethnic, cultural and linguistic needs. This is evident in the school's ethos (which states the pride taken in the school's diverse cultural community); the planning (which promotes the teaching, sharing and celebrating of all festivals from the five main religions practiced by the pupils in our school); and in each individual lesson which all aim to be interactive, visual and widely differentiated.

Whilst studying for our Post Graduate Certificate of Education (PGCE), we each received about four hours of PE lectures, and this, combined with a small number of PE In-Service Education and Training (INSET), run by our school's

Teaching About Social Justice Issues in Physical Education, pages 121–132.
Copyright © 2019 by Information Age Publishing
All rights of reproduction in any form reserved.

coordinator, made up our Physical Education Teacher Education (PETE). It was our own enthusiasm and passion for the subject which inspired us to further our knowledge and skills of PE teaching through a number of courses including a Masters in Physical Education and Sport Pedagogy. Throughout the Masters, many social issues were discussed in a way that invited us to question how much we promoted equity in our classrooms. These questions ranged from 'At what age should a child start receiving sex education?' to 'When we group children according to gender for class routines (such as who is lining up better, boys or girls?) are we unintentionally highlighting gender differences?' Teaching children with EAL can be present in a classroom in different capacities. First, the composition of EAL speakers can vary. Perhaps, like in our school, there is a lingua franca— where most children have another language, but English is the common tongue. Occasionally, individuals are one in a group of children who have a common language or perhaps there are just one or two children with EAL and are therefore isolated by their difference. Second, the level of proficiency in English will vary between EAL learners, from beginner to fluent. This is measured by our EAL Team in 5 stages and an outline of these levels can be found on the Hounslow Language Service (HLS) website (2016).

In our school, individual, cultural and social differences are at the forefront of interactions between teacher and pupil. It becomes as important to be aware of ensuring inclusive practice for the White British children (just 4%), as it is to ensure inclusion for what one might imagine are your typical ethnic minorities in a school in Greater London. It is therefore important to ensure that all teaching has a low threshold and a high ceiling. Our topic based curriculum—the Earth Curriculum—is built around real life experiences, often outdoors, to ensure that children of all language proficiencies have a first-hand experience of the topic. The cross-curricular nature of all lessons taught at our school is a key strategy used to grasp the attention of children who have very little experience of the English language (or experience in England!), and to continue to invigorate the minds of children who have acquired a more competent level of English and who are ready for new challenges.

LESSON SET-UP

Introduction

The National Curriculum in the United Kingdom states that, in Key Stage 1, (ages 5–7), children should be taught 'basic movements including running, jumping, throwing and catching, as well as developing balance, agility and coordination' (Department for Education, 2013). They should also participate 'in team games, developing simple tactics for attacking and defending' (Department for Education, 2013). This lesson focuses on developing fundamental movement skills, such as running and balancing, in the context of a game. To challenge those pupils who are ready, simple defense tactics are explored. Skills-wise, this lesson would sit well at the beginning of the school year, when there is a need for pupils to develop their fundamental movement skills so they are competent and able to participate in more complex games later in the year. In our setting, pupils learn about the Hindu celebration of Diwali as part of their Literacy lessons, and so we decided that this could be our 'theme' for the lesson. In the United Kingdom, timetabling this lesson early in the academic year complements the timing of Diwali; thus, the skills focus and theme are in alignment.

Initial Planning Stages

When we began planning the lesson, the children were learning about the Hindu celebration of Diwali. We decided that a PE lesson that celebrated the cultures and beliefs of the pupils would be a great hook; as having a familiar subject gives the children an opportunity to be an 'expert'. In addition, we have observed in this age range that incorporating gross motor movements into lessons can spark interest, deepen pupils' understanding of concepts and improve pupils' memory of what has been taught. We therefore decided that focusing a PE lesson on the class topic, namely Diwali, would enrich pupils' learning and ultimately result in better outcomes in all areas of the curriculum.

Essential Elements in Every PE Lesson

PE lessons should be inclusive and appropriately pitched, just like for Literacy and Maths. We chose a 'Tag' game for the main activity, as for this age range, simple games with a small number of rules are appropriate. However, rather than simply playing 'Tag', we included thematic elements such as the 'tagger' pretending to be the character of 'Ravana' from the Diwali story of Rama and Sita. This added a layer of excitement and thrill, giving the game meaning and making it more memorable. Another advantage of playing simple games is that they can be easily replicated in pupils' independent play, allowing further skills development. Activities that develop fundamental movement skills—or ABCs (Agility, Balance and Coordination)—are highly important. It could be argued that the development of these key skills has, in the past, been overlooked in the pursuit of teaching 'real PE' in the form of traditional school games. But in order to play these games, children need to have a sound level of Physical Literacy. Therefore, we attempted to deliver activities that develop Physical Literacy skills, such as hopping and skipping in the Warm Up, and balancing challenges later in the lesson.

Another essential feature of an effective PE lesson is to maximize opportunities for movement and to minimize sedentary activities like queuing and spectating. This was why, instead of playing the 'Tag' game and having pupils simply be 'out' if they were caught, we had timed 'challenges' to complete before rejoining the game. This way, children were expected to be moving and participating fully in the lesson at all times. Importantly, by being allowed to play again, they had lots of opportunities to practice and improve.

Additional Considerations for Teaching Effective PE Lessons for Pupils with EAL

In preparation for the lesson, we ensured that the story and key vocabulary for the lesson had been pre-taught; the story was read every day that week in the run up to the lesson so that it was familiar. We prepared visual picture prompts which we could show throughout the lesson. We considered our modelling of the activities, trying to balance teacher input with the need to allow pupils to be imaginative, problem solve and explore. This is evident in the Warm Up section of the lesson, where children were asked to move as various characters from the story. We thought it important that children have the opportunity to be imaginative with their movements at the beginning, without the teacher explaining 'how to do' an activity. This also provides a challenge for more able pupils to be creative and display their own prior knowledge. This teaching concept can be difficult for teachers of learners with EAL, as it can be tempting to explain and model exactly what pupils need to do. However, by ensuring pupils are well prepared with vocabulary, and key visuals are on display, the need to do this can be reduced. We also considered ways to make all parts of the lesson relate to the story; for example, 'making circles' was a theme of the challenge activities, as physically enacting language from the story with gross motor movements would deepen their understanding of the vocabulary.

LESSON PLAN

Lesson—PE (Multiskills) Theme—Diwali (The Story of Rama and Sita)
Year One (ages 5–6 years) Lesson One

Learning Objective

Play a running game as part of a large group.

Success Criteria and Teaching Points

For the Running Activities:

Practise running skills – head up and looking forward, trunk stable, hands move from 'pocket to mouth', high knees.

Practise stopping, starting, changing direction and moving safely in own space.

Explore ways of travelling imaginatively like characters in the story of Rama and Sita.

Participate in games, developing simple tactics.

For the Challenges:

Develop agility, balance, and co-ordination.

Hold a still position with quality and control, naming specific balances.

Personal/Social/Emotional

Listen to and follow instructions.

Work on simple tasks independently.

Try several times if at first they do not succeed.

Enjoy participating in games and reflect on how they can improve.

Personal Best philosophy – 'Practise to improve'.

Discuss how they feel before, after and during exercise and changes to the body when they exercise.

Resources

Visual Resources to Support Learners with EAL:

Pictures of characters from the story of Rama and Sita, pictures of challenges to go in the 'Challenge Zones'.

PE resources:

Cones for marking out 'zones', ribbons one per child, 1-minute sand timers, a ball, music (optional).

Introduction and Warm Up

Ensure pupils have been introduced to Diwali and are familiar with the story of Rama and Sita before the lesson.

Introduce the Learning Objective.

Warm Up:

Find a 'bubble space'. Remind pupils that this is their space and they need to be careful not to 'pop' their bubble – eyes need to be looking and they should make their own 'pathway'.

Travel around the space in different pathways using fundamental movements – call out hop, skip, jump, side step, gallop, leap, jog. Encourage them to improve their travelling skills by pointing out good role models – "Look at how... has their head up and is looking where he/she is going."

Call out a body part and children touch the floor with that part of their body – for example, hand, elbow, knee - before moving on. Could have pictures to support.

Repeat the activity, however, this time, call out characters from the story. Ask: How could you move like this character?

Prince Rama; Princess Sita; Ravana (demon king); Hanuman (monkey king); Golden Deer

Allow pupils time to explore first and then point out positive examples to refine and develop. Display pictures of characters on an Interactive Whiteboard, or have large A3 pictures to hold up. Play traditional music for effect if possible. When the music stops or the bell rings, freeze like that character.

Touch base—discuss how they are feeling after the warm up and changes to the body.

Increase in temperature, heartbeat, breathing, feeling thirsty. Discuss why it is important to warm up before exercising – gently increases heart rate, gets muscles ready, prevents injury.

Skills Development and Application

Skills Development

Read this part of the story to the pupils – *Sita saw a beautiful, golden deer in the forest and asked Rama to capture it for her. Rama drew a circle around Sita and told her not to leave the circle. Rama went away to capture the deer. But it was a trick – Ravana, the demon king, had created the golden deer. When Sita stepped outside of the circle, Ravana took her away.*

Explain that we are going to play a 'catch' game about this part of the story. In the game, if somebody is out, they need to do different challenges so that they are still participating and developing their PE skills.

Explain the challenges and try them out so that children are familiar with them. (In both challenges there is a link to 'circles' like the circle Rama drew for Sita in the story.)

Challenge 1: Seated balance on bottom. (Use hands to support if needed, challenge more able children to balance without hands). Make circles in the air with their feet for 1 minute (have sand timer to show them how long 1 minute is.)

Challenge 2: Stand up and hold both arms out to the side. Make circles by rotating arms—(either big or small circles – they can choose how much they want to challenge themselves.) They need to do this for 1 minute (again have sand timers as a visual.)

Practise the challenges. You could make it into a game by playing music and doing the challenges you call out in time to a song. Have lots of repetition so that they fully understand what they need to do in the 'Challenge Zones'. Extension for more able children: Make up their own circle challenges (e.g., Hop in a circle.)

Skills Application – Game

Play the Ravana Chase Game.

Mark out a circle in the centre of the space with cones and recap the two Challenge Zones on either side (outside the circle) where pupils will complete the challenges if caught before re-joining the game. Place pictures of the challenges in these zones for EAL pupils to refer to.

Pupils find a bubble space.

Explain that the teacher is Ravana and is going to try and catch them.

All pupils tuck a ribbon in the back of their shorts. They travel around the space like characters from the story (linking back to the Warm Up.) They can choose which character they want to be and how they will travel. Remind them – no sprinting and sensible noise level. Point out and praise pupils who are travelling around the space imaginatively like a character from the story.

Ravana 'chases' the pupils. If he gets their ribbon, they need do a challenge activity for one minute.

Once completed, they can retrieve their ribbon and re-join the game.

Extension for more able pupils. – How can they play tactically? (e.g. turn their back away from the catcher so that they cannot get their ribbon; change direction, stop and start to confuse the catcher).

Safety points: Remind children about space – stay in a bubble space. Look where they are going. Remind them to maintain a sensible noise level.

Cool Down and Plenary
Stand in a circle. Pass a ball around the circle saying names of the characters in a pattern (e.g. Rama, Sita, Sita, Rama) as they pass the ball around the circle.

When the teacher calls out 'change direction', change the way they are passing the ball and start again.

Evaluation
Sit down together. Ask them to close their eyes and think about the lesson.

Ask: What did you learn?

What did you have to do to play the game successfully?

What went well and what could you improve?

What part of the story could we do next time?

How are you feeling now? (Discuss changes to the body.)

INTERSECTIONALITIES

It is important to highlight the many factors that intersect with supporting children with EAL in an infant school. Intersectionality Theory is a tool for achieving gender and economic justice and it can also help to address issues like racism, classism and sexual identity (Samuels & Ross-Sheriff, 2008). Some poignant issues like these are more relevant than others in our setting and are discussed below. Many of these relate to the cultural diversity within our school community: 29 ethnic groups were identified by the school data collected at the start of the academic year of 2017–2018. Different cultural views and beliefs are hugely significant in our school and this raises many questions that should be considered to help provide the best and understand the most about our EAL learners.

The Relevance of Age

Our school is a large infant school, with seven form entry and an age range of 3–7. The children's age can be of an advantage: many have found that young children are especially prodigious learners, due to their flexible and exploratory minds (Gopnik, Griffiths, & Lucas, 2015), and often the less able children in a class have very similar needs to the children who have EAL as they all strive to learn new concepts and develop new skills. Interestingly, it has been shown that by the age of six, bilingual learners begin to exceed the abilities of their monolingual peers in many cognitive tasks (Blom et al., 2014). In contrast, their youth could be a challenging factor. For many of our children, youth comes with a lack of confidence and experience, leading to a lack of understanding in their situation. Many of our children are recent migrants and find themselves in difficult living situations, such as shared accommodation, while others may have close family members—parents or siblings –still in their home country. These can be difficult situations for young children to understand.

What is the Child's Prior Experience of the English Language?

Hounslow Language Service measures English speaking on 5 levels: from A: Beginner to E: Fluent (Hounslow Language Service, 2016). A child's confidence and competence at school is greatly affected by their means of communication. It is an asset of our school, that the EAL learners are never too isolated by their language; even if they are the only one with *their* language, they are not the only one who has EAL. In another school, it may be the case that there is just one child with EAL, and this child will need different support than if they were in a school that was more culturally diverse. There are some children who are learning more than two languages in our setting. In some children, this can be an advantage as they successfully develop proficiency in multiple languages with confidence. In contrast, it can overwhelm some children. A Reception child (aged 4–5 years) in our school was being spoken to at home by different family members in English, Dutch and Twi. The results were that at school his speech sounds were muffled;

he referred to himself as three different names; when frustrated about a social is-sue he would struggle to communicate his needs; and when he did speak, it was in sentences that were below his age expectation. In line with recommendations from our HLS experts, I advised the family to pick one language to speak all the time at home—not necessarily English, just consistent. Despite his speaking and language delay, this child quickly made a good friend in his class, who happened to be White British and fluent in the English language. With this linguistically convenient friendship and the consistently spoken language at home (the family did stick with English) the boy began to make rapid progress, first in his speaking and then everything else. Indeed, the language spoken at home has a great effect on language learning. The children whose families speak English at home tend to learn the language more quickly. This is a difficult issue, however, as parents risk their child losing their first language through lack of use. Another possibility, however, is if another child in a beginner's class speaks the same language, which serves to provide a great social support, especially if the teacher makes opportuni-ties to celebrate different languages. In addition to their language proficiency, the length of time that a child has been in the country has a huge effect on many of our children. The longer they are here, the more accustomed they become to the English culture, including linguistic factors like pragmatics and accents.

Does This Child's Culture Value PE as Highly for Girls as They do for Boys?

We have had many conversations with parents of certain Asian cultures, to stress the importance of physical education for their daughters. We have seen a lack of confidence when changing into their kit, joining in with games and during skills development in many young girls. This attitude then changed when the PE lesson was centered on Dance and Movement; they came to life, showing a natu-ral elegance, enthusiasm and creativity for movement and some children shared their knowledge of their own culture's dance styles. Incidentally, during these Dance lessons, many boys of a similar background become less engaged. The parents were often very supportive and began to encourage interest in PE at home. With the teacher's advice on board, they usually seem to find more value in PE as a subject, especially when the correlation to academic achievement is highlighted.

Prior Experience of School

The amount of schooling a child has had will also affect their learning behav-iour. Some children are very quiet and withdrawn around adults due to previous experience of very strict teaching methods in other schools. Others may have had no experience of school at all, which is a very common occurrence in our school. The parents' understanding of English schooling, too, plays a role, which is particularly lacking with their first child. It is paramount to make time for these parents, to offer guidance, reassurance and an approachability that makes them feel comfortable with the staff. Our senior staff also make themselves personally available every day. The school promotes a welcoming and open attitude that treats each individual with respect. If the parents are confident and trusting of the teaching staff, they can better encourage their children to feel the same.

Ability

On top of all of these issues that can intersect with the challenge of being in a school whilst trying to learn EAL, come the typical thoughts and feelings that all children have throughout their education: Am I good at this? Does it matter, in this game, if I can't speak English? Do I feel included? Will anyone notice me if I don't join in...

Indeed, an interesting question is which of these intersections are more important to our very young children? And which of them are they already aware of?

Ultimately, all we can do as teachers is to continue being aware of each child as an individual, but we should take care to be aware of groups of languages, religions and cultures, which can be used as a tool for promoting inclusion. Indeed, one of the best tools that our school has is the number of staff and students who have additional languages. Neither of us is a multilingual speaker, however it is easy to pick up a few key phrases in the required language—sit down, stop that, come here... and well done! Allowing an EAL learner to hear a few familiar phrases (probably pronounced poorly, with a funny accent, but with clear good intent!) will encourage them to take pride in their culture. In our experience, many children take great pride and pleasure in correcting the teacher's poor attempts at different languages, and these moments of teacher-pupil role-reversal allow them to become the expert, the teacher and one who feels valued as a member of a school community.

CHALLENGES AND POSSIBILITIES OF THE LESSON

Challenges of a 'Stand-Alone' Lesson

We would recommend teaching this lesson as part of a cross-curricular PE unit on Diwali, ideally over a number of weeks. The repetition is beneficial for both EAL learners and children of this age in general, who are only just learning 'how to learn'. For example, we found that the lesson took longer than anticipated, as we had to explain certain sections in more detail, such as the challenge section. Level of independence was also an issue, as the children needed reminders throughout that they were to go to a challenge station before rejoining the game. It is, however, important to note that this was their first experience of this style of learning. Through delivering a series of lessons in a similar structure, with some repetition of activities, or building on activities each time, pupils with EAL, and indeed all pupils, would get used to the language used and the expectations. Consequently, future lessons would run more smoothly, with less teacher input and more pupil activity.

Possibilities of a Sequence of Lessons Around the Theme

We agreed that there are many imaginative ways you can work with the topic of Diwali, however, we chose Multiskills as the PE area we wanted to focus on in the lesson. Deciding on the specific PE skills children learn within the thematic context is essential in ensuring that PE is at the forefront of the lesson and does not lose its value. In subsequent lessons, we would link the part of the story with Hanuman and his army in battle to partner games involving throwing, catching, and aiming for targets. We also considered possibilities for team activities and problem solving, such as using the context of Hanuman's army to pose the challenge of how to imaginatively 'cross the sea' in a team using a certain number of hoops. Telling the story progressively and doing PE activities around each significant part of the story over a number of weeks would create a rich physical learning experience, and also has the potential to lead to some great learning in other subjects. In addition to Multiskills, we see the potential of using Dance as the PE basis and have done so to retell stories about other themes, such as the Great Fire of London. Furthermore, the pupils that celebrate Diwali can contribute expertise of Dance from their home experiences to the lesson which would add further depth to the lessons.

Links to Other Subject Areas

The lesson highlights that teaching gross motor activities alongside core subjects has the potential for rich learning outcomes. Pupils had the chance to experience BEING the characters from the story, rather than just reading about them, which, given their limited experience at this age, can be powerful. Through experience, pupils of all levels usually have something to say about the story after the lesson. For practitioners who teach early writing, it is widely understood that speaking is the first stage of writing; pupils need to be able to say what they want to write and have the ideas formulated in their heads before they can be expected to write independently. Lessons that offer first-hand experiences are therefore perfect for both learners with EAL as well as English pupils in this age range, as they provide memorable opportunities to develop ideas and key speaking skills. This lesson would be a particularly good basis for Literacy; after the lesson, pupils could write character profiles, discuss how characters felt at different points in the story, or think of an alternative event or ending.

REFERENCES

Blom, E., Küntay, A. C., Messer, M., Verhagen, J., & Leseman, P. (2014). The benefits of being bilingual: Working memory in bilingual Turkish–Dutch children. *Journal of Experimental Child Psychology*, *128*, 105–119.

Department for Education. (2013). *Physical education programs of study: Key stages 1 and 2*. [online]. Available at: https://assets.publishing.service.gov.uk/government/

uploads/system/uploads/attachment_data/file/239040/PRIMARY_national_curriculum_-_Physical_education.pdf

Gopnik, A., Griffiths, T. L., & Lucas, C. G. (2015). When younger learners can be better (or at least more open-minded) than older ones. *Current Directions in Psychological Science, 24*(2), 97–92.

Hounslow Language Service. (2016). *Leaders in EAL training.* [online]. Available at: http://www.ealhls.org.uk/wp-content/uploads/2017/10/Assessing-Proficiency-in-English-sample.pdf

Samuels, G. M., & Ross-Sheriff, F. (2008). Identity, oppression, and power: Feminisms and intersectionality theory. *Journal of Women and Social Work, 23*(1), 5–9.

CHAPTER 12

WHAT WE TALK ABOUT WHEN WE TALK ABOUT GENDER

Constructing and Deconstructing Gender Through Physical Education Teacher Education

Leigh Sperka, Rachel O'Brien, and Eimear Enright

Rather than simply repeating the common narrative about Physical Education (PE) being a problematic site for the reproduction of gender norms in schools, this chapter focuses on the unique position of the subject to actively explore, question, and critique understandings of gender. Part of the rationale behind this decision is an appreciation that where one starts, and with what assumptions, can partially determine one's destination (Enright, Hill, Sandford, & Gard, 2014). Moreover, similar to others (e.g., Oliver & Kirk, 2016), we are cognizant of how, even with the best of intentions, it is possible for research that focuses on gender inequalities in PE to inadvertently reproduce existing gender divisions. Starting from a place of possibility rather than pessimism has the capacity to reframe how PE is viewed and its relationship with gender. In doing so, we endeavor to nuance how we think, talk, and teach gender in PE and in PE Teacher Education (PETE) specifically. For us, this involves 'confront(ing) the challenge of generating new meanings, of becoming poetic activists' (Saltzburg & Davis, 2010, p. 87) as:

Teaching About Social Justice Issues in Physical Education, pages 133–143.
Copyright © 2019 by Information Age Publishing
All rights of reproduction in any form reserved.

new patterns of social life are not secured simply by refusing or rejecting the meanings as given—for example, avoiding sexist...language. Rather, the strong invitation
is for the emergence of new forms of language, ways of interpreting the world,
patterns of representation. Invited are generative discourses, that is, ways of talking and writing (and otherwise representing) that simultaneously challenge existing
traditions and offer new possibilities for action (p. 87).

We believe that taking on such a challenge in PE and PETE requires a 'multi-
vocal' approach, that is, one that values the perspectives of all stakeholders (e.g.,
PE students and practicing teachers, PETE pre-service teachers, and PE teacher
educators). This is because we hold the view that gender is a 'lived process rather
than a proper object that we are each magically endowed with as an unwritten
consequence of our sex' (Nayak & Kehily, 2013, p. 5). Thus, everyone has unique
experiences and understandings of gender which should be told and heard, and
sometimes argued with. An approach to teaching and learning that values young
people's knowledge and their emic perspectives and is democratic, inclusive, and
collaborative is therefore necessary. The specific purpose of this chapter, then, is
to highlight an example of a modest, but potentially powerful, pedagogical practice that supports generative conversations about gender in and beyond PETE.

ACTION RESEARCH AND REFLECTION

Gender in PE and PETE

PE is arguably distinct as it is the only formal curriculum site where bodies
are privileged over 'minds' (Vertinsky, 1992) and where 'the body is explicitly
used, displayed and talked about' (Paechter, 2003, p. 49). This focus on the body
in PE is implicated in the (re)construction of gender subjectivity. Building on
feminist research in the 1980s (Griffin, 1983, 1984, 1985a,b), scholars in PE (and
health education) have contributed to the identification and naming of practices
that produce and reproduce gender and have established that PE is an active site
for acting out hyper-masculinities and femininities (see for example, Azzarito &
Solomon, 2005; Chepyator-Thomson & Ennis, 1997; Kirk, 2002; Talbot, 2017).
Examples of practices that have been identified as (re)producing gender inequities and inequalities in PE include: teaching boys and girls separately, citing concerns about the quality of student experience, teacher preferences, and resources;
making assumptions about the suitability of sports based on gender stereotypes;
and adopting different teaching styles, including favoring having male teachers
teaching boys and female teachers teaching girls (Hills & Croston, 2012). Many
of these processes originate from a problematic and limited view that PE, and
more broadly sport and physical activity, is a male domain that is incompatible
with femininity. These processes and practices teach about gender, even if this
teaching is not explicit or intentional. Like many others, we believe we need to go
beyond identifying these harmful views and practices and take seriously our role
in 'troubling' them. After all, if PE is a site in which miseducative pedagogical

work can be done, it is also a site that offers the potential to do powerful, critical pedagogical work on and about gender. More on that later.

In a similar vein, if we consider the research that has been undertaken on gender in PETE, it would be quite easy to arrive at the conclusion that PETE too is a site in which limiting norms are more likely to be perpetuated rather than disrupted. There is scholarship that does indeed reveal PETE as a site of reproduction. This includes, for instance, Dowling's (2006) study of four PE teacher educators in Norway in which she found that gender equality was not perceived to be central to the professional work of PE teacher educators. More recently, O'Connor and colleagues' (2016) development of a 'Stereotypical Attitudes in HPE Scale' suggests that identifying and better understanding pre-services teachers' stereotypical attitudes and limiting pretexts remains a challenge for PETE. However, identification alone will never be enough. Almost two decades ago, Griffin (1989) argued it is a:

> naïve assumption that once teachers are aware of the errors of their ways and change, the problem will be solved. It's only a matter of providing the appropriate instructional resources to help teachers make the transition from gender discrimination and bias to gender fairness. (p. 222)

It would also be naïve to reduce 'gender equity to a cognitive, technical issue' that can be measured, because it 'belies the complexity of gender power relations in society, their embodiment in individuals, and their modes of practical transmission in sport and physical education' (Brown & Evans, 2004, p. 50). Instead, it seems integral to take a relational view (Browns & Evans, 2004; Brown & Rich, 2002; Goldner, 1991) where we acknowledge that 'gender develops in and through relationships with gendered others' (Goldner, 1991, p. 262). Such an approach means the gendered subjectivities of teachers and students become 'a significant pedagogical resource' (Brown & Rich, 2002, p. 80).

More recent discussion and reflections on PETE and social justice provide encouraging examples of how this might be done (Hill et al., 2018). This work includes rare but promising examples of PETE programs where pre-service teachers experience 'having a switch' or 'eye-opener' critical moments of realization that disrupt their previous 'discursive formations regarding the body and health' (Varea & Tinning, 2016, p. 1012), and having their gendered subjectivities shifted or challenged. Moreover, there are also an increasing number of studies in schools and universities that seek to move beyond description and critique towards interruption and resistance. This work tends to privilege students' perspectives and value collective action.

Youth Voice and Gender

While 'youth voice research' is quite a broad term that encompasses many studies that vary in scale and focus, there are some consistent attributes. The studies reflect a shift away from 'consulting' young people, which often merely positions them as data sources, towards creating authentic, dialogic conditions in which students co-construct and/or lead the framing or identification of research problems and questions that interest and impact them, and the quest for solutions. Youth Participatory Action Research (YPAR) is one pedagogical and research approach that aligns with the youth voice movement by facilitating student opportunities to 'begin to re-vision and denaturalize the realities of their social worlds and then undertake forms of collective challenge based on the knowledge garnered through their critical inquiries' (Cammarota & Fine, 2008, p. 2). YPAR recognizes that students are experts on their own lives and reflects a commitment to the democratic impulse of education.

YPAR, and youth voice research more broadly conceived, is increasingly utilized to understand and respond to students' gendered experiences of PE (see for example, Enright & O'Sullivan, 2010, 2012, 2013; Hill, 2013; Oliver & Kirk, 2016; Oliver & Lalik, 2001). There is also youth voice research beyond our field that examines how students articulate and express their understanding of gendered characteristics and subjectivities (e.g., McIntyre, Chatzopoulos, Politi, & Roz, 2007; Saltzburg & Davis, 2010). This research often aims to dispel unitary conceptions of gender and instead acknowledge that there are multiple ways of being male and female, as well as question how we theorize and talk about differences and commonalities between diverse girls and boys (Flintoff, Fitzgerald, & Scraton, 2008). Significantly, however, this research is also biased towards activism and change (Enright & O'Sullivan, 2012; Oliver & Kirk, 2016).

From the research that has been undertaken *with* rather than *on* students of PE, we have multiple, rich examples of playing up/with/along gender (Fitzpatrick, 2013), 'undoing gender' (Hills & Croston, 2012), and identifying and challenging gender stereotypes (Enright & O'Sullivan, 2013; Oliver & Kirk, 2016) in PE. These cases represent pockets of innovative research and pedagogical activity, and suggest that opportunities do exist within current curricular provision to do things very differently.

In Australia, for example, where PE and health are taught as one combined subject (i.e., HPE), students are prompted to take a critical inquiry and strengths-based approach to understand 'identities' (Australian Curriculum, Assessment and Reporting Authority [ACARA], 2018). This includes an explicit focus on gender in the junior secondary school years (i.e., Years 7–10 where students are aged 12–16). More specifically, in Year 7 and 8, students are asked to examine 'the impact of physical changes on gender, cultural and sexual identities' (ACARA, 2018). In Year 9 and 10, they can both analyze 'how societal norms, stereotypes and expectations influence the way young people think about their bodies, abilities, gender, sexuality....' and examine 'how diversity and gender are represented in the media and communities, and investigating the influence these representations have on identities' (ACARA, 2018).

In summary, research, pedagogical, and curricular innovations all highlight how essential it is for both current and pre-service PE teachers to firstly, recognize that the subject is indeed not 'unproblematically androgynous, or gender-neutral' (Kirk, 2002, p. 25), and secondly, to understand that PE is a space where disempowering gender practices and ideologies can be actively questioned and disrupted through critical practice (Gray, 2018, p. 174). This deconstruction of dominant discourses around gender can and should involve active collaborations and partnerships with the young people on and through whom often narrow and damaging gender discourses are operating. Supporting pre-service and practicing teachers in doing this important but challenging pedagogical work is, however, a difficult undertaking. Oliver and Oesterreich (2013), for example, have found that:

> While pre-service teachers frequently learn the rhetoric of including students' voices [about gender] in their teaching and spout that they will put the student at the 'center' of the learning process, most pre-service teachers leave teacher education without an inkling of how they will do this (p. 396).

It is, therefore, important to devise and implement learning experiences in PETE that develop pre-service teachers' knowledge and skills in this area. We now turn to our own modest practice to offer some examples of how we teach gender through PETE.

CONTEXT

Two of us (Eimear and Leigh) teach a course entitled 'Youth, Sport, and Physical Culture'. This is a core course for third year students on a four year Bachelor of Health, Sport and Physical Education (Teaching) Degree, as well as being an elective for students studying journalism, primary education, and other degrees. The course aims to create opportunities for university students to use social theory to interrogate contemporary youth identities and youth, and physical cultures in the context of the flows of globalization. This course is not explicitly focused on gender, and neither is it specifically targeted at pre-service teachers.

ACTIVITY SET-UP

'Storying Youth' Learning Experience

Rather than choosing one lesson on this course to be illustrative of the kinds of learning experiences that might privilege gender, this particular learning experience is an assessment task that requires weekly engagement from the students. Titled 'Storying Youth', this task has three parts.

ACTIVITY

Part A

Firstly, students are required to construct and curate a Pinterest[1] board that centers on a fictional young person's engagement with physical culture (Part A).

In the first tutorial, students develop a profile or short biography for a fictional young person, which they pin on their Pinterest board. During the development of their fictional character, students are explicitly invited to consider their character's age, gender, sexuality, class, ethnicity and religion. At this early stage, while we discuss each of these categories as social constructions, the emphasis is very much on the character development. For six weeks following the biography development, we work together (through lectures and tutorials) to interrogate and advance understandings of youth, sport, and physical culture by engaging with case-studies of a diversity of youth identities and cultural spaces. At the end of each week, key prompts are shared with the students to help them 'flesh out' their characters, and consider, for example, the main spaces in which they function (fields), the valuable resources they have access to (capital), and the self-evident rules that might limit their mobility (doxa). The prompts, therefore, seek to bring the 'Grand Theory'[2] into dialogue with the characters being constructed. In response to the weekly prompts, students may choose to pin media of their choosing (e.g., images, excerpts from articles, quotations, video links) to their board. Students are asked to upload or save at least five pins in response to these prompts to their Pinterest pinboard. The short biographies the students develop in week one, as well as what they pin in response to the weekly prompts becomes the 'data' for analysis and critique.

Part B

Students are then asked to present a summary of their Pinterest board and provide an outline of their proposed digital story/essay, including their working title and how they are beginning to make sense of their data (their Pinterest board) in relation to some of Bourdieu's theoretical tools[3]. This assessment point serves as an important feedback mechanism for the final assessment.

Part C

The final part of this assessment task requires students to tell a sociological story about their character. Students may choose between creating a 'digital story' (i.e., a multimedia movie that combines photographs, video, animation, sound, music, text, and a narrative voice) or writing a more traditional essay (i.e., a scholarly piece of writing that presents an author's argument). These stories must engage with the data (each student's curated Pinterest board), the course themes (e.g., youth identities, equity), relevant literature, and Bourdieu.

INTERSECTIONALITIES

The above task has proved powerful for a number of reasons. Firstly, it encourages students to move away from the idea of taken for granted and neat social categories towards an appreciation of the complex ways that gender intersects and interacts with other markers of social difference such as age, class, sexuality, and so on. Holding and managing this complexity is not always easy for the undergraduate students, many of whom have asked as the semester proceeds how they might make their characters less complex:

> I'm not sure what aspect of my fictional character's story matters most. Should I focus my discussion on [Tia's] gendered, ethnic identity, or should I focus on her role as the eldest daughter in the family and what that means culturally, or how she's not in the in-group in school, and the reasons for that?... I think I get Bourdieu, better than I did, when we did the presentations. I'm not as afraid of the theory anymore, but Tia's life is a mess, and even when I try to narrow it down to looking at how she operates in two fields (Home and School Sport), I'm struggling to write the essay how I usually do. And I usually like writing essays! (Sarah, 3rd year student).

> Can I change my fictional character's bio? I've made him too complicated. (Jim, 4th year student).

While these students are clearly struggling to some extent with the task, there are lessons being learnt through these struggles. Stories of human experience are rarely simple, nor should they be. As students see and begin to articulate how personal and social contexts are always acting on the individual, they come to appreciate their characters' subjectivities as complicated and fluid and 'always in relation, always in a social context' (Clandinin & Connelly, 2000, p. 2).

Secondly, and this is facilitated by thinking with Bourdieu, the task often results in students naming and confronting the multiple biases that some young people face in relation to interwoven identity dimensions such as gender and religion.

> [Aisha] is a girl and she's Muslim. So, depending on what field she's hanging out in, she could be discriminated against for two reasons straight up. (Ann, 3rd year student).

What we see in Ann's reflection is not only a developing awareness that in the cultural spaces which young people inhabit social inequalities associated with gender and religion, for example, are always interacting, but also, an acknowledgement that different dimensions of identity become more or less problematic as one moves between social spaces.

CHALLENGES AND POSSIBILITIES

The title for this chapter references United States novelist Raymond Carver's short story, 'What we talk about when we talk about love', a celebrated work, which has been interpreted as a reflection on how difficult it is to define what love is. Gender is a similarly complex construct. The strength of the abovementioned learning experience is that it allows students to talk about gender (and other markers of social difference), reflect on their talk, be challenged and affirmed, tell and retell stories, and construct and deconstruct assumptions. Creating a character affords them the opportunity to speak as another, to reveal problematic, limiting, and subconscious assumptions without being afraid that they are revealing or announcing personal biases. The characters come to act as a bridge to discussion. They are straw (wo)men intended to generate discussion and debate about various norms and stereotypes (Part A), and to provoke the reconstruction of gender in ways that reflect our collective engagement with social theory over the 13-week course. When they begin talking about the experiences and identities of their characters, their language is 'saturated with values, frequently [their] own' (Fielding, 2004, p. 297). In the beginning, much of this talk is constructed 'in such a way that it supports, firstly, the way those groups are currently conceived of and treated and, secondly, the validation of the dominant group's position and the consolidation of its power' (Fielding, 2004, p. 299). This is a challenging context as this talk is often littered with damaging and limiting assumptions. However, this talk lays the foundation for the beautiful, critical, pedagogical work that will ensue. Cannella (2008) discusses how YPAR has the potential to 'give collaborators a chance to *unlearn*' (emphasis in original) any personal filters that 'dehumanize others and ourselves' (p. 191). Ultimately, the task and the other learning experiences on the course facilitate opportunities for the interruption of harmful stereotypes, and the telling of different, more complicated, nuanced, and balanced stories of different groups and identities.

We have already shared that this is not a course that is squarely focused on gender. However, we argue that we are all teachers of gender. The biomechanist, the anatomist, the professional experience coordinators that teach into, or facilitate aspects of the PETE student experience all have a role to play in terms of what is learned about gender in and through PETE. Further, the future PE teachers in our course will themselves be teachers of gender, whether consciously or not. As we have mentioned, PE has more often been a place of narrow gender reproduction than problematization. Examples of teachers 'playing up' gender demonstrate the potential for PE to be a space of critical engagement and learning where 'narrow, racialized, and gender norms can be exposed and challenged' (Fitzpatrick, 2013, p. 189). We hope this learning experience enables students to talk about gender, and in doing so ignites a critical spark; that they rethink and reimagine ways of thinking, talking, and doing gender. The learning experience outlined here is just one example of how we teach gender. We offer it up as a case for interrogation, and as an example of the incidental but not insignificant pedagogical work that can be done in and through many of the courses that comprise our PETE programs.

NOTES

1. Pinterest is a social curation website that functions as a digital pinboard. It allows users to 'pin' (i.e., link back to the original website it was saved from) digital images and videos to their virtual pinboard to form an organized collection of items. At the time of writing, the site was being used by 200 million people with 100 billion pins (Pinterest, 2018).

2. 'Grand Theory' can be understood as an 'abstract and normative theory of human nature and conduct' (Skinner, 1985, p.1) that is generic in nature and that can be applied to different circumstances and areas of research. In this respect, Bourdieu's Theory of Practice is the Grand Theory we recruited.

3. Bourdieu's theories were deliberately selected for this course as they are particularly generative in making sense of how young people construct and negotiate subjectivities in social arenas such as PE and school sport (Brown, 2005; Hunter, 2004).

REFERENCES

Australian Curriculum, Assessment and Reporting Authority. (2018). *Health and physical education.* Retrieved from https://www.australiancurriculum.edu.au/f-10-curriculum/health-and-physical-education/

Azzarito, L., & Solomon, M. A. (2005). A reconceptualization of physical education: The intersection of gender/race/social class. *Sport, Education and Society, 10*(1), 25–47. doi: 10.1080/135733205200028794

Brown, D. (2005). An economy of gendered practices? Learning to teach physical education from the perspective of Pierre Bourdieu's embodied sociology. *Sport, Education and Society, 10*(1), 3–23. doi:10.1080/135733205298785

Brown, D., & Evans, J. (2004). Reproducing gender? Intergenerational links and the male PE teacher as a cultural conduit in teaching physical education. *Journal of Teaching in Physical Education, 23*(1), 48–70. doi:10.1123/jtpe.23.1.48

Brown, D., & Rich, E. (2002). Gender positioning as pedagogical practice in teaching physical education. In D. Penney (Ed.), *Gender and physical education: Contemporary issues and future directions* (pp. 80–100). London, UK: Routledge.

Cammarota, J., & Fine, M. (2008). Youth participatory action research: A pedagogy for transformational resistance. In J. Cammarota & M. Fine (Eds.), *Revolutionizing education: Youth participatory action research in motion* (pp. 1–12). New York, NY: Routledge.

Canella, C. M. (2008). Faith in process, faith in people: Confronting policies of social disinvestment with PAR as pedagogy for expansion. In J. Cammarota & M. Fine (Eds.), *Revolutionizing education: Youth participatory action research in motion* (pp. 189–212). New York, NY: Routledge.

Chepyator-Thomson, J., & Ennis, C. D. (1997). Reproduction and resistance to the culture of femininity and masculinity in secondary school physical education. *Research Quarterly for Exercise and Sport, 68*(1), 89–99. DOI: 10.1080/02701367.1997.10608870

Clandinin, D. J., & Connelly, F. M. (2000). *Narrative inquiry: Experience and story in qualitative research.* San Francisco, CA: Jossey Bass Publishers.

Dowling, F. (2006). Physical education teacher educators' professional identities, continuing professional development and the issue of gender equality. *Physical Education and Sport Pedagogy, 11*(3), 247–263. doi:10.1080/17408980600986306

Enright, E., Hill, J., Sandford, R., & Gard, M. (2014). Looking beyond what's broken: Towards an appreciative research agenda for physical education and sport pedagogy. *Sport, Education and Society, 19*(7) 912–926. doi:10.1080/13573322.2013.854764

Enright, E., & O'Sullivan, M. (2010). 'Can I do it in my pyjamas?' Negotiating a physical education curriculum with teenage girls. *European Physical Education Review, 16*(3), 203–222. doi:10.1177/1356336x10382967

Enright, E., & O'Sullivan, M. (2012). Physical education "in all sorts of corners": Student activists transgressing formal physical education curricular boundaries. *Research Quarterly for Exercise and Sport, 83*(2), 255–267.

Enright, E., & O'Sullivan, M. (2013). "Now, I'm magazine detective the whole time": Listening and responding to young people's complex experiences of popular physical culture. *Journal of Teaching in Physical Education, 32*(4), 394–418.

Fielding, M. (2004). Transformative approaches to student voice: Theoretical underpinnings, recalcitrant realities. *British Educational Research Journal, 30*(2), 295–311. doi:10.2307/1502226

Fitzpatrick, K. (2013). *Critical pedagogy, physical education and urban schooling.* New York, NY: Peter Lang Publishing.

Flintoff, A., Fitzgerald, H., & Scraton, S. (2008). The challenges of intersectionality: Researching difference in physical education. *International Studies in Sociology of Education, 18*(2), 73–85. doi:10.1080/09620210802351300

Goldner, V. (1991). Toward a critical relational theory of gender. *Psychoanalytic Dialogues, 1*(3), 249–272. doi:10.1080/10481889109538898

Gray, S. K. (2018). *Biological differences or social constructions? The entanglement of sex and gender in health and physical education* (Unpublished doctoral dissertation). University of Toronto: Toronto.

Griffin, P. (1983). 'Gymnastics is a girl's thing': Student participation and interaction pattern in a middle school gymnastics unit. In T. Templin & J. Olson (Eds), *Teaching in physical education* (pp. 71–85). Champaign, IL: Human Kinetics.

Griffin, P. (1984). Girls' participation in a middle school team sports unit. *Journal of Teaching in Physical Education, 4,* 30–38.

Griffin, P. (1985a). Boys' participation styles in a middle school physical education team sports unit. *Journal of Teaching in Physical Education, 4,* 100–110.

Griffin, P. (1985b). Teachers' perceptions of and responses to sex equity problems in a middle school physical education program. *Research Quarterly for Exercise and Sport, 56,* 103–110.

Griffin, P. (1989). Gender as socialising agent in physical education. In T. Templin & P. Schempp (Eds.), *Socialisation into physical education: Learning to teach* (pp. 219–234). Indianapolis, IN: Benchmark Press.

Hill, J. (2013). Using participatory and visual methods to address power and identity in research with young people. *Graduate Journal of Social Science, 10*(2), 132–150.

Hill, J., Philpot, R., Walton-Fisette, J. L., Sutherland, S., Flemons, M., Ovens, A., . . . Flory, S. B. (2018). Conceptualising social justice and sociocultural issues within physical education teacher education: International perspectives. *Physical Education and Sport Pedagogy, 23*(5), 469–483. doi:10.1080/17408989.2018.1470613

Hills, L.A. & Croston, A. (2012). 'It should be better all together': Exploring strategies for 'undoing' gender in coeducational physical education. *Sport, Education and Society, 17*(5), 591–605.

Hunter, L. (2004). Bourdieu and the social space of the PE class: Reproduction of doxa through practice. *Sport, Education and Society, 9*(2), 175–192.

Kirk, D. (2002). Physical education: A gendered history. In D. Penney (Ed.), *Gender and physical education: Contemporary issues and future directions* (pp. 24–37). London: Routledge.

McIntyre, A., Chatzopoulos, N., Politi, A., & Roz, J. (2007). Participatory action research: Collective reflections on gender, culture, and language. *Teaching and Teacher Education, 23*(5), 748–756. doi:https://doi.org/10.1016/j.tate.2006.12.025

Nayak, A., & Kehily, M. J. (2013). *Gender, youth and culture: Global masculinities and femininities.* Basingstoke, UK: Palgrave Macmillan.

O'Connor, J. P., Penney, D., Alfrey, L., Phillipson, S., Phillipson, S. N., & Jeanes, R. (2016). The development of the stereotypical attitudes in HPE scale. *Australian Journal of Teacher Education, 41*(7), 70–87.

Oliver, K. L., & Kirk, D. (2016). Towards an activist approach to research and advocacy for girls and physical education. *Physical Education and Sport Pedagogy, 21*(3), 313–327. doi:10.1080/17408989.2014.895803

Oliver, K. L., & Lalik, R. (2001). The body as curriculum: Learning with adolescent girls. *Journal of Curriculum Studies, 33*(3), 303–333. doi:10.1080/00220270010006046

Oliver, K. L., & Oesterreich, H. A. (2013). Student-centered inquiry as curriculum as a model for field-based teacher education. *Journal of Curriculum Studies, 45*(3), 394–417. doi:10.1080/00220272.2012.719550

Paechter, C. (2003). Power, bodies and identity: How different forms of physical education construct varying masculinities and femininities in secondary schools. *Sex Education: Sexuality, Society and Learning, 3*(1), 47–59.

Pinterest. (2018). *Business.* Retrieved from: https://business.pinterest.com/en

Saltzburg, S., & Davis, T. S. (2010). Co-authoring gender-queer youth identities: Discursive tellings and retellings. *Journal of Ethnic & Cultural Diversity in Social Work, 19*(2), 87–108. doi:10.1080/15313200903124028

Skinner, Q. (1985). *The return of Grand Theory in the human sciences.* New York, NY: Cambridge University Press.

Talbot, M. (2017). A gendered physical education: Equality and sexism. In J. Evans (Ed.), *Equality, education, and physical education* (pp. 74–89). London, UK: Routledge.

Varea, V., & Tinning, R. (2016). Coming to know about the body in Human Movement Studies programs. *Sport, Education and Society, 21*(7), 1003–1017. doi:10.1080/13573322.2014.979144

Vertinsky, P. A. (1992). Reclaiming space, revisioning the body: The quest for gender-sensitive physical education. *Quest, 44*(3), 373–396. doi:10.1080/00336297.1992.10484063

CHAPTER 13

REFLECTIONS ON AND STRATEGIES TO CREATE GENDER PARITY IN PHYSICAL EDUCATION LESSONS

Alexandra Baird

ACTION RESEARCH & REFLECTION

I became increasingly aware of a growing lethargy and disinterest displayed by many teenage girls towards Physical Education (PE), many of whom had fully engaged in both the curriculum and extra-curricular opportunities earlier on in their school careers. This pattern seemed to be evident in both single-sex and co-educational schools, but more prominent within a mixed setting where girls became increasingly self-conscious over what they wore and being judged, particularly by the boys, within the public arena of the PE setting. I observed, as supported by (Larsson, Redelius, & Fagrell, 2010), that many of the girls were inhibited to participate or avoided appearing competitive in order to preserve their feminine appearance to those around them. Furthermore, given the inextricable link that society makes between femininity and heterosexuality, (Lenskyj, 1991), their reluctance to engage also avoided them being labelled as 'butch' or 'lesbian' if they were not able to serve a clear heterosexual marker. I was also struck by how

Teaching About Social Justice Issues in Physical Education, pages 145–169.
Copyright © 2019 by Information Age Publishing
All rights of reproduction in any form reserved.

often girls tended to underestimate their ability and this was surprisingly common even amongst the most-able performers. Girls' hesitancy to engage and a lack of perceived competence resulted in lower participation levels at both GCSE (General Certificate of Secondary Education taken by pupils in England, Wales and Northern Ireland where PE is one of a range of optional rather than compulsory subjects) and A Level (Advanced Level post-16 qualification required for University entrance and valued by employers, where students combine any subjects they wish to take). Lower entries of girls compared to boys in examination PE is also shown on a national scale (DfE 2017a,b).

The gender issue, however, is not just a female issue, as boys also experience similar frustrations. Bramham (2003) presents several accounts of boys' diverse experiences of PE, which considers the impact of dominant hegemonic masculinity on their behaviour and levels of involvement. Wright (1999) suggests hegemonic forms of masculinity can alienate boys with lower levels of skill or those who do not display the appropriately competitive and aggressive behaviour. I was conscious of boys often needing to prove their masculinity through their dominant behaviour within lessons and the language they used in the changing rooms to reinforce their heterosexuality and gain the approval of their male peers. A heteronormative culture, which promotes heterosexuality as the normal and preferred sexual orientation, clearly affects everyone regardless of their sexuality. Fitzpatrick and McGlashan (2016) suggest that PE, through its practice and pedagogy, remains too "straight." Youdell (2005) highlights the limits of what a student can be through the sex-gender-sexuality constellation. This suggests sex, gender and sexuality are joined together in complex constellations, involving both body and discourse, setting limits of 'who' a student can actually be. Wright (1999), Flintoff and Scraton (2001) and Oliver and Lalik (2004) suggest the analysis of the gender issue should go beyond just portraying girls as the problem and instead deconstruct what it means to be both masculine and feminine, break down the binaries of masculinity and femininity and demonstrate the benefits of an egalitarian society for everyone. Oliver and Lalik (2004) present the findings of a small scale study which aimed to develop a PE curriculum, built upon post-structural feminism, which would help girls understand the discourses that shape their lives and regulate their body.

Gender is a social construction, as it is through our interactions with one another and the environment in which we are exposed which create gender roles and defines masculine and feminine appropriate behaviors (Oakley, 1972). Bain (1990) highlights how pupils learn a powerful 'hidden curriculum' through their relationships with other pupils and their teachers. Flintoff and Scraton (2006) suggest PE is one of the most sex differentiated subjects and it is within this environment that ideological forms of masculinity and inferior forms of femininity are transmitted (Humberstone, 2002).

I began to critique both the explicit and implicit messages I was communicating about gender through the medium of PE. This occurred gradually over my teaching career, initially within my own pedagogy as I became more proficient and able to cope with the primary concerns of teaching, pupils and the curriculum and able to look for the first time beyond these factors. However, as I became a Head of Department, I recognized I was able to make a much more comprehensive strategic impact at both a departmental and whole school level. This encouraged me to become increasingly reflective, particularly as I found myself at this time in a male dominated school environment (due to the disparity in numbers of girls to boys), where values appeared further reinforced by the historic school traditions. In order to maintain my own confidence within such an environment, I developed important alliances with other female teaching staff who provided valuable support but who also probed and challenged what I was doing to challenge male hegemony and deconstruct gender binaries. Teaching solely traditional activities, I recognized, built a hierarchy (e.g., football over gymnastics and dance) reinforcing gender stereotyping within these activities. Assessing pupils' learning based upon performance outcomes benefitted the more-able boys who generally came with greater experience and in doing so often highlighted the girls' subordinated position (Flintoff & Scraton, 2006). It also reinforced hegemonic masculinity (Connell, 2005) by explicitly measuring performance based upon male standards in sport including, strength, dominance and competition (Bramham, 2003; Fleming, 1991; Light & Kirk, 2000; Parker, 1996) and presenting only the values held by this dominant group (Shire & Hardman, 2011). This encouraged the girls to only be welcomed if they had a similar attitude and skill to the boys.

Restructuring the curriculum and extra-curricular program to ensure equal access to a diverse range of activities beyond just competitive sports did challenge gender division and this was demonstrated by an increased uptake of examination PE amongst the girls. However, it was a slow process, not without conflict, often with and amongst pupils, as I attempted to challenge beliefs deeply embedded. Crucially, all members of the department were supportive and contributed fully to the shared objectives and I was able to acquire further assistance from Senior Management to fund the required teacher training for all members of the department as well as new equipment needs. Lorber (2000) advocated for the benefits of encountering sporting activities not traditionally associated with that gender to blur gender boundaries. Choosing appropriate activities involved listening to all pupils' feedback over a sustained period of time to ensure the activities held a relevance to them; however, I also had to be mindful that the choice of activities was not dictated by the very culture I wished to change. Girls' questionnaire responses, for example, were often in favor of girls-only activities and whilst I did offer opportunities such as these to fuel their interest (e.g. girls-only fitness gym sessions), I also felt it was important to show how the culture could be challenged more successfully within co-educational activities and I also wanted all pupils to feel equally free to use the free weights, sports hall and astro-turf space. This drew upon Hills and Croston's (2012) recommendation of 'undoing gender' through mixed activities, offering illustrations of boys' and girls' similarities and shared experiences to be highlighted as well as developing a growing awareness of girls' capabilities. Boys' questionnaire responses offered a narrow response of opinions, suggesting they were less prepared to offer their own individual opinions or did not value the impact they could have through the questionnaire, assuming it was put in place to gage female rather than male opinions. Williams, Bedward, and Woodhouse, (2000) large scale study that examined pupils' perception of PE revealed clear differences of activity preferences amongst boys compared to girls. Boys were far more positive than girls towards winter games, but dance was less well received by boys. The study also exposed a lack of continuity between curricular and extra-curricular opportunities for girls. Flintoff and Scraton (2001) argue that young women are in fact active, but not always in traditional sporting activities, and consequently view PE as irrelevant to them. Coakley and White (1992) suggest we need to go beyond the confines of just PE to consider how women negotiate physical activity in the wider society, which may include their own choice of clothing. I found team games were still positively received as long as I followed a learner-centered pedagogical model which gave my learners more control of their own learning. I also encouraged collaboration over competition, but included modifications within each activity to engage and develop learners at all levels of ability. Private rather than public assessment needed to provide pupils with personalized on-going feedback in terms of reaching cognitive, affective and social learning objectives as well as psychomotor ones.

Research surrounding whether classes should be segregated by sex or co-educational has long been debated and remains equally split. On the one hand, single sex classes can negatively reproduce and reinforce gender ideologies, (Scraton, 1993) by focusing upon differences between the genders rather than commonalities. On the other hand, single sex classes have been shown to benefit less able girls, particularly in ball games where boys might otherwise dominate, excluding the girls and limiting the amount of time they have to practice (Hills & Croston, 2012). Lyu and Gill (2011) showed perceived competence, enjoyment and effort of girls was higher in single sex classes compared to co-educational classes partly because it eliminated teasing, but also because the girls showed the tendency to support one another more readily within this environment. McCaughtry (2006) suggests that whilst removing girls from a co-educational setting may offer a safe space away from boys, in reality this may be more of a 'band aid approach' rather than a long term solution to changing the culture of PE. Separating pupils by gender would also suggest that gender is binary, in so far as, gender and sex are two opposite and disconnected forms of masculinity and femininity when Butler (2006) contends that gender identity is fluid, unstable and ambivalent.

Gender equity in co-educational classes is difficult and 'just' integrating boys and girls in the same setting will not guarantee equality of access and opportunity. Flintoff and Scraton (2006) suggest coeducation classes have in fact become a male re-modelling of PE. Research has also shown that boys can negatively impact girls' learning and dominate both teacher attention and the teaching space, which affirms their position (Evans, 1989; Evans et al, 1985; Griffin, 1984; Office for Standards in Education, 1995; Scraton, 1992). Co-educational settings do however provide the chance to understand one another by listening to different perspectives. In reality, of course, the decision around timetabling and staffing will often not be decided by individual subject heads and in fact mixed PE timetabling has been historically guided by resources rather than a clear educational rationale (Evans et al., 1985). The choice of grouping within each individual lesson plan, may instead offer the opportunity for particular grouping within a co-education class.

In an attempt to plan and deliver an inclusive lesson, I would follow Table 13.1, giving careful consideration to a number of factors. These factors may include the choice of activity, the choice of learner-centered pedagogical model, teaching skills, groupings, modifications and assessment. I would then foster positive cultural values within the classroom by, firstly, trying to enhance the social and emotional development of my learners. Later I would model this within my own behaviour which may include intervening and challenging inappropriate remarks and demonstrating how to conduct a fair and amicable debate. I would ask explicit questions to make the gender issue visible, engaging my learners to consider gender equality and to question the world in which they live and the concealed messages they may be taking in. My confidence in creating a safe space in lessons to challenge gender stereotypes, contest inequality and celebrate difference has grown, but is dependent upon successfully attaining pupils' trust and developing a positive rapport with the group. To create a sense of belonging for all my learners and present multiple perspectives to the rest of the group, I would ensure all voices are heard by posing questions in turn to different learners. I would incorporate a roundtable discussion where each learner in the circle takes a moment to talk and I would ensure all learners have a pen when adding ideas to a shared discussion board. Providing opportunities to reflect on gender discourses and encouraging more gender inclusive behaviors should allow the possibility of a real shift in the culture. To sustain the progress made in the lesson, I would consider how the curriculum may be linked to promotional events and extra-curricular activities.

My activation button to scrutinize and tackle gender inequality came from my own personal experience as a gender non-conforming pupil and as a lesbian PE teacher trying to function in some PE departments, which conveyed clear gender boundaries (Clarke, 2002). I have looked at research focused upon girls' and boys' experience of PE, not to inadvertently create gender division or view either as a homogenous group, but to consider barriers which may restrict their access to physical activity and to challenge my own assumptions and practice. Oliver and Kirk (2016) suggest it is essential individuals are able to find activities that suit their particular needs that are localized and relevant to them and that they also learn how to feel about their own bodies. In attempting to readdress gender inequality, it was crucial that I reflected upon my own responses to boys and girls and consider how my unintentional bias and use of language may have positioned girls and boys differently (Wright, 1997). I also reflected upon my own lived experiences and how this had influenced both my practice and who exactly I might represent to my pupils. Whilst my presence could disrupt feminine stereotypes and challenge the male and female binary, I did not want that to present only one perspective or identity to my pupils. I also became increasingly aware of the generational gap between how I, and the girls I taught, chose to negotiate the world in which we live (Williams & Bedward, 2001).

CONTEXT

I would address the gender issue slightly differently depending upon the specific educational setting in which I was teaching. I would begin by examining the micro-culture of the school by considering the norms, values and discourse which prevail to influence pupils' construction and reinforcement of gender identity. I would then consider the specific dynamics of the unique group of pupils in the class. The needs and abilities of each individual in the group, the demographics represented, their attitudes, interests, how they interact with one another and also with me.

The volleyball lesson plan, which follows, considers how I might have planned for this when teaching in a co-educational Independent Upper School in North London, England (13–18 year olds) where the number of boys made up a significant majority (70%) of the school population. Extra-curricular sport was highly valued in the school, but this was often to the detriment of the value placed by pupils on their PE lessons. Equal status and attention was given to both boys' and girls' individual and team performances by staff in an attempt to counterbalance the gender disparity. The hegemonic masculinity and occasional marginalization of females in the school was reinforced by the historic traditions surviving from the school's previous existence as a single sex boys setting. The classes arriving at PE were dictated by their setting for Mathematics. This meant that classes were mixed ability in terms of their physical performance and experience; however, those individuals streamed in a lower ability set often had lower self-esteem generally and frequently held a fixed mindset in terms of their inability to achieve cognitive learning objectives. As Head of Department, I had the freedom to construct a PE curriculum that reflected pupil feedback and utilized the specific knowledge and experience of the teachers within the department whilst also being mindful of balancing the extra-curricular opportunities already offered and encouraging pupils to take the subject at GCSE and A Level. The lesson plan however does fulfill the National Curriculum for PE (taught in all local-authority-maintained schools in England) at Key Stage 4 (Years 10 and 11, pupils aged 14 and 16) by introducing defending tactics to overcome opponents in a net/wall game. The lesson plan follows a Teaching Games for Understanding (Bunker & Thorpe, 1982) pedagogical model by placing them within a series of modified games. Their knowledge of tactics is developed through specific questioning and this knowledge is then linked to the specific skills and movements required to become competent and proficient games players.

The steeplechase lesson plan demonstrates how I might have delivered the same topic when teaching in a single sex Independent girls' school in South London, England (10–18 year olds). The school population was culturally diverse and academic performance was valued by most above participation and achievement in PE and sport. Classes were timetabled by mixed ability tutor groups; however, the close intimacy of the group on a daily basis meant the group generally responded well to collaborative tasks. The lesson plan fulfills the National Curriculum for PE at Key Stage 3 (Years 7–9, pupils aged between 11–14) by developing pupils' technique and performance in athletics as well as focusing upon their ability to analyze performance in order to improve their own and others' personal bests. The lesson plan follows a Co-operative Learning pedagogical model (Dyson & Casey, 2012) incorporating positive interdependence (pupils depend upon one another to succeed), individual accountability (each pupil is assessed to show involvement), promoting positive face-to-face interaction time, encouraging and relying upon interpersonal and small group skills and group processing (open dialogue and group discussion about learning).

LESSON SET-UP, PLANS AND RESOURCES

The volleyball lesson below requires four volleyball courts and space for discussion around a whiteboard. The attacking tactics of a net/wall game should be delivered prior to the lesson, so pupils are aware of the tactics they are trying to overcome in defense. I would begin by highlighting the learning objectives and assessment criteria for the session. This would include explaining how their social and emotional skills will enable them to express their own perspectives and provide a supportive environment for other learners to provide theirs. I would also state that learners will be expected to provide constructive peer feedback in terms of their understanding and application of defensive tactics as well as self-reflecting upon their own understanding. The delivery and discussion surrounding the three sensitive questions including pupils reflecting upon the groups they have situated themselves in, how male/female ideologies may have presented a barrier to them engaging in certain activities and whether sports should be segregated by sex, may require some prior thought.

TABLE 13.1.

Activity: Volleyball	Learning Objectives (Psychomotor, Cognitive, Affective, Social):	Pedagogical Model: TGfU—Bunker & Thorpe (1982)
No of learners: 18 (M) 6 (F) 24 (Total) **Age of learners:** 14 (Year 10) **Ability:** Mixed **Duration:** 1 hour	• Identify and apply defending tactics in a net/wall game • All learners will be able to express their own perspective regarding gender equality in sport • All learners will be able to listen to and consider one another's perspective • All learners will be able to work together effectively and value each other's unique contribution	**How will you consider the cultural values of the classroom?** Allow all voices/perspectives to be heard, challenge gender stereotypes **How will you encourage sustainability of activity?** Offer extra-curricular mixed volleyball activity, Inter house mixed volleyball tournament

Time:	Task:	Grouping/Resources/ Modification:	Key Learning Points:	Personalized Assessment of LOs:	Justification:
9:00	Register, explain learning objectives building upon previous experience of setting up the attack in a net/ wall game.	Learning objectives placed on large whiteboard. Allow pupils to choose groups of 3. Groups of 3 amalgamate with one other group to form a 6 for the first activity.	LOs	Discussion Q & A	Allow groups to gain confidence by working in friendship groups initially. I would predict the class chooses to work in single sex groups which will allow discussion later however those pupils who are non-gender conforming as well as LGBTQI pupils are free to choose where they feel most comfortable.

Time:	Task:	Grouping/Resources/ Modification:	Key Learning Points:	Personalized Assessment of LOs:	Justification:
9:05	Warm up activity: **Empty the court.** 3v3 on one volleyball court, 1 ball per player. Objective is to empty your side of the court from balls. Balls should be thrown underarm, over the net and not directly at players. Game stops when your court is free of balls or when the teacher blows the whistle. Question key learning points as a whole group and then return to play again. Provide feedback to peers.	4 courts 24 soft volleyballs Assessment criteria (footwork, movement, anticipation and returning to base) placed on whiteboard.	How do we score in the game? *Empty the court of balls* What defending tactic does your team need to use? *Defend space on court* What skills will you be using? *Positioning of players, footwork, movement, anticipation* What should you do after playing the ball? *Return to base (original position on court)*	Identify the defending tactics and skills required Feedback provided by teacher and peers when teams are playing again (footwork, movement, anticipation, returning to base)	First activity is accessible to all and allows all learners to experience the defending tactics and skills required in the game. The questions chosen will help learners to identify these tactics and skills and apply them when playing again.
9:15.	**3 v 3 game** • Initiate game with a playable throw (free ball) • Alternate free ball (rotate before each free ball your team gives) • Up to 3 touches on a side • Setter in ready position (by net) • Low catch as first contact (emphasis ball must be caught below waist rather than caught and moved to low position) • Two contacts score a point	Modified to suit individual ability: • Pupil can allow ball to bounce once • Pupil can catch the ball before performing set or hit • Pupil can perform set or hit technique straight away	What is the goal of the game? *To make 2 touches* How have you achieved this (tactic)? *Defend space on court, consistency* What do you do as free ball comes over? *Digger anticipates ball arriving and moves into position to be able to catch the ball low, setter opens up, hitter balances the court*	Identify key learning points Express their own perspective regarding how they feel playing sport in this environment.	Demonstration of 3v3 game provided. Modification and small-sided game allows full inclusion. Questions chosen to elicit key learning points from learners. Segregation of groups explicitly identified to allow individuals to consider the impact of this. Discussion between whole group. Clear expectations of how debate should be conducted set down. Including modelling how all voices/perspectives should be heard and valued.

Time:	Task:	Grouping/Resources/ Modification:	Key Learning Points:	Personalized Assessment of LOs:	Justification:
	Question key learning points as a whole group.	Discussion as a whole group. If pupils are reluctant to offer perspectives, they may be encouraged to do so by sharing ideas initially with a peer.	What should you do after playing the ball? *Return to base position*		
	Then ask pupils why they have chosen to work in the groups they have? *Familiarity, friends, ability, lack of confidence.* Does this separation affect how you interact together? Will it reinforce gender stereotypes? Do we want to emphasize the difference between ourselves or do we want to treat/ understand one another as individuals?		What should set be like? How do we perform it? *Face team, high ball*		
	How have you experienced working in this group playing the activity? Modifications offered allow full inclusion regardless of ability. Gender equality demands parity of esteem. Move groups around. May keep groups of 3 together dependent upon feedback provided by group.				

Time:	Task:	Grouping/Resources/Modification:	Key Learning Points:	Personalized Assessment of LOs:	Justification:
9:20	**Practice Phase.** • 3 consecutive balls to one team and then other team feeds, rotate roles within team • Passer slaps ball to initiate the start of play and Digger calls free • Emphasis contain dig in your own court. Learners given autonomy over which modification they choose. • Setter opens up (faces team) and calls 'here' • Attempt pass, set, hit	Modified to suit individual ability: • Allowed to catch ball before performing skill if required • Catch ball low and throw to setter • Dig to self to catch and then throw to setter • Dig straight to setter P H S H S D		Achieving pass, set, hit using modification to suit ability. Feedback provided by both teacher and peers.	Demonstration provided. Developing individual cognitive and psychomotor skills as well as empathy and social interaction (through co-operative activity).
9:30	**Return to 3v3 game.** -2 contacts score a point Rotate groups around again.	Modifications to suit individual ability still apply		Feedback provided by peers and teachers. Outcome of activity.	Opportunity to apply previous skills and tactics in a competitive situation as well as playing with/ against other individuals.

Time:	Task:	Grouping/Resources/ Modification:	Key Learning Points:	Personalized Assessment of LOs:	Justification:
9:35	**Defending against attack** in 6v6 game Add serve. 2 contacts score a point. Defending players set up triad. If certain individuals dominate game with their serve, ask them to serve underarm or choose who serves.	2 full size volleyball courts Modified to suit individual ability: • Server can throw the ball from close to the back line • Underarm serve • Overarm serve • Players can still use other choice of modifications for dig, set and hit	How can we defend against the attack (serve/hit)? *Intercept the attack at net, leave space open to condition the attack*	Outcome of activity. Self-reflection based upon criteria set (footwork, movement, anticipation, returning to base) Feedback provided by peers and teacher.	Opportunity to experience and consider how to apply previous skills in a more complex tactical situation, 'defending against an attack'. Questions asked to elicit new learning.
9:40	**Defend as a team tournament**. Timed 3 minute games. Consider position of 6 players. Objective is to achieve a five-point winning margin. Rotate teams. Again if certain individuals dominate game with their serve, ask them to serve underarm or choose who serves.	• 6 players on court (Heterogeneous) Start game with a serve (using above modifications) • If ball lands on floor/out of area point is over • Team that wins rally wins the point and gains the next serve • Rotate clockwise when you regain the serve		Outcome of activity. Self-reflection based upon criteria set Feedback provided by peers and teacher.	Opportunity to apply previous skills and tactics in a game which resembles volleyball more closely due to the rules now added.

Time:	Task:	Grouping/Resources/ Modification:	Key Learning Points:	Personalized Assessment of LOs:	Justification:
9:50	**Plenary** **How many teams achieved a five-point winning margin? What did you need to do to defend effectively as a team?** Historically sport has both reinforced and challenged gender inequality. Gender is a social construct. Discuss in groups the following questions and present both sides of the argument to the rest of the group... **1) From your own experience has the pressure of what is suitably masculine and feminine presented a barrier for you in a sporting setting? What is the role of volleyball within your immediate family, school and community 2) Should all sport be segregated by sex?** Key expectations regarding listening to and valuing other people's views and learners also asked to consider how this was modelled previously	Whole group 3 x mixed sex groups (2 girls in each) 6 white boards & pens Key questions placed on whiteboard	*Cover the space, communicate effectively; intercept attack, leave space open to condition attack* 1) Role models, opportunities presented, social influences, *fear of evaluation.* 2) **Competitive advantage**— *'the top women can't take on the top men'. (10% performance gap, highest in weightlifting, typically more level in aerobic events).* *Women's performance improved recently more than men. Sports research increasingly specifically designed around women.* *Does that mean women can't play on the same team as men or men can't play on women's teams?* **Fairness?** **Safety?** *Variations between individuals on a men's team anyway. Could the activity be structured to be inclusive? Integrating team sports could do a lot to challenge the way we value one another.*	Identify key learning points Express to whole group or share ideas within their smaller group.	Privilege is invisible to those who have it. Making gender issue visible is the first step to engaging pupils to consider gender equality. Challenging potential resistance to equality and examining why an egalitarian society is good for everyone. Offering a diversity of voices so that not just one view is held as the opinion of all men or women.

The steeplechase lesson below requires pupils to be placed in mixed ability, which may be organized by the teacher prior to the lesson or pupils may be asked to identify their current level of experience of athletics, from which the teacher may then place them in appropriate heterogeneous groupings. The equipment for the lesson will be set up by the pupils themselves during the lesson, but the first activity requires a laptop and projector with internet access set up in the sports hall or adjoining classroom. I would address the learning objectives as well as how each individual learner will be expected to enhance and support the cultural values of the classroom. I would emphasize the requirement of each individual to contribute to their group, and how their contribution will be assessed both individually and collectively, by interacting and communicating successfully to one another. The explicit questions asked will require a suitable discussion space and whiteboard. The questions surrounding women's accessibility to certain events in athletics, how gender is constructed and how this is embodied in terms of the girls' confidence in their own bodies to perform certain activities may require some careful consideration before the lesson.

Activity: Steeplechase	Learning Objectives (Psychomotor, Cognitive, Affective, Social):	Pedagogical Model: Co-operative Learning— Dyson & Casey (2012)
No of learners: 24 (F)	• All learners will be able to identify the key skills required for steeplechase and apply these successfully to the final team challenge	**How will you consider the cultural values of the classroom?**
	• All learners will be able to express their own beliefs and values regarding gender equality in sport	Allow learners to have autonomy of their own learning. Creating a sense of belonging by encouraging all voices to be heard which may offer different perspectives. Contest inequalities and celebrate difference.
Age of learners: 12 (Year 8)	• All learners will be able to listen to and learn from other people's beliefs and values	
Ability: Mixed	• All learners will be able to work together effectively to solve the final team challenge	**How will you encourage sustainability of activity?**
Duration: 1 hour		Challenging how gender identity is constructed and reinforced. Ask pupils' views about which activities they would like on curriculum/extra curriculum

Time:	Task:	Grouping/Resources/Modification:	Key Learning Points:	Personalized Assessment of LOs:	Justification:
Previous lesson covered: Hurdling technique					
9:00	Register. Explain learning objectives and expectations regarding empathy and listening to others.	All Heterogeneous/mixed ability to groups (4)	Los	Q & A	Steeplechase activity chosen to create inclusion because often all learners will come with little prior knowledge.
9:05	Play video of Coburn winning Steeplechase at World Championships London 2017 and complete team challenge. Discuss why women's steeplechase was only added to the Olympic Program in 2008? Is there complete parity in all athletic events for women—heptathlon (not decathlon), 100m (not 110m) hurdles over shorter barriers, lighter implements in the field, men running 10k cross country and women running 6k. Discuss as a group what changes you would make and why?	6 pupils in each group 4 whiteboard and pens	How far is the steeplechase event? How many barriers per lap? Total number of clearances in a 3000m race?	**Team Challenge:** 1500m/ 2000m/ 3000m 4 barriers and a water jump (35 total clearances) 7 ½ laps = 3000m (no barriers in first half lap)	Collaboration encouraged to develop social and emotion skills and generate a greater number of perspectives. Idea of equality introduced by discussing accessibility to certain events. Equalizing race distance however may not ensure equality—dominance of female Kenyan athletes in World Cross Country Championship 2017 (where both women and men raced 9.8K).

Time:	Task:	Grouping/Resources/ Modification:	Key Learning Points:	Personalized Assessment of LOs:	Justification:
	Rio Olympics (45% of participants female). Saudi Arabia's presence (4 athletes) but denial at home, Qatar and Brunei (1 athlete each). 56 openly LGBT athletes at Rio Olympics—highest recorded.		In what year was the women's steeplechase added to the Olympic program? Three specific skills required to perform the steeplechase? Ancient Olympic Games 1896 was limited by Baron de Coubertin to male athletes only. They first competed in Paris 1900 (tennis, golf, croquet, sailing). 1928 competed in track and field.	2008 Beijing Hurdling, endurance running, race tactics	
9:20	**Students expected to carry out 3 tasks without direct and immediate supervision.** Teacher facilitating learning (keeping close eye on hurdling group).	2 members of each 'home' group are allocated to go and learn about one cognitive/psychomotor skill required for steeplechase and bring back to practice with their group in the set order. Task sheets, 3 stop watches, 12 flat spots, 12 barriers/ hurdles (obstacle to be hurdled can be modified by learner) Performance criteria differentiated for individual ability by outcome (equal split)	Task 1: Circle Relay (on task sheet) Task 2: Hurdling technique (on task sheet) Task 3: Tactical understanding (on task sheet)	Team should keep running collectively for 5 minutes, pupils can run at their own steady pace to achieve this. Ensure trail leg foot is not pointed down. Get foot to floor as quickly as possible. Lift up knee of leading leg and drive heel down to ground Lean slightly forward.	Elements of Cooperative Learning accounted for: teacher frames task but does not teach pupils how to complete it, positive interdependence, Individual accountability, promotes face to face interaction and interpersonal and small group skills Modifications and success criteria allows autonomy and pupils can progress at their own pace. Encourages cognitive as well as psychomotor, social and affective learning outcomes.

Time:	Task:	Grouping/Resources/Modification:	Key Learning Points:	Personalized Assessment of LOs:	Justification:
				Ensure lead arm is raised and moves backward. Trail arm is moves forward. Shoulders kept level.	
				Ensure an equal split Try to anticipate the barriers.	
				Keep a low flight over barriers and regain running action as quickly as possible.	
				Keep a good running and hurdling form throughout.	
9:50	**Problem solving task as a team**		Try to achieve the lowest team time over 12 laps (groups can arrange team members however they wish). Team asked to reduce their time by 5 secs.	By outcome	Group processing (open dialogue about learning)

Time:	Task:	Grouping/Resources/ Modification:	Key Learning Points:	Personalized Assessment of LOs:	Justification:
9:55	**Plenary** Which team managed to reduce their time by 5 secs? How did you/could you do this? **Should success be based purely upon time/strength/ speed? Do you enjoy competition yourself? What does athletics mean to you? Gender embodiment—shape of the body—does muscularity benefit performance in PE or is it more important to express femininity? Are there any particular sports which are only socially acceptable for just men/women? Are you worried if you play these sports?**	Ask each group in turn and ensure all voices are heard Ask learners to reflect with a partner first to encourage them to offer ideas Ask groups to discuss and share ideas with the other groups	Improving running, hurdling, tactical aspects, utilizing all members of the group effectively Are these masculine qualities? Are we contradicting gender norms by pursuing in athletic participation? Can we enjoy physical activity without being competitive? Can we reframe what it means to be feminine? Could we consider masculinity and femininity on a spectrum where individuals could exhibit aspects of both qualities?		Identifying how gender is constructed and reinforced. Understanding of which activities pupils enjoy and would like to have access to on curriculum/extra-curriculum.

TASK 1: CIRCLE RELAY

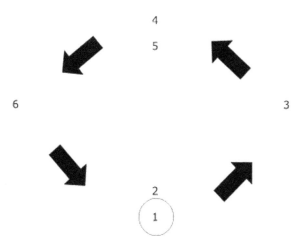

Key Points

- This activity considers the cardiovascular and muscular endurance required for steeplechase
- Ensure you organize your group safely (only one person running at any one time) and position the activity away from hazards, walls, other groups etc.
- Incorporate a variety of movement to keep your group motivated e.g. sidestep, skips, small steps, leaps

Criteria for Success

- Your team should keep running collectively for 5 minutes so keep an even steady pace to allow for this

TASK 2: HURDLING TECHNIQUE (10 MINS)

Key Points

- Set out 4 indoor hurdles/barriers 2m apart
- Make sure you are travelling over hurdles/barriers the correct way
- All drills should be carried out at walking pace
- Only one participant at a time

Criteria for Success

1. **Trail Leg Isolation Drill:** Stand to the side of the hurdle, lift your leg closest to the hurdle do lower leg is parallel to the floor, ensure toe is not pointed down, drive towards opposite arm, get foot to floor as quickly as possible and get back into walking action, repeat at next hurdle. Repeat technique over all 4 hurdles on opposite side of the hurdle.

2. **Hurdling Walking:** Lift up knee of leading leg, drive heel down to ground followed by trailing leg (following previous criteria). Lean slightly forward. Repeat on the next hurdle. Attempt with alternative lead leg and decide upon favored lead leg.

3. **Lead Arm:** Carry out the previous drill but ensure lead arm is raised to allow trail leg to come through. Lead arm should move backward to counterbalance forward motion of trail leg. The trail arm is moved forward to counterbalance forward motion of trail leg. Shoulders should be level.

TASKS 3 AND 4: TACTICAL (5 MINS EACH)

Continuous Relay (anti-clockwise)

- Set up 2 hurdles (equidistant)
- Only one team member running at any one time (others remain inside track

Set up 4 barriers (equidistant

- Each runner now runs 4 laps each (alternate lap run outside hurdles, then over all 4 barriers)

Key Points
- Ensure safety of all team members at all times
- Ensure barriers/hurdles are set up the correct way
- Waiting runners should remain in one place inside the track

Criteria for Success

- Ensure a steady pace throughout (equal split—so first lap is the same speed as last lap)
- Try to sight/anticipate the barriers rather than decelerating and then accelerating
- Decide upon whether you will use the same lead leg or whether this will make you fatigue quicker
- Keep a low flight over barriers and regain running action as quickly as possible
- Keep a good running and hurdling form throughout

INTERSECTIONALITIES

To include and account for all my learners, I would consider whether the lesson context holds a cultural relevance to them all as well as being accessible to each of them individually. The activities chosen for both lessons are global sports and may be easily adapted to account for the needs of pupils with a disability (e.g., changing the activity to sitting volleyball and providing ways to sustain the activity outside of the curriculum), which will help all pupils to reevaluate the abilities of Paralympic athletes. Equally, the steeplechase lesson may be modified by incorporating ramps rather than hurdles. Stride (2014) suggests each individual must then be given the opportunity to consider how they experience the activity, what meaning they give to it and how they negotiate the activity. For example, in the volleyball lesson, pupils are asked how they have experienced the activity working in their groups and the impact of their family, school, community on the meaning they give to volleyball. In the steeplechase lesson, pupils are asked how they view competition, what meaning they give to athletics and how their experiences are embodied in their confidence to engage in the activity. This will allow students to make connections to their cultural experiences, upbringing, interests and involvement in physical activity outside of the curriculum, which will make PE more meaningful to them. It will encourage pupils to recognize barriers to their engagement, offering insight of how gender, race, class and ability affect the classroom and give the teacher the opportunity to act upon it to improve the curriculum (Azzarito & Solmon, 2005). Encouraging pupils to speak up about their lived experiences will encourage pupils to recognize, value and celebrate the differences of other social identities. It may also allow students to consider reasons why they have become disengaged in physical activity and become involved again in other ways.

Intersectionality requires us to move outside of gender to consider the interplay of race, class, sexuality, ethnicity and ability (Flintoff & Scraton, 2006). Listening to the diverse experiences of each pupil will allow pupils to begin to recognize and accept the variety of ways of being in terms of their race, class, sexuality, ethnicity and ability and allow the teacher to explain the fluidity and contradictory nature of these intersecting categories (Azzarito & Solman, 2005). Intersectionality Theory illustrates how the multidimensional and interconnected nature of race, class, gender and sexuality are more visible for someone who faces oppression by more than one dimension of inequality. Experiences of gender are therefore racialized, sexualized and classed. This will be crucial in pupils' understanding their own identity and how their beliefs may be influenced and embodied by certain social and historical issues in sport (e.g., segregation of sport by sex, inaccessibility of certain events, male hegemonic values). Given the sensitive nature of looking at how they have embodied this, I have only asked this explicitly within the single sex group, but the mixed group have been asked to reflect upon this or could alternatively blog their feelings privately. By becoming critical of the way sport can both support and oppress different groups (e.g., through the influence of media (Azzarito, Simon, & Mattinen, 2016), will help young people become active agents in resisting racialization, classist and gendered barriers in sport.

CHALLENGES AND POSSIBILITIES

The questions outlined certainly require a level of emotional intelligence from the whole group; however, having specifically outlined the expectations of behaviour from the outset, I was often encouraged by learners' willingness and maturity to engage fully and consider the issues appropriately. Quickly and softly challenging inappropriate comments from a few pupils was often enough to steer all my learners to consider the issues at a deeper level. A greater challenge was often encouraging learners to express their opinions, particularly within a mixed environment, which I tried to encourage through the cultivation of a safe space, offering a means of private reflection, allowing them to work in small groups, offering prompts, responding positively to suggestions and trying to support learners to develop ideas further. This was particularly important given I was also trying to present multiple perspectives and identities. I ensured I was fully knowledge-able about the issue I was addressing and this often involved anticipating dif-ficult conversations (e.g., boys instantly wanting to highlight their competitive advantage and why this warrants sex segregation in sport). By accepting this as a valid reason for segregating sport showed how I valued their perspective, but I equally challenged whether this was true in all sporting activities and how the gap is closing partly due to increased sports science research focused specifically upon women's performance. My confidence to challenge inequalities grew even in conservative school environments, where I felt even more passionate about disrupting the discourses and values held by some pupils. I did not experience any negative repercussions, but felt at times frustrated by the impact other parts of the school and experiences outside the school had on the pupils.

REFERENCES

Azzarito, L., Simon, M., & Mattinen, R. (2016). 'I guess people are more attracted to white people than black people'. Shedding light on racial prejudice, misrepresentation, and (in)visibility of ethnic minority bodies. In D. B. Robinson & L. Randall (Eds.), *Social justice in physical education: Critical reflections and pedagogies for change* (pp. 15–35). Toronto, CA: Canadian Scholars' Press Inc.

Azzarito, L. & Solmon, M. A. (2005). A reconceptualization of physical education: The intersection of gender/race/social class. *Sport, Education and Society, 10*(1), 25–47.

Bain, L. (1990). A critical analysis of the hidden curriculum in physical education. In D. Kirk & R. Tinning (Eds.), *Physical education, curriculum and culture: Critical is-sues in the contemporary crisis* (pp. 19–34). Basingstoke, UK: Falmer.

Bramham, P. (2003). Boys, masculinity and PE. *Sport, Education and Society, 8*(1), 57–71.

Bunker, D., & Thorpe, R. (1982). A model for the teaching of games in secondary schools. *Bulletin of Physical Education, 18*(1), 5–8.

Butler, J. (2006). *Gender trouble: Feminism and the subversion of identity*. New York, London: Routledge.

Clarke, G. (2002). Difference matters: sexuality and physical education. In D. Penney (Ed.) *Gender and physical education: Contemporary issues and future directions* (pp. 41–56). London, UK: Routledge.

Coakley, J., & White, A. (1992). Making decisions: Gender and sport participation among British adolescents. *Sociology of Sport Journal, 9*, 20–35.

Connell, R. W. (2005). *Masculinities*. Cambridge, UK: Polity Press.

Department for Education. (2017a). *National statistics—A level and other 16 to 18 results: 2016 to 2017 (revised)*. Retrieved from https://www.gov.uk/government/statistics/a-level-and-other-16-to-18-results-2016-to-2017-revised.

Department for Education. (2017b). *National statistics—Revised GCSE and equivalent results in England: 2016 to 2017*. Retrieved from https://www.gov.uk/government/statistics/revised-gcse-and-equivalent-results-in-england-2016-to-2017

Dyson, B., & Casey, A. (Eds.). (2012). *Cooperative learning in physical education: A research-based approach.* New York, NY: Routledge.

Evans, J. (1989). Swinging from the crossbar: equality and opportunity in the physical education curriculum. *British Journal of Physical Education, 20*(2), 84–87.

Evans, J., Lopez, S., Duncan, M., & Evans, M. (1985). Some thoughts on the political and pedagogical implications of mixed sex PE grouping in the PE curriculum. *British Educational Research Journal, 13*(1), 59–71.

Fitzpatrick, K., & McGlashan, H. (2016). Rethinking "Straight Pedagogy." Gender, sexuality and physical education. In D. B. Robinson & L. Randall (Eds.), *Social Justice in Physical Education: Critical reflections and pedagogies for change* (pp. 102–118). Toronto, CA: Canadian Scholars' Press Inc.

Fleming, I. (1991). Sport, schooling and Asian male youth culture. In G. Jarvie (Ed.), *Sport, racism and ethnicity.* London, UK: Falmer.

Flintoff, A., & Scraton, S. (2001). Stepping into active leisure? Young women's perceptions of active lifestyles and their experiences of school physical education. *Sport, Education and Society, 6*(1), 5–22.

Flintoff, A., & Scraton, S. (2006). Girls and physical education. In D. Kirk, D. Macdonald, & M. O'Sullivan (Eds.), *The handbook of physical education* (pp. 767–795). London, UK: Sage.

Griffin, P. (1984). Girls' participation patterns in a middle school team sports unit. *Journal of Teaching in Physical Education, 4*, 30–38.

Hills, L. A., & Croston, A. (2012). 'It should be better all altogether': Exploring strategies for 'undoing' gender in coeducational physical education. *Sport, Education and Society, 17*(5), 591–605.

Humberstone, B. (2002). Femininity, masculinity and difference: What's wrong with a sarong? In A. Laker (Ed.), *The sociology of sport and physical education* (pp. 58–78). London, UK: Routledge/Falmer.

Larsson, H., Redelius, K., & Fagrell, B. (2010). Moving (in) the heterosexual matrix. On heteronormativity in secondary school physical education. *Physical Education and Sport Pedagogy, 16*(1), 67–81.

Lenskyj, H. (1991). Combating homophobia in sport and physical education. *Sociology of Sport Journal, 8*(1), 61–69.

Light, R., & Kirk, D. (2000). High school rugby, the body and the reproduction of hegemonic masculinity. *Sport, Education and Society, 5*(2), 163–176.

Lorber, J. (2000). Using gender to under gender: a feminist degendering movement. *Feminist Theory, 1*(1), 79–95.

Lyu, M., & Gill, D. L. (2011). Perceived physical competence enjoyment and effort in same-sex and co-educational physical education classes. *Educational Psychology, 31*(2), 247–260.

McCaughtry, N. (2006). Working politically amongst professional knowledge landscapes to implement gender-sensitive physical education reform. *Physical Education and Sport Pedagogy, 11*(2), 159–179.

Oakley, A. (1972). *Sex, gender and society.* London, UK: Temple-Smith.

Office for Standards in Education. (1995). *Physical education and sport in schools: A survey of good practice.* London, UK: HMSO.

Oliver, K. L., & Kirk, D. (2016). Towards an activist approach to research and advocacy for girls and physical education. *Physical Education and Sport Pedagogy, 21*(3), 313–327.

Oliver, K. L., & Lalik, R. (2004). Critical inquiry on the body in girls' physical education classes: A critical poststructural perspective. *Journal of Teaching in Physical Education, 23*,162–195

Parker, A. (1996). The construction of masculinity in boys' PE. *Gender and Education, 8*(2), 141–157.

Scraton, S. (1992). *Shaping up to womanhood: Gender and girls' physical education.* Buckingham, UK: Open University Press.

Scraton, S. (1993). Equality, co-education and physical education in secondary Schooling. In J. Evans (Ed.), *Equality, education and physical education* (pp. 139–153). London, UK: Falmer.

Shire, J., & Hardman, J. (2011). Physical Education. In M. Cole (Ed.), *Equality in secondary schools—Promoting good practice across the curriculum* (pp. 195–209). London: Continuum.

Stride, A. (2014). Let US tell YOU! South Asian, Muslim girls tell tales about physical education. *Physical Education and Sport Pedagogy, 19*(4), 398–417.

Williams, A., & Bedward, J. (2001). Gender culture and the generation gap: Student and teacher perceptions of aspects of national curriculum physical education. *Sport Education and Society, 6*(1), 53–66.

Williams, A., Bedward J., & Woodhouse, J. (2000). An inclusive national curriculum? The experience of adolescent girls. *European Journal of Physical Education, 5*, 4–18.

Wright, J. (1997). The construction of gender contexts in single sex and co-educational physical education lessons. *Sport, Education and Society, 2*(1), 55–72.

Wright, J. (1999). Changing gendered practices in physical education: Working with teachers. *European Physical Education Review, 6*, 102–118.

Youdell, D. (2006). Sex-gender-sexuality: how sex, gender and sexuality constellations are constituted in secondary schools. *Gender and Education, 17*(3), 249–270

CHAPTER 14

INDIGENEITY AND PHYSICAL EDUCATION

Culturally Relevant and Socially Just Possibilities

Daniel B. Robinson and Kate Jadis

REFLECTION AND SHARING CIRCLE RESEARCH

There are two of us. One of us is a white settler man and the other is an Indigenous Mi'kmaq woman. One is also a physical education teacher education professor while the other is a physical education teacher. Most importantly, together we are also co-learners.

Our co-learning has been related to many topics over the past five years: physical education, pedagogy, mentorship, and—most related to this chapter—the often ignored or unconsidered space of Indigeneity and physical education. Together, we have made a concerted effort to learn more about what and how our nations' (i.e., Canada's and Indigenous First Nations') elementary and secondary physical education students ought to learn about Indigenous peoples, as well as their ways of being, knowing, and moving. Such knowledge, we believe, is important for all students—settlers and Indigenous peoples. That is, it is our shared belief that educating settlers as well as attending to the immediate and long-term strengths and needs of Indigenous children and youth are worthwhile and necessary tasks if

Teaching About Social Justice Issues in Physical Education, pages 171–183.
Copyright © 2019 by Information Age Publishing
All rights of reproduction in any form reserved.

we are to achieve a more culturally relevant and socially just physical education, and society.

Oftentimes, our co-learning exercise has seemed as though we have been on a long journey of discovery. The path for this journey has rarely, if ever, seemed to be straight or straightforward. At times, it has felt as though we have been making this path by walking it. Notwithstanding this feeling, we also know that we have not been walking it entirely alone, nor without some guidance from others. Indeed, many others have provided us with some important direction(s). For example, in Canada we have learned from Kalyn (2006, 2014), as well as from Halas (1998, 2002, 2006, 2011) and her colleagues (Halas, McCrae, & Carpenter, 2013). We have similarly gained knowledge from our colleagues in countries that share, somewhat, Canada's discomfiting history of colonization. These peers include Whatman and her colleagues in Australia (Hart, Whatman, McLaughlin, & Sharma-Brymer, 2012; Whatman, Quennerstedt, & McLaughlin, 2017; Whatman & Singh, 2015) as well as Hokowhitu (2008, 2016) and Salter (1998, 2000, 2002, 2003) in New Zealand/Aotearoa. Certainly, these peers have shaped our own understanding of cultural relevance and social justice, especially as they relate to Indigenous students' physical education (see Robinson, Barrett, & Robinson, 2016; Robinson, Lunney Borden, & Robinson, 2013).

Perhaps most importantly, those who have informed us include local Elders and knowledge keepers. These individuals' contributions to our own understandings have occurred largely through their participation in a three-year sharing circle research project—one in which we aimed to co-create knowledge about Mi'kmaq ways of knowing as they relate to the physical education of Mi'kmaq children and youth. It is largely the results of these sharing circles that have informed us here of some culturally relevant and socially just movement possibilities for physical education. Accordingly, the lesson suggestions herein aim to reflect some possibilities related to the four broadly summarized suggestions from these Elders and knowledge keepers: offer nature-based/land-based physical education, invite Elders/knowledge keepers into physical education, ensure physical education includes traditional and contemporary Mi'kmaq/Indigenous activities, and include medicine wheel teachings in physical education.

CONTEXT

We both teach within Nova Scotia, a small province on the east coast of Canada that borders the Atlantic Ocean. Nova Scotia is located within Mi'kma'ki, the ancestral and unceded territory of the Mi'kmaq people. The province, like most others within Canada, has a shameful history of cultural genocide through, among other things, forced residential schooling for Indigenous children and youth (see Benjamin, 2014; Knockwood, 2015). The immediate trauma borne by residential school victims and survivors, many of whom suffered abject neglect and abuse at the hands of the Church and/or State, is compounded by the intergenerational trauma suffered by survivors' descendent families and communities (Bombay,

Matheson, & Anisman, 2014). To many, including to us, Milloy's (1999) labelling of the residential school experience as a 'national crime' is appropriate and justified. Particularly because of this history, aiming for reconciliation and decolonization within schools and school systems is both necessary and difficult.

Canada's history and historical relationships with its Indigenous peoples have clearly been shameful. The future must be better. Of this we are certain. Nationally, we have seen one recent and notable development that suggests better days are indeed upon the horizon: The Truth and Reconciliation Commission of Canada (TRC). This TRC recently released a final report that includes, among other things, 94 calls to action (see TRC, 2015). These calls include seven related to education, seven related to health, and five related to sport.

More locally, we have seen another development that has given us hope for the future of Mi'kmaq students. Within Nova Scotia, Mi'kmaq peoples have reclaimed responsibility for educating many of their children and youth, largely through the establishment of the self-governed educational authority Mi'kmaw Kin'matnewey (MK). In these MK schools, Mi'kmaq children and youth (and communities) are experiencing many benefits from this self-governance, including improved graduation rates and stronger feelings of cultural identity and inclusion (MK, 2016; Orr, Robinson, Lunney Borden, & Tinkham, 2017).

It is in this context that the two of us find ourselves—Dan as a physical education teacher education professor who prepares pre-service physical education teachers to teach settlers and Indigenous students, in both public and band-operated schools, and Kate as a physical education teacher who teaches Mi'kmaq students in one of these band-operated schools. We believe our work-life contexts are rich with individuals and also with potential.

LESSON SET-UP

Herein we aim to share some of our own learnings, hoping that they might be educative and/or valuable for others like us. Moreover, our hope here is that readers might come to see possibilities for consideration within their physical education programs, rather than lessons meant to be replicated. In other words, the context we have outlined matters, as do all contexts. So, readers will need to similarly consider their own context(s) before envisioning related possibilities for their own practice. Additionally, the two suggested lesson ideas offered here are only being made *after* we first listened to local Elders and knowledge keepers. We believe it is ever-essential to always respect and observe the 'nothing about us without us' ethic and ethos when making decisions or taking actions that are meant to have an impact upon Indigenous peoples. So, while we offer these lesson suggestions, we also offer this cautionary note: these are suggestions from and for our contexts. Others who recognize familiar characteristics and/or who share our concerns related to Indigeneity and physical education might similarly confer with their local Elders and knowledge keepers before engaging in similar teaching and learning exercises.

We offer two lesson possibilities here. Both are meant to provide an example of the sorts of things that ought to occur in physical education classes. It is also important to note that we are not suggesting that one-off lessons like these will do much (good). Rather, an inclusive and social justice-oriented mindset might welcome possibilities like the ones we offer here.

1. Lesson Idea 1 (Teaching for Cultural Relevance) is an example of the sort of lesson that might be normalized within a class with all (or some, or one, or no) Indigenous student(s). It is meant to highlight what a physical education lesson might look like if a teacher aims for cultural relevance in her/his instruction. It is also meant to occur within a lacrosse (or invasion/territory games) unit, ideally after students are familiar with the 'formal' rules of the adult or near-adult form of the game. We believe this lesson can occur with models-based practice (e.g., Sport Education, Teaching Games for Understanding, Teaching for Personal and Social Responsibility). This lesson would likely require more than one 'normal' class period.
2. Lesson Idea 2 (Teaching for Social Justice [Content] in Physical Education) is an example of the sort of lesson that might be taught with a class of (particularly settler) students. It is meant to highlight what a physical education lesson might look like if a teacher aims to address social justice (as it relates to Indigeneity) in her/his instruction. We believe this lesson can also occur with models-based practice (e.g., Cooperative Learning, Reciprocal Teaching, Teaching for Personal and Social Responsibility). This lesson would likely require more than one 'normal' class period.

LESSON IDEA 1: TEACHING FOR CULTURAL RELEVANCE

Lesson Purpose

Our province suggests/requires (as outcomes or suggested learning experiences for elementary and secondary physical education) the following: "explore ways to be physically active with respect to a variety of cultural backgrounds" (Government of Nova Scotia, 2016, p. 4) and "create and present a modified game…organize a game using…rules" (Government of Nova Scotia, 1999, p. 94). This lesson serves as an opportunity for students to learn about lacrosse, an historically meaningful and traditional game from/for Indigenous peoples. In addition to learning sport-specific skills related to lacrosse, this lesson is (primarily) meant to focus upon cultural teachings that might also be taught alongside or through lacrosse.

Lesson Materials

Required materials include modified/developmentally appropriate lacrosse equipment (e.g., soft lacrosse equipment), an outdoor space, mini white boards or chart paper, markers, and natural objects (e.g., branches, stones, trees, etc.).

Anticipatory Set

In small groups (of 4–5 students), have students brainstorm and record responses to the following four prompts: 1) What are the rules of lacrosse? 2) Who decides upon the rules for sports (like lacrosse, hockey, basketball)? 3) How are group decisions (that respect the input of all individuals) best made? 4) What equipment do we need to play lacrosse? These small group responses should be recorded and available for viewing by others (e.g., on mini white boards or on chart paper).

Body of Lesson

At the beginning of the class, students may be taught, as they normally are, lacrosse-related skills with opportunities to apply those skills in authentic applied task scenarios and/or small-sided games. Whatever the focus of initial movement instruction (e.g., passing, defensive tactics, etc.), the subsequent focus of this lesson is meant to be placed upon having students create, play, and present a modified game of lacrosse.

Before this 'create, play, and present' task can begin, the small group responses to the four anticipatory set questions need to be addressed. Allow students to share their responses to all four questions and, afterwards, offer them these important pieces of information:

1. Regarding 'What are the rules of lacrosse?' and 'Who decides upon the rules for sports?': The formal rules of lacrosse are dependent on time and circumstance. For example, lacrosse existed long before any current (Western) rules or organizations. Ask students what they think the rules used to be and why would they change with time and place.

2. Regarding 'How are group decisions best made?': Often within the West, we think that voting and accepting the position of the (voting) majority is the best way to make a fair decision. Ask students what potential harms might be associated with this decision-making method and also invite students to share examples where minority rights, for example, are not respected when majority decisions are made. There are plenty of examples that might be shared here (e.g., with Indigenous peoples, sexual and gender minorities, racialized minorities, etc.). Ask the students to explain in what other ways group decisions can be better made (and introduce the notion of consensus).

3. Regarding 'What equipment do we need to play lacrosse?': Remind students that although they may have listed nets and gymnasiums (or sports fields), lacrosse existed before any of these things existed as we know them today. Have them brainstorm what might be used instead of nets and gymnasiums/sports fields. Encourage them to think of ways to creatively include natural objects.

Share with students the history of lacrosse. This sharing might rely upon an age-appropriate text (e.g., Calder & Fletcher's [2011] *Lacrosse: The Ancient Game* or Coulson's [2013] *The Creator's Game: A Story of Baaga'adowe/Lacrosse*). Among other things, it is important to highlight the following: 1) Lacrosse is also known as The Creator's Game and it comes to us from Indigenous peoples in North America who would at times come together with others to play. 2) There were very few familiar formal rules to The Creator's Game (e.g., players could not touch the ball with their hands) and so players from competing teams or nations would come together and, through consensus, come to decide upon the rules (related, for example, to the number of players, size of the playing field, ways of scoring, etc.).

Partnering with another small group (i.e., now 8–10 students), students should then be given the task of creating, playing, and presenting a modified game of lacrosse, while also aiming to observe and respect a historically Indigenous way of decision making. Students should record their responses on a teacher-created form, like the one presented in Figure 14.1.

Once the games are created, student groups should play them. After students have played their games, they should all come together to present their games to their peers in the rest of the class.

Task: Your two teams will need to come together to create, play (test), and then present your version of Lacrosse to the rest of the class. You will need to do determine answers to all questions on the table below. **These decisions should be made as a group. To make these group decisions, please sit in a circle and take turns speaking. We need to make everyone feel free to share their ideas and so all students need to also be respectful listeners. Let's try to find consensus—where 100% of the group comes to agree on all game decisions.**	
What is the name of your version of Lacrosse?	
What are the playing boundaries?	
How can a team score a goal? Is there more than one way to score? How many points is a score worth?	
How should the game start and end?	
Are there any penalties? What happens if a penalty occurs?	
In what ways can players demonstrate fair play when playing?	
In what ways will you need to use things found in nature (e.g., stones, logs, trees, hills) for your game?	
Other important points:	

FIGURE 14.1.   Lacrosse game creation record form.

Closure/Checking for Understanding

After students share their games, they should be encouraged to also engage in guided discussion about the following: 1) consensus as a decision-making strategy (e.g., how it welcomes all views to be heard and (often) heeded, 2) how to respectfully use nature within games (e.g., returning objects back to their places), 3) in what other ways they see their culture in lacrosse and/or any other sports.

Extending the Learning

- Elders and/or knowledge keepers might come into the class to share oral histories (e.g., related to sport and recreation) with students.
- Students and/or teachers might investigate other games with Indigenous histories.
- Students and/or teachers might consider how lacrosse can enable players to develop physically, culturally, mentally, and/or spiritually.

LESSON IDEA 2: TEACHING FOR SOCIAL JUSTICE (CONTENT) IN PHYSICAL EDUCATION

Lesson Purpose

Our province suggests/requires (as an outcome) the following: "identify social injustices in Canadian sport and articulate steps that would help address each of the injustices they identify" (Government of Nova Scotia, 2010, p. 2). This lesson serves as an opportunity for students to learn about social injustices in sport, particularly as they relate to Indigenous peoples. More specifically, this lesson focuses upon offensive imagery (e.g., logos, mascots) and terminology used by high profile sports teams and it encourages students to react, as social justice advocates and/or allies, to those images and terms.

Lesson Materials

Required materials include a video player, loose-leaf paper, access to internet, and small tablets (e.g., iPads, smart phones).

Anticipatory Set

Play the following video for students: http://www.changethemascot.org/proud-to-be-video/ (a two-minute version, which is highly recommended, can also be found online on YouTube). Invite students to independently record their responses to the following two prompts: 1) What does this video tells us about who Indigenous peoples/Native Americans are? 2) Why do you think the Washington Redskins' name and logo are offensive to Indigenous peoples/Native Americans? These individual responses should be recorded on loose-leaf paper.

Body of Lesson

With their responses, students should come together and engage in a think-pair-share (TPS) activity. In this activity, they should listen to their partners' responses and they should share their own. Together, partnered pairs should then also brainstorm, and record, responses to the following two questions: 1) What other teams similarly have offensive names and/or logos/mascots? (Allow them to use the internet, if necessary, to address this question.) 2) What should our (re) action be in response to these sports teams using these sorts of offensive names and/or logos/mascots?

Examples of sports teams using these sorts of names and logos/mascots are plentiful. They include the following: Atlanta Braves (MLB), Chicago Blackhawks (NHL), Cleveland Indians (MLB), Edmonton Eskimos (CFL), and Kansas City Chiefs (NFL). There is also evidence of (re)actions from social justice advocates and/or allies. For example:

- Two major American NFL broadcasters (Phil Simms and Tony Dungy) have refused to say the (Washington) team name 'Redskins' in their broadcast of football games. Some NFL players have taken the same stance (e.g., Allen Barbre [a Native American], A. J. Francis). And, at least one NFL referee (Mike Carey) has refused to officiate games in which Washington plays.

- One mayor Canadian MLB broadcaster (Jerry Howarth) has refuses to say the (Cleveland) team name 'Indians' in his broadcast of baseball games. Additionally, the team recently decided to not use their Chief Wahoo logo while competing in Toronto, Canada—though it is still in use for games played in the United States.

- Canada's University of Saskatchewan recently passed a resolution ending the use of all school mascots and logos that depicted Indigenous peoples. In the United States, a number of NCAA colleges have also recently removed all reference to Indigenous peoples. Some colleges have been granted waivers so that they may continue to use such mascots and logos (e.g., Florida State University Seminoles, University of Utah Utes); in all of these cases the waivers were granted only after individual Indigenous tribal nations exercised Tribal Sovereignty (i.e., they supported the continued use of the terminology and/or imagery).

Once students have shared some possible (re)actions, they should join another pair (i.e., now groups of four) and then begin to create an action plan. Possibilities for action plans might include, but are not limited to, the following:

- An in-school educational message (e.g., hallway/gymnasium bulletin board, school-wide announcement, etc.).

- A specific petition and/or letter campaign, directed at a local team that continues to use offensive terminology and/or imagery.
- A name and/or logo design task that requires students to create an alternative name/logo and, more importantly, provide a rationale for the updated name/logo (see/search Mike Ivall's Blackhawks logo as an exemplar).

Closure/Checking for Understanding

Students' final products should be evaluated with respect to their developed knowledge about the importance of knowing about and respecting Indigenous peoples. A critically reflective question might also enable deeper and more meaningful considerations (e.g., In what ways were you uninformed before? Could some of the things you once said or wore suggest to some that you may have been contributing to racism? What will you do, moving forward? Can not saying something when you see these things also say something about you?).

Extending the Learning

- Elders and/or knowledge keepers might come into the class to share their perspectives on Indigenous names, images, and terminology (e.g., Aboriginal, Indigenous, Métis, Inuit, etc.).
- Students and/or teachers might investigate how some teams have changed or introduced Indigenous imagery in a more positive and respectful manner (e.g., Seattle Seahawks [NFL], Vancouver Canucks [NHL]).
- Invite students to research notable past or current Indigenous sporting icons (e.g., Tom Longboat, Carey Price, Jim Thorpe, etc.) and (among other things) have them determine how these individuals identify/label themselves (and/or how others identify/label them).

INTERSECTIONALITIES

The introduction in this chapter includes a brief mention of our own intersectional identities. Again, Dan is a white settler man and Kate is an Indigenous Mi'kmaq woman. Additionally, we are also both heterosexual, cisgender, able-bodied, middle class, and Canadian. These intersecting identities do not exist without one another. We can see and feel the shifting power and privilege that comes with some of them—shifts that sometimes occur as we move (literally) into different spatial and/or temporal circumstances.

Similarly, our focus upon Indigeneity cannot be made with an assumption that our students' Indigenous (or settler) identities are lone or singular ones. True, an Indigenous identity might be proudly proclaimed by some to be a primary cultural marker (and, as we have unfortunately seen, might be denied or downplayed by others). Still, the intersection of Indigeneity with a number of other identities (e.g., sex, gender, sexuality, [dis]ability, socio-economic status, citizenship, etc.) must always be recognized and attended to. We must endeavor to see and welcome attention to all of our students' intersectional identities if we are to also aim to create safe spaces for them.

Relatedly, we must also avoid making statements or drawing conclusions that relate to *all* Indigenous peoples. There are many Indigenous peoples and nations, often within a small geographic area. Attending to and respecting this observation is important. There is no 'single story' narrative for Indigenous students or peoples.

CHALLENGES AND POSSIBILITIES

From experience, we know that our desire to identify and aim for what is just for all may come with some resistance from others. Indeed, we have come across many people in our work (i.e., students, teachers, and teacher educators) who seem unable to recognize their own (often White) privilege and/or who ascribe to colour blind discourses rather than colour conscious ones. For these sorts of individuals, resistance might be expressed or actualized in a myriad of ways, including guilt, denial, and/or anger. Though eliciting these sorts of emotions and feelings is not our primary goal, we believe learning and unlearning may necessarily be a discomforting experience for some. What we really want are allies who are able to recognize their own intersectional privileged (and marginalized) identities and, with that recognition, who can then see a need to take (re)action. Relatedly, we want power to be afforded to others (particularly to those who have been othered)—something that can only be achieved when those in power are able and willing to let go of what has been unearned.

We see great possibilities for physical education, especially if our local physical education teachers attend to the learnings made possible by our local Elders and knowledge keepers. For us, we are hopeful that our local physical education programs (particularly those within MK communities) will offer nature-based/land-based physical education, invite Elders/knowledge keepers into physical education, ensure physical education includes traditional and contemporary Mi'kmaq/Indigenous activities, and include medicine wheel teachings in physical education. It is these sorts of things that might signal to Indigenous students (and settlers) that being Indigenous matters—to what and how physical education is taught within culturally relevant and socially just milieus.

AN ACKNOWLEDGEMENT OF LOCAL ELDERS AND KNOWLEDGE KEEPERS

Lastly, we believe it is also important to recognize the influence many Elders and knowledge keepers have had upon us. While our sharing circles have enabled us to sit down and listen to over two dozen individuals, we are especially appreciative to the following people: Clifford Paul, Danny Paul, Kerry Prosper, Levi Denny, and Michael R. Denny. That these five were willing to offer so much of their time to share their wisdom and knowledge related to culturally relevant physical education for Mi'kmaq children and youth speaks to their passion and desire for ensuring the wellbeing of those within their communities. While the words included herein may be ours, so many of the ideas and ideals expressed with them are theirs. We are humbly appreciative and eternally grateful to all five of these men. Wela'lin.

RESOURCES

1. www.downiewnjack.ca: This website includes information and resources related to Secret Path, an educational program meant to teach children and youth about the impact of residential schools and the treatment of Indigenous people.
2. www.orangeshirtday.org and www.safeandcaring.ca/orangeshirtdayresources: These websites include information and educational resources related to Orange Shirt Day, an event held in Canada on September 30 to recognize the residential school experience, witness and honor the healing journey of survivors, and contribute to the ongoing reconciliation process.
3. www.changethemascot.org: This website includes information and resources related to racial equity, especially as it relates to the offensive use of Indigenous-themed names and images.

REFERENCES

Benjamin, C. (2014). *Indian school road: Legacies of the Shubenacadie Residential School*. Halifax, CA: Nimbus Publishing.

Bombay, A., Matheson, K., & Anisman, H. (2014). The intergenerational effects of Indian Residential Schools: Implications for the concept of historical trauma. *Transcultural Psychiatry, 51*(3), 320–338.

Calder, J., & Fletcher, R. (2011). *Lacrosse: The ancient game*. Toronto, CA: Ancient Game Press.

Coulson, A. (2013). *The creator's game: A story of baaga'adowe/lacrosse*. St. Paul, MN: Minnesota Historical Society Press.

Government of Nova Scotia. (1999). *Physical education curriculum: Grades 7–9*. Halifax, CA: Author.

Government of Nova Scotia. (2010). *Specific curriculum outcomes physical education 11*. Halifax, CA: Author.

Government of Nova Scotia. (2016). *Physical education 4–6 streamlined curriculum*. Halifax, CA: Author.

Halas, J. (1998). "Runners in the gym": Tales of resistance and conversion at an adolescent treatment school. *Canadian Native Education Journal, 22*(2), 210–222.

Halas, J. (2002). Engaging troubled youth in physical education: An alternative program with lessons for the traditional class. *Journal of Teaching in Physical Education, 1*(3), 267–286.

Halas, J. (2006). Developing a white race-consciousness: A foundation for culturally relevant physical education for Aboriginal youth. In E. Singleton & A. Varpalotai (Eds.),

Stones in the sneaker: Active theory for secondary school physical and health educators (pp. 155–182). London, CA: The Althouse Press.

Halas, J. (2011). Aboriginal youth and their experiences in physical education: "This is what you've taught me." *PHENex Journal/Revue phénEPS, 3*(2), 1–23.

Halas, J., McCrae, H., & Carpenter, A. (2013). The quality and cultural relevance of physical education for Aboriginal youth: Challenges and opportunities. In J. Forsythe & A. R. Giles (Eds.), *Aboriginal peoples and sport in Canada: Historical foundations and contemporary issues* (pp. 182–205). Needham Heights, MA: Allyn & Bacon.

Hart, V., Whatman, S., McLaughlin, J. & Sharma-Brymer, V. (2012). Pre-service teachers' pedagogical relationships and experiences of embedding Indigenous Australian knowledge in teaching practicum. *Compare: A Journal of Comparative and International Education, 42*(5), 703–723. doi:10.1080/03057925.2012.706480

Hokowhitu, B. (2008). Understanding the Mäori and Pacific body: Towards a critical physical education pedagogy. *New Zealand Physical Educator, 41*(3), 81–91.

Hokowhitu, B. (2016). Indigenous bodies: Ordinary lives. In D. B. Robinson & L. Randall (Eds.), *Social justice in physical education: Critical reflections and pedagogies for change* (pp. 164–182). Toronto, CA: Canadian Scholars' Press.

Kalyn, B. (2006). *A healthy journey: Indigenous teachings that direct culturally responsive curricula in physical education* (Unpublished doctoral dissertation). University of Alberta, Edmonton, Canada.

Kayln, B. (2014). Indigenous knowledge and health and physical education. In D. B. Robinson & L. Randall, *Teaching physical education today: Canadian perspectives* (pp. 152–176). Toronto, CA: Thompson Publishing.

Knockwood, I. (2015). *Out of the depths: The experiences of Mi'kmaw children at the Indian Residential School at Shubenacadie, Nova Scotia* (4th ed.). Halifax, CA: Fernwood Publishing.

Mi'kmaw Kina'matnewey. (2016). *Annual report 2015–2016*. Retrieved from http://kinu.ca/sites/default/files/doc/2014/Feb/mk_annual_report_2016.pdf

Milloy, J. S. (1999). *A national crime: The Canadian government and the residential school system, 1879 to 1986*. Winnipeg, CA: University of Manitoba Press.

Orr, J., Robinson, D. B., Lunney Borden, L., & Tinkham, J. (2017). "There is a difference": Mi'kmaw students' perceptions and experiences in a public school and in a band-operated school. *Journal of American Indian Education, 56*(1), 55–80.

Robinson, D. B., Barrett, J., & Robinson, I. (2016). Culturally relevant physical education: Educative conversations with Mi'kmaw Elders and community leaders. *Education, 22*(1), 2–21.

Robinson, D. B., Lunney Borden, L., & Robinson, I. (2013). Charting a course for culturally responsive physical education. *Alberta Journal of Educational Research, 58*(4), 526–546.

Salter, G. (1998). Me ako ki nga tikanga Mäori i te reo kori: Culture and learning through te reo kori. *Journal of Physical Education New Zealand, 31*(1), 18–21.

Salter, G. (2000). Culturally responsive pedagogy and the renaissance of a Mäori dimension in physical education. Te reo kori as cultural taonga. *Journal of Physical Education New Zealand, 33*(2), 42–63.

Salter, G. (2002). Locating 'Mäori Movement' in mainstream physical education: Curriculum, pedagogy and cultural context. *Journal of Physical Education New Zealand, 35*(1), 34–44.

Salter, G. (2003). Mäori culture and tradition in the mainstream: Teaching te reo kori in sport education. *Journal of Physical Education New Zealand, 36*(1), 27–42.

Truth and Reconciliation Commission of Canada. (2015). *Honouring the truth, reconciling for the future: Summary of the final report of the Truth and Reconciliation Commission of Canada*. Ottawa, CA: Author.

Whatman, S., Quennerstedt, M., & McLaughlin, J. (2017). Indigenous knowledges as a way to disrupt norms in physical education teacher education. *Asia-Pacific Journal of Health, Sport and Physical Educ ation, 8*(2), 115–131. doi:10.1080/18377122.2 017.1315950

Whatman, S. L., & Singh, P. (2015). Constructing health and physical education curriculum for indigenous girls in a remote Australian community. *Physical Education and Sport Pedagogy, 20*(2), 215–230. doi:10.1080/17408989.2013.868874

CHAPTER 15

EQUALITY AND DIVERSITY IN TEACHER EDUCATION

Developing an Understanding of Race and Ethnicity in the Classroom

Jason Arday

INTRODUCTION

Teacher education within the United Kingdom (UK) has historically been situated within a White majority context. The primacy for this context has been underlined within a Eurocentric curriculum, which prioritizes particular types of knowledge above others. Traditionally, this has been aligned to developing an understanding of pedagogical approaches (James & Pollard, 2014). However, these approaches are not reflective of the post-modern diverse landscape of learners in education (Maylor & Williams, 2011). The diversification of the classroom continues to be an evocative stimulus towards challenging the notion that we now operate within a post-racial global society, which embraces diversity as a symbolic reference to multi-culturalism and egalitarianism. The individuals best placed to advance this narrative are often the educators themselves and by proxy the initial training of trainee teachers then becomes even more imperative (Hicks et al., 2010). Teacher education has consistently failed to address the wider scope of diversity and the

Teaching About Social Justice Issues in Physical Education, pages 185–196.
Copyright © 2019 by Information Age Publishing
All rights of reproduction in any form reserved.
185

varying complexities of this discourse (Lander, 2011; Mirza, 2008). Narrow understandings of diversity among teacher educators have often been compounded by the lack of attention given towards exploring the nuances of 'race' and how this covertly and overtly plays out within the classroom (Aveling, 2002). A clear omission in the vernacular of teacher education discourse, 'race and diversity' is often overlooked in favor of pedagogical proficiency. This is contradictory to an over-arching landscape which posits that we reside in a colour-blind society (Ladson-Billings & Tate, 1995). Importantly, Maylor (2009) states that newly qualified teachers in England have often expressed feelings of inadequacy in being prepared to teach and engage ethnic minority children, despite the rhetoric proffered that multi-cultural education has been a continuous feature of teacher education.

The importance attributed to developing trainee teachers' and teacher educators' understanding of equality and diversity and drawing praxis links with the plight of ethnic minority learners in the UK education system is significant in recognizing the forms of marginalization and oppression that these learners may encounter on a continuous basis (Lander, 2011). An understanding of the societal constructs and binaries which suppress the endeavor of young ethnic minorities from an attainment and ambition perspective allows educators to engage in a brand of pedagogy which is very much aligned to social justice, inclusivity and the opportunity for social mobility (Amico, 2015; Chubbuck, 2010). This echoes the sentiments of Solomon et al. (2005, p. 149) who note that with such demographics it is imperative that pedagogues examine personal attitudes related to their 'racial ascription and social positioning,' as this directly informs classroom practices. The all-encompassing remit of teacher education programs and the time-constrained nature of the initiation process for trainees present a challenge for developing a sufficient and conceptual understanding of equality and diversity issues (Lander, 2011).

This chapter aims to provide a snapshot of pertinent considerations for advancing equality and diversity discourse by teacher educators, in supporting the professional development of trainee teachers preparing to enter the classroom. Further, this chapter argues the importance of developing cultural awareness among trainees as an essential tool in being equipped to facilitate and manage the multi-faceted needs of ethnic minority learners, who reside within a backdrop of societal and institutional constraints, barriers and binaries. Conclusions drawn will highlight recommendations for how teacher education can become more progressive and cognizant of equality and diversity issues in preparing trainees to teach in culturally and ethnically diverse classroom spaces.

UNDERSTANDING THE PROBLEM

One of the salient features of teacher education is the knowledge that is packaged as 'priority' and essential for what is needed to facilitate learning within the classroom (Amico, 2015). Traditionally, this model has often been aligned with having an understanding of pedagogical approaches towards learning and engaging with reflexivity as a tool for professional and personal development as a trainee pedagogue. Governmental pressures regarding the National Curriculum have also played a pertinent role in the lack of attention given towards prioritizing diversification as a valuable instrument for trainee teachers (Maylor & Williams, 2011). The emphasis placed on satisfying the Standards required to achieve Qualified Teaching Status (QTS) can be problematic, often resulting in the neglect of perhaps more pertinent equality issues (Maylor & Williams, 2011; Tomlinson, 2011). The wide remit for developing trainee teachers presents a challenge for teacher educators and students alike due to the need to compress 'priority' knowledge within such a short time period. Maylor and Williams (2011) suggest that such permeations impact upon developing a conceptual understanding of equality issues within teacher education, particularly in adequately preparing trainees to enter the multi-diverse classroom.

Developing an understanding of diversity and more importantly anti-racist teaching is aligned to a concern about developing an awakening of the challenges which many learners from ethnic minority backgrounds encounter (Amico, 2015). Critical pedagogy encourages pedagogues to challenge their world view; this is a diluted concept in teacher education due to what is prioritized as 'essential' knowledge (Amico, 2015). The reservoir of diversification within a teaching context, regards anti-racist approaches as value-laden enterprise underpinned by the principles of social justice and equity (Bhopal & Rhamine, 2014). The refining of this understanding challenges the status quo and hegemonic normativity that pervades through a largely dominant White and Eurocentric curriculum, which perpetuates racial inequality and advances in many cases White dominance (Gillborn, 2008). Much of the dialogue presented also dovetails with a lack of coherent of racialized contexts or the necessary tools to arrest the overwhelming attainment gap in relation to academic achievement for ethnic minorities within the UK education system, particularly for young black boys (Rhamie 2007). Contrastingly, there have been some significant changes regarding equality policy in relation to equality and inclusion in England, which has not been reflected through initial teacher education training programs (Bhopal & Rhamie, 2014).

The Ajegbo Report was published in 2007 and emphasized the complexity associated with understanding diversity and inclusion. Essentially, this report was collated as a navigational tool for recognizing the different understandings of the term 'British' and acknowledged that people construct identities in multiple and plural ways (Ajegbo, 2007). The impact of this report illuminated that the Training and Development Agency for Schools (TDA) should review and evaluate the effectiveness of education for diversity across initial teacher training (ITT) providers, with an emphasis to develop teachers that are culturally cognizant and aware of diversification issues (Ajegbo, 2007; Bhopal & Rhamie, 2014). Conversely, there have also been commentaries (Mills, 2009; Osler, 2009), which suggest that elevating diversity discourse could inadvertently create considerable inequality due to the ideal that this discourse should be prioritized above other inequitable discourses, thus further perpetuating the cycle of inequality. Osler (2009) asserts that in promoting diversification, which has a focus around predominantly ethnic minorities, this may isolate other homogenous groups (for example, White British; Looked-After Children; Individuals with Disability and Traveler Communities) that also require the attention of prospective teachers in truly embracing and facilitating multi-culturalism and multi-diversity.

The present context recognizes an emerging discourse, which encourages an examination of trainee teachers understanding of race, diversity and inclusion in the classroom (Ambe, 2006; Santoro & Allard, 2005). Emerging commentaries (Amico, 2015; Bhopal & Danaher, 2013; Maylor & Williams, 2011; Smith & Lander, 2012) identify a palpable disconnect, which transpires through all tiers of education that reflects a disparity between teaching populations and ever-increasing ethnically diverse student populations. While attempts to address issues of 'race' and inclusion on ITT courses have transpired, which have included engaging trainees in cycles of reflexivity to examine how their own identity or privilege may impact on the classroom space; much of these attempts still lack the penetrative direction required to truly best prepare trainee teachers for negotiating and understanding issues associated with race, diversity and inclusion (Causey, Thomas, & Armento, 2000).

ACTION RESEARCH & REFLECTION

The articulation of diversity remains problematic. There is perhaps a difficulty in articulating how diversification awareness is developed in trainee teachers, that has often been submersed within a fear of being politically incorrect, which can sometimes result in sweeping generalizations about ethnic minority learners (Lander, 2011; Mirza, 2008). Importantly, Ladson-Billings (2011) notes that it has sometimes been difficult to articulate what exactly is wrong about racialized mainstream beliefs and often arduous to argue against negative stereotyping and unconscious or conscious racist practices. Further, Ladson-Billings posits that there is little agreement on how race is defined or what it means in the training of teachers or classroom practices. In essence, we are obstructed by an unwavering paradox which resembles a largely White teaching staff population whose practices, consciously or not, contribute to racial achievement gaps and this becomes particularly evident when teachers have not examined or reflected on their own positionality in relation to issues regarding race, diversification and inclusion (Ladson-Billings, 2011). The utilization of theoretical lenses such as Critical Race Theory (CRT) or Critical Whiteness Studies (CWS) on initial teacher training programs could serve as a bridge towards exploring and deepening an understanding of the racial barriers faced by ethnic minorities, as well as exploring how teachers can help to equip learners to overcome these barriers and build resilience in negating potential racialized societal challenges (Chubbuck, 2010; Ladson-Billings, 2004; McIntosh, 1990).

An intriguing narrative often proffered by educators aligns with the 'language' used to examine issues associated with ethnic minority learners. Lander's research (2011) found that the language used by trainee teachers when examining issues associated with Black and Minority Ethnic (BME) pupils is considered in relation to 'otherness' and a feeling associated with this that many trainees feel unequipped to deal with issues concerning 'race' (Lander, 2011, p. 362). Furthermore, Lander's research revealed that this became more evident with students that resided in predominantly White areas where there is a dearth of ethnic diversity. Significantly, this places further emphasis on developing more inclusive policy-making, in addition to questioning whether initial teacher training operates within a 'neutral, colour-blind and liberal context,' which fails to recognize the impact of Whiteness and dominant Eurocentricity in the initiating of teachers (Lander, 2011, p. 362). Whiteness provides us with an interesting point of departure in examining the advancing of race and diversification in initial teacher training. In considering notions of hierarchy and meritocracy, Whiteness has traditionally operated within an inequitable paradigm, where power relations are often unfair. This vehicle for inequity becomes quite a pertinent consideration when understanding how the conscious or unconscious racist assumptions of a teacher impact their pedagogical identity within a classroom setting (Smith & Lander, 2012). Stereotypical rhetoric concerning ethnic minorities in education is very much facilitated and perpetuated by racist assumptions, particularly in the context of experiencing overt racism during school placements (Taylor, 2009). Conversely, Wilkins and Lall (2011) report contrasting experiences for BME trainee teachers who report positive experiences on ITT courses. Conversely, they also reported feelings of marginalization and experience of stereotypical attitudes regarding overt examples of racism from White peers.

While recent social and academic commentaries (Amico, 2015; Ladson-Billings, 2004; Ladson-Billings, 2011) have highlighted a need for greater race, diversity and inclusion interventions on ITT programs, there still remains a lack of urgency to address the chasm in knowledge regarding trainees' understanding of key diversification issues within an education context. Bhopal and Rhamie (2014) recognize that future educational policy-making must acknowledge the important issues related to race, diversity and inclusion by making this a compulsory component of initial teacher training provision. The prioritization of this issue is central to developing awareness in teacher educators and trainee teachers about the importance of equality, equal opportunity and significance attributed to examining one's own value and belief systems and how this impacts an educator's positionality. This point becomes further exacerbated when we consider recent Ofsted frameworks which have removed the requirement to inspect race equality from school and teacher education provision (Ofsted, 2012). This is indicative of the low institutional priority status given towards addressing diversification issues in teacher education in the United Kingdom more generally (Tomlinson, 2011).

CONTEXT: CHALLENGING BELIEFS AND VALUES SYSTEMS OF TEACHER EDUCATORS AND TRAINEE TEACHERS ABOUT EQUALITY AND DIVERSITY

As reiterated within this chapter, pedagogical identity is paramount to understanding and challenging belief and value systems. This becomes imperative when engaging in cycles of reflexivity to examine how equality and diversity issues affect firstly the teacher, and secondly and perhaps more pertinently the student. As teacher education has largely operated within a large White majority context, it is pertinent to consider White privilege. White privilege is often referred to as a 'form of domination' (McIntosh, 1990). It positions one person or group over another person or group. It is a concept of racial domination that enables us to see this relationship from the perspective of those who benefit from such domination (Amico, 2015). The eminent question which arises from this phenomenon, queries what are the privileges or advantages to which White individuals readily have access over ethnic minorities? The questioning of these societal constructs is essential in determining a level of understanding for the fluid inequity that transpires and continues to disadvantage particular groups which remain on the periphery of social mobility within British society (Davies & Crozier, 2006). An important intervention which could perhaps facilitate greater racial dialogue is the utilization of reflection as a tool for teacher educators and trainees to observe how aspects of their own privilege advantage them (Lander, 2011), in addition to considering how cultures of inequity function to facilitate racism in overt and covert forms. Encouraging educators to consider the effect on the ethnic minority learning experience is integral with regards to residing in an ever-increasing multi-cultural society.

Teacher education has traditionally adopted a hierarchical approach towards the transmission and facilitation of knowledge, which typically asserts that the experienced practitioner is the disseminator of knowledge while the novice teacher becomes the subservient recipient of this 'expert' knowledge (James & Pollard, 2014: Le Cornu, 2005). Perhaps, it is this normative orthodoxy that has been a contributing factor towards teacher educators facilitating a challenging of beliefs and value systems regarding equity and diversity in relation to trainees' understanding the nuances and complexities of ethnically diverse teaching environments (Ladson-Billings, 2004). The cycle of reflexive engagement which very much underpins a cyclical evaluation of pedagogical beliefs and values in initial teacher training could additionally be the catalyst for overtly addressing 'race' and anti-racism on ITT programs. The primacy of 'race' and diversity for some ITT programs has often been an after-thought or a symbolic, tokenistic gesture (Davies & Crozier, 2006). The initiation of trainee teachers situates them onto a path of continuing professional development and for inherent beliefs to be developed and challenged, equality endeavor needs to be prioritized by teacher education providers and trainee teachers themselves tasked with facilitating learning in ethnically diverse learning environments (Bhopal & Rhamie, 2014; Maylor, 2009). Central to developing a broad understanding of diversity, its effectiveness can only be penetrative when we consider the impact on structural diversity, informal interactional diversity and classroom diversity (Ambe, 2006; Gurin et al., 2002). In further unpacking this discourse, the operative lies with an intrinsic motivation to learn about how obtaining a comprehensive understanding of diversity contexts provides a teacher with capital to engage ethnic minority learners, whilst being mindful of their plight and the racialized terrain they navigate on a daily basis (Gillborn 2008).

The unpacking of power and privilege while delicate remains an essential tenet of critical reflexive engagement regarding Whiteness and understanding how this social construct is regarded as normative orthodoxy (Smith & Lander, 2012). For teacher educators and trainee teachers, the acknowledgement that Whiteness represents the universal connation of acceptance and privilege is integral when examining positionality and the conscious or unconscious privileges that ethnic minorities are not readily able to access (Bhopal & Rhamie, 2014). The absence of consideration in acknowledging this plight becomes problematic when we explore notions of 'otherness' and illegitimacy for Black and Minority Ethnic teachers. As such, Blackness (or 'otherness') continues to be posited as a category of deficiency in relation to, or more accurately, in opposition to Whiteness (Ladson-Billings, 2004; Smith & Lander, 2012; Picower, 2009). Smith and Lander indicate that this has serious consequences for the Black teacher whose identity is constituted by students as Black first, teacher second.

The prevailing orthodoxy has inherently always asserted that the majority of teachers are White, therefore where Black teachers are encountered this conflicts with normativity, thus breaking cycles of familiarity among school pupils used to regularly engaging with and being taught by White educators (Smith & Lander, 2012). Smith and Lander (2012) suggest that by exposing complicity in racialization processes which favor Whites and heralds their presence within a teaching construct as normative, we attempt to dismantle the cycle of orthodoxy which pervades within education. Further, they note that we must situate pupils as change agents responsible for transformative practice, by developing mindsets and challenging stereotypes and taken-for-granted assumptions about who delivers, facilitates and engages with the knowledge construction process in education. For educators the focus must be on creating transformative cultures for ethnic minority learners to flourish within an education system in the UK that has traditionally failed ethnic minority learners, in particular young Black boys (Mirza, 2008). These transformative cultures require educators to examine their own value and belief systems, in addition to becoming socially cognizant of the issues that permeate ethnic minority lives from a communal and societal perspective; and the institutional structures that function to disadvantage this particular group

CHALLENGES AND POSSIBILITIES: FUTURE CONSIDERATIONS AND MOVING TOWARDS CHALLENGING NORMATIVITY IN TEACHER EDUCATION

Symbolic gestures towards equality and diversity discourse within the classroom can, in essence only be advanced by prospective teachers, who have the pedagogical agility to challenge and examine their own value and belief systems (Mirza,

2008). Developing an awareness of the dynamics of power and its affiliation with 'Whiteness' becomes essential in recognizing how this privilege and inequity serves to undermine notions of equality and social justice. This awareness becomes an integral instrument towards developing anti-racist educators that sought to acknowledge or disrupt White privilege (Hytten & Warren, 2003; McIntosh, 1990). The gap between words, images and policy makers is evident as we still operate within a society that perceives BME teachers as a novelty, where judgements are based on physical characteristics such as skin colour, which become a dominant feature in rendering an ethnic minority teacher as 'illegitimate' and therefore not as capable as a White counterpart (Ahmed, 2012; Smith & Lander, 2012). This particular rhetoric can be challenged within teacher education by encouraging trainees to examine their own identity and explore how this impacts the classroom and learner context.

STRATEGY/ACTIVITY/LESSON

Importantly, this identity must be interwoven into an over-arching understanding of intersectionality, which encompasses race, class, disability and gender to inform their own experiences in negotiating the subtle complexities and variances of the diverse classroom environment (Gillborn, 2015). Importantly, educators can challenge misinformation about race by creating and developing curricula that encourage the exploration of identity. A tectonic shift is required which changes the narrative from dominant Eurocentric knowledge to a more inclusive multi-cultural curriculum which is reflective of the multiple identities that frame our education system within the UK. Activities could focus on exploring how our multiple ethnicities support tolerance and acceptance within a global society, by tapping into learners' lived experiences as a stimulus for creating conversation and endorsing more inclusive cultures.

Initial teacher education (ITE) providers must bear a significant amount of the responsibility for not advancing this agenda, as there is autonomy outside of Government legislation (in the UK) from the Department for Education (DfE) to tailor knowledge for trainees with the intention of eventually satisfying teaching benchmarks and gaining qualified teacher status (QTS). We can safely assert, that ITE providers have not overtly advocated or prioritized for trainee teachers to be suitably equipped with specific strategies to negotiate racism and acknowledge their own privilege and positionality, in preparation to navigate learners through the racialized, changing societal and political landscape.

LESSON SET-UP

Education policy needs to centralize this issue and reflect the urgency required in better preparing teachers to navigate overt and covert racism within schools, in addition to developing an understanding of racialized contexts that many ethnic minority pupils encounter on a daily basis. Teacher training within Physical

Education requires a re-examination of its practices for engaging ethnic minority learners which recognizes the importance of diversification within lesson preparation and development, as the current model does not examine racial inequality and discrimination in any depth to suitably inform trainees on how they can better engage learners of colour. Issues concerning diversity and racism must stand alone rather than being conflated within an inclusive discourse. The legacy of racism and its centrality are enduring and as such this requires concentrated attention, discussion and analysis to consider how this legacy can be dismantled through a pedagogical paradigm.

Practitioners could develop lessons or set them up in the following ways to facilitate the challenges of dominant Eurocentric practices within Physical Education:

1. Develop Physical Education lessons theoretically and practically that explore physical activity and sport from a more global perspective. This may involve engagement with external agencies in the physical activity sector.

2. Explore the impact of Black and Minority Ethnic sportspeople globally and examine their contribution to sport within curricula. Examples should be used to challenge stereotypes about ethnic minorities within society, particularly stereotypes about young Black boys.

3. Practitioners should look to develop curricula that engages with sports from different cultural diasporas to provide learners with a more global perspective of physical activity engagement. This engagement should extend beyond your own country and focus on physical activity engagement with indigenous populations throughout the world and the types of sporting activity that they engage with.

4. Historical contexts through sociological lenses associated with race, class and gender should be provided which help to position race and ethnicity as something that can be a barrier to accessing physical education/physical activity. Practitioners should also examine the colonial impact of the British Empire on sport historically and how this has impacted the modern context. This can be achieved through open and inclusive dialogue which encourages learners to critically engage in the historical narrative and how racial inequality underpins this.

5. The development of learning materials for teachers to use in Physical Education that are culturally diverse and representative of multi-cultural pupil populations should be carefully considered. In addition, practitioners should be engaged in sessions that specifically address the importance of racial inequality within a Physical Education and Sport context, highlighting how this disadvantages ethnic minorities. Further, lessons should focus on supporting the development of advocacy skills which challenge and disrupt the Eurocentric nature of Physical Education.

6.   Practitioners should endeavor to ensure that textbooks and resources used to engage learners in Physical Education must be culturally representative and diverse in order to reflect a multi-cultural society. This can be achieved through positive and inspiring images that reflect people of colour in a positive light.

EXPANDING THE DIALOGUE

Open discussions perhaps in the focus of focus groups must be encouraged amongst trainees which facilitate reflexive engagement regarding an examination of identity and how a teacher may negate interactions with ethnic minorities who may not have access to the same types of privileges that some trainee teachers may have been afforded. Teacher educators also have a responsibility to challenge the cyclic and normative nature of Whiteness by examining their own belief and value systems and reflecting on how this impacts their understanding of critical pedagogy and the implications for preparing trainees to flourish in the diverse classroom (Gillborn, 2015; Picower, 2009). This could be best exercised through the use of reflexive assignments designed to challenge belief and value systems.

Generally, higher education and the plethora of vocational programs within the Academy such as initial teacher education purport to be a haven for multi-culturalism and diversity. This is often contradictory to the cycle of inequality which continuously pervades as outlined throughout this chapter in education and more specifically concerning the training of teachers. Potential interventions suggested and future recommendations to be implemented must recognize the importance for all educators to acknowledge and prioritize diversity awareness, as a penetrative instrument towards understanding and dismantling fluid inequity, discrimination, power and privilege. Targeted interventions could include teacher educators and trainees having bespoke compulsory modules focused on exploring racism within education and ensuring that school placements are more diverse with regards to staff and student populations. Teachers are an essential tool in advocating this discourse and creating the next generation of agents for change. Fundamentally, initial teacher education has a responsibility to develop culturally aware pedagogues that are receptive to the ever-changing diverse classroom context.

REFERENCES

Ahmed, S. (2012). *On being included: Racism and diversity in institutional life.* Durham & London, UK: Duke University Press.

Ajegbo, K. (2007). *Report the diversity and citizenship curriculum review.* London, UK: DfES.

Ambe, E. (2006). Fostering multicultural appreciation in pre-service teachers through multicultural curricular transformation. *Teaching and Teacher Education, 22,* 690–699.

Amico, R. P. (2015). *Anti-racist teaching.* New York, NY: USA: Routledge.

Aveling, N. (2002). Student teachers' resistance to exploring racism: Reflections on 'doing border pedagogy.' *Asian-Pacific Journal of Teacher Education, 30,* 119–130.

Bhopal, K., & Danaher, P. A. (2013). *Identity and pedagogy in higher education: International comparisons.* London, UK: Continuum.

Bhopal, K., & Rhamie, J. (2014). Initial teacher training: understanding 'race,' diversity and inclusion, *Race, Ethnicity and Education, 17*(3), 304–325.

Causey, V., Thomas, C., & Armento, B. (2000). Cultural diversity is basically a foreign term to me: The challenges of diversity for preservice teacher education. *Teaching and Teacher Education,* 16, 33–45.

Chubbuck, S. M. (2010). Imperatives for social justice in teacher education: Realization in theory and practice, *Teacher Education & Practice,* 23(4), 462–465.

Davies, J., & Crozier, G. (2006). *Diversity and teacher education: Research into training provision in England.* London, UK.

Gillborn, D. (2008). *Racism and education: Coincidence or conspiracy?* London, UK: Routledge.

Gillborn, D. (2015). Intersectionality, critical race theory, and the primacy of racism: Race, class, gender, and disability in education, *Qualitative Inquiry, 21*(3), 277–287.

Gurin, P., Dey, E. L., Hurtado, S., & Gurin, G. (2002) Diversity and higher education: Theory and impact on educational outcomes. *Harvard Educational Review,* 72(3), 330–366.

Hicks, M., Smigiel, H., Wilson, G., & Luzeckyj, A. (2010). *Preparing academics to teach in higher education final report.* Sydney, NSW: Australian Learning and Teaching Council.

Hytten, K., & Warren, J. (2003). Engaging whiteness: How racial power gets reified in education. *Qualitative Studies in Education, 16*(1), 65–89.

James, M., & Pollard, A. (2014). *Principles for effective pedagogy: International responses to evidence from the UK teaching & learning research programme.* New York, NY: Routledge.

Ladson-Billings, G. (2004). Just what is critical race theory and what's it doing in a nice field like education? In G. Ladson-Billings & D. Gillborn. (Eds.), *The Routledge-Falmer reader in multicultural education* (pp. 49–67). Abingdon, UK: Routledge-Falmer.

Ladson-Billings, G. J. (2011). Asking the right questions: A research agenda for studying diversity in teacher education. In Ball, A. & Tyson, C. (Eds.), *Diversity in teacher education* (pp. 383–396). Lanham, MD: Rowman & Littlefield.

Ladson-Billings, G., & Tate, W. F. (1995). Toward a critical race theory of education, *Teachers College Record,* 97, 47–68.

Lander, V. (2011). Race, culture and all that: an exploration of the perspectives of White secondary student teachers about race equality issues in their initial teacher education. *Race, Ethnicity and Education, 14*(3), 351–364.

Le Cornu, R. (2005). Peer-mentoring: Engaging pre-service teachers in mentoring one another, *Mentoring and Tutoring: Partnership in Learning, 13*(3), 355–366.

Maylor, U. (2009). 'They do not relate to Black people like us': Black teachers as role models for Black pupils. *Journal of Education Policy, 24*(1), 1–21.

Maylor, U., & Williams, K. (2011). Challenges in theorising 'Black middle-class' women: Education, experience and authenticity. *Gender and Education, 23*(3), 345–356.

McIntosh, P. (1990). *Interactive phases of curricular and personal re-vision with regard to race.* Working Paper No. 219.

Mills, C. (2009). Making sense of pre-service teachers' dispositions towards social justice: Can teacher education make a difference? *Critical Studies in Education, 50*(3), 277–288.

Mirza, H. S. (2008). *Race, gender and educational desire: Why black women succeed and fail.* London, UK: Routledge.

Office for Standards in Education (OFSTED). (2012). *Initial teacher education inspection handbook.* Manchester, UK: OFSTED.

Osler, A. (2009). Citizenship, democracy and racial justice: 10 years on. *Race Equality Teaching, 27*(3), 21–27.

Picower, B. (2009). The unexamined whiteness of teaching: How white teachers maintain and enact dominant racial ideologies, *Race, Ethnicity & Education, 12*(2), 197–215.

Rhamie, J. (2007). *Eagles who soar: How black learners find paths to success.* Stoke on Trent, UK: Trentham Books.

Santoro, N., & Allard, A. (2005). (Re) examining identities: Working with diversity in the pre-service teaching experience. *Teaching and Teacher Education, 21*, 863–873.

Solomon, R. P., Portelli, J. P., Daniel, B. J., & Campbell, A. (2005). The discourse of denial: How white teacher candidates construct race, racism and 'white privilege', *Race, Ethnicity and Education, 8*(2), 147–169.

Smith, H. J., & Lander, V. (2012). Collusion or collision: Effects of teacher ethnicity in the teaching of critical whiteness. *Race, Ethnicity and Education, 15*(3), 291–309.

Taylor, E. (2009). The foundations of critical race theory in education: An introduction. In E. Taylor, D. Gillborn, & G. Ladson-Billings (Eds.), *Foundations of critical race theory in education* (pp. 1–13). New York, NY: Routledge.

Tomlinson, S. (2011). More radical reform (but don't mention race) gaps and silences in the government's discourse, *Race Equality Teaching, 29*, 25–29.

Wilkins, C., & Lall, C. (2011) You've Got to Be Tough and I'm trying': Black and Minority Ethnic Student teachers' Experiences of Initial Teacher Education, *Race, Ethnicity and Education, 14*, (3): 365–386.

CHAPTER 16

STRATEGIES AND LESSONS IN PHYSICAL EDUCATION RELATED TO RACE

Julie Fimusanmi

ACTION RESEARCH & REFLECTION

According to the Department for Education (2015), English schools (primary and secondary) had more than 8 million pupils of whom over 28 percent were classified as being of ethnic minority origin. However, when it came to those potentially training to be Physical Education (PE) teachers through both dedicated and related courses at University, that percentage dropped by well over 10 percent. For ethnic minority teachers working as PE staff in schools, this fell to less than seven percent.

As advocated by authors such as Alexander and Arday (2015) and organizations including the Office for Standards in Education and Children's Services and Skills, it is important to have a diverse range of backgrounds of staff in schools for the benefit of the community, teachers, parents and pupils. The diversity can encourage greater participation, challenge racist views and abuse, support the learning of ethnic minority pupils and appreciate the learning needs of an increasingly diverse pupil population (Department for Education and Skills, 2007). It is also

Teaching About Social Justice Issues in Physical Education, pages 197–206.
Copyright © 2019 by Information Age Publishing
All rights of reproduction in any form reserved.

important to enhance and celebrate diversity in order to provide an all embracing positive environment and curriculum for all.

Coupled with this, research by authors including Parekh (2006) and Fimusanmi (2010), highlight the issues ethnic minority young people state as negatively affecting physical education (PE) experiences, participation in sport and involvement in school sport, such as racism by staff and officials, a lack of cultural awareness and a lack of role models. This chapter examines the implications of the lack of a diverse teaching population and recommends strategies that can be used to address issues raised by children and in an attempt to create a more level playing field for all.

The author has over twenty years' experience working and teaching in a variety of primary and secondary schools in the north of England, UK, and has worked specifically with ethnic minority young people throughout the north, establishing activities and pathways to alleviate some of the overarching issues, such as racism and a lack of role models. Research and intervention continues to play a large part in her current work, whilst working in a Higher Education setting training future Physical Education teachers. The information contained here stems from ongoing action research, which is part of daily activity.

CONTEXT

Racism is part of the lived reality for an increasing number of children in schools in the United Kingdom. Whilst the population is constantly changing, it could be argued that schools are merely reacting at best and ignoring at worst the global changes that young people are facing. Despite many years of acknowledgement on both sides of the Atlantic regarding racism and its detrimental effects (Fimusanmi, 2010), it can be argued by Macauley (2000), Maylor (2014) and others that issues still exist and rather than problems going away, they are exacerbated and entangled with wider global issues, for example, the rise in Islamaphobia.

Whilst race related issues sit within and alongside subjects such as religion, disability, gender and sexuality, amongst others, there is a notion of intersectionality in which all these have a part to play. The author acknowledges that race cannot be regarded in isolation, but rather than attempt to address all areas, this selection of recommendations addresses primarily race and barriers for young people in schools. Critical race theory, a theoretical framework that is used to examine society and culture as they relate to categorizations of race and power is key to the thinking behind these suggestions. The need for redress is fundamental in these suggestions with diversity and equality at the heart of the changes. Indeed, authors such as Hylton (2012) would go further and state that in order to begin to address white supremacy within PE requires changes in terms of the curriculum, head teachers and even the balance of power within education nationally.

As an academic or teacher, that notion may seem a little far-fetched or out of reach. Therefore, these recommendations are intended to address imbalances at a local level, if you like, at the grass roots. By targeting initiatives bottom up and top down the hope is that they will eventually meet and really have a societal impact.

The children that the initial study was based on were from ethnic minority backgrounds, either first or second generation immigrants totaling over 100 young people across the city of Sheffield, a northern industrial city with a population of over 500,000. Over 50 percent of these young people were either of African or African Caribbean descent. Whilst the experiences of the young people's involvement were subtly different due to factors such as socio-economic income and religion, the experiences in PE were largely similar.

The issues the young people raised fell into five broad categories, which are listed below.

1.   Racism in sport
2.   A need for more recognized role models
3.   Lack of referees and officials from ethnic minority backgrounds
4.   A greater awareness of different cultures
5.   More readily available exit routes into clubs and squads

Although the principle issues and intersectionality can be unpicked further, this chapter focuses on the race element and what can be done within a PE department to address these issues and have a positive effect on diversity. It should be noted that although these measures can be adopted by one department, it takes a school wide effort to make inroads on a significant issue.

STRATEGY/ACTIVITY/LESSON

Throughout my time in schools, much of the teaching was in establishments where those who were regarded as ethnic minorities were in the minority (less than 15 percent of the population). Many felt they were marginalized and the examples used of ethnic minorities across the school were regarded as 'a bolt on' or where individuals were seen as overcoming issues (particularly slavery) and were successful despite oppression. Consequently, the recommendations in this chapter are designed to be cross curricula in nature and planned so that the message throughout the school year is one that advocates diversity as a state of normality rather than exceptionality. It is important to initially talk to all young people and find out from them what works and what does not. This may be in the form of focus groups or questionnaires, and use this as a starting point. By obtaining these perceptions there is a sense of buy in and not being 'done to' but 'with'. It is also worth hearing the view of parents and careers as their involvement can be critical for success. Although the ethnic minority population within a specific school or geographical area may not be high, it is just as important for young people to acknowledge and see the positive contribution all sectors of society can make in the sporting arena.

Recommendations—Role models

The lack of role models is an issue that arises constantly amongst ethnic minority young people from all walks of life. It can be just someone who looks different than the norm, someone who looks like a particular ethnic minority group, someone famous, someone who supports or is an advocate or it could be a referee or an official. I was fortunate that for me a role model who was to become a very famous ethnic minority took me under his wing when he attended an athletics fun day at my school when I was just twelve years of age. Did my teachers know what effect that would have on me? To this day I do not know if the event was planned or a happy coincidence, but it had a positive effect on me and my International sporting involvement for over two decades. The ideas below are designed so that the use of role models is not just a one off event, but a different initiative can be planned each term to accommodate a range of different activities. Some individual steps are provided to assist in achieving these.

Using Role Models from Ethnic Minority Background	How Can This be Achieved ?
• Use famous people such Olympians / Paralympians to talk to pupils • Invite athletes to take part in Q&A sessions • Invite athletes to work in small groups • Invite parents • Use high level athletes who are likely to be less busy, cheaper or free to teach / coach. Think outside the box and rather than sticking with traditional sports why not invite a Latin American dancer in. • Use referees or officials from different backgrounds • Ask trainee PE teachers to offer their services throughout the year • Ask PE students to offer their services and enhance their CV • Introduce a new sport such as Kabaddi with its roots firmly related to the South Asian community. Invite players to demonstrate and teach the activity.	*Contact National Governing Bodies of Sport by email, letter or phone to find out who in the sport does work with young people, what type of work is done and when.* *Use the internet to research individuals who may have an interest in this type of work. Find individuals who attended local schools or clubs or live in the city or county.* *Look at newspapers and see who is doing work in the local community. Many team members are contracted to do a number of hours community work. If you are aware what and who is out there you can extend opportunities that may be mutually beneficial.* *Contact local Universities and use their knowledge of potential students, clubs and local volunteers. They are a vast resource.*

Steps to Take to Use Role Models from an Ethnic Minority Background

Step 1—Choose a sport or activity (e.g. Football, Salsa, Cricket)

Step 2—Search online to obtain names of local athletes from an ethnic minority background who currently play the sport.

Step 3—Contact athletes by phone, e-mail or letter to introduce yourself and the school and what you are trying to achieve. Make it clear in your initial contact what you can offer (e.g., time, payment) and also what type of commitment you are looking for (time, public speaking, intervention work and how many students).

Step 4—Be prepared to meet the athlete both where they train and at school.

Step 5—Work with the athlete to devise a short resume that can be used for any publicity plus gain a recent photograph.

Step 6—Organize what is going to be done at the school, with which pupils and when. It is important to establish what will be done after the initial event as arguably this is where the real benefits can be made (e.g., follow up visits, invites to fixtures, intervention work). A lead in time of at least a month is desirable.

Step 7—Publicize when the athlete is visiting your school. Use posters, fliers, letters to parents for information, letters to the local press, information on the internet, utilize social media.

Step 8—On the day of the event make sure there are photos or videos of the athlete and pupils engaging in activities.

Step 9—After the event send thank you letters to all who have contributed.

Step 10—Make sure all who need to know are informed of any follow up activities.

Step 11—Publicize the success of the initial event so parents, pupils, staff, the media, etc. are aware that the event took place and what will be achieved.

Diversification of the Curriculum

One of the arguments cited by students within Higher Education is that the curriculum is an alienating concept and is dysfunctional being overwhelmingly white, middle class and predominantly male. It is not a reflection of the population in modern day Britain and serves to alienate ethnic minorities by its limited diversification (Ogunbawo, 2012; Paechter, 2000). The same can be said of much of the Physical Education curriculum which centers on a predominantly white curriculum in terms of examples and activities. There are noticeable changes in textbooks, but many schools do not use these often and for an activity performed outside with an inclement climate this is rarely practical. By staff having an arsenal of examples to hand, worksheets and a broader understanding of issues will go some of the way to addressing issues about the curriculum.

Diversification of the Curriculum	How Can This Be Achieved ?
• At Key stage 3 introduce a range of activities which serve to diversify experience such as Movement to music where different styles are introduced such as Salsa and Argentinian Tango. • Use classroom based or wet weather lessons to explore the origins of sports or sports people. • For practical lessons integrate well known ethnic minority sports people as examples. • At Key Stage 4 explore issues that may arise for ethnic minority participants and look at potential solutions. • Use video clips of ethnic minorities participating in sports	*Search the internet for relevant examples of activities that can be used in schemes of work such as through Equality and Diversity organizations.* *Explore examples of good practice. In the United Kingdom these are available through Sport England. Rather than trying to reinvent the wheel adapt and modify others work in order to help diversification of your curriculum.* *Design a range of worksheets that can be used for wet weather lessons that explore the historical context. This could be linked to styles of dance such as Salsa, specific sports e.g. Cricket or sports people such as Alex Scott and Oliver Skeete.*

Steps to Diversify the Curriculum (Designing Wet Weather Worksheets)

Step 1—Design a logo that can be incorporated on worksheets that celebrates diversity. This could be either text, a symbol or a picture, but keep it simple. This can be added to all worksheets, posters, etc. so pupils are aware that diversity has been considered and is reflected in the contents.

Step 2—Take a subject (e.g., styles of dance). Use photos and videos from places such as You Tube to make the subject come to life.

Step 3—Provide a brief section of text to explain issues such as where the dance originated, why it originated, where you may see it today.

Step 4—If the internet is available, it is worth providing questions for pupils to search to find answers such as who are the current world champions, what country has the most dancers of that particular style. A useful starting point is Wikipedia for different styles of dance.

Step 5—If no internet is available, written questions may stem from slightly longer text (e.g., In which country did the dance originate, why are there so many types of this dance (Salsa).

Historical Exploration of New Activities

With the increasing use of league tables based on exam success there are many who will argue that the curriculum is becoming narrower as schools focus on key activities in order to drive standards up. At a similar time with the rise in obesity and a reduction in lifelong participation in sport, there are multiple arguments for a need to diversify the range of activities offered in order to appeal to as many students as possible and promote a healthy lifestyle. The introduction of different activities therefore can be fraught with issues, but for ethnic minorities the potential benefits can be enormous.

New Activities	How Can This Be Achieved ?
• Introduce different activities which provide a wide range of opportunities rather than staying with traditional activities.	*Take a look at the existing curriculum and see what you could add or replace*
• Use a simple questionnaire to find out what the children actually do out of school. Bring these activities into school.	*Ask other staff or older students in school if they have skills to offer, sometimes you may be amazed at what people do in their own time*
• Have a day when new activities take over the curriculum	
• Have taster days / hours	
• Invite new faces to deliver session from a local club or gym	*Visit a taster day or afternoon at a school or sports club to see how mass participation can be achieved and the links that can be made with new organisation.*
• Identify a new activity or sport, e.g. Kabaddi, and include it as a curriculum area or extracurricular activity. Invite pupils, parents and friends to get involved	
• Be realistic about the range of activities you could offer.	

Steps to Take to Encourage New Activities (Organizing a Taster Day)

Step 1—Planning is critical. Make sure the event is on the school calendar. It is worth leaving several months from deciding to do the event to it actually happening.

Step 2—Assign various tasks within an organizing committee. This may only be a handful of people, but do not try to do everything yourself.

Step 3—Agree on a format of what you plan to do. Decide if the activity is in or outside and which year groups are to be involved.

Step 4—Undertake a SWOT analysis of what has worked and weaknesses from the past. A useful tool is to do activities during curriculum time, thereby ensuring that participation will be high.

Step 5—Visit other schools or clubs to see how they organize taster days. An easy way to find out when and where these are happening is to send emails.

Step 6—Arrange for staff, coaches, teachers, etc. to lead the activities. Often a different face is just as exciting for pupils as a new activity.

Step 7—Publicize the event. Use posters, fliers, letters to parents for information, letters to the local press, information on the internet, utilize social media.

Step 8—On the day of the new activities, make sure there are photos or videos of the pupils enjoying the new experience.

Step 9—Distribute fliers to everyone so they know where they can continue to be involved in the activity.

Step 10—After the event, send thank you letters to all who have contributed. Publicize the event on the school website so parents can see what was happened.

Subliminal Messages

According to Fred Barnard in the late 1920s, 'a picture is worth ten thousand words'. It is true that many perceptions of people playing sport originates from images they see on a daily basis. For institutions across the country, there is a reliance on stock photographs or images that can be bought easily often featuring stereotypes such as speedy black wingers in football. Even though many textbooks have moved on, it is fair to say poster and image companies are not so fast moving. Have a look around your workplace and see what messages are being depicted. A simple solution is to alter the sporting images on display around the school. Not only can you have an impact during lesson time it is an opportunity to challenge stereotypes for anyone who sees the images at any time.

Posters/Videos	How Can This Be Achieved?
• Use images in notice boards which celebrate diversity • Display images of ethnic minorities in nontraditional sports. • Display young ethnic minority participants in a range of different activities • Profile a famous ethnic minority athlete, providing information about their background as well as their sporting attributes	*If you are struggling to find the images you want, why not create your own. Through a keen amateur photographer or School photography club, write a clear brief for the images you want.* *A sense of ownership can be created plus this may be a far cheaper way of getting the images you need, royalty free and images you can use on other school based literature.*

Steps to Take to Increase Subliminal Messages

Step 1—Design a logo that celebrates diversity. This could be either text, a symbol or a picture, but keep it simple. This can be added to all posters and website material so pupils are aware that diversity has been considered and is reflected in the contents. It is a great way of subliminally reinforcing a message.

Step 2—Take a look at all posters in the department. For each one with an image, is it possible to change, amend or add another image in order to diversify the message.

Step 3—As each display is changed, consider racial and gender diversity. Make sure displays reflect society and not just the population of the school.

Step 4—Use notice boards to profile a famous athlete or cause (e.g., Jesse Owen, The Williams sisters, Mohammed Ali).

A useful starting point is www.complex.com and Wikipedia.

Adopting Different Learning Styles

Stacking is a term which has gained much currency within the USA and is often witnessed in the UK. For example, many black athletes are deemed to be fast or strong, but are less likely to be in decision making positions such as a scrum half in Rugby Union. In order to challenge this, there needs to be interventions across a range of activities with young people given the belief that they can play in whatever position they want. It is not a quick or fast solution, in fact, it may take several years for ethnic minority young people to believe they are capable of participation in nontraditional roles or officiating. But you can do your part.

It is easy to fall into familiar habits and deliver similar content each year, because it appears to work. However, this may not be received as positively by all pupils. The idea behind the recommendations below is to adapt and change and make the activities which are delivered more student centered. The pupils have more ownership of the delivery, language used, and timing. This can be achieved through using different teaching styles as described through the work of Mosston and Ashworth (1994).

Adopt New Teaching Styles	How Can This Be Achieved ?
• Become familiar with a range of teaching styles and provide opportunities for ethnic minority young people to undertake organizational roles such as a decision maker, organizer or referee • CPD for staff to actively see different approaches in action and to work with other experienced staff to adapt schemes of work.	*For a scheme of work you are familiar or comfortable with adopt a Teaching Games for Understanding (TGfU) or Sport Education approach. Give ethnic minority young people roles which challenge stereotypes.*

Steps to Take to Use a Range of Teaching Styles

Step 1—Become familiar with the range of teaching styles that can be used in PE.

Step 2—Reflect on your own practice. Analyze what you do in which sports / activities.

Step 3—Visit and observe in other schools how Teaching Games for Understanding (TGfU) can work.

Step 4—Actively incorporate TGfU into a scheme of work. Initially, this may involve a fair amount of work, but in subsequent years this will pay off.

Step 5—Assign specific roles to members in each group. Orchestrate for those who are less likely to be vocal to adopt teaching / coaching roles and those who are less likely to be in decision making locations on the pitch, such as a winger to change position.

A useful starting point for TGfu is www.playsport.net

CHALLENGES AND POSSIBILITIES

Although many ideas are suggested here, each one requires thought and sensitivity before implementing. It may also be one activity combines several different areas such as taking pictures of children learning a new activity, assisted by community coaches and supported by parents and friends.

There are many challenges schools face to even think about making changes such as time, money, ideology and philosophy. The challenge is to incorporate changes into the curriculum so that the onus is not on one individual, but the collective being the children and staff. With each new academic year curricula are modified, and it is within this context that changes can take place. Maybe each member of staff takes an area they are familiar with and adaptations are made. Maybe a whole department works collaboratively to achieve change. Maybe a staff, student working party work together to make changes. The choice is yours, however there needs to be buy in from staff and students to make this work. As previously mentioned the starting point is the exploration of the views and perceptions of the pupils. This could be followed up by forming a working party formed of students, staff and parents. The group can decide what the priorities are and who will do which part. Active membership of a working party is something to add to CV's and is a starting point for a school population to buy in to a worthwhile cause.

Any changes that are made are likely to have a long term effect, so do not expect immediate Eureka moments. Staff need to start to think outside of the box, start to address concerns and produce a generation that are able to coexist in an ever changing dynamic world. In order to tackle the issues cited by young people, it will take a generational change.

REFERENCES

Alexander, C., & Arday, J. (2015). *Aiming higher race, inequality and diversity in the academy.* London, UK: Runnymede Trust.

Department for Education (DfE). (2015). *SFR 16/2015 School pupils and their characteristics.* London, UK: HM Treasury.

Department for Education and Skills (DfEs). (2007). *Department for Education and Skills departmental report 2007* London, UK: HM Treasury.

Fimusanmi, J. (2010). *Diversity and divergence: perspectives on inclusion through sport for ethnic minority young people.* London, UK: British Library EThOS.

Hylton, K. (2012). *Talk the talk, walk the walk: Defining critical race theory in research.* London, UK Routledge.

Macauley, B. (2000). Raising the attainment of ethnic minority pupils, what strategies are recognised? *IIMPROVING SCHOOLS, 3*(1), 56–60.

Maylor, U. (2014). *Teacher training and the education of black children. bringing color into difference.* Abingdon, New York: Routledge.

Mosston, M., & Ashworth, S. (1994). *Teaching physical education.* New York, NY: Macmillan.

Ogunbawo, D. (2012). Developing black and minority ethnic leaders: The case for customized programmes. *Educational Management Administration & Leadership, 40*(2), 158–174.

Paechter, C. (2000). *Changing school subjects: Power, gender and curriculum.* Buckingham, UK: Open University Press.

Parekh, B. (2006). *Re-thinking multicuturalism: Cultural diversity and political theory* (2nd ed.). London, UK: Profile Books Ltd.

CHAPTER 17

WELCOMING (STUDENTS')
GOD(S) INTO THE GYMNASIUM

PETE Possibilities for Introducing Religiosity
and/or Spirituality into Physical Education

Daniel B. Robinson and Lynn Randall

BACKGROUND

Like many other contributors to this text, in all of our time as academics, we
have embraced a social justice/critical pedagogy orientation in our work. We note,
too, that this embracement has steadily increased over the course of our careers,
as issues related to social justice/critical pedagogy have garnered an increasing
amount of our attention and (re)action. Some of our earliest and continuing influences include Fernández-Balboa (1997), Freire (1970), Kincheloe (2008), Kirk
(2006), and Tinning (2002), among others.

While we have long embraced this orientation, and attended to these scholars'
work, not until our publication of *Social Justice in Physical Education: Critical
Pedagogies for Change* (Robinson & Randall, 2016a) did we focus, closely, upon
religious minorities as a consideration within physical education. Within that text,
we offered a position that, largely, suggested religious minorities might be best
(i.e., most justly) served when the power and privilege of religious majorities are

Teaching About Social Justice Issues in Physical Education, pages 207–220.
Copyright © 2019 by Information Age Publishing
All rights of reproduction in any form reserved.
207

challenged, interrogated, and/or eliminated. While we continue to believe this to be true, we have since come to also see a/the place for/of religiosity or spirituality within physical education. This emerging position is accentuated by a suggestion recently offered by Robinson (2019):

> ...all our students' identities are multi-layered ones. Prohibiting the expression of religion, even if such a prohibition is meant to make a safer space for religious minorities, denies all students the ability to see, experience and interpret their PE experiences as whole ones. We need PE spaces that welcome the whole student. Religion- or spirituality-free measures cannot achieve this for those who are religious or spiritual. (p. 16)

Our task (and struggle) then is to address the following sorts of questions: How do we make the convincing case to invite and include students' religiosity and/or spirituality into physical education? That is, on what basis can we make such a suggestion for inclusion? Also, given this possibility, how can students' religiosity and/or spirituality be authentically included within physical education? That is, what does such an effort look like in physical education teacher education (PETE) practice? Lastly, how can this all be done while simultaneously protecting the rights and safety of all students? That is, how do we ensure that such efforts will still embrace social justice/critical pedagogy for those who have traditionally suffered the consequences of being othered (see Borrero, Yeh, Cruz, & Suda, 2012) within (physical) education?

CONTEXT

We both teach, research, and serve within PETE programs in Atlantic Canada. One of us works in a province where there is only one PETE program (Daniel at St. Francis Xavier University in Nova Scotia) while the other works in a province where there are only two PETE programs (Lynn at the University of New Brunswick in New Brunswick). Though both of our universities are now secular public ones, St. Francis Xavier University maintains some ongoing Catholic traditions (e.g., priest-led prayers at ceremonies).

Within Canada, most schools are publicly funded and secular. The exceptions include the publicly funded Catholic schools that exist in three provinces (Alberta, Ontario, and Saskatchewan) as well as a small number of secular or religious charter or private schools. Consequently, most of our PETE graduates who remain within the region after graduation will teach in publicly funded secular schools. Some of our graduates who relocate or return to Ontario or the West (as many do) will have opportunities to teach in publicly funded Catholic schools. However, no matter the eventual location or context of our graduates, until recently we have given minimal thought and little-to-no instruction related to considering, inviting, or introducing religiosity and/or spirituality within physical education.

Our longstanding inattention here was largely related to our values about ensuring a safe learning environment for minoritized students (including those students who have been minoritized due to their religious/spiritual beliefs or non-beliefs). With these values, we simply did what many others have also been doing. That is, we ignored religion and spirituality as though they were unwelcome intrusions within secular public primary/secondary and higher education.

While Canada does not have the constitutional separation of Church and State that the Unites States boasts, "any discussion about, or expression of, religion must respect the values and principles embodied in the *Canadian Charter of Rights and Freedoms*" (Clarke, 2005, p. 352). For many, this has meant avoiding religion within schools—in an effort to also avoid accusations of indoctrination and/or a Charter violation. However, we believe such avoidance of risk also misses opportunities to reap the "good philosophical, pragmatic and educational" (Clark, 2005, p. 352) benefits that religious or spiritual attention might offer (some) students. We have come to recognize that this avoidance of risk has also been preventing physical education students from more fully living and embracing wellness, holistically.

Finally, we must offer some insight into our own positionality (Hearn, 2012; Leistyna, Woodrum, & Sherblom, 1996). Elsewhere we have very clearly provided an account of this, especially as it relates to religion (see Robinson & Randall, 2016b). Summarized most simply here: we carry plenty of privilege related to a number of our identities. We are white, able-bodied, heterosexual, native citizens, educated, and relatively affluent. However, we also note that we are both secular, non-religious in all ways—a religious minority.

Our earlier work required us to address perceived potential bias (i.e., humanists suggesting religion ought not to be in public schools might be seen to be self-serving [in addition to or instead of being seen as concerned for all]). However, here we see that, if anything, this identity provides additional license. That is, we are non-religious PETE faculty suggesting that religion and/or spirituality does, indeed, have a place within physical education. We are speaking up for others— that is, for those others who are religious majorities as well as for those who have been othered as religious minorities.

THE CASE FOR INVITING AND INCLUDING RELIGIOSITY AND/OR SPIRITUALITY

We have noted two emerging happenings within Canadian schooling in general, and within physical education in particular, which have been providing an impetus and an avenue for, as our title suggests, welcoming (students') God(s) into the gymnasium. These two happenings have been the following: 1) a multidimensional focus upon health and wellness within (physical) education and 2) a monist and embodied conception of the self, as it is suggested by authentic and foundational physical literacy conceptions (particularly as it has been taken up by Indigenous peoples).

Multi-dimensional Focus upon Health and Wellness

For many years, multi-dimensional models for wellness have been used to frame and fashion health and wellness initiatives and programs. Though variations exist in the number of dimensions within each model (from as few as two to seven or more), most common are five- to seven-dimensional models (Corbin & Pangrazi, 2001). The most common six-dimensional model (see Figure 17.1) includes the following dimensions: emotional, intellectual, occupational, physical, social, and *spiritual* (Miller & Foster, 2010). Given that some emerging theoretical perspectives that underpin physical education are increasingly focused more holistically upon wellness, we see that spirituality can, and likely should, be a part of a wellness-orientated physical education program.

Scholars who have also recently recognized this potential include Kilborn (2014), McCuaig, Quennerstedt, and Macdonald (2013), and McGuire, Cooper, and Park (2006). Relatedly, some of Canada's provinces (which have the jurisdiction and responsibility for public education) are currently redesigning physical education curricula with a "wellness-oriented philosophical perspective" (Kilborn, Lorusso, & Francis, 2016, p. 35). Given these possibilities and happenings, it is clear to us that such a multi-dimensional focus upon wellness within physical education necessitates some attention be given to religiosity and/or spirituality.

Physical Literacy's Monist and Embodied Self

Another more holistic notion of what might be achieved through physical education has garnered great attention within Canada's physical education communities in recent years: physical literacy. Introduced initially by Whitehead (1990), physical literacy has increasingly been embraced by many within the physical

FIGURE 17.1. Six Dimensions of Wellness. Retrieved from http://delraycommunity-wellness.org/about-us/

education (and sport and recreation) sector(s) (see Sheehan, Robinson, & Randall, 2019). Shaped largely by Whitehead's initial and ongoing influence, sector leaders within Canada recently joined together to draft a shared definition of physical literacy (Robinson & Randall, 2017). This consensus definition included four intertwined elements: motivation and confidence (affective), engagement in physical activities for life (behavioral), knowledge and understanding (cognitive), and physical competence (physical) (ParticipACTION et al., 2015).

Notwithstanding the potential of this multidimensional view of physical literacy, it still comes short of meeting Whitehead's articulated foundations related to monism and embodiment, whereby, for example, she cautions against dualist conceptions that may lead to pedagogies that "focus on the body as an instrument" while departing from "whole-body engagement" (Active for Life, 2015, para. 8).

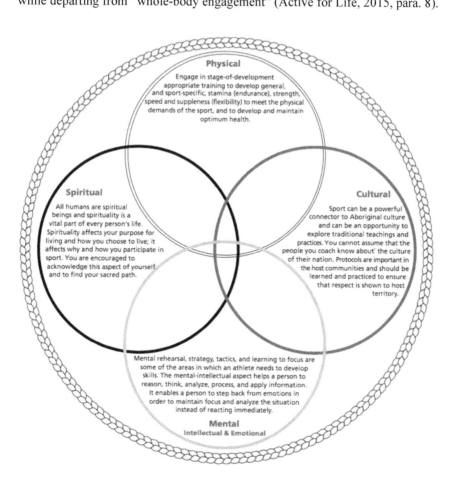

FIGURE 17.2. The Holistic Model. Created by Rick Brant for the Aboriginal Sport Circle (Sport for Life Society, 2016, p. 8).

To this omission, we have been more than pleased to see that Canada's Indigenous leaders have (re)broadened what physical literacy entails with the introduction of their physical literacy-related holistic model (see Figure 17.2). Again, with a more holistic notion of the self and physical literacy, it is clear to us that spirituality ought to be a part of physical-literacy informed physical education programs.

AUTHENTICALLY INVITING STUDENTS' RELIGIOSITY AND/OR SPIRITUALITY: PETE LESSON IDEAS

Let us first remind readers that, as is the case with many issues of social importance, one or two lessons do not necessarily afford students enough time to develop all necessary pedagogical content knowledge and/or deep understanding related to a topic. Still, we are hopeful the ideas presented here will be recognized as ones that may help PETE students *begin* the necessary process of questioning their current practices and assumptions so that they may, in turn, create inclusive lessons and spaces that respect all students' religious and spiritual beliefs and identities. We would also suggest that many of these tasks might be tied to journal/ reflective responses.

LESSON SET-UP

The lesson ideas presented below are intended to be completed in a classroom setting, ideally where an atmosphere of trust has already been developed. We would not suggest conducting the activities at the beginning of the year before students have had an opportunity to get to know one another and feel comfortable with their classmates. Prior to engaging with the ideas below, we suggest the instructor be prepared with the necessary materials (e.g., chart paper, markers, etc.) and consider possible student responses and questions, so they can conduct some independent research based on the possibilities their students may present. Instructors may want to complete the activities themselves prior to using them in a classroom with their students. Instructor responses may provide other areas that may require additional attention and/or research.

LESSON IDEA(S) I: RECOGNIZING RELIGIOUS/SPIRITUAL BIAS AND PRIVILEGE

We believe that students are more likely to participate and actively engage in lessons related to social justice-related topics if they are able to recognize and admit they are biased and/or privileged in the first place. This first lesson includes a word association activity meant to highlight students' biases as well as a Christian privilege survey/walk activity meant to highlight Christian privilege.

Step I. Begin the lesson by asking students to take out a piece of paper. Students cannot complete this activity on electronic devices; they must have a piece of paper and a writing utensil. Instruct students *not* to put their names on their paper. Beginning at the top left-hand margin and continuing down the page, ask students to write the numbers 1–20 (or 30 depending on how many words you decide to use) down the side of their blank piece of paper (one number per line). You will call out a word and the students will write the first word or words that come to mind. With each word called out, students respond in writing, progressing down the page. Begin this process slowly; after approximately five to seven words, begin to speed up the pace at which you are calling out words (i.e., decrease the amount of time students have to react and write). By beginning relatively slowly with the first words and then speeding up (still ensuring enough time for students to write words), there is an increased likelihood that by the time the religious/spiritual words are called out students will be comfortable with the process and will write the first word or words that come to mind (rather than 'thinking' of best answers). Word suggestions for this task include the following (again, we suggest 20–30 words): chair, pen, computer, house, home, school, phone, stick, car, nose, sand, water, cross, bottle, loud, Jew, rain, table, Mormon, clouds, heaven, spoon, Muslim, Christian, soul, Islam, spirit, Catholic, God, Protestant. You can add or remove words you feel would be more applicable to your students' specific context(s).

Step II. Collect the students' papers. On a board, overhead, or chart paper (some method by which all students can see), select a few of the non-religious/spiritual words and compile the student responses. Then, working in columns, with a religious/spiritual word at the top of each column, continue to record each student response to the religious/spiritual words in each of the appropriate columns.

Step III. Analyze the results with students (looking for 'themes', commonalities, original responses, etc.). Consider, for example, posing questions such as, "Do some columns/words tend to have more words that conjure up negative connotations than others? Why is this?" Begin an open discussion about the perceived origins of these connotations and what the implications might be for teaching. As 'homework', students should be tasked with finding stories/examples that counter prevailing or common ideas about a specific religion. Additionally, students can attempt to find a description of a specific religion. For example, in researching 'Christian', 'Muslim', or 'Jew', one is likely to learn, quite quickly, that there are various traditions within each category and attempting to characterize all with a single description is very difficult—not to mention, an oversimplification.

Step IV. Once the idea of bias is presented, introduce students to the notion of religious (Christian) privilege. Using Clark, Vargas, Schlosser, and Alimo's (2002) Christian privilege statements, engage students in an individual survey or blind privilege walk (whereby steps are taken forward for affirmative responses and steps are taken backwards for negative responses). These statements parallel McIntosh's (1988) more familiar "40 Examples of White Privilege" (see also Robinson & Randall, 2016b). At the conclusion of this activity, small and/or large group discussions about observations (e.g., related to oneself and/or the group) ought to explore implications for (physical) education.

LESSON IDEA(S) II: ACCOMMODATING RELIGIOUS/SPIRITUAL MINORITIES IN PHYSICAL EDUCATION

After completing lesson one, it is not uncommon for students to recognize or admit they hold some bias and/or privilege related to religion or spirituality. They may also suggest that they really want to make their classes more inclusive. It is normal, for example, for students to pledge to be (more) open and accepting of religious difference within their teaching spaces. This second lesson includes a 'test' (of sorts) intended to gauge the degree to which students are willing to accommodate religious 'difference', an opportunity to share homework findings from last class, and an introductory activity related to religious/spiritual-based exclusions within physical education.

Step I. Begin the lesson as you normally would, by stating, for example, "We're going to begin today's class by sharing the stories and examples you researched from last class. Who would like to begin?" However, before calling upon a student, quickly interrupt the lesson with an announcement similar to the following:

> By the way, before we begin, I want to share some news. I was at the Department of Education yesterday attending curriculum meetings and, as is often the case when a number of educators get together, our conversations got off-topic. One of the Minister's assistants shared the news that the Department is seriously considering altering the school calendar. Instead of the two-week break at Christmastime and the Easter long weekend, the province/state is looking at rotating the breaks. One year, students will have Christmas and Easter as their main holiday breaks. The following year, Purim, Passover, Shavuot, Rosh Hashana, Yom Kippur, Sukkot, and Hanukkah will be province/state-wide school holidays. In the third year, Al-Hijra, Ashura, Ed Al-Adha, Ramadan, and Eid Al-Fitr will all be public school holidays. This way, no one major religion is privileged over the others. So, within the next year or so, we will be the first province/state to rotate on a three-year cycle.

This script needs to be followed with an invitation for students to share their reactions to this new rotation of holidays. Using the students' responses to this script, introduce the following sorts of observations: 1) we may not be as willing—at least as we verbally profess we want to be—to accommodate religious differences, 2) religion, more specifically Christianity, dominates our life schedules (e.g., Sundays are 'off', main Christian holidays are often national holidays where businesses are closed, etc.). Use this reactive discussion as an entry into considering how others may have to take time off of work or school in order to participate in their own religious traditions (or else, they have to abandon some religious observances to fully participate in public schooling)—all the while others are automatically accommodated. Ask students, for example, "(Why) is this problematic?"

Step II. Revisit students' findings from the end of last class (i.e., have students share the stories/examples they found that counter prevailing or strong ideas about a specific religion).

Step III. Begin by asking why, for the most part, we tend to ignore the need for religious accommodation(s). This could be due to the fact that unless there are specific or obvious signs of religious affiliation (e.g., wearing a bonnet [a head covering worn by some Amish or Mennonite women], hijab [a head scarf worn by some Muslim women], kippah [a cap worn by some Jews], or turban [a long head-cloth worn by some Sikh or Shia Muslim men), teachers are not always aware of the religious orientations of their students. Or, it could be due to the fact that in most Western countries, there is a belief about (or policy or law enforcing) the separation of Church and State. In such environments, education is supposed to be free of religious bias, or presence.

Brainstorm a list of religious practices that may require accommodations and invite students to share ways they can be addressed in physical education. Some of these may relate to the following sorts of questions:

- What accommodations are required for students who elect to adhere to any of the dress codes discussed above, and/or others? Are some unreasonable or impossible?
- Do prescribed physical education uniforms or dress codes interfere with religious dress codes? What could, or should, be done?
- Fasting is often required of Jews and Muslims during specific observances and/or celebrations. What possible accommodations might be possible within physical education?
- Some religions prohibit boys and girls from being together, or touching one another, or being taught by someone of the 'opposite' sex. What accommodations could, or should, be made for these students?

If time permits, you may also want to begin a discussion about how the physical education teacher's religious beliefs can (consciously or unconsciously) impact what and how they teach.

LESSON IDEA(S) III: INVITING RELIGIOSITY/SPIRITUALITY INTO INCLUSIVE PHYSICAL EDUCATION

As previously noted, spirituality is included as an aspect of many multi-dimensional models of health and wellness (as well as in emerging Indigenous physical literacy applications) that are familiar to physical education. We believe, then, that rejecting spirituality within physical education is not ideal—that students' spirituality (including religiosity) ought to then be welcomed within physical education. This lesson includes discussions about possibilities for recognizing the place of religiosity/spirituality within physical education.

Step I. Invite students to perform internet searches of 'wellness models' or 'health and wellness models'. This will yield several results and different (yet largely similar) models. Using a few as examples, note the similarities in models, eventually noting that 'spirituality' is an element of several, if not most, of them.

(We note, too, that students may already be familiar with a model, such as the one presented in Figure 17.1).

Step II. Discuss common notions of spirituality and why students think many teachers avoid directly addressing the topic in class. Topics for discussion may include the following:

- Traditionally, spirituality has been associated with religion. Here, spirituality has often meant developing a relationship with a higher being (e.g., God) and finding meaning in the belief in, and devotion to, a higher being.
- For others, spirituality is also associated with finding meaning in one's life and many have found meaning in life without also having devotion to, or belief in, a higher being.
- Because of the association many make between spirituality and religion, many teachers have intentionally avoided related discussions for fear of offending students and the potential backlash from parents/guardians.
- In health or physical education (i.e., the typical classes where health and wellness are discussed), curricular outcomes generally focus on physical health, healthy eating, social relationships, and mental health. Even where more holistic messages are espoused, rarely can one find curricular outcomes related to spiritual health. However, where there are outcomes related to health and wellness, the teacher can (we would argue, should) introduce and discuss spirituality from a health and wellness perspective.

If class discussion does not adequately address the observation that spirituality is a more 'universal' concept, consider also offering the following:

- More recently, spirituality is understood to be a much broader concept than that associated with religion. Instead of being tied exclusively to those who would describe themselves as religious, spirituality is considered a more universal human experience. Spirituality is broadly understood to be one's personal beliefs, values, and practices that influence the ways in which we come to know, understand, experience, and live in the world. One's spirituality can foster a sense of connectedness to the world around them. This connectedness can be with nature, one's self (e.g., inner peace through meditation), art, et cetera. Spirituality is not a static concept; it changes over the course of one's life. Religious beliefs and customs can and often do influence one's spirituality but spirituality is not dependent upon religious beliefs. Religious beliefs, traditions, and customs are often inherited, whereas practicing spirituality is a conscious choice to find one's sense of place in the world.
- With a more holistic understanding of spirituality, you can begin to invite the exploration of students' personal spirituality. Possibilities include asking students to think about their core values and about the types of experiences that connect them to something larger than themselves. For example,

consider asking, "What makes you whisper, 'wow'?" (e.g., certain spaces in nature, music, an amazing feat of athleticism).
• Begin to explore with students their place in the world and type of person they want to become. Sample questions to begin the discussion include: "When you leave here (i.e., graduate from university), how do you want to be remembered?" "What do you hope people say about you?" "What actions and behaviors do you exhibit in trying to be the person you want to be?" "What types of people do you like to be around and why?"

Step IV. Conclude the lesson by inviting all students to connect their own spirituality to their overall health and wellness. This might be best done by way of a written reflective response.

INTERSECTIONALITIES

Religion is often associated with national or ethnic identity. For example, over 20% of the countries in the world have an official state religion, with similar statistics for countries with a preferred or favored religion (Pew Research Center, 2017). In the Middle East and some North African countries, Islam is the most common state religion while Christianity is the most preferred or favored religion in North America. Of course, this does not mean that all residents of countries with an official state religion practice that religion, but it often adds a layer of oppression particularly when one practices a religion that differs from the state-sponsored or preferred religion of the country in which they reside. Additionally, religion is not restricted to a place, race, gender, sexual identity, or socioeconomic status. For some, religion can be another social marker that contributes to varying levels of inequity.

Note, too, that a recent literature review related to physical education and religion found that most authors purposely attended to the important intersectionalities that exist, especially with respect to gender and culture (Robinson, 2018). Herein, then, we echo the following:

A singular focus upon one identity or issue risks dismissing or misunderstanding the place

> and significance of others. So, though a consideration of the failings and inequities related to social power and influence might focus upon a lone identifier, that consideration must also always recognize the intersectionality of various other and othered identities. (Robinson, 2019, p. 2)

Our advice, then, is to consider the content of this chapter alongside all other content within this text. We would also encourage readers to actively look for intersections between our suggestions (and these identities) and those presented by others in other chapters.

CHALLENGES AND POSSIBILITIES

Religion is complex. It is steeped in history, politics, and culture. Religion is not static; it continuously evolves. To effectively teach about religion, teachers must have a strong background in history, politics, and culture, as well as be knowledgeable in a variety of religious traditions and the variations that exist within each tradition. The background knowledge required to teach about religion is extensive and teachers may feel they do not possess the requisite knowledge to do so. This, combined with the fear of offending students (and/or their parents/guardians) or of being reprimanded if the teacher's words or messages are misconstrued or misunderstood, are primary reasons teachers often give for avoiding religion or religious topics. However, as Sears and Herriot (2016) note, "religion is a ubiquitous and persistent part of modern societies: in other words, it is everywhere and will be a key feature of social interaction into the future" (p. 286). For social justice and equity to be a possibility, we must stop avoiding discussions about religion. Rather we must embrace and thus begin to engage in such discussions for the purposes of educating ourselves and our students, and creating more understanding relationships and inclusive spaces in our schools.

POSSIBLE RESOURCES

1. Christian privilege statements can be found within Clark et al.'s (2002) journal article or Robinson and Randall's (2016b) book chapter. These statements should be shared with students to highlight the idea of religious (Christian) privilege.
2. Project Implicit (https://implicit.harvard.edu/implicit/) offers a number of implicit bias 'tests' for participants. Some address religion. This activity might be used to highlight for students the idea of religious bias.

REFERENCES

Active for Life. (2015). *Margaret Whitehead on physical literacy, the term she invented.* Retrieved from https://activeforlife.com/margaret-whitehead-interview/

Borrero, N. E., Yeh, C. J., Cruz, I., & Suda, J. (2012). School as a context for 'othering' youth and promoting cultural assets. *Teachers College Record, 114*(2), 1–37.

Clarke, P. (2005). Religion, public education and the Charter: Where do we go now? *McGill Journal of Education, 40*(3), 351–381.

Clarke, C., Vargas, M. B., Schlosser, L. Z., & Alimo, C. (2002). Diversity initiatives in higher education: It's not just "Secret Santa" in December; Addressing educational and workplace climate issues linked to Christian privilege. *Multicultural Education, 10*(2), 52–57.

Corbin, C. B., & Pangrazi, R. P. (2001). Toward a uniform definition of wellness: A commentary. *President's Council on Physical Fitness and Sports Research Digest, 3*(15), 3–10.

Fernández-Balboa, J. M. (1997). Physical education teacher preparation in the postmodern era: Toward a critical pedagogy. In J. M. Fernández-Balboa (Ed.), *Critical postmod-*

ernism, human movement, physical education and sport (pp. 121–138). Albany, NY: SUNY Press.

Freire, P. (1970). *Pedagogy of the oppressed*. New York, NY: Continuum.

Hearn, M. C. (2012). Positionality, intersectionality, and power: Socially locating the higher education teacher in multicultural education. *Multicultural Education Review, 4*(2), 38–59.

Kilborn, M. (2014). *(Re)conceptualizing curriculum in (physical) education: Focused on wellness and guided by wisdom* (Unpublished doctoral dissertation). University of Alberta, Canada.

Kilborn, M., Lorusso, J., & Francis, N. (2016). An analysis of Canadian physical education curricula. *European Physical Education Review, 22*(1), 23–46.

Kincheloe, J. (2008). *Critical pedagogy*. New York, NY: Peter Lang.

Kirk, D. (2006). Sport education, critical pedagogy, and learning theory: Toward an intrinsic justification for physical education and youth sport. *Quest, 58*(2), 255–264.

Leistyna, P., Woodrum, A., & Sherblom, S. A. (Eds.). (1996). *Breaking free: The transformative power of critical pedagogy*. Cambridge, MA: Harvard Educational Review Reprint Series.

McCuaig, L., Quennerstedt, M., & Macdonald, D. (2013). A salutogenic, strengths-based approach as a theory to guide HPE curriculum change. *Asia-Pacific Journal of Health, Sport and Physical Education, 4*(2), 109–125.

McGuire, B., Cooper, W., & Park, M. (2006). Pastoral care, spirituality and physical education. *Pastoral Care in Education, 24*(4), 13–19.

McIntosh, P. (1988). *White privilege and male privilege: A personal account of coming to see correspondence through work in women's studies*. Wellesley, MA: Wellesley College Center for Research on Women.

Miller, G., & Foster, L. T. (2010). A brief summary of holistic wellness literature. *Journal of Holistic Healthcare, 7*(1), 4–8.

ParticipACTION, Sport for Life Society, the Healthy Active Living and Obesity (HALO) Research Group at the Children's Hospital of Eastern Ontario Research Institute, Physical and Health Education (PHE) Canada, Canadian Parks & Recreation Association, & Ontario Society of Physical Activity Promoters in Public Health. (2015, June). *Canada's physical literacy consensus statement.* Retrieved from http://stage. participaction.com/sites/default/files/ downloads/Participaction-CanadianPhysical-Literacy-Consensus_0.pdf

Pew Research Center. (2017). *Many countries favor specific religions, officially or unofficially: Islam is the most common state religion, but many governments give privileges to Christianity.* Washington, DC: Author. Retrieved from http://www.pewforum. org/2017/10/03/many-countries-favor-specific-religions-officially-or-unofficially/

Robinson, D. B. (2019). Religion as an other(ed) identity within physical education: A scoping review of relevant literature and suggestions for practice and inquiry. *European Physical Education Review, 25*(2), 491–511.

Robinson, D. B., & Randall, L. (Eds.). (2016a). *Social justice in physical education: Critical reflections and pedagogies for change*. Toronto, CA: Canadian Scholars' Press.

Robinson, D., B., & Randall, L. (2016b). (Un)holy spaces: A consideration of religious minorities in health and physical education. In D. B. Robinson & L. Randall (Eds.), *Social justice in physical education: Critical reflections and pedagogies for change* (pp. 206–247). Toronto, CA: Canadian Scholars' Press.

Robinson, D. B., & Randall, L. (2017). Marking physical literacy or missing the mark on physical literacy? A conceptual critique of Canada's physical literacy assessment instruments. *Measurement in Physical Education and Exercise Science, 21*(1), 40–55.

Sears, A., & Herriot, L. (2016). The place of religion in education for citizenship and social justice. In A. Peterson, R. Hattam, M. Zembylas, & J. Arthur (Eds.), *The Palgrave international handbook of education for citizenship and social justice* (pp. 285–304). London, UK: Palgrave MacMillan.

Sheehan, D., Robinson, D. B., & Randall, L. (2019). Physical literacy in Canada. In M. Whitehead (Ed.), *Physical literacy across the world*. New York, NY: Routledge.

Sport for Life Society. (2016). *Aboriginal long-term participant development pathway.* Retrieved from http://sportforlife.ca/portfolio-view/long-term-participant-development-pathway-1-1/

Tinning, R. (2002). Toward a "modest pedagogy": Reflections on the problematics of critical pedagogy. *Quest, 54*(3), 224–240.

Whitehead, M. (1990). Meaningful existence, embodiment and physical education. *Journal of Philosophy of Education, 24*(1), 3–13.

REFERENCES

Azzarito, L., MacDonald, D., Dagkas, S., & Fisette, J. L. (2017). Revitalizing the physical education social-justice agenda in the global era: Where do we go from here? *Quest,* 69(2), 205–219.

Bain, L. (1975). The hidden curriculum in physical education. *Quest* 24(1), 92–101.

Bain, L. (1990). A critical analysis of the hidden curriculum. In D. Kirk & R. Tinning (Eds.), *Physical education curriculum and culture: Critical issues in the contemporary crisis* (pp. 23–42). New York, NY: Falmer Press.

Dodds, P. (1985). Are hunters of the functional curriculum seeking quarks or snarks? *Journal of Teaching in Physical Education, 4*, 91–99.

Evans, J. (Ed.) (1993). *Equality, education and physical education*. London, UK: Falmer.

Fernandez-Balboa, J. M. (1993). Sociocultural characteristics of the hidden curriculum in physical education. *Quest, 45*(2), 230–254.

Fernández-Balboa, J. M. (1997). Physical education teacher preparation in the postmodern era: Toward a critical pedagogy. In J. M. Fernández-Balboa (Ed.), *Critical postmodernism in human movement, physical education, and sport* (pp. 121–138). Albany, NY: State University of New York Press.

Freire, P. (1970). *Pedagogy of the oppressed*. New York, NY: Herder and Herder.

Kirk, D. (1986). A critical pedagogy for teacher education: Toward an inquiry-oriented approach. *Journal of Teaching in Physical Education, 5*, 230–246.

Robinson, D. B., & Randall, L. (2016). An introduction. In D.B. Robinson and L. Randall (Eds.), *Social justice in physical education: Critical reflections and pedagogies for change* (pp. 1–14). Toronto, CA: Canadian Scholars' Press.

Tinning, R. (2002). Toward a 'modest pedagogy': Reflections on the problematics of critical pedagogy. *Quest, 54,* 224–240.

Walton-Fisette, J. L., & Sutherland, S. (2018). Guest editors on special issue: Exploring social justice issues in physical education teacher education. *Physical Education and Sport Pedagogy, 23*(5).

CHAPTER 18

HAVING FAITH IN RELIGION AND/OR SPIRITUALITY WITHIN PHYSICAL EDUCATION

Samantha Zanini

ACTION RESEARCH AND REFLECTION

As a student, I attended elementary, junior high, and senior high school in an urban publically-funded Catholic school board. I never questioned why or how my religion was connected to an entire school district and I was certainly unaware of the religious diversity that existed within public schools. As a pre-service teacher, I enjoyed a diverse array of placements. I was placed in an urban public junior high and senior high school, an urban charter elementary school, a rural Catholic elementary school, a rural public middle school, and an Australian urban public elementary school. At the time, I was aware of religious differences in the schools, but I was not 'reflective' enough at the time to consider the influence of my students' intersectional identities on their own learning. Upon graduation, I was hired at a private non-denominational school in an urban Canadian community. After my fifth year of teaching in 2016, I started my Master of Education (MEd) degree. There, my peers and I were formally introduced to social justice issues and how we can start addressing them in physical education (PE). The very first course started with us considering our own invisible knapsack of the privileges and per-

Teaching About Social Justice Issues in Physical Education, pages 221–235.
Copyright © 2019 by Information Age Publishing
All rights of reproduction in any form reserved.

spectives we carried into our teaching practice (MacIntosh, 1990). One identity that I had never considered, until then, was my religious denomination and how it afforded me power and privilege within education and PE contexts.

I was very intrigued by this self-discovery so for my first assignment, I selected religion as an identity to investigate. This assignment required me, among other things, to offer suggestions for inclusive and just PE teaching practices. Though I was certainly pushing my comfort levels with the topic, in hindsight, I was just 'scratching the surface' by researching best practice for teaching Muslim students. In Robinson's (2018) scoping review, it was noted that, "almost all research and conceptual articles related to religion have focused upon Islam/Muslims" (p. 11). When I thought about all the religions there are to learn about and consider (particularly as those considerations related to inclusive PE), I knew there had to be a better way to address religion. Or, rather, I knew I could do more.

As I continued in the MEd program, I felt more empowered to identify and "challenge the role of the majority religion, Christianity" (Robinson & Randall, 2016, p. 214). I had gained insight on my own faith's impact on my teaching practice and considered a handful of specific religions' voices in PE. But, I was still not confident in addressing the topic with my students. I wanted my students to understand how their own religion might impact their involvement in PE and, moreover, their motivation to be active for life. But what about students that did not adhere to a religion? How can you create a fair and inclusive learning environment for all degrees of religiosity?

For example, in 2017, I had a few students observing Ramadan during the last month of school. After conversations with each of them, I realized their fasting practices varied. Some students fasted the entire day, some had shorter time frames because of their age, and some were allowed certain snacks throughout the day based on their expected energy exertion. This solidified for me the idea that students of a similar religion cannot be treated the same when making a classroom inclusive. The most important element is creating a safe space for religious identities, or any identity, to be discussed, welcomed, and accepted.

Fortunately, the concept of spirituality, which is open to a broad scope of interpretation, is absolutely individualized and can encompass religious identity, denomination variance, and those who have no religious affiliation. The conversation about religion and/or spirituality can therefore be approached in PE a few different ways. At the 2013 International Physical Literacy Association (IPLA) Conference in Banff, I heard Margaret Whitehead speak about monism and embodiment as a philosophical foundation for physical literacy, which I took away as a reason (or license) to teach about the connection of the mind and body through activity. This is the most basic and approachable idea for students, especially for those that do not identify as religious or spiritual. Benn, Dagkas, and Jawad (2011) presented a similar idea, though more affiliated with religion in stating, "attention to embodiment, faith and physical education could help to increase understanding for more inclusive practice" (p. 23). Although they discussed the Islamic religion specifically, the concept gives many students a chance to consider their religious identity and their bodies. Finally, the Aboriginal Sport for Life manual presents a Holistic Model based on the medicine wheel comprised of balancing the physical, mental, cultural and spiritual elements. Herein, spirituality is prominent because it "affects our purpose for living and how we choose to live it" (Sport for Life Society, 2016, p. 11). This model is one that all Canadian students can learn about regardless of their own religious background. Students can consider their own spiritual beliefs and have the opportunity to learn more about the Indigenous community of Canada.

My goal, most simply, is to make PE an inclusive space that welcomes the whole student (Robinson, 2018). To do this, all students' identities and intersectionalities must be considered. In PE, students can have the opportunity to acknowledge their religious or spiritual identity when considering their participation and motivation to be active for life.

CONTEXT

This is my seventh year at the private non-denominational school I was hired at after finishing my Bachelor of Education (BEd) degree. I have taught in the classroom, in the gymnasium, and from elementary to senior high. Currently, I teach a racially diverse and high academic group of Grade 7, 8, and 9 students aged 12 to 15 years old. The subjects I teach are PE and Health Education (HE). Though I have carried the assumption noted by Kahan (2011) that, "religion, ethnicity, and national origin are often intertwined" (p. 22), until recently I have only openly discussed ethnicity and national origin with my students. Religion was somehow a taboo topic and never addressed in my teaching practice. Robinson (2018) brings to light the idea that religion is still an identity of students that teachers need to consider in their practice. In attempts to make a more inclusive learning space and to help students identify their own intersectional identities, I have pondered and found an area in our curriculum where religion and/or spirituality can be addressed.

Within my province (Alberta), the *Do It Daily for Life* general curriculum outcome for PE aims to have students assume "responsibility to lead an active way of life" (Alberta Education, 2000, p. 28). "Effort" is the first category in that section and has the following specific curricular outcomes:

> D 9.1 Students will participate regularly in, and realize the benefits of, an active lifestyle, and
>
> D 9.2 Students will develop a personal plan that encourages participation and continued motivation. (Alberta Education, 2000, p. 28)

These outcomes present an opportunity for students to first reflect on their own religion and/or spirituality. Once they consider their individual values and beliefs, there will then be an opportunity to consider the physical, mental, cultural, and spiritual benefits described in the Holistic Model (Sport for Life Society, 2016). Ideally, if planned and carried out in a lesson, students will then have a model to follow for their lives. Students can then recognize the connection between their values and physical activity, and make an individual plan for participation and motivation for life. We as PE teachers can plan activities and lessons where the goal is religious and/or spiritual identity fulfilment.

LESSON SET-UP

- This lesson is one way to introduce the concept of wellness within a PE or HE class. It builds a caring community within the class at any point in the school year. If you have already introduced a wellness model, you can take certain activities and use them where suitable.
- The lesson is designed to be completed in two sixty-minute block classes for twelve to fifteen year old students. It can be taught in a classroom, outside, or in a gymnasium.
- A labyrinth can be created outside on a tarmac surface with chalk (see Figure 18.1). The following website gives a step-by-step classic pattern to follow: https://labyrinthsociety.org/make-a-labyrinth. If you are not able to go outside or do not have a tarmac area, the labyrinth walk could be done in a classroom between desks by putting them together sporadically beforehand with student assistance (see Figure 18.2). It could also be done in a gymnasium and students could select a line colour to walk along.

FIGURE 18.1.   Fenty, C. Chalk classic labyrinth. From The Labyrinth Society, Labyrinth in places. Retrieved from https://labyrinthsociety.org/labyrinths-in-places.

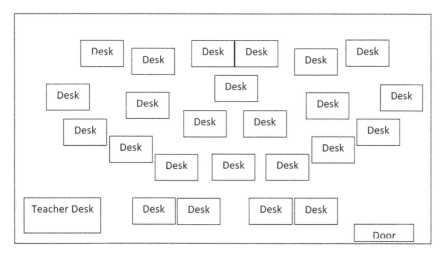

FIGURE 18.2. Desk labyrinth in a classroom.

• Organizationally, have a system for students to store Exploring Wellness Dimensions and four copies of the Post-Activity Reflection handouts (see Appendix A, B, and C) after the activity classes (such as a duo-tang, folder, or simply stapled together).

THE LESSON(S)

Lesson Part 1: Introducing the Dimensions of Wellness and Personal Values

Materials—Class copies of Exploring Wellness Dimensions (Appendix A and B), three index cards per student, labyrinth

Objective—Explain to students that the objective is to understand wellness and spirituality, embrace the diverse benefits of physical activity, and consider motivation needed to participate for life.

Hook—What is wellness? Ask students to talk to their neighbor about the question for two minutes. Have students raise hands to share their answers and thoughts.

Introducing and Understanding the Dimensions—Give students a copy of the Exploring Wellness Dimensions handout and read aloud the multi-definition of wellness. Explain that the visual for wellness is often a circle to represent the balance needed among the dimensions (see Figure 18.4 in Appendix A). Have student volunteers read aloud the information about each dimension (see Figure 18.5 on Appendix A). Explain to the students that each dimension will be discussed, but the focus will be on the spiritual dimension. Note that spirituality can be interpreted differently for all individuals. It is often glossed over because religion is viewed as a sensitive subject and the two, spirituality and religion, are intertwined. Explain that we need to create a space that everyone feels comfortable considering their own connection to all the dimensions of wellness.

Think, Pair, Share Responses—Have students individually write or draw responses to the two questions on the second page of Exploring Wellness Dimensions (see Appendix B). On the closest section to the central figure, they will be considering ways they find wellness in that dimension. On the outer section, they will be writing general barriers or groups of people that would be challenged to find fulfillment. Next, have the students pair with someone who is not next to them to discuss both responses to the physical, intellectual, and emotional dimensions. Then, ask if any groups would like to share their responses on how they find wellness in the physical dimension. Follow up by asking them to share their responses to challenges or groups that would be challenged to achieve satisfaction. Continue the class discussion in the same way with the intellectual and emotional dimension. Next, have the students find a new partner to discuss both responses to the occupational, social, and spiritual dimensions. Then, follow in the same way by asking the groups to share their responses about the two questions for each dimension of the remaining three dimensions. Below are examples from the Canadian Mental Health Association (2016) for each dimension, should you want to supplement their responses:

- Physical wellness: "get plenty of sleep and rest, do relaxation techniques, eat healthy, drink water, play sports, walk or run, go for a bike ride, exercise."
- Intellectual wellness: "learn something new that you want to, read or write, ask for help, problem solve, set realistic goals, look for areas to grow, create."
- Emotional wellness: "set time for yourself, listen to music, read, watch a movie, be creative, journal, keep a sense of humour, think positively."
- Occupational wellness: "talk to teachers or counsellors, use daytimers and calendars, balance school and leisure activities, learn new study strategies, join a club, team, or activity, ask for help, take breaks."
- Social wellness: "talk about your feelings, find someone who understands, volunteer in the community, spend time with loved ones, ask for help, be around pets."
- Spiritual wellness: "enhance the things that give a purpose to life, practice religious or spiritual beliefs, be grateful for something every day, do what you believe is ethical and right, read a religious or spiritual text, yoga, travel, think positively."

Why Be Well?—Have students consider the six dimensions and ask them which dimension influences their motivation to achieve wellness the most? Perhaps they will say occupational to ensure they make enough money to accommodate for a lifestyle of wellness or perhaps they will say social as their friend group will influence their choices in many of the dimensions. Guide them to the spirituality dimension which forces everyone to consider the bigger question of, "Why should we try to achieve wellness?" Explain that it comes down to individual values. Ask students where people learn values. If no one says religion, explain that it is an influencing factor for many people. Interpretation of religion and/or spirituality is individually unique as even those of the same religion may not understand or practice it in the same way. A religious person can be considered spiritual, but a spiritual person may not necessarily be religious. Some people would not identify as either religious or spiritual, but they still have values that guide their life. Brainstorm a list of values on the board or share a list of values.

Labyrinth Walk—Explain that they will now do a reflective labyrinth walk to consider two questions: "What are my values?" and "How do they guide my life and purpose?" Labyrinth walks are an active way to contemplate individually so there should be no talking in respect for each other's thoughts. Tell students to think about their family, religion, and childhood lessons or memories while walking along the path. Explain that this activity will be done for a set time (depending on your time frame) so there is no rush nor is it a race. When the time is finished, students will come back and write down their top three values, each on a separate index card so they can be shared with the class through a gallery walk.

Closure—Have students put their index cards face up on a central table, gather around to gallery walk, and read each other's values. Note aloud the diversity and similarities in the responses. Summarize that today we looked at the dimensions of wellness and how we can fulfill them, focusing on the values. We acknowledged the spiritual dimension and the question, "Why be well?" Share that the next day, we will then take our understanding of values and consider what is personally the best activity to aim for spiritual fulfilment.

Lesson Part 2: Religion and/or Spirituality, Values, and Physical Activity

Materials—Sheet of paper describing each aspect of the Sport for Life (2016) Aboriginal Holistic Model (see Figure 18.3), eight blankets or tarps, signs of the top eight general values from last class, four pages and pens for group brainstorm of activities.

Objective—Consider the impact of spirituality on a model designed to support participation in activity for life and connect how students' values can be fulfilled through participation in diverse physical activities by highlighting elements of those activities beyond the physical skill set.

Hook—Start class by sitting in a circle (around the centre circle of the gym) and introduce the Aboriginal Holistic Model. Have the circle divided into four sections and have the four aspects described on sheets of paper in the sections for students to read as they arrive (physical, cultural, spiritual, and mental—intellectual and emotional). Ask students to think about and then share with others in their section of the circle why the aspect they are sitting in front of would be important for people when developing as a participant or competitive athlete in sports. Have students recall the six dimensions of wellness from last class and consider similarities.

Value Blanket—In both models, there is affiliation with a spirituality component. This model's objective is helping people understand how to be active for life

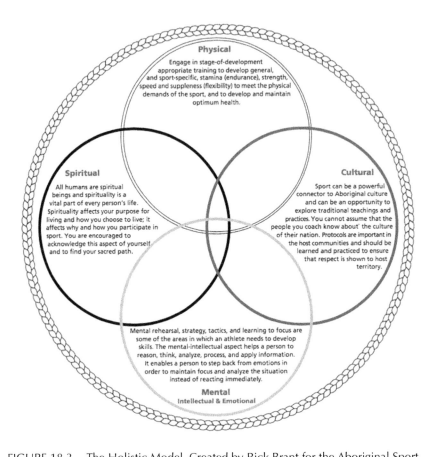

FIGURE 18.3.   The Holistic Model. Created by Rick Brant for the Aboriginal Sport Circle (Sport for Life Society, 2016, p. 8).

by addressing each aspect while the model from last class was aimed at achieving overall wellness. As discussed last class, individual values must be acknowledged when understanding spirituality. Explain that around the gym are blankets that represent the top eight general values shared last class. Students are to consider which value is most important to them when participating in activity. Share a personal example as a guide. For example, I value community as it was a big part of my Catholic faith growing up. I have felt spiritual fulfillment from team sports, because it places an emphasis on working together and helping each other. I also value gratitude, so going for a run outside allows me to value my able body and nature. Ask students to consider the question, "How is spirituality being fulfilled in the elements of the activities you do, or could do for life?" Have students walk around to see the value options (one being "other" for students who do not feel their value is represented by the majority) and then sit on the blanket with the value they connect most with or want to connect with during activity. Once everyone has selected a blanket, each person will share (or choose to not share) why they sat at that blanket. They could give an example of when they felt the value was fulfilled in an activity or why that value is important to them without relation to activity. Encourage students to talk about their families, childhoods, and religions if they practice, or why they do not follow a religion. After all the students have shared, ask one spokesperson from each blanket to share a summary of the conversation at the blanket with the class.

Activity Brainstorm—Keeping the insights from the blanket sharing opportunity prevalent, students will now consider how to select activities that will help them fulfill the spirituality component. Have students break off into the four earlier sections of the Holistic Model. Assign each group a broad PE activity category of body management (yoga, dance, martial arts), individual sports (cross country running, singles badminton, tennis, golf), team sports (soccer, volleyball, basketball), or low organized games (tag, capture the flag, rock paper scissor challenges). Have groups brainstorm as many activities they can for that category and then select one that can be carried out in class. Explain that one activity will be selected each day and then at the end of class, there will be a period of reflection on the fulfillment of each dimension of wellness by showing and explaining the Post-Activity Reflection (see Appendix C) to the students. They will first list the activity of the day, rate their fulfillment in each dimension (see Figure in Appendix C), and write about their values from previous brainstorms.

Closure—Applaud the students for their efforts, sharing, and brainstorming. Explain that we are just skimming the surface of everyone's diverse value set and only sampling the many activities that can bring fulfillment in the spiritual dimension. Note that we are carving steps to take when considering how to select activities for life, and the ways and reasons to be motivated to be active for life. As an exit activity, have students share with a partner one activity that they have yet to try, but would like to at some point in their life.

Activity Classes—For upcoming classes, select an order for the four activities and trying one each day. For the last ten minutes of class, have students fill in a copy of the Post-Activity Reflection. Once all activities have been completed, have the students compare their four reflections and consider which type of activity would be best to help them fulfill their spiritual dimension of wellness and why that would be important to them for the future. Have students share their findings with a partner and then share as a class.

INTERSECTIONALITIES

Religion cannot be viewed as only one piece of the puzzle in isolation. To quote Aristotle, "the whole is greater than the sum of its parts," meaning the interaction of diverse identities are what make a student whole, rather than separating the parts and then adding them together. Religion is especially connected to other identities, because it is through religion that values are learned and expectations are set regarding other identities. One of Robinson's (2018) main findings was that the intersection of religion with gender and culture is increasingly prevalent in today's literature.

The Islamic Koran teaches men and women to dress modestly, but to also match gender-appropriate attire. This affects boys and girls differently in PE with clothing pieces, such as a hijab, being suitable for girls but not suggested for boys. This teaching would also affect anyone whose gender does not align with biological sex. Watson, Weir, and Friend (2005) look back at Christian influence on sport and there is only reference to boys and improving manliness. The absence of female presence through history of sport and Christianity speaks volumes. In both examples, gender and religion intersect to subtly exclude girls from PE.

Sexual orientation is another area of religious teaching. For example, the Christian Bible dictates that homosexuality is sinful. This was a challenge for an athlete I coached at a Catholic school who was dating another girl on the team. Her parents were not accepting of her sexual orientation and she felt extreme guilt, which in turn, negatively affected her athletic enjoyment. Religion affects culture through their spoken and unspoken expectations, which are engrained into all facets of identity. How these identities interact with each other make the whole student and need to be considered.

CHALLENGES AND POSSIBILITIES

The first challenge of this lesson is understanding the dynamic relationship between intersectional identities for each student and creating a community of respect. Depending on students' previous experiences talking about religion and spirituality, there will be variation on the apprehension or willingness to discuss and share. Students may already have negative perspectives about bringing up their religion outside of their family. Sparking an interest, making it relatable to the group of students, and ensuring an environment of respect is essential. There may also be parental concerns with religion or spirituality in PE. If parents contact you with concerns, first and foremost, consider it a success, because that means students are talking to their parents about the lesson! Next, embrace the opportunity to share the concept with parents and be willing to have an open conversation. By hearing their perspective, you also gain insight as to how their child may understand religion or spirituality, which can help you connect with that student in their learning.

In general, addressing the social issue of religion in schools is challenging because of "Christianity's foundational influence and ongoing privilege" (Robinson, 2018, p. 9) in Western schooling contexts. We need to be reflective and critical thinkers about the current structure to ensure "different" religions are welcome in PE. Twietmeyer (2008) suggested that PE needs to move from traditional Christian ideas of dualism to modern Christianity's perspective of monism, uniting the mind and body. Once this is accomplished, the next step is uniting the mind, body, and spirit as attempted in the lesson. Another area of dissonance to consider is 'new' PE and HE curricula that may conflict with Christian-influenced teachers' own beliefs.

Most often, these teachers will follow their own value set rather than fulfill their obligation as a teacher to achieve the mandated student outcomes (Macdonald & Kirk, 1999). Although it is professionally challenging to extract and analyze these cataleptic situations in PE, a concerted effort must be made in acknowledging and accommodating religious diversity. Herein lies the possibilities and hope.

It is common for PE teachers to accommodate for diverse physical abilities. If a student uses a wheelchair, we can modify the rules to a game to maximize participation. If a student was excelling at a skill, we can layer on challenges, Or, if a student was not finding success at a skill, we can modify the equipment. In the same way, we can make religious accommodations while maintaining active participation, designing challenging opportunities, and developing confidence. A few examples that Robinson (2018) suggests for Islamic/Muslim students are to allow students to wear hijabs in class, offer modest PE clothing options, organize classes to have a female instructor if available on staff, choose electives that do not involve revealing attire (e.g., swimming), and arrange PE classes to the morning so students who eat early breakfast before fasting will have more energy. Another accommodation would be arranging an annual plan so lower intensity units are during fasting periods as well.

Accommodations stem from thinking outside of the box and having conversations with the student to discover what can be changed so everyone has the opportunity to be involved in PE. I hope this chapter has encouraged you to start that discussion with all your students. Talk about the taboo topic of religion, discuss the glossed over spiritual component of wellness, and have faith that your classroom can become even more accepting and inclusive.

APPENDIX A:
EXPLORING WELLNESS DIMENSIONS (PAGE 1)

"Wellness is:
- an active process through which you become aware of, and make choices towards, a more balanced life
- a conscious, self-directed and evolving process of achieving your full potential
- a multi-dimensional and whole-self lifestyle
- positive and self-affirming"

(University of New Hampshire, 2018)

FIGURE 18.4 Six dimensions of wellness. Retrieved from http://delraycommunity-wellness.org/about-us/

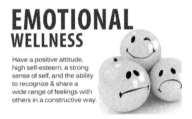

FIGURE 18.5. Definition of dimensions. Retrieved from http://www.unh.edu/health/ohep/wellness

APPENDIX B: EXPLORING WELLNESS DIMENSIONS (PAGE 2)

1. In the inner section, closest to the figure, write or draw ways that you find satisfaction in that dimension of wellness.
2. In the outer section, furthest from the figure, write or draw general challenges or groups of people who would be challenged to find satisfaction in that dimension of wellness.

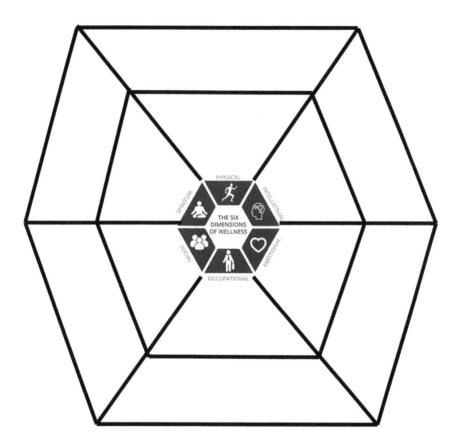

APPENDIX C: POST-ACTIVITY REFLECTION.

Today' Activity: _____

1. Check a number in each dimension to indicate how satisfied you are after the activity. The higher the number, the more fulfilled you are in the dimension. Draw a line across at the number to make a trinagle and new edge on the hexagon.
2. Are your dimensions balanced? If not, which are highest and lowest?
3. Why were you balanced, or had some high and some low?
4. What values did you feel were satisfied in the spiritual dimension?

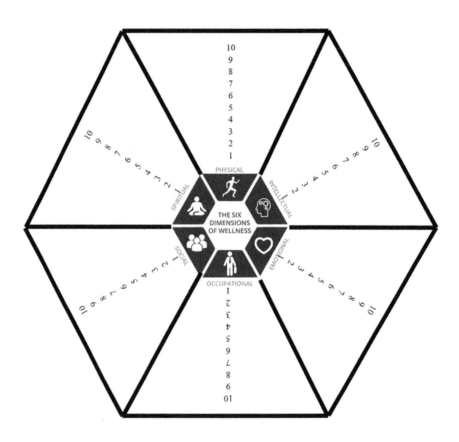

REFERENCES

Alberta Education. (2000). *Physical education program of studies*. Retrieved from https://education.alberta.ca/media/160191/phys2000.pdf

Benn, T., Dagkas, S., & Jawad, H. (2011). Embodied faith: Islam, religious freedom and educational practices in physical education. *Sport, Education and Society, 16*(1), 17–34. doi: 10.1080/13573322.2011.531959

Canadian Mental Health Association. (2016). *Youth mental health education: Stress management junior high 2017*. Retrieved from http://cmha.calgary.ab.ca/youth-mental-health-education/

Definitions of Dimensions [Image] (2018). Retrieved April 12, 2018, from http://www.unh.edu/health/ohep/wellness

Fenty, C. (2018). *Chalk classic labyrinth* [Photograph]. Retrieved July 8, 2018, from https://labyrinthsociety.org/labyrinths-in-places.

Kahan, D. (2011). AAA roadmap for navigating religion in physical education. *Strategies 24*(4), 20–24. doi: 10.1080/08924562.2011.10590939

Macdonald, D., & Kirk, D. (1999). Pedagogy, the body and Christian identity. *Sport, Education and Society, 4*(2), 131–142.

MacIntosh, P. (1990). White privilege: unpacking the invisible knapsack. *Independent School Winter 90, 49*(2), 31–36.

Robinson, D. B., & Randall, L. (2016). (Un)holy spaces: A consideration of religious minorities in health and physical education. In D. Robinson & L. Randall (Eds.), *Social justice in physical education* (pp. 206–247). Toronto, CA: Canadian Scholars' Press Inc.

Robinson, D. B. (2018). Religion as an other(ed) identity within physical education: A scoping review of relevant literature and suggestions for practice and inquiry. *European Physical Education Review*, 1–21. doi:10.1177/1356336X17747860

Sport for Life Society. (2016). *Aboriginal sport for life long-term participant development pathway*. Retrieved from http://sportforlife.ca/portfolio-view/long-term-participant-development-pathway-1-1/

Six dimensions of wellness [Image] (2018). Retrieved April 12, 2018, from http://delray-communitywellness.org/about-us/

Twietmeyer, G. (2008). The theology of inferiority: Is Christianity the source of kinesiology's second-class status in the academy? *Quest, 60*(4), 452–466.

Watson, N.J., Weir, S., & Friend, S. (2005). The development of muscular Christianity in Victorian Britain and beyond. *Journal of Religion & Society, 7*(1), 1–21.

CHAPTER 19

SOMEWHERE OVER THE RAINBOW...

Queer(y)ing Physical Education Teacher Education

Leanne Coll

THE QUEER POTENTIALS OF PHYSICAL EDUCATION

How can we [as teacher educators] teach ourselves and our students to deconstruct what is "there," what is not "there," and that, in fact, there may be multiple "theres"?

—*Loutzenheiser (2005, p. 125)*

My work is largely centered on how concepts of normality (heteronormativity) are embedded in the spaces, places, pedagogies and everyday moments of schooling (including physical education settings). I am interested in the ways in which (cis)gender and (hetero)sexual norms are ignored or left unchallenged by both students and teachers. My thinking has been shaped by scholarship which has documented the heteronormative landscape of physical education (Clarke, 2006; Larsson, Redelius, & Fagrellet, 2011), the effects these norms have on students' and teachers' experiences irrespective of their sexual identity (Gard, 2003; Lars-

Teaching About Social Justice Issues in Physical Education, pages 237–249.
Copyright © 2019 by Information Age Publishing
All rights of reproduction in any form reserved.

son, Quennerstedt & Öhman, 2014; Sykes, 2011) and the queer potentials of physical education (Landi, 2018; lisahunter, 2017).

As a researcher and pedagogue, I am passionate about the conditions and possibilities of transformation and what it might mean to work collaboratively with pre-service students and young people to interrogate heteronormativity. Interrogating norms, as well as re-iterating them, is not something that only adults-researchers-educators do (Renold, 2017). Queer moments are also led or initiated by young people and pre-service teachers (Coll & Charlton, 2018; Harris & Farrington, 2014; Larsson, Quennerstedt & Öhman, 2014; McGlashan & Fitzpatrick, 2017). These creative capacities warrant not only the attention, but the response of researchers-educators who are open to being transformed by their students' perspectives and priorities (Coll, O'Sullivan & Enright, 2017; Enright, 2013).

For me, navigating and exploring the thresholds between research-activism-pedagogies is important. Theories are not just something I think or read about, they 'slip and slide against personal histories, ways of knowing, and the lived experiences' (Childers, 2013, p. 600). A queer theoretical perspective, as described by Piontek (2006), is rooted 'not in an identity, but a questioning stance, a cluster of methodologies that let us explore the taken for granted and the familiar from new vantage points' (p. 2). The notion of queer pedagogy constantly circulates in my work and frames my thinking about sexuality, identity, teaching and learning. Queer pedagogy is not about teaching and learning about queer identities; rather, queer pedagogy is an inquiry approach into the conditions that make learning possible or prevent learning. Focus is not on 'what knowledge matters?,' but instead on 'what is the matter with this knowledge?' (Britzman, 1995). Queer pedagogy, according to Britzman (1995, p. 13), identifies 'questions concerning what education, knowledge, and identity have to do with fashioning structures of thinkability and the limits of thought'. This suggests that teachers and students become less interested in 'reporting existing knowledge' and more interested in 'inquiring into the ways knowledge becomes available, the ways knowledge is structured, and the ways identities are continually formed through curriculum identifications' (Sumara & Davis 1999, p. 204). Queer pedagogies necessitate a shift away from understanding or 'learning' towards a focus on 'unlearning', towards uncertain and daring directions for curriculum and pedagogy.

Through my work, I encourage my students to explore how their own everyday experiences are imbued with various degrees of heteronormativity, and to consider the problematic effects of these understandings for all young people not just those who find themselves on the margins of strict (hetero)sexual and (cis) gender boundaries. My aim is to foster opportunities to collectively question how educators-students come to know, how knowledge is produced (Luhmann, 1998) and to doubt the knowledge on offer (Britzman, 1995). I am interested in the potentials of being irritated, unsatisfied, and even uncomfortable in classroom spaces (Alexander, 2014; Quinlivan, 2012). I raise questions regarding, what it might mean to be surprised, shocked, thrilled into new forms of knowing?

CONTEXT

Queer(y)ing Physical Education Teacher Education (PETE)

For the past eight years, I have worked in various capacities and roles in Physical Education Teacher Education (PETE). Durig this time, I have been afforded invaluable opportunities to work with pre-service teachers around topics of gender, sexuality, and their relationships to teaching and learning. In my current role as a Lecturer in Health and Physical Education (HPE) at Deakin University, Melbourne, Australia, I work with pre-service teachers enrolled in the Bachelor of Health and Physical Education (BHPE) course. As a teacher educator my focus is on interrogating pedagogical approaches to HPE in units such as 'Introduction to HPE', 'Professional Issues in Teaching HPE' and 'Teaching Sexuality Education'. I also work with graduate students in an online MEd 'Social Justice and Difference' unit and through various supervisory roles engage with Masters and PhD students.

In my engagements with students, I encourage them to question how norms surrounding gender-sexuality impact young people's experiences of physical education. Drawing students' attention to the norms of their own/my own pedagogical practice provides us with opportunities to collectively consider what might be missing or who/what is privileged in our pedagogical approaches as educators. In my 'Professional Issues in Teaching HPE' unit, the first four weeks is dedicated to engaging with the potentials and challenges of transformative pedagogies (including queer pedagogies) for HPE. In my Teaching Sexuality Education unit, the focus is placed firmly on troubling concepts such as sex, gender, sexuality, privilege and power, and pedagogical approaches to sexuality in and through education. Regardless of what I teach, I always place a strong emphasis on disrupting traditional notions of Physical Education with my students and believe that prospective teachers need to be given opportunities to understand how they have been both oppressed and privileged by the content and pedagogical practices that make up schooling systems. I think that prospective teachers need to be encouraged to be creative thinkers and critical consumers of curriculum.

Engagement with queer forms of praxis thread through both my pedagogical and research encounters. Most recently, I have been working on a participatory activist project with a group of 12 pre-service teachers "Working Beyond Binaries". The purpose of this project is to work towards interrogating aspects of heteronormativity in everyday teaching practices through a critical and collaborative engagement with critical norm and queer based pedagogies. In actively engaging 'with' pre-service teachers beyond the scope of university-based courses and into classroom spaces I have been afforded opportunities to explore the boundaries, challenges and potentials of norm critical work. These stories have carried through and are enmeshed in my own teaching. The sequence of activities that follow are a combination of activities/provocations that I have used both in my teaching and participatory based research engagements (Coll & Charlton, 2018; Coll, Enright & O'Sullivan, 2014) .

SET UP AND LESSONS

Queer Pedagogical Tools, Strategies and Provocations

The primary purpose of the sample lessons, provided in this chapter, is to work collaboratively with pre-service teachers to challenge taken for granted assumptions surrounding sex-gender-sexuality and to think a little differently about how matters of sex-gender-sexuality play out in physical education settings. Each lesson has been designed to provoke teacher educators and pre-service students to rethink and queer their pedagogical approaches to, and experiences of, physical education. Lesson one focuses on deconstructing normative associations and conflations between sex assigned at birth, gender identity, gender expression and sexual identity. Lesson two shifts attention towards (a) the heteronormative landscape of physical education and (b) pedagogical potentials to disrupt heteronormativity that too often go unnoticed. Lesson three will engage with the transformational potentials of physical education and opportunities for educators and students to collaboratively create, rethink and queer physical education.

Lesson One: Deconstructing Sex-Gender-Sexuality
Introduction Activity: Brainstorming Sex, Gender & Sexuality
(Adapted from Ollis, Harrison, & Maharaj, 2013)

Materials Needed: Poster paper (A3 or larger), pens/markers, tacks

Activity Process: In groups of 3–4 students, write down as many words, definitions or phrases that they can think of that fit under each of the following headings:
• Sex
• Gender
• Sexuality
When groups are ready, stick each sheet of paper to the wall so students can look at the different responses to the task. This activity is an opportunity to start where students are and will act as a springboard/reference point for subsequent activities.

Activity Debrief Questions:
a. Are there any differences and similarities in your responses?
b. Are there any terms, words or phrases that you struggled to place under a specific heading?
c. What do you think the purpose of a task like this might be?

Key Considerations:
In my experience of this task, I have noticed that students often conflate sex assigned at birth with gender identity in their responses. For example, they may list body parts (e.g., breasts or penis) under the gender heading. In facilitating this activity, it is important to discuss how these terms are distinct. Sex assigned at birth (by a medi-

cal practitioner) is largely determined by physical and biological attributes such as chromosomes, hormones and internal and external sexual organs. Common understandings would suggest that there are only two sexes, but this is not the case. Someone who is intersex is born with variations in hormones, chromosomes or sexual organs that differ from conventional ideas about what it means to be female or male. It might be worthwhile to discuss the following question "where does the category of 'male' end and 'intersex' begins, or where 'intersex' ends and 'female' begins?" On the other hand, gender identity relates to an individual's sense of themselves as non-binary, man, woman, both, or neither. It's important to make the distinction that sex assigned at birth and gender identity do not always neatly align, this distinction is particularly important in recognition of intersex and trans identities.

Activity Process continued:
In the same groups, give students one/two of the following terms and ask them to place them in the appropriate heading(s). If students are unsure, give them some time to do some research on their assigned term(s) online.
- Cisgender
- Intersex
- Demi-romantic
- Asexual
- Gender-queer

This additional task allows students to explore how sex-assigned at birth, gender identity, gender expression, sexual identity and romantic/sexual attraction do not always neatly align. It also provides an opportunity to disrupt dominant understandings of and intersections between feelings, behaviours, and identities.

Activity Debrief Questions:
a. What might have been the decision-making process behind assigning these additional terms?
b. Was there anything about this task that surprised you or challenged your thinking?
c. If you identified/identify as any of the terms listed, how might this task make you feel?
d. As educators, how might we approach a task like this differently? What norms are challenged? What norms are reinforced?

Additional Resources:
The following are useful teaching resources that will assist in the planning, preparation of and engagement with this activity. Specifically, accessible ways to engage with definitions of sex, gender and sexuality and challenge dominant ways of knowing with students:
- Gender Unicorn (useful handout on sex, gender and sexual identity, expression and behaviour): http://www.transstudent.org/gender/
- All of Us Resource (Building blocks of identity pages 24, 34, 38): https://www.studentwellbeinghub.edu.au/docs/default-source/all-of-us-online-version-may-2016-v3-pdf2af89fb756c645d9b8492a68a39765f6.pdf?sfvrsn=0
- TomGirl Documentary (a useful resource to trouble the conflation between gender identity and gender expression): https://vimeo.com/147551380

Activity Two: Gender Expression and Sexuality
(Adapted from RFLS Ungdon, 2012)

Materials Needed: Depending on group size, 4 or 5 copies of picture cards pages 18–31 from the RFLS Ungdon (2012) resource 'Break the norm', Whiteboard, Whiteboard pen/marker, Computer with AV data projector and audio kit

Activity Process: In groups of 4-5, give students a set of picture cards (RFLS Ungdon, 2012, pages 18–31). Each group should spread the pictures out on a large table or on the floor in plain view of all. Ask each group to compile a selection of pictures of all the individuals who they think "look heterosexual/straight". Encourage the groups to talk about their selections and keep note of their decision making-process. As a whole group, compare and contrast how the pictures were selected and list the words on the board – e.g., clothes, background, job, family, etc.

Key Considerations: What tends to happen in the facilitation of this task is that groups (a) struggle to make decisions or refuse to complete the task and (b) create two piles of pictures (those who they believe to be homosexual and those they believe to be heterosexual) even though this was not the task allocated to them. It is important to emphasize how this task is more about raising and holding the right questions as opposed to generating the 'right answers'. It is also important to use this task to challenge some of the normative assumptions surrounding the alignment between gender expression and sexuality. Gender expression relates to how individuals express various masculinities and femininities through for example clothing, demeanor, movement etc. How one expresses their gender is not necessarily related to their gender identity. Both gender expression and gender identity can be fluid and change over the course of one's life, and they need not change together. Gender expression may be a way of playing with external gender performance and exploring roles, while gender identity relates to a sense of self. Those who break gender roles or expectations are often presumed to be homosexual, while this may not be the case. Sexual identity refers to individuals' romantic and sexual attraction to others, or lack of attraction. The idea behind this task is to complicate understandings of sex-gender-sexuality. For example, a person whose sex assigned at birth is male, but whose gender identity is woman, may identify with a full range of sexual identities including (but not limited to): heterosexual, queer, bi-sexual, pansexual, etc. Gender identity or expression does not determine sexual or romantic attraction.

Activity Debrief Questions:
a. How do norms specific to femininity and masculinity impact our decision-making processes for this task?
b. How might norms which surround race, ability, class, age or ethnicity impact our decision-making processes?
c. How difficult/easy was this task to complete? What made this task difficult/easy?
d. Why might it be easier to talk about deviators from norms as opposed to the norm itself? What are the implications of this?
e. Was there anything about this task that surprised you or challenged your thinking?

f. As educators, how might we approach a task like this differently? What norms are challenged? What norms are reinforced?

Lesson Two: Queer(y)ing Physical Education
Activity One: Tango Role-play
(Adapted from Coll, Enright, & O'Sullivan, 2014)

Materials Needed: Computer with AV data projector and audio kit, Tango music, Whiteboard, Whiteboard pen/marker

Activity Process: Tell the students you are going to role-play a dance lesson scenario. Depending on group size you might like to ask for six volunteers or divide the group into pairs, facing each other. Ask each pair to assign the role of 'female dancer' and 'male dancer'. The facilitator assumes the role of 'teacher'. As the 'teacher', organise the students and tell them that the focus of today's lesson will be on "Relationships & Body Dynamics" through Tango. Get the group to brainstorm words/phrases they might associate with the relationship between dancers in the Tango (e.g. good chemistry, natural flow and movement). Now work with the group to brainstorm the ideal body dynamics that they would expect for each role. Here are some examples to work with:

Female Dancer	Male Dancer
Submissive	Dominant
Follower	Lead
Elegant	Aggressive
Compact	Sharp
Dramatic	Strong
Silky foot movements	Defined Movements

Tell students that when you play the Tango music they are to try to emulate the relationship and the body dynamics listed for their assigned role through their movements. As they move, the 'teacher' should circulate, reinforce and provide feedback on how the female dancers and male dancers are working to the criteria you have set. When giving instructions or feedback make sure to refer to the students as "female dancers" and "male dancers".

Key Considerations: This role play is an opportunity to interrogative some of the norms and expectations that often go unnoticed within the most mundane and incidental moments of physical education. Heteronorms are so embedded within physical education rituals, practices and routines that many young people, teachers and members of school communities accept them without questioning their implications. I have used this activity in the past to discuss how physical educators teach about gender, sexuality, race, ablism and class when we teach about bodies, movement and physical culture. Recognising the unintentional normative aspects of our teaching is important not only in order to reconsider the learning opportunities we provide students but also the role physical educators play in larger movements towards socially justice educational practices.

Activity Debrief Questions:
a.   What story or stories are we told about sexuality in this role-play? (What are the hidden messages, assumptions, norms, or expectations about sexuality?)
b.   What story or stories are we told about gender in this role-play? What do your answers so far highlight about the relationship between gender expression and sexuality?
c.   Was there anything about this role-play that surprised you or challenged your thinking?
d.   As educators, how might we approach a role play like this differently? What norms are challenged? What norms are reinforced?

Activity Two: Physical Education Case Study
(Drawing on Larsson, Quennerstedt, & Öhman, 2014)

Materials Needed: Copies of pages 142 & 143 from Larsson, Quennerstedt, & Öhman (2014), Whiteboard, Whiteboard pen/marker

Activity Process: In pairs, ask students to read pages 142 and 143 and discuss what is going on in the classroom scenario. Once they have had time to discuss in their pairs, bring the group together and debrief.

Key Considerations: In this short extract from their data, Larsson, Quennerstedt, & Öhman (2014) emphasise the queer potentials and queer moments in a dancing lesson and opportunities for students to discuss the heteronormative structure of the lesson. What is particularly poignant in this case, however, is the teacher's openness and willingness to change their practice based on students' suggestions. In order to challenge heteronormativity with young people, Larsson, Quennerstedt, & Öhman (2014) suggest more teachers should create spaces for discussions about the normative underpinnings of the subject and practice in question, including cultural norms that engender, and privilege, certain behaviours and identities while marginalising others. Larsson, Quennerstedt, & Öhman (2014) stress how some young people are already challenging heteronormativity, but educators are struggling to keep up or even at times to recognise it. There are "challenges that often fizzle out" if educators are not aware of the cultural implications of their teaching, of students learning and of subject areas within which these assumptions are based.

Activity Debrief Questions:
a.   What are the core issues this scenario raises?
b.   What surprised you and/or challenged your thinking?
c.   What are the implications of this scenario for (1) you as a professional, (2) the profession of Physical Education, and (3) students that you work with?

Lesson Three: Pedagogies of Possibility for Physical Education
Activity One: Activist Movement(s)

Materials Needed: Students will need Laptop/Tablet devices

Activity Process: In addition to what needs to be challenged in Physical Education, it is important to work with students to consider what can be transformed through Physical Education. From public flash mobs to live theatre, dance activism can play a powerful role in communicating experiences that are sometimes difficult to put into words. In groups of 4–5, students must research different ways that people have shared and taken action on gender-sexuality related social justice issues through dance. To help them in their search, facilitators might like to provide them with an inquiry starter pack pointing them in the direction of relevant hashtag campaigns, dance flash-mobs or dance productions (some samples included below). This task will allow students to engage with projects that have made a difference in their own communities, home country and beyond.

Sample Dance Activisms:
- http://www.ballez.org/
- https://www.dv8.co.uk/projects/archive/to-be-straight-with-you
- https://fellowsblog.ted.com/a-dance-for-transgender-lives-on-the-margin-2941bf246efa

Activity Debrief Questions:
a. From your research, is there anything that inspired you, surprised you or challenged your thinking?
b. What are the implications of your research for (1) you as a professional, (2) the profession of Physical Education, and (3) students that you work with?
c. How might we use an inquiry-based task like this with students in schools? What might we need to do differently?
d. Are there any extensions to this activity that might be productive?

Activity Two: Stop and Start
(Adapted from Renold, 2016)

Materials Needed: Red and green paper plates, string, pegs, markers/pens

Activity Process: Building from the previous task, give each group three green START plates and three red STOP plates. Ask the group to list on each of the STOP plates three things that they think needs to be challenged in Physical Education around gender-sexuality (based on experiences from various tasks and discussions). Once they have done this, ask them to list on each of the START plates three things related to gender-sexuality that they would like to transform through Physical Education. Using these STOP-START plates and their research from the previous task, ask the group to create a dance which represents the journey from STOP to START. They can draw inspiration for their movement sequence from their research on dance activism. The facilitator might select a piece of music for the group or allow each group to select their own.

Activity Debrief Questions:
a. Tell us about the dance that you have choreographed, what inspired you? What did you find challenging?

b. How might you use a movement based task like this with students in schools? What might we need to do differently?

c. Are there any extensions or alterations to this activity that might be productive?

TEACHING FOR DISRUPTION AND DISCOMFORT

Too often pedagogical approaches to sexuality tend to fall 'under the guise of settling controversy, celebrating difference, and teaching for tolerance' (Sandlos, 2012, p. 285). Britzman (1998) has argued that concepts such as empathy and tolerance can mobilize in ways that are pedagogically problematic. Teaching for tolerance or grasping for empathy often translates into 'already privileged' (Quinlivan, 2012). In contrast, Alexander (2014) emphasizes how:

> ... the call to 'work' or think queerness in the classroom should not focus solely on introducing our many straight students to queer lives and stories; rather, working queer- ness in the writing classroom should be an invitation to all students—gay and straight—to think of the 'constructedness' of their lives in a heteronormative society. (p. 375)

Inspired by queer pedagogues and queer theorists, the series of lessons provided in this chapter are an attempt to interrupt normative understandings of and privileges surrounding sex-gender-sexuality with pre-service teachers. It is also an attempt to critically and creatively explore how norms and privileges impact on pedagogical approaches to physical education. The dialogic, critical and reflective nature of this lesson points toward a pedagogical philosophy rather than a particular set of teaching strategies.

Putting queer pedagogy 'to work' has forced me to consider the extent to which the enactment of queer ideas 'provokes emotions that not only need to be acknowledged and negotiated, but also attended to and worked with as part of the pedagogical process' (Quinlivan, 2012, p. 512). It is important that the activities suggested are approached with an awareness of the emotionality associated with the potential discussions that might be generated and the potential impact they may have on teacher-student and student-student relationships and/or learning (Quinlivan, 2012). This lesson demands teacher educators and their students 'to do much more than learn that which affirms how they already understand themselves and what they already believe' (Kumashiro, 2002, p. 69).

Engaging with privilege in classroom spaces is tricky. It is often difficult for educators and students who are privileged by norms to see how others might be affected by them, and sometimes even hard for individuals to recognize that norms exist. For educators-researchers-students, often the hardest task is to maintain an obligation to those by whom we feel ourselves to have been injured, or whose difference from us seems severe (Coll & Charlton, 2018). Kumashiro (2004, p. 113) suggests that 'one barrier to anti-oppressive teaching is the very notion that good teaching happens only when students respond in ways the that we want them to respond'. Kumashiro (2004) suggests that teaching paradoxically involves teaching not with the intent to change our students, but with the intent to unlearn in conjunction with them. My experience has been that queer pedagogical approaches can and will give rise to negative reactions. Some of these reactions and associated affective intensities have the potential to injure. Therefore, in raising and holding the right questions, it is equally important to respond to reactions without shutting down the conversation. Being able to incorporate difference and conflict in productive ways in the classroom is the most difficult, yet also the most necessary task for educators.

Much takes place in classrooms, teacher education programs, and research communities and processes that, despite our good intentions, actually contributes to oppression (Kumashiro, 2002). One of the most difficult things to reconcile as a queer pedagogue has been the exercise of my own authority and queering of my own practice. Norm critique, while exposing certain norms, also inscribes or reinforces other norms. One of the key learning experiences for me has been questioning the target/audience of norm-critical work. There is a risk in assuming that those who are learning about marginalization are not marginalized themselves. For example, in norm critical work on sexuality too often it is assumed that there are only straight people in the discussion.

It is important to be aware of how we are telling and showing our queer pedagogies to students. Larsson et al (2014) emphasize that 'few teachers critically reflect on how their teaching, its content and pedagogy, express norms that the students have to deal with' (p. 144). This is a key consideration for teacher educators as well as the pre-service teachers that they work with. Teacher educators should also create spaces for discussions about the normative underpinnings of their own practices, including cultural norms that engender, and privilege, certain behaviors and identities while marginalizing others. Larsson et al (2014) stress how some students are already challenging heteronormativity, but educators are struggling to keep up or even at times to recognize it. Teacher educators must also be open to being transformed by students' perspectives and priorities.

The hope in sharing these points of reflection is to encourage other researchers-educators-students to work through often-unvoiced concerns, misconceptions, confusion and discomfort related to the queer pedagogical possibilities for/of physical education. In accordance with Allen (2015), I would argue that 'perhaps it is in the pursuit of queer pedagogy's boundaries, rather than the securing of them, that the concept of queer's possibilities lie?' (p. 773).

REFERENCES

Alexander, K. (2014). Teaching discomfort? Uncomfortable attachments, ambivalent identifications. *TransFormations: The Journal of Inclusive Scholarship and Pedagogy, 22* (2), 57–71.

Britzman, D. (1995). Is there a queer pedagogy? Or, stop reading straight. *Educational Theory, 45*(2), 151–165.

Britzman, D. (1998). On some psychical consequences in AIDS research. In W. Pinar (Eds.), *Queer theory in education*. New York, NY: Psychology Press.

Childers, S. M. (2013). The materiality of fieldwork: An ontology of feminist becoming. *International Journal of Qualitative Studies in Education, 26*(5), 599–609.

Clarke, G. (2006). Sexuality and physical education. In K. D. McDonald & M. O'Sullivan (Eds.), *Handbook for research in physical education* (pp. 723–739). London, UK: Sage.

Coll, L., & Charlton, E. (2018). Not yet here, queer and now for sexualities and schooling. *Sex Education: Sexuality, Society & Learning, 18*(13), 307–320.

Coll, L., Enright, E., & O'Sullivan, M. (2014). 'The dangers of a single story': Heteronormativity in physical education. In Flory, S. B., Sanders, S., & Tischler, A. (Eds.), *Social and cultural issues in physical education: Case studies for teachers* (pp. 101–114). Lanham, MD: Rowman & Littlefield.

Coll, L., O'Sullivan, M., & Enright, E. (2017). The trouble with normal: (Re)Imagining sexuality education with young people. *Sex Education: Sexuality, Society & Learning, 18*(2), 157–171.

Enright, E. (2013). Young people as curators of physical culture: A metaphor to teach and research by. In L. Azzarito & D. Kirk (Eds.), *Physical culture, pedagogies and visual methods* (pp. 198–211). Oxon, UK: Routledge.

Gard, M. (2003). Moving and belonging: Dance, sport and sexuality. *Sex Education: Sexuality, Society and Learning, 3*(2), 105–118.

Harris, A., & Farrington, D. (2014). 'It gets narrower': Creative strategies for re-broadening queer peer education. *Sexuality, Society and Learning, 14*(2), 144–158.

Kumashiro, K. (2002). *Troubling education "Queer" activism and anti-oppressive pedagogy.* New York, NY: Routledge.

Kumashiro, K. (2004). Uncertain beginnings: Learning to teach paradoxically. *Theory into Practice, 43*(2), 111–115.

Landi, D. (2018). Toward a queer inclusive physical education. *Physical Education and Sport Pedagogy, 23*(1), 1–15.

Larsson, H., Quennerstedt, M., & Öhman, M. (2014). Heterotopias in physical education: Towards a queer pedagogy? *Gender and Education, 26*(2), 135–150.

Larsson, H., Redelius, K., & Fagrell, B. (2011). Moving (in) the heterosexual matrix: On heteronormativity in secondary school physical education. *Physical Education and Sport Pedagogy, 16*(1), 67–81.

lisahunter. (2017). What a queer space is HPE, or is it yet? Queer theory, sexualities and pedagogy. Sp*ort, Education and Society,* 1–12. DOI: 10.1080/13573322.2017.1302416.

Loutzenheiser, L. (2005). The ambivalences and circulation of globalization and identities: Sexualities, gender, and the curriculum. *Journal of Curriculum Theorizing, 21*(2), 117–139.

Luhmann, S. (1998). Queering/querying pedagogy? Or, pedagogy is a pretty queer thing. In W. Pinar (Ed.), *Queer theory in education* (pp. 141–155). New York, NY: Psychology Press.

McGlashan, H., & Fitzpatrick, K. (2017). LGBTQ youth activism and school: Challenging sexuality and gender norms. *Health Education, 117*(5), 485–497.

Ollis, D., Harrison, L., & Maharaj, C. (2013). *Sexuality education matters: Preparing pre-service teachers to teach sexuality education.* Melbourne, AU: Deakin University.

Piontek, T. (2006). *Queering gay and lesbian studies*. Chicago, IL: University of Illinois Press.

Quinlivan, K. (2012). Popular culture as emotional provocation: The material enactment of queer pedagogies in a high school classroom. *Sex Education, 12*(5), 511–522.

Renold, E. (2016). *Agenda: A young people's guide to making positive relationships matter*. Cardiff University, Children's Commissioner for Wales, NSPCC Cymru, Welsh Women's Aid and Welsh Government. Retrieved from www.agenda.wales

Renold, E. (2017). 'Feel What I Feel': Making Da (R) Ta with teen girls for creative activisms on how sexual violence matters. *Journal of Gender Studies, 27*, 1–18.

RFLS Ungdon. (2012). *Breaking the norm: Methods for studying norms in gender and the heteronorm in particular*. The Swedish Youth Federation for Lesbian, Gay, Bisexual and Transgender Rights. Retrieved from http://www.includegender.org/wp-content/uploads/2014/02/BreakTheNorm.pdf

Sandlos, K. (2012). Another telling representational effect. In E. Meiners & T. Quinn (Eds.), *Sexualities in education: A reader. Counterpoints: Studies in the postmodern theory of education* (pp. 285–289). New York, NY: Peter Lang.

Sumara, D., & Davis, B. (1999). Interrupting heteronormativity: Toward a queer curriculum theory. *Curriculum Inquiry, 29*(2), 191–208.

Sykes, H. J. (2011). *Queer bodies: Sexualities, genders, & fatness in physical education*. New York, NY: Peter Lang.

CHAPTER 20

DISRUPTING THE HETERONORMATIVE AND HOMOPHOBIC CULTURE WITHIN PHYSICAL EDUCATION

Creating Inclusive Spaces in the Gymnasium

Rachael Harrison and Charlotte Shipley

ACTION RESEARCH AND REFLECTION

As is the case with all other contributors to this text, we approach this chapter through a social justice lens. Drawing upon our similar yet unique work-lives within education and social work, we acknowledge and rely upon the influences of feminist and queer theory as we take a critical look at physical education's (PE's) problematic culture, particularly as it relates to sexuality and gender. Through our discussion in this chapter, we hope to unpack not just the "what" of this topic, but more importantly the "why" and "how" related to a need for urgent attention in today's PE class. To gain a comprehensive understanding of these discussions, it is important to acknowledge that change needs to happen on both a micro-level

Teaching About Social Justice Issues in Physical Education, pages 251–262.
Copyright © 2019 by Information Age Publishing
All rights of reproduction in any form reserved.   **251**

(intrapersonal and in the classroom) and at the macro-level (curriculum, policy and administration).

The culture within the PE field can be incredibly heteronormative and homophobic. Larsson, Redelius, and Fagrell (2011) describe heteronormativity as the presupposition that heterosexuality is the expected and desired sexual disposition and that certain behaviors and movements are tied to the presumption of heterosexuality. Homophobia is the fear, hatred, discomfort with, or mistrust of people who are lesbian, gay, or bisexual (Planned Parenthood, 2018; Warriner, Nagoshi, & Nagoshi, 2013). In other words, heteronormativity is assuming everyone is/ ought to be heterosexual and homophobia is the fear of or negative association with not being heterosexual. These terms are not mutually exclusive of one another. Oftentimes, extreme heteronormativity (refusing to accommodate or be proactive with inclusive language or ideas) can be perceived as homophobia.

Starting at a young age, students gradually learn cultural norms about what it means to be a boy or girl and the appropriate gender roles associated with each. The culture surrounding PE can create heteronormative expectations and norms. These expectations connect with the term Oliver and Kirk (2016) label as compulsory heterosexuality. Compulsory heterosexuality encompasses not just the homophobic notion that all relationships should be heterosexual, but also prescribes *how* women and men are to display their heterosexuality. These gender role expectations are very present in PE classes, and in our society as a whole. Compulsory heterosexuality is very evident in PE through implicit and explicit messages. Implicit messages are often harder to notice as they can be products of traditional ways of thinking and using language. Harmful implicit messages can be found through the use of heteronormative assumptions made in daily interactions with colleagues and students (e.g., all men are expected to be tough and strong and, likewise, all women are to be soft and feminine). Explicit messages are obvious signs that there are heteronormative expectations. A common example of this would be within a dance unit context when the PE teacher instructs males and females to get into pairs. The expectation is that pairs are dichotomous (one male and one female) and that the males are automatically the lead. Anything outside of these limits is rarely acknowledged and usually only through an insult or inappropriate joke.

With our understanding of how the world of sport is saturated with heteronormative ideas and expectations, it would be reasonable to anticipate that many athletes (and therefore many PE teachers) may have internalized this heteronormative culture. Research supports this very point. For example, O'Brien, Shovelton, and Latner (2013) explored the relationship between university students' (i.e., 199 PE students and 210 non-PE students) physical/sporting identity and athletic self-concept-related constructs and homophobia. Findings showed that anti-gay and anti-lesbian prejudice was greater in PE students than it was among non-PE students. The finding that physical/sporting attributes and identities are related to greater homophobia is consistent with suggestions that homophobia is closely linked with physical characteristics central to masculinity and males, rather than femininity and females (O'Brien et al., 2013). Knowing this, it is the responsibility of readers of this text to take an open and honest look at how they understand gender and sport and how that understanding influences their pedagogy and practice.

With the above definitions in mind, PE teachers have a central role in confronting heteronormativity and homophobia in sport and PE settings. It is important to address the following sorts of issues: How do we create a culture within PE that does not revolve around gender performance? How do we include and encourage these conversations within a PE setting? What do these lessons look like in practice? Which inclusive language and policies can help form an inclusive and safe school culture for all students? How do we eliminate these stereotypes while still embracing the diverse characteristics that some will have (e.g., strong female who identifies as lesbian that is great at sport)? How do we ensure that such efforts will embrace social justice pedagogy while some students will be opposed to such ideas based on religion, culture, family, internalized homophobia, et cetera?

CONTEXT

The first contributor, Rachael, is an occasional teacher for a public school board in Ontario, Canada. She is currently studying for her Master of Education degree (with a focus on physical and health education) through St. Francis Xavier University. Rachael is passionate about social justice as she is a public speaker and LGBTQ advocate who presents workshops for a variety of teachers and students focused upon creating inclusive spaces for LGBTQ individuals and understanding/addressing the effects of homophobia.

The second contributor, Charlotte, has been working in the social work field with children and youth for close to 10 years. Although her roots are in education, her passion for creating change emerged through the marriage of education and social justice while pursuing her Master of Social Work degree. Charlotte recently started her own business (Positive Space Consulting) as a platform for creating social change for the LGBTQ community and society as a whole through education and advocacy.

Sexual Health Education in Ontario

Within Ontario, where we both live and work, there is substantial controversy over the government updating the sexual health curriculum in 2015 for the first time since 1998. A lot of the controversy stems from fear and misinformation and revolves around discussions of sexuality and gender in the earlier elementary years. Changes included children learning about visible (e.g., race) and invisible differences (e.g., sexual orientation) in Grade 3 (ages 8–9). In Grade 6 (ages 10–11) and 8 (ages 13–14), students will be explicitly taught what is sexual orientation and gender identity/expression and assess the effects homophobia and gender roles has on positive self concept. The nature of these changes to the curriculum were not made in haste and were agreed upon by a committee of professionals, who determined that the curriculum covered appropriate topics for all students' emotional, social, cognitive, and biological development. This new curriculum was presented in 2015, but was faced with criticism from religious groups who advocated against revisions that take a harm-reduction approach rather than an abstinence approach. Justification for these revisions from the provincial government recognized that youth "now have widespread access to the internet, social media, and smartphones, giving them easy access to both helpful and potentially harmful and incorrect information" (Ontario Ministry of Education, 2018, para. 5). Curriculum does not replace the role of parents in educating their children about sexual health, but will provide teachers with resources to establish a foundation of mutual respect and acceptance of diverse perspectives in the classroom. At the secondary level, each grade includes at least one outcome that specifically addresses an LGBTQ issue within the human development and sexual health section of the physical and health curriculum. We believe (through a best-practice, research-informed lens) these changes have the potential to alleviate confusing and potentially harmful internalized homophobia felt by young LGBTQ students.

To put this into a national context, there are only four provinces and one territory (British Columbia, Manitoba, Ontario, Quebec, Yukon) out of 13 provinces/ territories that provide a combined physical and health curriculum. We believe this to be a beneficial approach as this provides another context to be consistent with and openly discuss the conversations and learning that takes place in health class. Other Western countries seemingly recognize this same value. Consider, for example, New Zealand's position about the place of sexual health education within PE:

> While most sex education will be taught in health education classes, PE classes have a role to play in establishing a supportive environment and keeping messages consistent with the school's approach. International research suggests that physical education classes are often not inclusive of diverse students and can reinforce rather than question gender and sexuality stereotypes. (New Zealand Ministry of Education, 2015, p. 13)

Intersectional Positionality, Elaborated

We also feel it is important to offer some information around our own intersectional positionality. We both share some familiar privileged social locations. We are both Caucasian settlers who were raised in middle/upper class nuclear families, and we both went on to receive university educations.

Notwithstanding the privilege that these identities afford us, our positionality also differs a great deal in terms of our identity and how we, as youngsters, perceived and experienced PE. This can offer a well-rounded perspective on this topic. Rachael is an able-bodied cisgender woman who has played sport at the university level; she identifies as a lesbian. Charlotte is a cisgender woman who has had a physical disability since birth and is therefore not able-bodied; she identifies as queer. Our experiences within PE are different due to how we both internalized the heteronormative expectations and compulsory heteronormative ideals as two different individuals at different places in our journeys.

Upon reflection, Rachael remembers that she struggled with accepting her sexual orientation. She feels that this internalized homophobia was precipitated through the culture of sport, which then led to issues in middle school. Realizing that being athletic rejected the ideals of heteronormativity, she began to not want to perform at her full potential in order to avoid being targeted and labelled as a lesbian. As her journey progressed, Rachael was conscious and, at times, consumed by the pressure to properly perform her gender by proving her femininity in other ways. Although her overall experience was positive in PE, she can recognize this is not the case for all individuals. Charlotte experienced PE from the sidelines. This meant that she spent a great deal of time absorbing these heteronormative ideas and expectations. What is truly fascinating is that as Charlotte is more comfortable in her traditional display of femininity, she was confused once she began to unpack her queer identity. Could she be a lesbian, if she was *not* into sports? These two experiences offer unique insights into how heteronormativity negatively affects students. This then offers another exciting opportunity—to disrupt this heteronormative culture and to make change through PE.

LESSON SET-UP

Before one delves into a lesson with potentially emotional content, it is important to reflect both personally and professionally. The idea of reflecting on this subject matter requires not just a one-time conversation, lesson, or discussion. Rather, it requires a commitment to ongoing reflection, learning, discussions, and both proactive and reactive actions. We recommend that prior to teaching these lessons, you spend some time self-reflecting and asking yourself the following questions: Do I have an emotional response to this topic? What kind of emotional reaction do I have (e.g., positive, negative, neutral)? What might be causing or contributing to these feelings or lack of feelings? How will these feelings affect my ability to teach about this topic and maintain a safe space?

It is important that when asking these questions, you be honest about your reaction. If you have a negative reaction, then it would be appropriate to do some research and work on your negative reaction towards the LGBTQ community. If, however, you experience positive emotions surrounding this topic or you feel passionate about creating and maintaining change, then we are confident that these lessons will help provide some ideas for moving forward with your commitment to fostering a safe and inclusive space.

Preparing the Physical and Emotional Landscape

It is our hope that these lessons will be woven into your usual curriculum on an on-going basis and thus providing space to normalize these discussions. It is crucial that a safe and inclusive space is consciously created and maintained from day one in PE. The culture of inclusivity, and therefore emotional and physical safety, is derived from both implicit and explicit gestures. Using inclusive language when referring to the class such as "everyone" or "folks" instead of "guys" or "boys and girls" is an example of an implicit gesture. Another implicit way of creating safe and inclusive spaces is to reject the idea of grouping students by their sex or gender. Try grouping students by assigning group names, birthday months, or likes/dislikes. Display a Positive Space rainbow sticker or poster somewhere prominent in your gym/classroom (ask your administration for one, order one online, or even make one by hand). These signs are a visible and explicit reminder that this is a space where everyone is respected.

We suggest a collaborative approach with students in creating this environment. On the first day of your PE program it is important to ask your students what an inclusive and safe space looks, sounds, and feels like. Have students define what respect and inclusion means to them and what it looks like through actions and words. Through these discussions, we recommend creating a class agreement that is posted and visible so they can be referred to throughout the term.

STRATEGY/ACTIVITY/ LESSON

Elementary Level (Ages 8–11) Lesson Idea: Recognizing and Questioning Gender Stereotypes in Sport

At a very early age, children are aware of what it means to be a boy or girl in society. We need to address these topics at the elementary level to help students realize their full potential and disallow stereotypes to limit their choices. This lesson includes a visualization activity meant to highlight students' assumptions and stereotypes about family, sport, and gender. A read aloud book is presented that leads into discussions about girl and boy stereotypes in sport and ends with a community circle to provide space for sharing their thoughts and feelings.

Step I. To begin the lesson, explain to the students that as a class they will be doing a visualization activity that will lead into what they will be learning today. You will describe a scenario of a family participating in a physically active day. All character names will be gender neutral and students will try and figure out the family dynamics based on the descriptions given. We have provided an example below. However, we encourage you to write your own if you wish. Ask students to close their eyes if they are comfortable, and try to imagine who the characters are and what each character is doing as you read the following scenario:

Scenario: Alex and Jamie Smith and their two children, Kelly and Sam, are packing up their family mini-van for an action-packed day at the beach. They packed sunscreen, a beach umbrella, sand toys, a football, and a hula hoop. Alex and Sam had a great time throwing around the football while enjoying the sun while Jamie and Kelly were excited to swim and try out their new hula hoops!

Ask students to open their eyes, turn to their neighbor, and discuss the following questions: What did you visualize? Describe each person in the family. What did they look like? Who was doing what? Bring the group back together and facilitate a group discussion. Ask students to share their discussions with the class. You can ask questions such as: "Why did you think that?" or "How did you know?" Help the ideas of gender stereotyping and family diversity emerge through critical questioning and probing: "What is a stereotype?" "Why did you think it was a mom and dad?" "Why were the mom and daughter doing the (blank) activity?"

Step II. Read aloud *Allie's Basketball Dream* by Barbara E. Barber and Darryl Ligasan (2002). Pause and discuss certain parts of the book that would be important to focus on such as, "My brother says basketball is a 'boys' game" "Some guys think girls shouldn't be playing basketball" "Some girls think boys shouldn't be jumping rope"

Ask students what they learned from the book. What was the moral of the story? The moral was: You can be anything you want to be, regardless of what people think and say. Reflect back on the sentence, "My brother says basketball is a 'boy's' game." Ask students what they think about this statement. Split the class into two groups, ask one group to come up with stereotypical characteristics and sports specific to boys and the other group to do the same for girls. Remind students what a stereotype is. After the students have created both lists, share as a whole class and facilitate discussion based on the answers. Ask questions such as, "Where do these stereotypes come from?" "Are they sometimes correct?" "What names or put downs are boys and girls called when they do not fit this list?" "How can stereotypes hold us back from doing what we want/feel or how are they harmful for kids? How do these stereotypes make you feel?" Discussing language and gender insults will naturally lead to students bringing up anti-LGBTQ epithets. Teachers need to be prepared to discuss the harmful history of anti-LGBTQ language. These words become insults when individuals defy gender roles and expectations. Discussing how gender norms and the expectations associated with them as well as how harmful using anti-LGBTQ epithets can help students be aware of their language and how harmful stereotypes can be.

Step III. Conclude the lesson by forming a circle with your class. Review previous key points from earlier in the lesson such as stereotypes and remind students that they do not have to subscribe to stereotypical roles or expectations as previously discussed. Have each student take turns sharing one way a person can defy their gender stereotype or sport they play (or wish to have/play) that they have been told they should not because of their gender. Each student will have the 'right to pass' or may repeat others' comments. Make sure to encourage all students to listen and respect all shared answers.

Intermediate-Secondary (Ages 11–18) Level Lesson Ideas:
Unpacking Homophobia and Gender Stereotypes in Sport

As students enter their adolescent years, the pressures to conform to societal norms increases. The norms based on gender role expectations, stereotypes, and sexual orientation can be quite limiting for students within PE. Often the root cause of discrimination or prejudice is simply a lack of understanding or awareness. We believe the lessons provided herein will guide teachers on how to educate their students on these topics, disrupt these expectations, and create inclusive spaces for all.

LESSON IDEA 1: TEACHING PRIVILEGE THROUGH GAMES

In this first activity, we are randomly assigning less privilege to a number of students with no rational explanation. This experience and the ensuing discussion is meant to help students understand the concept of privilege and then discuss how this could be compared to the experience of being marginalized through no fault of your own, as is the case with the LGBTQ community.

Step I. Choose a game to play with your students that they enjoy and are very familiar with. For the purpose of this lesson, we will use basketball as an example. Divide your class into two teams (e.g., blue and red). Between the two teams, randomly select one of the teams (e.g., red) that will have to play by a separate set of rules. Inform the students that the red team may only walk and are not allowed to jump during the game of basketball. The students will naturally ask why and have questions. However, encourage them to try their best and to follow the rules. Observe how each team and their individual members handle this situation; these observations will be useful for discussion.

Step II. Allow this scenario to naturally play out and then come to a point where discussion needs to happen. Gather the students for a group discussion. Begin the discussion by allowing the students who were on the red team to describe how it felt to be in their situation. Ask questions such as, "What were some emotions you felt while playing?" "Did these feelings change throughout the game?" "Did this feel fair?" Then, encourage other students to describe their experience. Ask questions such as "How did it feel to see your classmates in this situation?" As the teacher, use the observations you made during the game to add to the discussion.

Step III. This should prompt some discussion and would be a good time to introduce the word privilege and ask students what they think it means and how it relates to this activity. Remind your class of the agreement made to be respectful and inclusive at the beginning of the year. Encourage the students to think of how this game of basketball can relate to life experiences. Ask them if they can think of any groups of people who might not benefit from the same privileges as the majority of society (e.g., religious minorities, racialized individuals, LGBTQ community). Ensure the LGBTQ community is mentioned and prompt the students to think of examples of how LGBTQ people's experiences might be relatable to this activity. Also remind them that there are probably people in our PE class who identify as part of the LGBTQ community or have friends or family members who do. Some examples would be how the LGBTQ community has limited representation in professional sport, or how the transgender community is excluded from sport as a whole. LGBTQ individuals lack proper representation in the media and/or advertisements and they can be excluded from or hated by some religious groups. Some students might be able to make the connection as to how heteronormativity affords heterosexual people privilege by just being included in society's "norms" and how this therefore places the LGBTQ community as an "other" and lacking such privilege.

Step IV. Have students reflect on today's activity. Ask guiding questions such as "Reflect on the activity we did today and how it relates to society as a whole and specifically the LGBTQ community. Thinking about our group discussion today, what is one thing you can do to help support the LGBTQ community?"

LESSON IDEA 2: UNPACKING HOMOPHOBIA AND GENDER STEREOTYPES IN SPORT

We recommend completing this lesson fairly soon after the previous lesson as we believe they build upon important concepts. This lesson asks students to think about the culture within sports and athletics and discuss its potential implications.

Step I. Write the word stereotype on the board. Create discussion around this topic and ask students for examples of gender stereotypes. Ask questions such as "How 'should' each gender act and behave?" "Have you found yourself having stereotypical ideas about gender and sport?"

Step II. Identify stereotypical characteristics and sports related to male and female athletes. Place students into groups to make a list of stereotypes for male and female athletes. Ask the students to further think about these lists by saying something such as: "Now we are going a little further and I want to ask you how these stereotypes could be related to sexual orientation and homophobia (discuss gay/lesbian stereotypes)?" "What is sexual orientation and homophobia?" "How does it affect athletes (fear of rejection, discouraging, suppress identity for acceptance)?"

Step III. Watch The Sports Network (TSN)'s "ReOrientation Part One: The Culture of Casual Homophobia and Part Two: The Transition Phase" which can be found on YouTube. Engage in a discussion with your class around these videos. Ask them to think critically by prompting them with questions such as: Why is it so uncommon for professional athletes to be openly gay while playing (pro athletes can risk their careers by coming out e.g., Michael Sam (NFL) and Jason Collins (NBA)? What about sports where the opposite is assumed such as figure skating, gymnastics (male), softball (female), etc.? The assumptions associated with these sports is that they are LGBTQ. What are the similarities and differences of these? Ask what their thoughts are on the fact that many gay and lesbian athletes stay in the closet for fear of being harassed, demeaned, or even physically harmed. Ask if athletes should solely be judged on skill, talent, and character?

Step IV. Have the students create a social justice in sport project. Students can work independently (or with a partner) to research and create a presentation (poster/slideshow) about an athlete who was/is out during their athletic career. Inform students that you will use these projects to create a billboard to inspire other students outside of your gymnasium to highlight all of the talented athletes who are brave enough to live their authentic truth.

Examples:

Out Male Professional Athletes	Out Female Professional Athletes
Robbie Rogers (NSL)	Erin Mcleod (Olympic soccer player)
Tom Daley (Olympic diver)	Elena Delle Donne (WNBA)
Gus Kenworthy (Olympic skier)	Lauren Lappin (Olympic softball player)
David Denson (MLB)	Liz Carmouche (UFC fighter)
Gareth Thomas (rugby)	Billie Jean King (tennis)

INTERSECTIONALITY

When discussing LGBTQ topics, it is important to keep in mind that there is the potential for some students to be resistant to these discussions as they may associate with a certain religion or culture that denounces the LGBTQ community. While it is important for open dialogue to take place, it is crucial that the emotional safety of everyone involved be paramount. This might look like reminding students before and during discussions that respectful language must be used and that religious opinions need to be kept in the context of opinions. Canada's laws protect the LGBTQ community and afford them the same official rights as others. However, though these laws are in place to protect the LGBTQ community, many still face discrimination and violence every day. It is also important to remember that members of the LGBTQ community have varying levels of ability and could also come from different socioeconomic backgrounds. Existing within multiple intersectionalities as an LGBTQ individual (e.g., queer woman with a disability) can make that person feel incredibly vulnerable. Creating a safe space within your PE classroom can help alleviate some stress for that individual and open doors for the student to reach out for further support.

CHALLENGES AND POSSIBILITIES

The topics of sexual orientation, homophobia, and gender can be sensitive ones for many teachers and students as they have not been traditionally discussed in the education system. Teachers might report having a fear of backlash from administration or parents. This could be in large part because teachers and administrators have faced this type of backlash in the past in regard to discussing topics of diverse nature. If teachers or administrators identify with the LGBTQ community themselves, they may be accused of pushing their own agenda, which is a cultural narrative that has no basis in fact. Holding all students and teachers accountable to use inclusive and safe language is important. With all of the above considered, imagine how it might feel for LGBTQ students or students from LGBTQ families in your classroom to hear potentially negative comments being made during class discussions.

Prior to having these conversations, it is very important to have a list of local resources students can access for support. We would also advise you to inform your colleagues or administration that these topics are being discussed, so that they might be prepared to answer student's questions in other contexts. There are a number of organizations both locally and nationally that exist to help support educators in having these conversations. Teachers typically rely on these external organizations exclusively. However, teachers need to have the knowledge and tools themselves in order to properly create a safe and inclusive PE program, therefore, it is important not to rush into anything before feeling you are prepared.

Addressing these topics within PE starting at an early age can lead to a number of possibilities. Homophobia in sport has the potential to limit all students, gay or straight. By creating an environment where students and teachers are free to be their authentic selves provides a feeling of freedom and can minimize the stress felt by LGBTQ individuals who are existing within a heteronormative culture. We also believe it is imperative that these discussions happen at the elementary (i.e., not just secondary) level in order to help normalize these ideas and topics within the school culture and help potentially decrease the issues of homophobia in middle and high school. Administrators are always very busy therefore they typically wait for a situation to unfold or for a student to 'come out' before addressing issues such as homophobia. A proactive versus a reactive approach can limit the prevalence of bullying, self-harm, depression, addiction, and low self-esteem that members of the LGBTQ community experience in greater numbers than their non-LGBTQ peers (Dyck, 2012). This will build an inclusive community for all and teach students to question heteronormative culture as they continue to be active for life.

ADDITIONAL RESOURCES

1. The Always commercial "Like a Girl" (https://www.youtube.com/watch?v=XjJQBjWYDTs) is another video that can be shown to deconstruct the assumptions and stereotypes society makes about girls.
2. Outsports.com is a sports news website focusing on LGBT personalities and issues in amateur and professional sport students can use to help them with their project.

REFERENCES

Barber, B. E., & Ligason, D. (2002). *Allie's basketball dream.* New York, NY: Lee and Low Books.

Dyck, D. R. (2015). *Report on outcomes and recommendations: LGBTQ youth suicide prevention summit 2012.* Canada: Egale Canada Human Rights Trust.

Larsson, H., Redelius, K., & Fagrell, B. (2011). Moving (in) the heterosexual matrix. On heteronormativity in secondary school physical education. *Physical Education and Sport Pedagogy, 16*(1), 67–81.

New Zealand Ministry of Education. (2015). *Sexuality education: A guide for principals, boards of trustees and teachers.* Wellington, NZ: New Zealand Ministry of Education.

O'Brien, K. S., Shovelton, H., & Latner, J. D. (2013). Homophobia in physical education and sport: The role of physical/sporting identity and attributes, authoritarian aggression, and social dominance orientation. *International Journal of Psychology, 48*(5), 891–899.

Oliver, K. L., & Kirk, D. (2016). *Girls, gender and physical education: An activist approach.* London, UK: Routledge.

Ontario Ministry of Education. (2018). *Sex education in Ontario.* Retrieved from https://www.ontario.ca/page/sex-education-ontario#section-2

Planned Parenthood. (2018). *What is homophobia?* Retrieved from https://www.plannedparenthood.org/learn/sexual-orientation-gender/sexual-orientation/what-homophobia.

Warriner, K., Nagoshi, C. T., & Nagoshi, J. L. (2013). Correlates of homophobia, transphobia, and internalized homophobia in gay or lesbian and heterosexual samples. *Journal of Homosexuality, 60*(9), 1297–1314.

CHAPTER 21

TEACHING PRE-SERVICE TEACHERS ABOUT SOCIOECONOMIC STATUS

Sara Barnard Flory

ACTION RESEARCH & REFLECTION

As a physical education teacher educator who grew up in a lower-middle-class family, I had an entire childhood to "gather data" regarding a variety of social issues, including socioeconomic status. My community was located just outside of a large, urban city in the Midwestern United States, and boasted a broad spectrum of diversity. Residents hailed from a variety of racial, ethnic, religious, and socioeconomic backgrounds. In fact, our high school was highlighted by a well-known reporter on the national news during a meeting of the Group of Seven (G7) Summit (a group of industrialized, democratic nations) in the mid-1990s, because our student population represented a microcosm of the rest of the world. I identified as lower-middle-class because of my parents' income level. We were by no means "rich" so I wore hand-me-down clothes, and there was a period of time where parents shared one car, my mother worked the midnight shift at a restaurant so my father could take the car to his job during the day—but we never went without

Teaching About Social Justice Issues in Physical Education, pages 263–271.
Copyright © 2019 by Information Age Publishing
All rights of reproduction in any form reserved.

basic needs like food, water, and utilities like electricity, heat, and gas. I was able to attend a prestigious state university for my undergraduate degree, and received a few scholarships, but most of my undergraduate education was paid for through federal financial aid, grants, and a few loans.

While in graduate school, I worked as a research assistant for a grant program that worked with physical education teachers in an urban school district, where I learned a great deal about social issues in education. Driving into the neighborhoods to visit the schools revealed so much about the living conditions of residents. For every house that was in good condition, there were usually three to four others that were abandoned, damaged by fire, or partially torn down. Teachers shared multiple challenges that their students faced in their communities, such as relying on the meals received at school for daily nutrition, or homelessness. While my own upbringing provided some insights to a variety of social issues, my work in urban schools provided a much deeper understanding of the (major) differences between the "haves" and the "have nots" in schools.

The PETE program where I prepare pre-service teachers is somewhat similar to the community where I grew up. The university is located in a large, urban city in the southeastern United States, and the university serves residents from diverse backgrounds (including race, ethnicity, religion, and socioeconomic status). The school district where I work with local students, teachers, and PETE students is one of the 10 largest districts in the U.S. I attempted to weave several social issues into the courses I taught within the PETE program, however, a few incidents prompted a more focused commitment to teaching about social issues within my first three years of teaching in the program. First, most graduates of our program were getting hired in Title I schools. Title I schools in the U.S. are defined as those schools with a high number or a high percentage of students from low-income families, where at least 40% or more of the students qualify for free or reduced-price lunch. These schools receive additional funding from the government to help students reach educational goals. I received many emails, text messages, and phone calls from former students who felt like they knew *what* to teach, but they were struggling with *how* to teach their students given the challenges they faced outside of school. Questions about management strategies, establishing relationships with students and their families, and conflict resolution concerns were common from recent graduates. I felt honored that our graduates were comfortable enough to reach out for advice, but it quickly made me realize that PETE students needed more specific content about social issues.

The second incident occurred during a middle school methods course one spring seventh and eighth [12–14 years old] twice per week. Throughout the 14-week semester, the female PE teaching position at the middle school had to be filled and re-filled a total of four times because teachers hired for the position did not stay for various reasons. The original teacher was pulled to another site within the district because of a specific certification she held. The second teacher worked for three days before resigning. The third teacher hired spent approximately four weeks at the school before moving out of state for graduate school. The fourth teacher had experience at another urban elementary school, and has remained in the position for several years. The male PE teacher that the PETE students and I worked with shared with us that the teachers who did not stay were not prepared for the challenges of teaching in an urban school.

These incidents prompted my thinking about what issues I needed to address in my courses, and how I could do so within the constraints of credit hours and timelines. My "short list" of issues included considerations for teaching in urban schools, and for teaching students from diverse backgrounds, however both of these issues were complex and interwoven with many other issues that arise in schools and communities. I started thinking of ways to ensure that the PETE students had experiences in diverse, urban schools for both coursework and internships. I began designing course meetings and assignments that involved conversations and experiences regarding the complexities of teaching in diverse or urban schools, and teaching students from a variety of socioeconomic status. I started considering ways to help PETE students understand their own privilege and avoid taking on a "savior complex" with students from lower socioeconomic status. In short, I had my work cut out for me!

CONTEXT

The university where I teach is a large, metropolitan, urban university in the southeastern U.S. The university enrolls over 50,000, and the College of Education where the Physical Education program is situated, enrolls over 2,500 students. The region has been described as experiencing "urban sprawl" and public transportation is not reliable or plentiful in the area. The Physical Education program faculty has excellent relationships with district administrators in the three surrounding counties where our graduates are hired. PETE majors enter the program after completing other general education coursework in the fall semester of their junior year (3rd year in a 4-year degree program). They progress through as a cohort for five semesters (Fall I, Spring I, Summer, Fall II, Spring II).

I address issues of socioeconomic status in multiple courses via the physical location of the class, discussions, and specific assignments. These include three methods courses, two internship experiences, and the "Capstone" senior seminar course. The table below provides a broad overview of the scope and sequence where socioeconomic status is addressed within the five-semester program.

Course	Semester	Teaching Methods
PET 3441 Instructional Design & Content: Middle School PE	Spring I	• Immersion Experience
PET 4742 Instructional Design & Content: Physical Activity & Fitness Opportunities	Summer	• Unit Plan Activity Portfolio: Required to find low cost or free resources within the community for students
PET 4442 Instructional Design & Content: High School PE	Fall II	• Case study readings, responses, and discussions • Unit Plan Activity Portfolio: Required to find low cost or free resources within the community for students
PET 4944 Pre-Internship in PE: Secondary	Fall II	• Rotation at middle and high school settings • At least one of the rotations is at a diverse/urban school setting
PET 4947 Final Internship in PE: Secondary	Spring II	• One rotation at either a middle or high school— usually a diverse/urban school setting • Lesson planning to fit the needs of student population
PET 4929 Senior Seminar in PE	Spring II	• Weekly meetings to review a variety of topics, share experiences from internship • At least one planned seminar discussion regarding teaching diverse students, culturally relevant teaching (including SES)

SECTION 3: LESSON SET-UP

Although there are several places within the PETE curriculum where I address social issues and specifically socioeconomic status, I will focus on the one assignment that I believe has the most profound influence on PETE students' development and understanding of social issues. This is the Immersion Experience, which is assigned during the spring semester of the junior year in the Instructional Design & Content: Middle School PE course.

To prepare for this assignment, it is helpful for the instructor to have a working understanding of their own social identity, the demographics of the broad community where you teach or live, the smaller communities that exist among specific school sites or areas, and the definition of privilege. This assignment is one that I give about halfway through the semester within the course. The students are juniors, and have had some experiences in elementary schools at this point, and they participate in a methods course at a diverse middle school close to campus and have observed me teach students from diverse backgrounds for several weeks prior to giving this assignment. I make sure to discuss "teachable moments" from each class session at the end of the class with the PETE students so they can understand why I did or did not do certain things during lessons. I am also very purposeful in slowly revealing my research interests and background during this first course with the cohort, so I do not overwhelm them or "turn them off" to working or teaching in urban schools.

SECTION 4: STRATEGY/ACTIVITY/LESSON

The purpose of the Immersion Experience is for students to experience life as an "Other." Most students in the PETE program would identify as White or Caucasian, and as students in college, almost all of the PETE majors would fall into the "middle class" category. Although the Immersion Experience assignment can be completed using a variety of experiences (attending different religious ceremonies, attending a club meeting for a culture other than their own, etc.), one of the most poignant experiences for students is to experience life as if they were not middle class—that is, I encourage the students to run weekly errands without the convenience of their own car—using public transportation or walking, doing a load of laundry at a Laundromat rather than relying on the washer and dryer they have in their apartment complex, house, or dorm, or to shop for their weekly groceries by only using items from the SNAP benefits approved list. The Immersion Experience assignment that I give is included below. PETE students are required to complete the experiences alone so that they can personally reflect on their own values, biases, and potential shifts in their teaching philosophy during and after each experience. Another reason I require PETE students to complete each experience alone is to prevent large groups of students from participating in activities together and creating instances of "poverty tourism" or the like. I take at least 30 minutes to go over the requirements and allow students to ask questions. The first portion of the assignment, the Social Identity Profile, was provided by Dr. Jennifer Walton-Fisette. While this assignment is not without issues (such as 'checking boxes' to determine social identity), it does seem to be a starting point for many undergraduate students for broadening their understanding of many social issues, including socioeconomic status.

PET 3441: Immersion Experience Assignment

Part of becoming an educator is learning to interact with students and teachers from a variety of backgrounds. My job as your professor is to help you learn about your own thoughts and feelings about entering the "unknown"—which is likely to happen when you are a new teacher.

For this assignment, you will first complete a "Social Identity Profile" and discuss what this might mean to your profession. Then, students must spend 10 hours (or more) "immersing" yourself in a community or cultural group where you are not currently comfortable, familiar, or the "majority." The purpose of this immersion experience is to build your awareness of the group's cultural norms, and to experience life as an "other." Although I cannot force you to experience life as another, my hope is that you will engage in the experience as genuinely as possible and in the spirit in which the experience was designed. Culture often implies race or ethnicity, however, there is much more to culture than the color of one's skin. Culture includes language, religion, family dynamics, socioeconomic status, sexual orientation, etc.

Immersion experiences should meet the following criteria:
1. The majority of the people there are from the focal group
2. You are on the "turf" of the focus group
3. It is a type of experience you have never had before
4. It takes place during this semester
5. Each experience lasts at least 2 hours
6. It pushes your comfort zone
7. You have face-to-face interaction with people from the focal group.

Examples of appropriate Immersion Experiences include:
- Attending a religious service unfamiliar to you
- Attending a meeting/function for a campus cultural club or group where you are not a member of the targeted cultural group
- Touring a school zone for a school in an impoverished neighborhood and noting access to major grocery stores, parks, green spaces, etc. (i.e., ability for residents to live a "healthy lifestyle")
- Running a typical weekly errand (grocery shopping, drug store, etc.) by using public transportation (NOT the campus bus service)
- Other experiences that you clear with Dr. Flory first!

You should keep a log of your experiences (attached) and plan to take notes during the experience or immediately after the experience (type these up).

You will hand in:
- Your Immersion Experience Hours Log
- Notes from each Immersion experience, and
- Reflection paper that encompasses the following:
  - A DETAILED explanation of EACH setting—so that I can clearly understand the context of your immersion experience. The more detailed, the better.
  - Your reaction during the immersion experience—what were your emotional responses? What were your cognitive responses? Did you have any physical responses? The more detailed, the better (hopefully this is getting my point across…).
  - Your "processing" after the immersion experience—how did you feel afterwards? How does this relate to your personal life? How does this experience make you feel about being a teacher of diverse students? How did this experience influence your teaching philosophy?

There is no page requirement to this assignment, however, you should spend as much time as possible discussing each experience and each question. If you hand in a final reflection paper that is only 3 pages long, you may want to re-read the description of the assignment.

A Few Notes:

- Immersion experiences need to be completed individually so that your peers, family, or friends do not influence your thoughts, attitudes, or the experience itself. It is perfectly acceptable to discuss your plans before or after, however.
- I encourage you to be as open and honest in your reflections and notes as possible. This is a judgment-free assignment. However, you must provide justification for any broad statements or reflections that you make—these should be based on what you see/observe/hear during the experience, not stereotypes or your personal values, whatever they may be. In other words, watch your language.... Try your best not to "judge" the environment or the participants. If you go into a situation with a negative outlook, you will probably only "see" negative things....

Social Identity Profile

Social Identities	Examples of Social Identities	Your Identity
Race	Black, White, Asian/Pacific Islander, Latino/a, Native American, Biracial	
Gender	Woman, Man, Transgender, Non-Binary	
Class	Poor, Working Class, Middle Class, Owning Class	
Physical/Mental/ Developmental Ability	Non-Disabled, Disabled	
Sexual Identity	Lesbian, Gay, Bisexual, Heterosexual, Questioning	
Religion	Catholic, Jew, Protestant, Buddhist, Hindu, Muslim, Baptist, Evangelical	
Age	Young, Old, Middle-Aged	
Other		

1. What is the meaning of one's social identity? How is it developed/formed? How do you think YOU identify this way and why?
2. Reflect upon how you felt completing this social identity profile.
3. Reflect upon **WHY** it would be important to know and reflect upon your identity as future professionals?
4. Record additional notes, comments, or questions you might have.

INTERSECTIONALITIES

The Immersion Experience assignment is full of intersectionality, because socioeconomic status has much to do with other social identities and social issues. Often, socioeconomic status intersects with race, ethnicity, gender, [dis]ability and sexual orientation. Rates of poverty are higher among people of color than among those who identify as white. On average, women earn less than men. Recent research identifies that individuals who identify as LGBTQ+ are more vulnerable to socioeconomic disadvantages compared to heterosexual individuals (Badgett, Durso & Schneebaum, 2013). I try to spend focused time on the concept of inter-sectionalities in the courses where I teach about social issues.

CHALLENGES AND POSSIBILITIES

When implementing the Immersion Experience assignment, I am often met ini-tially with resistance and questions about "why" this assignment is required, as well as a variety of questions to try to complete the assignment as quickly and painlessly as possible. Some of the other challenges to including this assignment in my courses is the PETE students not taking the assignment seriously. During one semester, three students turned in reflection papers that included an incident on a city bus about having a deep conversation with "Mr. Joe"—a man they had met while riding the bus who was doing so to save as much money as possible to try to send his daughter to college. It was difficult to determine whether all three students actually had this experience, or if students copied each other's work. This was disheartening, obviously, because the students who submitted that work did not find value in the assignment and the broader message was lost on them. In subsequent semesters, I made sure to remind students that these experiences were meant to be completed individually so that each student could consider how this would influence their teaching philosophy.

Another challenge with this assignment is overcoming the broad assumptions that PETE students may make about people and communities where they are un-familiar, which often surface in the reflection papers. For example, PETE students assuming that they are unsafe if they travel to or visit certain neighborhoods, or that the parents of K–12 students in urban schools do not care about their chil-dren's education are sometimes mentioned in reflection papers after Immersion experiences. I often address these assumptions with class discussions or questions during class sessions that take place in schools. I am fortunate to be able to take my PETE students to local schools for their methods coursework, and the PETE students are able to observe and assist me teach middle and high school students using the curricular models for that level (i.e., Sport Education, Adventure Edu-cation, etc.). After each class session, I host a short "debriefing" to discuss any notable events that occur during our sessions, such as management issues, transi-tions in between tasks, or student concerns that came up during the class. If the PETE students make statements or ask questions that reflect negatively on the students or community, I ask the PETE students why they may think that way. Often these attitudes or assumptions are based on stereotypes or personal bias. It is important to respectfully address these assumptions with PETE students rather than ignoring them, as these can lead to negative interactions in the future among teachers and students.

A final challenge that I have encountered when giving this assignment are defi-cit perspectives and savior complexes—both of which are equally dangerous in pre-service teachers. Deficit perspectives attribute things like school failure to a deficit within a student, their families, or their cultures. Savior complexes occur when PETE students, usually those from white, middle class backgrounds, want to help non-white students and "save" them from their circumstances, rather than identifying the strengths and benefits of their culture or trusting that people of color can solve their own problems. Unfortunately, since these assignments are typically handed in at the end of the semester, it is difficult to tell how much of the feedback given is absorbed or even read. This is why I attempt to give this assignment early on in the program, and re-address so many social issues in subsequent semesters. Having conversations and discussions with PETE students about valuing multiple cultures and thinking broadly about the many ways that education occurs is another strategy I use to prevent deficit thinking.

While there are several challenges to giving this assignment, the possibilities from this experience are also well-documented. Many PETE students discuss how "eye-opening" the assignment is in their reflection, as well as how grateful they are for the small luxuries they do experience every day, such as a washer and dryer in their apartment complex, or having their own car for transportation. Many PETE students also discuss how they had never even considered the challenges that students from disadvantaged socioeconomic status may face in their everyday lives. Several students discuss a shift in their teaching philosophy and seem more comfortable and open to teaching in urban schools after the assignment is completed. While it may not be a completely transformative exercise for all students, reading honest reflections about a shift in perspective is a small step that validates my teaching and research every semester.

REFERENCE

Badgett, M. V. L., Durso, L. E., & Schneebaum, A. (2013). *New patterns of poverty in the lesbian, gay, and bisexual community*. Retrieved from http://williamsinstitute.law.ucla.edu/wp-content/uploads/LGB-Poverty-Update Jun-2013.pdf

CHAPTER 22

A SPORT ACTIVIST MODEL OF WORKING WITH YOUTH FROM SOCIALLY VULNERABLE BACKGROUNDS

Carla Luguetti and Kimberly L. Oliver

ACTION RESEARCH & REFLECTION

Social vulnerability can be defined as the result of the negative relationship be-tween availability of material or symbolic resources and access to an opportunity that is structurally, socially, economically and/or culturally provided by the state, market and society (Misztal, 2011). Lack of access to education, work, healthcare, leisure and other forms of cultural capital decreases the chances of upward social mobility. Problematic to traditional views of youth from socially vulnerable back-grounds is the belief that any problem (e.g., poverty, educational failure, drug / alcohol abuse) faced by these youth is a result mainly of their own volition. Thus, we blame the victim for the victim's problems.

Authors use a variety of names for socially vulnerable youth, such as; under-served youth (Hellison, 2010), disaffected youth (Sandford & Duncombe, 2011), at-risk youth (Coalter, Allison, & Taylor, 2000), and marginalized young people (Kelly, 2011) to name a few. However, these different terms may not represent the

Teaching About Social Justice Issues in Physical Education, pages 273–285.
Copyright © 2019 by Information Age Publishing
All rights of reproduction in any form reserved.
273

complexities of social issues, because they tend to put the focus on the individual, rather than taking into account the wider social structures in which youth live (Haudenhuyse, Theeboom, & Coalter, 2012)but across a range of issues including education, employment and training, community leadership and healthy lifestyles. Although there are some indications that when working towards broader outcomes with socially vulnerable youth a specific methodology is required, it remains unclear what constitutes this specificity within a sports context. For this, a Flemish (northern region of Belgium. In this chapter, we use the term "youth from socially vulnerable backgrounds" because we do not want to "blame the youth". We have chosen an activist approach to working with youth from socially vulnerable backgrounds, because rather than blame the victim, we assert that young people have the capability to analyze their social context and to challenge and resist the forces that impede their possibilities for liberation (Cammarota & Fine, 2008; Freire, 1987, 1996; Lawson, 2005).

The first author's (Carla) experience in sports was fundamentally critical to her personal life and desire to understand how a sport program could create spaces to empower young people. Her coach and the environment he created in her adolescence inspired her to seek answers to fight against "social injustice". She wanted to work with young people in sport settings so that they could experience the type of empowering possibilities that she experienced through sport as a teen. Although her beliefs were related to social change and empowerment, her professional identity developed within a teacher-centered pedagogy. During Carla's PhD, she was introduced to the second author (Kim)—an expert in student-centered pedagogy and inquiry-based education centered *in* action. Kim accepted the challenge to help Carla in this project. Kim's expertise in activist research and in co-created curriculum possibilities was the complement that Carla was missing to seek answers to fight against "social injustice" in sport contexts. Kim was able to take the theory and make it concrete in pedagogical practice.

In this chapter, we are going to describe the experience the authors faced in working with 17 youth, 4 coaches, a pedagogical coordinator, and a social worker that were part of a soccer program designed for youth in a socially and economically disadvantaged neighborhood in Brazil. Our intent was to create empowering possibilities by assisting youth in learning to name, critique and negotiate barriers to their engagement in their sport context. It involved the youth and coaches identifying barriers to sport opportunities in their community; the youth, coaches, and researchers imagined alternative possibilities to the barriers identified; and we worked collaboratively to create realistic opportunities for the youth to begin to negotiate some of the barriers they selected.

CONTEXT

This project took place in a soccer program in a socially and economically disadvantaged neighborhood in Santos, Brazil. According to the Brazilian government (SEADE, 2010), this neighborhood is considered a high socially and economically disadvantaged area because there is low per capita household income, poor health conditions and low quality of the education system. This project is run by a non-governmental organization and serves approximately 250 boys and girls ages 6 to 15. The study included 17 boys between the ages of 13 and 15 years. The reason the participants were all boys was that the group we were working with only had boys. While it was not intended to be a study on boys only, there were no girls playing soccer that were within the age group we were targeting. In addition, four coaches, a pedagogic coordinator, and a social worker were part of the project. They boys were invited to participate in the project. Carla met with the boys for 40 minutes every Wednesday prior to their training sessions for a total of 18 work sessions. On Fridays Carla worked with the coaches, the pedagogical coordinator and the social worker for 1 hour for a total of 16 sessions.

LESSON SET-UP

In this topic, we are going to describe a prototype pedagogical model for working with youth from socially vulnerable backgrounds based in an activist approach (see Figure 22.1). The first part of the pedagogical model involved the youth and coaches identifying barriers to learning opportunities through sport in their community (Building the Foundation phase). In the second part of the process, the youth, coaches, and researchers imagined alternative possibilities to the barriers identified (Activist phase). The five critical elements (student-centered pedagogy, inquiry-based education centered in action, ethic of care, attentiveness to the community, and a community of sport) formed a patchwork of practice that formed the basis of the prototype model (Luguetti et al., 2015).

Student-centered pedagogy is the ability and willingness of adults to listen to youth and respond to what they are hearing. *Inquiry-based education centered in action* is a process through which the youth could name their experiences and work with the researcher and coaches to change the things that hinders their engagement in opportunities to play sports. That is, we work with the youth in order to challenge, negotiate and/or transform the barriers they identified and assist them to develop strategies to increase their sports participation. *Ethic of care* means that the coaches' role is showing interest in and respect for the youth's lives outside of sport. *Attentiveness to the community* describes that it is also essential to be aware of the problems that the youth encounter playing sports. Finally, when designing sport programs for youth from socially vulnerable backgrounds, it is required a collective action on the part of the community—a *Community of sport*.

When working with youth, these five critical elements should be considered 'non-negotiable' when attempting to *co-construct empowering learning possibilities through sport for youth from socially vulnerable backgrounds (key theme)*. It is important to highlight that while these critical elements must be present in order to faithfully implement the model, depending on the context, the critical elements will take different substantive forms in different settings. For example, the problems youth from socially vulnerable backgrounds face in Brazil (e.g. safety,

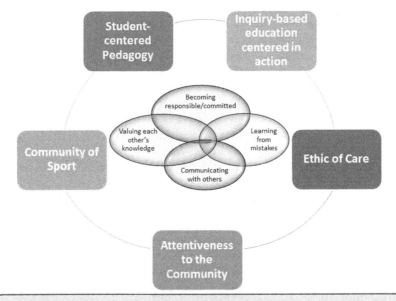

The Key-theme is to co-construct empowering learning possibilities through sport for boys from socially vulnerable backgrounds.

FIGURE 22.1.   Diagram of the Key Theme, the Critical Elements and the Learning Aspirations of the Prototype Pedagogical Model.

sanitation, opportunity to play) might be different in other countries, but teachers/coaches must consider the critical element "attentiveness to the community" to implement this model. What they have to attend to specifically, however, will depend on the specific features of their own local context. Through the Building the Foundation phase, researchers/teachers will seek to understand the form each of the critical elements takes in their specific context.

In the final part of the process (Activist Phase), we worked collaboratively to create realistic opportunities for the youth to begin to negotiate some of the barriers they identified in Building the Foundation phase. It was through the Leadership Program that the learning 'aspirations' for the prototype pedagogical model emerged (Luguetti et al., 2016). First, the youth became more responsible and committed when they had opportunities to be leaders. Second, participants learned that mistakes were areas for learning and growth. Third, participants learned to value different people's knowledge. Finally, the youth learned to communicate more effectively. The leadership program offered the youth an additional day each week to work in the soccer project, thus allowing them to manage what they identified as a serious risk (the life of crime). While it may seem that merely adding one day per week for the youth to engage in the sport program was insignificant, what is important to remember when working in activist approaches is that transformation begins at the micro level—small steps toward changing oppressive practices make a difference over time (Cook-Sather, 2002; Oliver et al., 2009). We believe that pedagogical models developed through activist approaches will always have learning aspirations that are context specific rather than predetermined. Although learning aspirations that will emerge when implementing this prototype pedagogical model in the future will always be context specific, we suspect they will always also center on the affective domain.

STRATEGY/ACTIVITY/LESSON

To begin the process, we engaged the youth in inquiry in order to help them better understand what facilitates and hinders their learning opportunities in sport. We started by inquiring into what the youth liked/disliked, their perceptions of school and family, their opinions about the soccer training sessions, and barriers to sport participation they encountered in both the program and their community as a whole. Below is a description of how the tasks developed in that phase (see Table 22.1).

Our first step in the model involved working with the youth and coaches to identify the barriers they experienced in their sport context. These barriers revolved around issues of safety, sanitation and opportunities to play sport (Luguetti et al., 2015). The second step involved working to imagine alternative possibilities to the various barriers that were identified. It started from things that the youth saw as important if they were going to develop strategies for negotiating the barriers they identified. Despite all the barriers, the youth described sport as a constructive activity in their lives and they believed that sport was an opportunity for not only them, but also younger children, in order to avoid a life of crime. As such, we worked to create additional sport opportunities with the youth that would allow them to be in a sporting context more days out of their week. The idea of creating a Leadership Program where the older boys would work to assist the coaches during the younger children's training sessions was one of the options put forth as a possible change project.

The Leadership Program became the site for change. It was through this last step that we worked with the youth and coaches to combine the five critical elements as we developed and implemented this Program. We worked with boys and coaches for four sessions to plan the Leadership Program. As part of their planning, they decided that in order to serve as role models for the younger children, the youth would need to alter their behavior. They also decided that each week two boys would work at each training session for the younger children. After the program was loosely organized, the youth started working with the coaches to serve as leaders. During this time we held not only the work sessions with the youth and with the coaches, but we also held joint work sessions with the youth and coaches together in order to discuss the specifics of how the Leadership Program was unfolding. Below is a description of the tasks in coaches work session and youth work session in Phase 2 (see Table 22.2).

TABLE 22.1. Schedule of the Tasks in Coaches Work Session and Youth Work Session in Phase 1

Coaches Work Sessions	Youth Work Sessions
Coaches Work Session 1 Task #1—Coaches' perceptions about the youth that participate in the sport project What do you think the youth like? What do you think the youth dislike? What do you think you know about their family environment? How do they view their school?	**Youth Work Session 1** Task #1—Interview each other about their lives Task #2—Share coaches' perceptions of the youth and check if the youths agree
Coaches Work Session 2 Task #1—What do you suggest so the kids talk to me more? Task #2—Share the youths' perception about the last meetings Task #3—What do you think the youth expect from the project?	**Youth Work Session 2** Task #1—Carla asked if the youths could help her to find ways to them to feel comfortable in the Work Sessions Task #2—Carla tried to understand about why the youths love soccer and what they believed an ideal coach would resemble
Coaches Work Session 3 Task #1—Share what the youth said about why they love soccer and their ideal coach *Task #2—What do you do during your training sessions that reflect the idea of caring (something that emerged in the youth's Work Session)*	**Youth Work Session 3** Task #1—Share the coaches' assumptions about the youth (the boys want to be a professional soccer player) Task #2—Play an adventure education game designed to help the youth get to know each other better in order to facilitate their being comfortable in the Work Sessions (e.g. what is nice in your personality? Do you like to call and be called by nickname? What do you love in your family? What do you like and dislike in your school? What do you like and dislike in your neighborhood?)
Coaches Work Session 4 *Task #1—Bring back the youth' comments on the coaches' assumptions about why they play soccer.* *Task #2- Designed to respond to the boys' ideal coach…brainstormed suggestions about how to motivate youth to want to learn game tactics* *Task #3—Coaches' perception about what facilitates and hinders the youth's engagement in the project and in playing sport in the community*	**Youth Work Session 4** Task #1—Write about what makes it easy and difficult to do sports in the project and in the community Task #2—Share the coaches' perceptions about *what facilitates and hinders the youth's engagement in the project and in playing sport in the community*

Coaches Work Session 5

Task #1—Designed to respond to the boys' desire to learn game tactics. Presented the Teaching Games for Understanding model as a possibility

Task #2—Share what the youth identified hindered their sport participation in both the project and the community (e.g., what can coaches do about safety, sanitation and opportunity to play?)?

Coaches Work Session 6

Task #1—Designed to respond to the youth' desire to learn game tactics. Planned various tasks with the coaches to teach game tactics in training sessions

Coaches Work Session 7

Task #1—Designed to recap with coaches everything the boys discussed across the previous Work Sessions. (e.g., what the kids like, dislike, their family, school, what they think about the training sessions, barriers and facilitators to doing sport in the project and community)

Coaches Work Session 8

Task #1—Carla showed the coaches the 2 funk songs that the youth created and asked coaches to discuss their perception

Task #2—Carla asked how the sport project could be used more specifically to assist the boys in seeing beyond their current life situations

Youth Work Session 5

Task #1—Carla identified barriers to participation in the training sessions (e.g., drug trafficking, lack of sanitation on the field, violent game play, drunk homeless man present at training session)

Task #2—We brainstorm ideas how to best negotiate these barriers

Youth Work Session 6

Task #1—Talk about barriers to participating in the sport project

Task #2—Make a list of songs that represent your view of your community (designed to help boys better name their experiences in their communities)

Youth Work Session 7

Task #1—Using lyrics from funk music, create a song that represents your community– divided in 2 groups

TABLE 22.2.   Schedule of the Tasks in Coaches Work Session and Youth Work Session in Phase 2

Coaches Work Sessions and Combine Coaches and Youth Work Sessions	Youth Work Sessions
	Youth Work Session 8 Task #1—Carla tried to better understand why the boys have not chosen a life of crime and what they would do with their lives if any choice was possible Task #2—Carla invited the youth to develop and implement a project within the soccer program to create better opportunities
Coaches Work Session 9 Task #1—Share with the coaches what the boys discussed in regard to where the boys hope their lives will go Task #2—Share with coaches what the boys wanted to do as a project and invited the coaches to participate. (e.g., design and implement a leadership program)	**Youth Work Session 9** Task #1—Carla told the boys that the coaches were hesitant to develop the Leadership Program. Carla asked if they know why the coaches were hesitant Task #2—We talk about how the leadership program should look like
Coaches Work Session 10 Task #1—Carla asked what are the qualities of an ideal young leader Task #2- Carla shared what the boys said about the ideal leader	**Youth Work Session 10** Task #1—Share with the boys the coaches concerns about the leadership program (e.g., boys behaviors during training sessions) Task #2—Designed to help the boys identify what they would need to do to alleviate the coaches concerns. (e.g., make a list of behaviors that facilitate and hinder their work in training sessions) Task 3 # We talked about what they could do differently in their training sessions to improve coach perception of youth behavior
Coaches Work Session 11 Task #1—Shared the critical elements that emerged (the analysis of data that Carla and Kim completed) and ask the coaches' perceptions (member check) Task #2—Carla brainstormed with coaches how to begin to implement the leadership program	**Youth Work Session 11** Task #1—Reflection about how the boys would behave in both the training sessions and the Leadership program. Came to an agreement about what they would
Coaches Work Session 12 Task #1—Designed to discussion assumptions coaches were making about the boys and how these assumptions would influence their behaviors toward the boys in the Leadership program	**Youth Work Session 12** Work Session with boys cancelled as Tim (drunk homeless man who is responsible for opening the building) lost the key to the facility

Coaches and Youth Work Session 13

Task #1—What do you think is the best part of the Leadership Program and why?

Task #2—What do you think is the most beneficial aspect of the Leadership Program?

Task #3—What would you like to see changed and why?

Task #4—How can you contribute?

Task #5 -What do we collectively think is most important in the Leadership Program?

Coaches Work Session 14

Task #1 Carla showed the coaches the schedule for the next two weeks of the leadership program

Coaches Work Session 15

Task #1—Reflection about the challenges and enablers Kim and Carla analyzed

Coaches and Youth Work Session 16

Task #1—What do you think is the best part of the Leadership Program and why?

Task #2—What do you think is the most beneficial aspect of the Leadership Program?

Task #3—What would you like to see changed and why?

Task #4—How can you contribute?

Task #5 -What do we collectively think is most important in the Leadership Program?

Youth Work Session 13

Task #1—We organized a monthly schedule for the leadership program

Task #2—Designed to discuss the possible levels of participation in the leadership program (e.g., attend Work Sessions only; attend Work Sessions and serve as leader in younger players training sessions; attend Work Sessions, work as leader in younger players training sessions; attend combined coaches and youth Work Sessions)

Task #3—We discussed how to help low skilled kids (designed to respond to the boys difficulty in working with low skilled children)

Youth Work Session 14

Task #1- Designed to respond to a problem identified in the coaches/youth Work Session regarding the leadership program (e.g., discussion and specific plan on what to do if a boy could not show up on his designated leader day)

Task #2- Designed to reflect on the boys' experiences in the position of leader from the previous week

Youth Work Session 15

Task 1 # Reflection about their experience as leaders

Task 2 # Designed to bring to the boys what the coaches and Carla had witnessed about the their behavior during training sessions and leadership program

Youth Work Session 16

Task# 1—Reflection about things that the youth might have an opportunity to learn in the leadership program (learning aspirations)—the youth gave us examples

(continues)

TABLE 22.2. Continued

Coaches Work Sessions and Combine Coaches and Youth Work Sessions	Youth Work Sessions
Coaches Work Session 17	**Youth Work Session 17**
Task #1—Double check the learning aspirations (the coaches gave us examples)	Task #1—Reflection about the last week as a leader
Task #2—Designed to discuss the incident that occurred around Kleiton being kicked out of the soccer program.	Task #2—Check if the youths learned anything else in relation to the learning aspirations
Coaches Work Session 18	**Youth Work Session 18**
Task #1- Designed to discuss what the coaches believed the leadership program did to how they worked with the boys	Task #1—Reflection about the last week as a leader
Task #2—Designed to discuss how the leadership program could be sustained	Task #2—Check if the youths learned anything else in relation to the learning aspirations
Task #3- Designed to share with coaches the relationship between the critical elements and learning aspirations that emerged through Carla and Kim's data analysis	Task #3—Discussion of how to sustain the leadership program
Coaches and Youth's Work Session 19	
Task #1—What do you think is the best part of the Leadership Program and why?	
Task #2—What do you think is the most beneficial aspect of the Leadership Program?	
Task #3—What would you like to see changed and why?	
Task #4—How can you contribute?	
Task #5 -What do we collectively think is most important in the Leadership Program?	

It was through the simultaneous development and implementation of the Leadership Program that we combined the five critical elements in our work with the youth. It was through this action that the 'learning aspirations' emerged. To be able to co-construct this prototype pedagogical model we had to trust that what was possible to learn would emerge when we implemented the critical elements and worked to create change.

In the process of working collaboratively to create realistic opportunities for the youth to negotiate some of the barriers they identified (action), the learning aspirations emerged. Our willingness to risk trusting the youth in the Leadership Program allowed them to learn about the importance of being responsible and committed, to learn from mistakes, to value each other's knowledge, and to communicate effectively. For a more elaborate explanation of these learning aspirations please see Luguetti et al. (2016).

CHALLENGES AND POSSIBILITIES

We had to negotiate two challenges. These included the adults' lack of trust in the youth, and the incommensurability between the culture of sport in Brazil and the articulated goals of the sport project to address the needs of youth from socially vulnerable backgrounds. What we think is important as we consider this process is that we must be cognizant of challenges that emerge as a result of taking an activist approach.

Our first challenge was a result of our efforts to work in student-centered ways. The lack of trust in the youth that the coaches initially felt could have prevented them from allowing the youth to work as leaders, thus preventing the transformative possibilities that emerged. Many of these assumptions emerged out of the fear about how the youth would or would not respond to being put in positions that required responsibility and maturity. This basic lack of trust in young people has developed through adults' need to control youth and to view them as passive recipients of what others determine is education (Cook-Sather, 2002, 2006). Kim's structural support was essential for the coaches and Carla to understand that in order to co-create a leadership program using an activist approach, we would need to trust the youth to be both responsible and mature.

The second challenge we experienced was the incommensurability between the culture of sport in Brazil and the articulated goals of the sport project for addressing the needs of youth from socially vulnerable backgrounds. This happened when the coordinators of the sport program were trying to influence the coaches by demanding that "winning" should be the main objective of the project. Although the project was run by a non-governmental organization and had as its mission to "promote and democratize access to educational sport", the coordinators insisted that "winning" would be the best way to bring more kids to the project. According to the youth, they were playing soccer to "have fun", "meet friends," and to "avoid a life of crime", reasons beyond "winning the competitions." Further, the coaches were engaged in the project because they believed in the value that sport could bring to youth from socially vulnerable areas. If we are going to succeed in developing a pedagogical model in a sport context, particularly in a sport that has important cultural significance, we will have to negotiate the value of "winning". Even though competition is an essential element in a sport context, an activist approach should challenge authoritarian visions that winning should be the most important part of a sport program.

REFERENCES

Cammarota, J. , and M. Fine. (2008). *Revolutionizing education: Youth Participatory Action Research in motion.* New York and London: Routledge.

Coalter, F., M. Allison, and J. Taylor.(2000). *The role of sport in regenerating deprived urban areas.* The Scottish Executive Central Research. Retrieved April 16, 2013 from http://www.cabdirect.org/abstracts/20003006275.html

Cook-Sather, A. (2002). Authorizing students' perspectives: Towards trust, dialogue, and change in education. *Educational Researcher, 31*(4), 3–14.

Cook-Sather, A. (2006). 'Change based on what students say': preparing teachers for a paradoxical model of leadership. *International Journal of Leadership in Education, 9*(4), 345–358.

Freire, P. (1987). *Pedagogia do oprimido* [Pedagogy of the oppressed] (17th ed.). Rio de Janeiro, Brazil: Paz e Terra.

Freire, P. (1996). *Pedagogia da autonomia: saberes necessários a prática educativa* [Pedagogy of autonomy: Necessary knowledge for educational practice]. Sao Paulo, Brazil: Paz e Terra.

Haudenhuyse, R., Theeboom, M., and Coalter, F. (2012). The potential of sports-based social interventions for vulnerable youth: Implications for sport coaches and youth workers. *Journal of Youth Studies* 15(4):37–41.

Hellison, D. (2010). *Teaching personal and social responsibility through physical activity.* Champaign, IL: Human Kinetics.

Kelly, L. (2011). 'Social Inclusion' through Sports-Based Interventions?. *Critical Social Policy* 31(1):126–50.

Lawson, H.A. 2005. Empowering people, facilitating community development, and contributing to sustainable development: The social work of sport, exercise, and physical education programs. *Sport, Education and Society* 10 (1): 135–60.

Luguetti, C., Oliver, K.L., Dantas, L.E.P.B.T., & Kirk, D. (2016). "The life of crime does not pay; stop and think!": The process of co-constructing a prototype pedagogical model of sport for working with youth from socially vulnerable backgrounds. *Physical Education and Sport Pedagogy*, 1–20.

Luguetti, C., Oliver, K. L., Kirk, D., & Dantas, L.E.P.B.T. (2015). Exploring an activist approach of working with boys from socially vulnerable backgrounds in a sport context. *Sport, Education and Society*, 1–18.

Misztal, B. A. 2011. *The challenges of vulnerability: In search of strategies for a less vulnerable social life*. United Kingdom: Palgrave Macmillan Ltd.

Oliver, K.L., Hamzeh, M., and McCaughtry, N. (2009). Girly girls can play games/Las Niñas pueden jugar tambien: Co-creating a curriculum of possibilities with fifth-grade girls. *Journal of Teaching in Physical Education* 28:90–110.

Sandford, R., and Duncombe, R. (2011). Disaffected Youth in Physical Education and Youth Sport. In K. Armour (ed.) *Sport Pedagogy: An Introduction for Teaching and Coaching,* 165–89. London: Routledge.

SEADE. (2010). Índice Paulista de vulnerabilidade social [Sao Paulo State index of social vulnerability]. Accessed 20 April 2013 http://www.iprsipvs.seade.gov.br/view/pdf/ipvs/metodologia.pdf

PART III

CURRICULUM DEVELOPMENT:
WHAT ARE THE POSSIBILITIES?

CHAPTER 23

CREATING A SOCIAL JUST AND EQUITABLE CURRICULUM IN PHYSICAL EDUCATION

Jennifer L. Walton-Fisette

Throughout Section II of this book, an eclectic array of transformative learning experiences were provided to guide you, physical education teachers, with practical pedagogical strategies that may be implemented into your physical education curriculum. In each of those chapters, the what and how of the individual lessons were included. However, what about the overall physical education curriculum? How is a socially just and equitable curriculum developed in PE?

Most resources in physical education that focus on curriculum development include some aspect of standards and outcomes, curriculum and unit goals, curriculum models and content and/or curriculum assessments (e.g., Kelly & Melograno, 2004; Lund & Tannehill, 2015; SHAPE America, 2018); providing physical education teachers a framework to guide their own PE curriculum. In addition to these variables, when developing a curriculum, other considerations may also include: number of teachers, number of students, equipment available, geographic location, gym and outdoor spaces, amount of time students have PE, and a teacher's philosophy. All of these components are certainly important when developing a curriculum in PE; however, a primary focus for this chapter is going to center on the teacher, since it is important to not only focus on the what of teaching, but who

Teaching About Social Justice Issues in Physical Education, pages 289–296.
Copyright © 2019 by Information Age Publishing
All rights of reproduction in any form reserved.

is doing the teaching (Timkin & Watson, 2015). Teachers' biases and assumptions, dispositions and attitudes and values and beliefs have the potential to explicate or perpetuate the hidden curriculum (i.e., messages teachers send to students with or without intent) (Timken & Watson, 2015, Bain, 1975). Teachers who are culturally aware and sensitive to the whole child tend to be culturally responsive teachers. Timken and Watson (2015) identify culturally responsive teachers who are socioculturally conscious, hold affirming attitudes towards students, embrace a constructive view of learning, learn about students and their communities and are committed to and develop the skills for being an agent of change. Examples of teaching characteristics and behaviors for each category are provided in Figure 23.1.

We understand that not every teacher (or potential teacher) reading this book may be culturally responsive right *now*. We know that for many of us, we need to enhance our content knowledge on social justice issues and/or pedagogical knowledge on how to educate students about social justice issues. To get you

Teaching Characteristics and Behaviors of Culturally Responsive Teachers
Sociocultural Consciousness—Has Cultural Content Knowledge
• Is aware of their own sociocultural history and identity. • Demonstrates, empathy, not pity, for students. • Works to build community within each class. • Creates social, psychological and emotional safety for students.
Holds Affirming Attitudes Towards Students
• Is aware of personal beliefs and values relative to student cultures and characteristics. • Embraces multiple approaches to learning, and different methods of thinking and interacting. • Builds on individual and cultural resources of students. • Thoughtfully considers student interests and varying abilities when planning. • Constructs learning experiences to accommodate for various learning needs.
Embraces a Constructivist View of Learning
• Focuses on learner capabilities, not deficits. • Believes that learners construct knowledge instead of absorbing it. • Uses real-life situations and applications instead of contrived situations. • Finds ways to make learning more problem-based whereby critical thinking skills are honed. • Utilizes assessment tools to propel student learning instead of simply evaluating it.
Learns About Students and Their Communities
• Works to connect with all students.
Is Committed to and Develops the Skills for Being an Agent of Change
• Is aware of and challenges institutionally inequities. • Collaborates with other teachers to focus on social change.

FIGURE 23.1. Adapted from the Culturally Responsive Teachers table in: Lund, J. & Tannehill, D. (2015). Standards-Based Education Curriculum Development, Jones & Bartlett: Burlington, MA.

started, you may want to consider some suggestions provided by Mitchell and Walton-Fisette (2016) on how to address social justice issues (see Figure 23.2).

Although there are numerous textbooks that include aspects of social justice and inclusive practices (e.g., Lund & Tannehill, 2015; Mitchell & Walton-Fisette, 2016) and valued resources that provide a scholarly focus on social justice (e.g., Ennis, 2016; Flory, Tischler & Sanders, 2015; Robinson & Randall, 2016), we have yet to identify how to develop a physical education curriculum that focuses on, integrates and/or addresses social justice issues. The Teaching Tolerance Organization (https://www.tolerance.org/) has created a comprehensive website for all content areas in schools (aside from PE, frustratingly) that focuses on "educating for a diverse democracy". On the website, there are extensive classroom

---

Creating a Socially Just and Equitable Learning Environment for All Students

- Encourage students to be positive with one another and supportive of each other's efforts.
- Openly address inappropriate name calling that targets and ridicules students.
- Develop appropriately challenging tasks for all students by utilizing modifications (e.g., simplifications/extensions) to meet the needs of all learners.
- Educate students about people's differences and provide learning opportunities to engage with other students who are similar and different from them (e.g., social identities, body types, hair and clothing styles).
- Implement lesson activities (see Section II) that explicitly addresses social justice issues in the physical education environment.
- Consider how you partner and group students in your classes.
- Limit the opportunities that students' performance and ability is on public display in front of others.
- Take into consideration students' social identities when constructing units of instruction (e.g., based on one's religion, students may engage in a dance unit differently).
- Provide learning opportunities about the physical and emotional body.
- Create safe spaces to allow students to engage in discussions about their thoughts, feelings and experiences.
- Do not include elimination games or activities that utilize students as physical targets in your curriculum.
- Create instructional materials that can be utilized by all students in the class (e.g., for ELL, visual and hearing impaired, etc.).
- Select units of instruction that do not perpetuate gender and racial bias (e.g., girls will participate in dance while boys participate in football/rugby).
- When implementing curriculum and instructional models, consider social justice issues to address that is specific to each model (e.g., in the Sport Education Model engage in conversations on how students select their roles and responsibilities—is the head coach the most skilled student and the record keeper the least skilled?).
- Allow a variety of students to answer questions and demonstrate tasks.
- Provide feedback to all students.
- Create/utilize written assignments and assessments that are accessible to all students.

FIGURE 23.2. Social Justice Issues to Address in Physical Education. Adapted from Mitchell, S. A. & Walton-Fisette, J. L. (2016). The Essentials of Teaching Physical Education: Curriculum, Instruction, and Assessment. Human Kinetics: Champaign, IL.

Teaching Tolerance Social Justice Standards and Domains
Identity
1. Students will develop positive social identities based on their membership in multiple groups in society.
2. Students will develop language and historical and cultural knowledge that affirm and accurately describe their membership in multiple identity groups.
3. Students will recognize that people's multiple identities interact and create unique and complex individuals.
4. Students will express pride, confidence and healthy self-esteem without denying the value and dignity of other people.
5. Students will recognize traits of the dominant culture, their home culture and other cultures and understand how they negotiate their own identity in multiple spaces.
Diversity
1. Students will express comfort with people who are both similar to and different from them and engage respectfully with all people.
2. Students will develop language and knowledge to accurately and respectfully describe how people (including themselves) are both similar to and different from each other and others in their identity groups.
3. Students will respectfully express curiosity about the history and lived experiences of others and will exchange ideas and beliefs in an open-minded way.
4. Students will respond to diversity by building empathy, respect, understanding and connection.
5. Students will examine diversity in social, cultural, political and historical contexts rather than in ways that are superficial or oversimplified.
Justice
1. Students will recognize stereotypes and relate to people as individuals rather than representatives of groups.
2. Students will recognize unfairness on the individual level (e.g., biased speech) and injustice at the institutional or systemic level (e.g., discrimination).
3. Students will analyze the harmful impact of bias and injustice on the world, historically and today.
4. Students will recognize that power and privilege influence relationships on interpersonal, intergroup and institutional levels and consider how they have been affected by those dynamics.
5. Students will identify figures, groups, events and a variety of strategies and philosophies relevant to the history of social justice around the world.
Action
1. Students will express empathy when people are excluded or mistreated because of their identities and concern when they themselves experience bias.
2. Students will recognize their own responsibility to stand up to exclusion, prejudice and injustice.
3. Students will speak up with courage and respect when they or someone else has been hurt or wronged by bias.
4. Students will make principled decisions about when and how to take a stand against bias and injustice in their everyday lives and will do so despite negative peer or group pressure.
5. Students will plan and carry out collective action against bias and injustice in the world and will evaluate what strategies are most effective.

FIGURE 23.3. Teaching Tolerance Social Justice Standards and Domains (www.tolerance.org/).

resources and professional development opportunities for us to access. To frame the work of the organization, social justice standards were developed, with the intention of the standards to be the foundation of establishing an anti-bias curriculum (see Figure 23.3 for the standards). The four domains of the teaching tolerance framework includes: identity, diversity, justice and action. We will utilize these domains as a segue to provide recommendations for how to create a social just and equitable curriculum in PE and also suggest you refer to the chapters in Section II for specific lessons and activities to align with these suggestions.

IDENTITY

In Chapters 4 and 5, numerous lessons were shared as to how students can explore their own social identities. A first step in establishing an equitable environment in PE is for students to understand who they are and how their identity and culture is positioned within their home, their school community and society at large. The following are suggestions on how teachers can access and explore students' identities in your classes.

1. Provide students with the opportunity to explore their own social identities. Who are they? Where do they come from? How do they identify? How are their cultures and identities accepted/rejected, privileged/marginalized in the local and global communities?
2. Create learning opportunities for students to research and explore their culture and identities, along with the cultures and identities of the students in their class, school and/or community.
3. Create spaces and opportunities for students to engage in discussions with their peers about who they are, where they come from and the influences that shaped their belief system.

DIVERSITY

Exploring self and social identities allows students to establish a foundational understanding about what identity actually is, how people may be viewed/perceived based on one's identity and hopefully a knowledge base of the power positioning that may occur simply due to how a person identifies. In building on their initial understanding, it is important for students to learn about the similarities and differences of individuals within the human race. Teaching about diversity is a necessary step in this learning process.

1. Allow students to share their feelings, thoughts and beliefs about people who are similar and different from them. The hope would be to engage in open and respectful dialogue to provide the opportunity to learn about and from one another, even if they have different perspectives.

2. Educate students on how people are similar and different, while attempting to deconstruct socially constructed messages that students gather through a wide variety of media outlets.
3. Formulate the expectation that students will be respectful, understanding and caring of others, regardless of their identities and similarities and differences.
4. Utilize current events and issues to engage in discourse about diversity. In physical education, sport is a pathway that may be utilized to address social issues, which can then be connected to education and other contexts.

JUSTICE

Teaching about identity and diversity is necessary to educate students about social justice issues and social inequalities. Educational experience begins with the self and expands to others, including their classmates, teachers, administrators and families. The next level, justice, increases the depth of their learning since the expectation is for the student to be more central and involved in the process. For students to be given opportunities to engage in justice initiatives, we suggest the following.

1. Create lessons that allow students to critique and question an image, context and/or situation. For example, images and media sources may be displayed to students and for them to identify potential stereotypes and or unfairness that a person may be experiencing. Another example would be to use scenarios in a physical education setting to address different social justice issues and have students identity who was privileged/marginalized in those situations and what steps could be taken to make the circumstance more equitable.

ACTION

Taking action requires a strong sense of self, compassion and empathy, a level of passion for justice and equity and courage. Often times, taking action is not easy and may result in a negative outcome or feeling. However, engaging in activist work provides opportunities to create change for others and can be quite rewarding. Here are some considerations for taking action in a PE context.

1. Establish a culture in your classroom where students feel respected and supported to take action. Inform your students that you want them to identify socially unjust issues and potentially address them as long as they are not harmful or disrespectful to someone else in the process.
2. Encourage students to stand up to peers if they verbalize or engage in a disrespectful or hurtful act.

3.   Allow students to explore and research injustices in physical education, sport and/or human movement with the goal to carry out and take action against the injustice.

CHALLENGES AND POSSIBILITIES

As you attempt to create a socially just and equitable curriculum, you may face some challenges along the way. For many of us, we are bounded by standards, assessments, policies, national curricula and accreditation boards that govern what we teach; although many of these socio-political networks includes, to some degree, content related to social justice (Ovens, et. al, 2018). Thus, these networks can support our argument for formulating a curriculum that focuses on social justice; however, their relationship to social justice may be minimal or lack overtness, which will demand extra time and energy from you to navigate these networks. Another challenge that you might encounter is that your programs, schools and/or administrators may not espouse a socio-critical perspective, leaving you to be the 'token' person advocating and educating about and for social justice. For many teacher educators in PETE, a lack of content knowledge and limited time are also reasons that prevent them from providing their students with a social justice education (Walton-Fisette, et. al., 2018). For those of us who are already or intending to engage in this work, even with best practices and best of intentions, we will have students that challenge us back, resist in engaging about social justice issues or potentially make limited inroads on their perspectives and beliefs about social issues.

Despite these challenges, the benefits far outweigh these barriers that we may encounter. In our attempt to teach about and for social justice, we are doing our share to create a more just and equitable world in which we live. The more that we can educate and potentially influence upcoming generations about equity and justice and teaching them how to question and critique what is or what always has been, the greater opportunity for positive change to transpire for the betterment of our collective society.

MOVING FORWARD

Our hope is that current and future physical education teachers will make philosophical, curriculum and instructional decisions to create a socially just and equitable learning environment for *all* students in physical education. For some of you, you are on this journey and are looking to enhance your content knowledge and pedagogical strategies on how to address a variety of social justice issues. For others, it may seem daunting to even know where to begin. Our goal was to provide you with a variety of suggestions and strategies for you to get started, in your own context, with your own students. When teaching for social justice, we know there is no 'one size fits all,' but we all believe in the importance of creating equitable learning opportunities and socially just experiences in physical education. Let's keep moving forward on creating change with our children and youth.

RESOURCES AND REFERENCES

Bain, L. (1975). The hidden curriculum in physical education. *Quest,* 24(1), 92–101.

Ennis, C. (Ed). (2016). *The Routledge handbook of physical education pedagogies.* New York, NY: Taylor and Francis.

Flory, S. B., Tischler, A., & Sanders, S. (2014). *Sociocultural issues in physical education: Case studies for teachers.* New York, NY: Rowman & Littlefield.

Lund, J., & Tannehill, D. (2015). *Standards-based education curriculum development.* Burlington, MA: Jones & Bartlett.

Kelly, L. E., & Melograno, V. J. (2004). *Developing the physical education curriculum: An achievement-based approach.* Long Grove, IL: Waveland Press.

Mitchell, S. A., & Walton-Fisette, J. L. (2016). *The essentials of teaching physical education: Curriculum, instruction, and assessment.* Champaign, IL: Human Kinetics.

Ovens, A., Flory, S., Sutherland, S., Philpot, R., Walton-Fisette, J. L., Hill, J., Phillips, S., & Flemons, M. (2018). How PETE comes to matter in the performance of social justice education. *Physical Education & Sport Pedagogy, 23*(5), 484–496.

Robinson, D. B., & Randall, L. (2016). An introduction. In D. B. Robinson and L. Randall (Eds.), *Social justice in physical education: Critical reflections and pedagogies for change* (pp. 1–14). Toronto, CA: Canadian Scholars' Press.

SHAPE America. (2018). *Curriculum in physical education.* Retrieved on April 26, 2018 from www.shapeamerica.org/publications/resources/teachingtools/teachertoolbox/curriculum.aspx

Teaching Tolerance Social Justice Standards and Domains. (n.d.) Retrieved on April 26, 2018 from www.tolerance.org/.

Timkin, G. L., & Watson, D. L. (2015). Teaching all kids: Valuing students through culturally responsive and inclusive practice. In Lund & Tannehill, (Eds.), *Standards-based education curriculum development* (pp. 137–165). Burlington, MA: Jones & Bartlett.

Walton-Fisette, J. L., Philpot, R., Phillips, S., Flory, S., Hill, J., Sutherland, S. & Flemons, M. (2018). Implicit and explicit pedagogical practices related to sociocultural issues and social justice in physical education teacher education programs. *Physical Education & Sport Pedagogy, 23*(5), 497–509.

CHAPTER 24

SOCIAL JUSTICE ISSUE

Critical Sport Pedagogy in Pre-PETE Courses

Michelle Flemons

ACTION RESEARCH & REFLECTION

I have worked with children and adults in education for many years; as a gymnastics coach, a teacher of physical education and as a senior lecturer involved with PETE and physical education undergraduate courses in the United Kingdom (UK). Although my own personal experience of living abroad, and to some degree my education, has contributed towards a broader awareness and appreciation of a global community rich in diversity; I did not feel fully equipped with the knowledge, skills and understanding of *how* to teach effectively in a culturally sensitive and inclusive way. Much of what I delivered within the curriculum focused on the subject specific requirements within physical education (Ovens, et al., 2018).

According to Tripp, Piletic, and Babcock (2004), inclusion in physical education can be described as meeting individual educational needs within the context of political and social justice. Involvement in a thoughtful and caring community of diverse learners promotes effective learning through the collaborative efforts of everyone. Specifically, inclusion in physical education honors all kinds of student diversity (not just disability) as an opportunity for learning about how everyone can become physically active through a variety of movement and fitness activi-

Teaching About Social Justice Issues in Physical Education, pages 297–306.
Copyright © 2019 by Information Age Publishing
All rights of reproduction in any form reserved.

297

ties (Webb & Pope, 1999). Inclusion has been described as 'an attitude, a value, and belief system, not just an action or set of actions' (Tripp, Rizzo, &Wibbert, 2007, p. 32). I recognized that in order to develop the 'whole' person, a more holistic approach towards teaching; with a particular focus on the affective domain through physical activity was needed. The affective domain refers to personal and social development, feelings, emotions, morals and ethics (Beane, 1990 cited by Martin & Reigeluth, 1999). My 'actions' in planning and differentiating subject specific tasks did not explicitly educate all learners to become socially and culturally sensitive. My interest and passion in valuing every individual I taught was unwavering, however, opportunities to develop my teaching in a way that would fully embrace this was limited.

Teaching and research opportunities in Higher Education provided a forum whereby teaching through and for social justice could be further explored. Following my involvement with the data generation for an international social justice research project, I listened to the accounts of other physical educators about their experiences and appreciation of equality and diversity within an education context (Walton-Fisette et al., 2018). The findings suggested that my experiences were not in isolation. Participants who had been discriminated against or marginalized for varying reasons had a heightened sense of its importance. Additionally, although some physical educators recognized that they had an opportunity to engage in discussions surrounding social justice in their own education, they did not always appreciate its relevance until they entered the workplace. This raised the question as to *how* social justice, inclusion and teaching through the affective domain can be made relevant and be explicitly embedded within pedagogical practices.

The cultural studies model has been adopted for this purpose. O'Sullivan and Kinchin (2010) observed that adolescents were being educated in a diversity of school contexts and as a consequence, there was a need for a pedagogical model that would better reflect and address a more contemporary life experienced today. The authors recognized that physical education in its current form was not really considered as a place to develop literate and critical consumers of sport, physical activity and movement culture. Drawing from this, they proposed the cultural studies model as a possible solution. Its purpose was to not only encourage participation in Sport and Physical Activity, but also encourage students to learn how sport and physical activity can contribute positively and negatively to individual wellbeing, and to group, community and national cultures. Furthermore, students are encouraged to challenge the status quo related to access and influence of physical activity and sport infrastructure by becoming 'cultural connoisseurs' (O'Sullivan & Kinchin, 2010; p. 334). Furthermore, Bheekie and Huyssteen (2015) inferred that affective responses to situations where inequalities arise are not always addressed in a formal curricula. The authors considered the notion that adopting a pedagogy of discomfort would allow students to examine their passive acceptance or non—acceptance of apparent social injustices that had already been shaped by the status quo. Gymnastics provides a forum through which students could critically examine these issues, as this is not always an environment that they were familiar with as it does not dominate the contemporary traditional physical education curricula.

Engaging learners with their thoughts, feelings and perceptions was central to teaching through and for social justice by making it relatable, regardless of each individual's life stories and experiences. This was achieved by combining pedagogy (i.e., child centered learning), with the five assumptions associated with a more andragogical adult centered approach (Knowles, 1984). Pedagogy and andragogy have been described as sitting at opposite ends of a continuum; pedagogy geared towards child and adolescent learners with andragogy being more conducive to adult learners (Merriam, 2001).

The five assumptions for adult learning are;

1. The self-concept of oneself as a more self-directed and independent learner,
2. Adults may have a broader catalogue of life experiences to inform learning,
3. A readiness to learn and having an awareness of the development of his/her own social role,
4. An ability to apply learning straight away
5. Foster a stronger internal motivation to learn.

This approach was adopted to encourage Higher Education students to reflect on their own lived/witnessed experiences and the feelings they evoked. The purpose was to develop well-rounded students that can flourish in a global community rich in diversity by encouraging empathy and an appreciation of those around them. This warranted a more experiential learning experience during practical gymnastics workshops, thus, allowing a safe space to explore pedagogies of discomfort (Boler & Zembylas, 2003; Zembylas, 2015).

CONTEXT

The teaching activities focused upon in this chapter were situated within a widening participation university in the UK. Widening participation universities actively recruit students from underrepresented groups. The community within the town and university is rich in diversity and culture.

I have taught students across a range of Sport and Physical Education courses including Teacher Education. There are a number of students who commute from surrounding towns and cities. Some are first generation Higher Education students and others are continuing a tradition within their own families in terms of pursuing a career in teaching. At the time of writing this chapter, social justice issues are embedded within a level 6 Critical Sport Pedagogy unit as part of the core pedagogy strand in BA and BSc Sport and Physical Education. This is delivered through practical workshops, seminars and lectures. They are also drawn upon in the sociology units in the course. This unit provides students with an introduction to the concepts of critical pedagogy and social justice as these relate to sport and physical education. Students experience practical physical activities in dance and gymnastics, and learn about the philosophy, pedagogy and role of dance in critical pedagogy. Through gymnastics, students engage with a range of social justice issues using the Cultural Studies pedagogical model and consider the possibility of these activities as forms of critical pedagogy. It expands existing knowledge of sport pedagogy and aims to critically examine contemporary issues in current forms of physical education and youth sport using a critical pedagogy approach. It also provides opportunities for students to reflect on their biography of experience in sport and physical education and examine it as a context for engaging in critical pedagogy. Additionally, students are encouraged to challenge the philosophy, pedagogy and practice of gymnastics and dance as forms of critical pedagogy.

UNIT/LESSON SET-UP

The unit has been created and underpinned by the cultural studies model by using class discussions and journaling to support reflective practice. The practical workshops are therefore not planned in isolation, but planned to complement topics addressed in the seminars and lectures. The following steps identify the considerations for devising and delivering the unit.

Step 1: An overview of the key topics relevant to the unit were considered and aligned with the most appropriate gymnastics based activity in the workshop (see Figure 24.1).

Step 2: The cultural studies model, movement culture and encouraging students to become cultural connoisseurs are introduced to the students in the first main lecture. This provides an opportunity to contextualize social justice and align it with topics that are relevant and personal to the students. Marginalization in physical education (Oliver & Kirk, 2014; Smith & Karp, 1996) is a concept that students may be aware of within the field of physical education. This is used as the initial 'hook' following their reflections during the lecture in order to make marginalization relatable by evoking the feelings associated with this. Drawing attention to what students had either witnessed or experienced facilitated this. By encouraging students to consider the activities they liked and disliked and why, these experiences were drawn upon in order to give social justice importance in teaching and encourage students to become more aware of the world around them.

Step 3: The content in the practical workshops are used as a vehicle to explore social justice in physical education and sport. Gymnastics was chosen in this instance as this was an activity that the majority of students felt uncomfortable with and had limited experience. There were very few 'experts', which meant that the choice of activity itself highlighted the discourses and the emotions attached to the discomfort. Gymnastics was used to demonstrate how we can teach through social justice. However, any content within physical education and sport may be

Week	Lecture	Practical Workshop	Reading	Reflection
41	Introduction to the Cultural Studies Model	Aerobic gymnastics and basic shapes	Kinchin, G.D. and O'Sullivan, M. (2003) 'Incidences of student support for and resistance to a curricular innovation in high school physical education', *Journal of Teaching in Physical Education*, 22: 245–260.	Note your initial feelings towards doing gymnastics. Consider how physical cultural issues impact on your pre-conceived ideas about gymnastics. (100 words)
42	Critical Pedagogy through gymnastics	Balance	Tischler, A., & McCaughtry, N. (2011). PE Is Not for Me: When Boys' Masculinities Are Threatened. *Research Quarterly for Exercise and Sport*, 82(1), 37–48.	Highlight your key thoughts about how the media representation of bodies affects young people's engagement with their body in gymnastics (150 words).
43	The Midway Model in Gymnastics	Rotation	Oliver, K. (2001). Images of the body from popular culture: engaging adolescent girls in critical enquiry, *Sport, Education and Society*, 6 (2), 143–164	a. Reflect on the sessions to date and note situations where gendered roles were reinforced/'undone' throughout your experience of gymnastics. b. Discuss what devices were used to maintain or challenge gendered boundaries. c. Consider whether gender can be 'undone' using gymnastics (150 words)
44	Inclusion issues in Gymnastics	Sports acro Pairs balances	Sykes, H., & McPhail, D. (2008) Unbearable lessons: Contesting fat phobia in physical education. *Sociology of Sport Journal*, 25, 66–96.	Reflect on this week's activities. Which role did you take within the pair/trio and why? How were you included in your group? (100 words).
45		Sports acro Trio balances (balance)		
46		Sport acro Group dynamic	Hills, L. and Croston, A. (2012) 'It should be better all together: exploring strategies for undoing gender in co-educational physical education' *Sport, Education and Society*, 17(5), 591–605	

FIGURE 24.1.   Unit Delivery Overview

(continues)

Week	Lecture	Practical Workshop	Reading	Reflection
47		Educational gymnastics sequence building with large equipment (creating, performing and appreciating)	MacPhail, A., & Kinchin, G. (2004). The use of drawings as an evaluative tool: Students' experiences of Sport Education. Physical Education & Sport Pedagogy, 9(1), 87–108. OR Mowling, C. M., Brock, S. J., & Hastie, P. A. (2006). Fourth grade students' drawing interpretations of a Sport Education soccer unit. Journal of Teaching in Physical Education, 25, 9–35.	AFTER SESSION: a. Work in groups or individually for this. Take your gymnastics movements out of the classroom (SAFELY!) and create some photographs of you and your group engaging in gymnastics in everyday spaces. Bring these to the next practical session. b. Using this experience reflect on the place of gymnastics in everyday life and the possibilities for bringing gymnastics into non-typical spaces. which movements you created (150 words)
48		Free gymnastics	View the photo slideshows provided in web links in the BREO Guided Learning section for Gymnastics Krane, V., Ross, S. R., Miller, M., Rowse, J. L., Ganoe, K., Andrzejczyk, J. A., & Lucas, C. B. (2010). Power and focus: self-representation of female college athletes. Qualitative Research in Sport and Exercise, 2(2), 175–195	Reflect on the physical cultural issues that influenced which movements you created (150 words)
49		Flight: Team gym	Wrench, A., & Garrett, R. (2012). Identity work: stories told in learning to teach physical education. Sport, Education and Society, 17(1), 1–19.	Conclude your gymnastics task with a reflection on your experiences and learning of gymnastics through the cultural studies model. Has your own embodied identity and sport participation supported or constrained your engagement in this unit and in gymnastics? (150 words)
50		Vaulting		

FIGURE 24.1. Continued

selected. This comprised of four main lectures and 10 x 90-minute practical workshops.

Step 4: Using the emotional feelings students attach to the activity may support their learning. However, care needs to be taken to ensure that the environment can become a comfortable one. There are many disciplines within gymnastics, therefore these were all experienced over the 10 weeks.

Step 5: Students are asked to write a 150 word reflection each week that aligns to their practical experience and highlights a particular social justice issue. A suggested reading is given to support their reflection.

STRATEGY/ACTIVITY/LESSON

The example used for the purpose of this chapter is one of the practical workshops focused upon 'undoing' gender through gymnastics. The gymnastics discipline was chosen because it encompasses strong stereotypes and preconceived ideas surrounding participation. The issues reflected upon during each session are evident in other sessions, therefore students could draw from different experiences for each of the reflective blogs as they encountered them. This highlighted the fluid nature of how the different issues impact upon and influence each other (e.g., body image and gender within sports acrobatics).

Step 1: The example below uses sports acrobatics as the gymnastics discipline through which 'gender undone' could be further explored. This has been delivered through cooperative learning. The purpose for this is that social learning is considered to be just as important as physical development (Dyson, 2001). The non-negotiables of the model include working in heterogenous groups, promoting interdependency within the group, face to face interaction, working towards a group goal, working together to construct new information and individual accountability. The teacher's role is to facilitate learning and give students the space to discuss and work through ideas (Dyson, 2001; Johnson & Johnson, 2009). Non- physical participants are also accounted for, which maximizes engagement. Additionally, students are more explicitly engaged with the affective domain via the emphasis on social learning.

Step 2: Heterogenous groups: the groupings for the activities provide opportunities to explore students' feelings and confidence towards the activities. Initially, I ask for the students to get themselves into heterogenous groups and justify how their group was heterogenous. In these instances, students would often make sure they grouped themselves with their friendship groups. In other workshops, I grouped them by moving them away from people they would naturally choose to work with. This had a positive effect on the engagement of the students during the sessions and facilitated different discussions amongst the groups by changing the dynamics. By giving each group member a role within their learning team such as feedback manager, safety manager, etc., the aim was to ensure that the interdependency allowed all students to interact with each other in a positive way.

Step 3: Group Processing is a non–negotiable when using the cooperative learning model. Students are encouraged to not only actively discuss the physical requirements of the session at certain points, but also consider how they could challenge their preconceived ideas of their role within their group in sports acrobatics; as a 'base' or as a 'top'. Furthermore, pre-planned questions allowed them to explore how as a group they could try alternatives and adapt the activity to challenge their existing views. Additionally, as a facilitator, I move around the class and speak to students on an individual basis to identify what they were hearing from other students, what those conversations meant to and for them, and how they related back to the reflective task set at the beginning of the session.

Step 4: Teacher as facilitator: The reflective task and reading is made available prior to the session in order to provide the focus for the session and then highlighted again within the group goal at the beginning of the session. Some of our students struggle with engaging in independent tasks, therefore providing them with a 'scaffold' of simple, more closed questions surrounding the learning objective for the practical workshop made the task easier for them to engage. Moreover, the tasks are linked to the assessment, therefore, non-engagement was not an option. The questions surrounding 'gender undone' are: a) Reflect on the sessions to date and note situations where gendered roles were reinforced or 'undone' throughout your experience of gymnastics, b) Discuss what devices were used to maintain or challenge gendered boundaries, and c) Consider whether gender can be 'undone' using gymnastics. This allows students to reflect on their own emotional feelings and responses towards the activity and the causes of those emotions (e.g., the pedagogical model used, the activity, the environment and peers). Further reflection on the session and aligning this with further research outside of the gym facilitated further thought and consideration.

Step 5: The final stage is consideration for assessment in and for learning. The students are required to keep a journal. This handwritten piece allows students to actively engage in the process of noting their thoughts, feelings and perceptions. They can express this through pictures and written reflections based on their practical experiences and readings. This is an on-going process throughout the unit and is submitted as a final piece.

CHALLENGES AND POSSIBILITIES

Many of the Sport and Physical Education students have been socialized through a traditional curriculum in physical education heavily dominated by games based activities (Green, 2002). This influences their thoughts, feelings and beliefs surrounding physical education, how it should be taught and how they engage with the tasks set for them (Dewar & Lawson, 1984).

Some students may focus on physical competence in the lessons as this is the way they have been socialized through physical education and in their sporting environments. The fact that gymnastics may be new to most of them created a level playing field and ensured that students became very aware of their feelings towards an activity that was relatively new to them. The activity itself held pre-conceived ideas regarding what a gymnast looks like and many students had pre-conceived ideas based on their previous experiences as to how the sessions would run. At this point, students have looked at various pedagogical models theoretically, so by teaching them a new activity using the model and creating an awareness of the sociocultural issues embedded within physical education, sport and gymnastics specifically, students can be provided with opportunities to engage in a unique experience whereby the issues could be raised and explored in a practical way. This suits kinesthetic learners, as they learn by 'doing' (Coker, 2013), experiencing as opposed to only accessing the theory.

A great deal of sensitivity is needed for those who struggle with negative memories of gymnastics lessons in school, as well as a more defensive 'jock culture' attitude towards the activities and misogynistic behaviors. This provides an opportunity to sensitively discuss the behaviors with the individuals involved and what impact it may have on those around them. Furthermore, this aides in developing the emotional intelligence by challenging behaviors in a positive way and exploring the feelings associated with the behaviors. The assessment task provides a medium through which feelings can be explored based on the literature provided and the tasks set. Students are asked to produce a handwritten 'diary' of the tasks including pictures, annotations, comments, and colour schemes to portray the topics, their reflections in relation to the topics and summarizes their awareness of what they learned and how they learned during the practical sessions. This enables each student to align their physical development with emotional and cognitive development by articulating their views and ideas towards the tasks in a positive way. Moreover, they could examine how the pedagogical approaches can explicitly support teaching in a socially just way. Additionally, BSc students argue that they do not have a sociology strand for their course, therefore they are at a disadvantage due to the 'quantitative nature' of their own course. For them, the importance of social justice within a global and real context needed explaining so that they could see its relevance outside of their learning and how it applies to day to day life.

REFERENCES

Beane, J. A. (1990). *Affect in the curriculum: Toward democracy, dignity, and diversity.* New York, NY: Teachers College Press.

Bheekie, A., & Huyssteen, M. (2015). Be mindful of your discomfort: An approach to contextualized learning. *International Journal of Research on Service-Learning and Community Engagement, 3*(1).

Boler, M., & Zembylas, M. (2003). *Discomforting truths: The emotional terrain of understanding difference.* In P. Trifonas (Ed.), *Pedagogies of difference: Rethinking education for social change* (pp. 110–136). New York, NY: Routledge Falmer.

Coker, C.A. (2013). Accommodating students' learning styles in physical education. *Journal of Physical Education, Recreation & Dance, 67*(9), 66–68.

Dewar, A. M., & Lawson, H. A. (1984). The subjective warrant and recruitment into physical education. *Quest, 36*(1), 15–25.

Dyson, B. (2001). Cooperative learning in an elementary physical education program, *Journal in Teaching Physical Education, 20*(3), 264–281.

Green, K. (2002). Physical education teachers in their figurations: A sociological analysis of everyday philosophies. *Sport and Society, 7*, 65–83.

Johnson, D., & Johnson, T. (2009). An educational psychology success story: Social interdependence theory and cooperative learning. *Educational Researcher, 38*(5), 365–379.

Knowles, M. (1984). *Andragogy in Action. Applying modern principles of adult education*, San Francisco, CA: Jossey Bass.

Martin, B. L., & Reigeluth, C. M. (1999). *Affective education and the affective domain: Implications for instructional design theories and models.* In C. M. Reigeluth (Ed.), *Instructional design theories and models, Vol. 2, A new paradigm of instructional theory.* New York, NY: Routledge.

Merriam, S. B. (2001). Andragogy and self-directed learning. *New Directions for Adult and Continuing Education, 89*, 3–14.

Oliver, K. L., & Kirk, D. (2014). Towards an activist approach to research and advocacy for girls and physical education, *Physical Education and Sport Pedagogy, 21*(3), 313–327.

O'Sullivan, M., & Kinchin, G. (2010). *Cultural studies curriculum in physical activity and sports.* In J. Lund & D. Tannehill (Eds.), *Standards-based physical education curriculum development* (pp. 333–365). Sudbury, MA: Jones and Bartlett.

Ovens, A., Sara B. Flory, S. B., Sutherland, S., Philpot, R., Walton-Fisette, J. L., Hill, J., Phillips, S., & Flemons, M. (2018), How PETE comes to matter in the performance of social justice education, *Physical Education and Sport Pedagogy, 23*(5), 484–486.

Smith, B., & Karp, G. (1996) Adapting to marginalisation in a middle school physical education class. *Journal of Teaching in Physical Education, 16*, 30–47.

Tripp, A., Piletic, C., & Babcock, G. (2004). *Including students with disabilities in physical education: A position statement.* Reston, VA: American Alliance for Health, Physical Education, Recreation and Dance.

Tripp, A., Rizzo T. L., & Webbert, L. (2007). Inclusion in Physical Education, *Journal of Physical Education, Recreation & Dance, 78*(2), 32–48.

Walton-Fisette, J. L., Philpot, R., Phillips, S., Flory, S. B., Hill, J. Sutherland, S., & Flemons, M. (2018). Implicit and explicit pedagogical practices related to sociocultural issues and social justice in physical education teacher education programs, *Physical Education and Sport Pedagogy, 23*(5), 497–509.

Webb, D., & Pope, C. C. (1999). Including within an inclusive context: Going beyond labels and categories. *Journal of Physical Education, Recreation & Dance, 70*(7), 41–47.

Zembylas, M. (2015). 'Pedagogy of discomfort' and its ethical implications: the tensions of ethical violence in social justice education, *Ethics and Education, 10*(2), 163–174.

CHAPTER 25

STUDENT-CENTERED INQUIRY AS CURRICULUM IN PHYSICAL EDUCATION TEACHER EDUCATION

Kimberly L. Oliver and Carla Luguetti

ACTION RESEARCH REFLECTION AND CONTEXT

In an attempt to answer the calls for better teachers and teacher education programs in an era of scrutiny, policy has demanded more field-based placements in pre-service teacher education (Levine, 2006; National Council for Accreditation of Teacher Education, 2010; National Council on Teacher Quality, 2010). Physical education teacher educators have indicated a need to intentionally structure field-based placements (Collier, 2006). McIntyre, Byrd, and Foxx (1996) warned us, however, that what occurs in field experiences requires attention to create any type of change to pre-service teachers' learning. If we hope to challenge the status quo in physical education (Fernandez-Balboa, 1997; Kirk, 2010; Oliver & Kirk, 2015) in order to better meet the interests and needs of today's youth (Enright & O'Sullivan, 2012; Oliver, Hamzeh, & McCaughtry 2009; O'Sullivan & MacPhail, 2010), then we must change what we are doing in our physical education teacher

Teaching About Social Justice Issues in Physical Education, pages 307–323.
Copyright © 2019 by Information Age Publishing
All rights of reproduction in any form reserved.
307

education (PETE) field-based placements and seek to understand what impact our practices have on our pre-service teachers' learning (Oliver & Oesterreich, 2013).

In this chapter, we will describe how we use a *Student-Centered Inquiry as Curriculum* (Oliver & Oesterreich, 2013) approach with pre-service teachers in a secondary physical education methods course in order to meet the challenges and realities of working with youth. The *Student-Centered Inquiry as Curriculum* (SCIC) approach to working with youth was initially developed as a way of preparing pre-service teachers to be inquiry oriented and student centered in their pedagogical practices in order to challenge the status quo of physical education. This approach emerged from 12 years of activist research with marginalized girls in physical education settings whereby we worked with girls to create curricula that better met their needs and interests (e.g., Oliver, 1999; Oliver & Hamzeh, 2010; Oliver, Hamzeh, & McCaughtry, 2009; Oliver & Lalik, 2000; 2004). At the heart of the SCIC approach is a commitment to listening and pedagogically responding to the needs and interests of a diverse student population in localized contexts.

Assisting pre-service teachers to utilize inquiry centered in student voice as a guide for understanding what facilitates and hinders young people's interests, motivation, and learning involved a theoretical shift in how we conceptualized curriculum for both teacher education and secondary physical education. As such, I (Kim) redesigned my secondary methods course to be school based. The course is designed as a 6-credit class (e.g. the equivalent of two courses) that meets for three hours two days per week. During this time, we work with one block scheduled freshman physical education class that meets 2 days per week for 75 minutes each day. Following the physical education class, the secondary methods class would meet for an additional hour and 15 minutes at the university.

As part of the design, I planned the course so I could model for my pre-service teachers how to use student data, derived through inquiry, to guide pedagogical decisions. The goal was to work with the youth to help them identify barriers to their physical activity, critically examine these barriers, and work with them to imagine and implement alternative types of activity possibilities within their physical education class that better facilitated their interest and learning. *Student Centered Inquiry as Curriculum* (Oliver & Oesterreich, 2013) is a *process* for working with youth in physical activity settings. In this chapter, we will briefly describe the SCIC process and provide more detail on the initial aspect of the approach, *Building the Foundation*, and how we use it within a secondary physical education methods course taught in a local high school. For a more detailed description of the entire process please see Oliver & Oesterreich (2013) and Oliver et al. (2015).

STUDENT CENTERED INQUIRY AS CURRICULUM

Building the Foundation. The foundation of *Student-Centered Inquiry as Curriculum* (see Figure 25.1) is to co-create an environment that allows for mutual

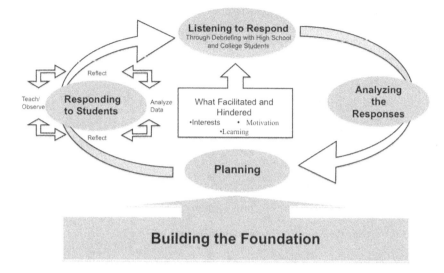

FIGURE 25.1. Student Centered Inquiry as Curriculum approach, by Oliver & Oesterreich (2013).

understanding, respect, and learning amongst all participants involved in the educational setting. We need to create valued spaces where students can speak, and where we as teachers re-tune our ears so that we can hear what they are saying and redirect our actions in response to what we hear. The foundation was designed to help the pre-service teachers understand the needs and interests of high school students with respect to physical activity, physical education, and the importance of a safe learning environment; help the high school students feel valued for their knowledge and perceptions of their worlds; and help the teacher educator to better understand the pre-service teachers' beliefs about youth and physical activity. This process involves two parts—a series of three lessons designed to gather data on students' perceptions, co-create a class environment that fosters learning and engagement, and seek input from students on areas of interest with respect to expected standards based learning (see sample lessons below).

INTERVIEW GUIDE—
BUILDING THE FOUNDATION LESSON #1: PEP 466

Goal: Your goal for this assignment is to gain some insights into students' perceptions of physical education. Modify this interview guide to suit your needs and the needs of the students you work with.

Suggested Interview Questions and Tips for Interviewing Adolescents:

- Writing before talking helps them to have time to think about what they want to say. The free writing exercises are a good way to start.
- Follow their leads. Let them go onto a tangent, you can gradually bring them back to the topic. Do not think you have to follow this guide in its given order…it is a guide.
- Remind them that there are no right or wrong answers. This is about understanding what they think and how they feel.
- ALWAYS ask them WHY, this helps them to elaborate.
- Tell them about yourself. If they are having a hard time answering a question tell them a story about some of your PE experiences.
- When you are talking with them try to use their words…this shows them that you are actually listening to them.
- Have fun with them…this is a great age group! ☺

Part I: Feelings During PE: Free writing exercises:

Give them 5 × 8 notecards and pencils and have them write on the following topics. Do one at a time. Give them about 2 minutes per question, or until you see them stop writing. Tell them to write as fast as they can whatever comes to mind about each topic. Tell them not to worry about spelling or grammar or complete sentences. Do not erase anything…it is ok to put a line through something if you don't want it there. When they are writing you too need to write with them. Just think back to your own PE experiences.

- Theme: PE, every sentence begins with: "Sometimes I wish…"
- Theme PE, every sentence begins with: "I get mad when…"
- Theme PE, every sentence begins with: "I get frustrated when…"
- Theme PE, every sentence begins with: "I get bored when…"
- Theme PE, every sentence begins with: "I get embarrassed when…"
- Theme PE, every sentence begins with: "I have fun when…"

Have them talk you through their cards, ask them to explain what they wrote in detail and let them talk together about their answers. LISTEN TO THEM and ask questions based on what THEY ARE SAYING.

Part II. Changes They Want in PE

- If you could change anything about PE what would you change? Why? If you could tell PE teachers 2 things to make PE better for people your age what you would say to them? Why?

Part III. Peer Interactions

- How do the young people get along in PE? Tell me about it.
- What problems do you see between the young people here? Tell me about them.
- What are some of the things that you enjoy most in PE that relate to other people your age? Tell me about them?
- If you could change anything about the way teens get along in PE what you would change? Why?

Building the Foundation—Lesson #2

CHS Lesson

1. Professor—share some of what we learned as a class from interviewing the CHS (just a brief overview of the main issues that influence student enjoyment and participation.) These are things that we will keep in mind as the semester moves forward.
    a. Students want variety in activities
    b. Students want to learn new activities
    c. Students want teachers to participate
    d. Students want all students to participate
    e. Students want to get to know each other so they can feel comfortable working with people
    f. Students want to be able to play with their friends
    g. Students don't want the entire class to be punished because of one student.
    h. Students want to be successful and not be singled out or made fun of
    i. Students want more time to play
    j. Students want more flexibility in the clothes they wear
    k. Students want the teacher to understand their needs, skill levels, fitness levels and interests better.
    l. Some students want less competition
    m. Students want teachers to listen to them
    n. Students want others to not bully or be disrespectful
2. And actually what you (high school students) have said sets up what we are planning to do next perfectly. Today I am going to ask you to get with another person that you do not know. The reason we are doing this is because you have collectively said PE is more fun when you are comfortable with your groups and this means you need more opportunity to get to know your classmates.
3. Like last time we are going to ask you to discuss things that influence your experience in PE. Today we will focus on class environment and what it means to create an environment where we all feel comfortable participating. From there we will come up with Ways of Working (what some people call rules but I detest that word as it assumes you can't behave). I'd prefer we agree to working in particular ways that allows us to all have opportunities to enjoy ourselves and learn.
4. When I say go get with 1 other person who you are comfortable with and two other sets partners you don't know well. Put NMSU folks with new people too.
5. NMSU students, working with your HS group, identify the main issues that influence how high school students experience their class environment. The big issues you will need to focus on include:
    a. How would you describe an emotionally and physically safe class environment? **(you might have to explain what this means)**
    b. What issues arise between students that influence whether a class environment is physically and emotionally safe?
        i. Why do these issues arise?
        ii. What can teachers do to prevent and/or stop these issues?
        iii. What can students do to prevent or stop these issues?

c. What issues arise between students and teachers that influence whether a class environment is physically and emotionally safe?
   i. Why do these issues arise (for both students and teachers)?
   ii. What can teachers do to prevent and/or stop these issues?
   iii. What can students do to prevent or stop these issues?
6. Depending on how the conversation goes you might ask the following specific questions—I think these might emerge from the bigger questions so start big and then move to these if they don't talk about bullying specifically.
   a. What does bullying look like?
   b. What do you want to see teachers do when students are bullying other students?
   c. What do you want to see students do when students are bullying other students?
7. Be prepared to share in a large group what you discuss in your small groups VERY briefly.
8. We will all come together in a large group and share what we discuss. We will talk about ways teachers and students can work together to create a positive learning environment. During this conversation, we will set up our class rules for how we will work together the rest of the semester. There needs to be something that deals with safety and respect for sure. Have students create a poster and sign their names.
9. You should take notes on what you are hearing to help you with your reflection/ assignment #1.

NMSU portion
1. Debrief what we did and why. Have students identify the strategies I was using and how I connected what we learned from the HS students to what we were doing that day.

BUILDING THE FOUNDATION—LESSON #2
DAY #6: STANDARDS LESSON

Lesson at the High School
1. Pass out name tags and pen and have everyone make a name tag and put it on. Explain that this is to help us all get to know each other's names. PLEASE keep your name tag for next class if possible.
2. Start by reminding students of the ways we have agreed to work together throughout the semester.
   ○ Be safe
   ○ Be open minded
   ○ Be respectful
   ○ Be supportive/helpful
   ○ Give your best effort

Let the class know that we trust that everyone will abide by these behaviors and if we have problems we will sit down as a class and figure out what we need to do differently to make class work better. But for now we will start here and assume that each of us will do the best we can do each day we are together. ☺

3. Explain what we will be doing with respect a process of identifying possible learning foci. Explain that students will start by working in a group of 2–3 students with 1 college person. For about 15 minutes spend time going over the NM PE Standards. These are what you should know and be able to do when you graduate from high school. Obviously this is not possible to cover in one year so we will focus our learning on a few areas that you as a class find interesting.
    a. On go get with a partner who you feel comfortable working with AND with whom you believe you share similar physical activity interests. If you are unsure or cannot find a partner come to me. Once you have a partner sit down next to your partner and wait for the next instruction. Let's try to do this in 15 seconds.
    b. In your group discuss the standards and possible learning themes…College students will lead this portion…each group will have a copy of the standards and a game card and an instruction sheet to refer to. Let's try to do this in no more than 15 minutes IF possible.
4. Once the groups have their learning themes written down and on their game card explain the game (see instruction sheet). When you have all groups' themes recorded come back and sit where you were with your college person.
    a. Have students play the game—about 20 minutes probably
    b. Once everyone is back in their groups college students will lead an analysis of the data. Working in your group come up with the 4 top themes for the boys and the top 4 themes for the girls. Next identify the top 4 common themes between the boys and girls. Be prepared to share your results with the large group.
    c. IF time—have groups share their results…If not have groups give their analysis information to their college person.
5. Talk about how we will use this information in our future planning and that next week we will start with sampler lessons that are designed to help broaden the youths' perspectives on what is possible content and possible teaching styles.
6. At NMSU—Start by going over what we did and why we did it.
7. Do group analysis of the data and brainstorm possible sampler lessons that cut across the standards

Task Sheets Needed for this Lesson
Instruction Sheet

Instructions— *Below are 5 Standards—These are things that the Department of Education in NM thinks high school students should know and be able to do by the time they graduate. Under each standard are examples of what you might learn if you were working toward meeting that particular standard. In your small group discuss each of the standards and what they mean with your college student.*

Once everyone in your group understands what the standards are and what is possible to learn, with your partner select the top 4 overall things you want to learn *and discuss why you want to learn these things.*

On your Game Card you will find a number in the top right hand corner....That is your group #. On the Game Card place your group number in each of your top choices of what you and your partner want to learn this semester. If you are confused ask your college student to show you what to do.

Standards and Learning Outcomes Task Sheet

Standard #1—Demonstrates competency in motor skills and movement patterns. What this means is that you are competent at different types of skills that are required for lifetime activities, dance and rhythms, and fitness activities.

In Standard #1 I want to learn:

_____Different skills that will allow me to participate in and enjoy different lifetime activities such as (tennis, self-defense, hiking, orienteering, golf etc.)

_____Different skills that will allow me to participate in and enjoy different dance and rhythm activities such as (e.g., line dancing, jazz dance, hip hop, ballet, social dance etc.)

_____Different skills that will allow me to participate in and enjoy different fitness activities such as (i.e., aerobics, Zumba, cardio kick boxing, circuit training, yoga, walking fitness, martial arts, etc.)

Standard #2—Applies knowledge of concepts, principles, strategies and tactics related to movement and performance. This standard means a variety of things. First it means that you know how to improve your sporting game play by using strategies to outmaneuver the other team (if a team sport—soccer) or opponent (if a dual sport—tennis). Second it means you know how to improve your performance (in dance or gymnastics) by applying different ideas related to moving. (e.g., keeping the beat to the music while doing aerobics or dancing; moving gracefully in a routine or dance). Third it means you know how to develop personal goals and practice plans related to improving physical activity performance or fitness levels.

In Standard #2 I want to learn:
___how to use complex movement concepts and principles to get better at the skills I need in sports or physical activities I like.
___how to develop the ability to learn, self-assess, and improve movement skills without help from others.
___how to develops an appropriate conditioning program for a self-selected game/ activity to engage in for life.
___how to develops realistic short-term and long-term physical fitness goals.

Standard #3—Demonstrates the knowledge and skills to achieve a health-enhancing level of physical activity and fitness.

In Standard #3 I want to learn:
___about the significance of physical activity in the maintenance of a healthy lifestyle.

___how to develop the skills, knowledge, and interest to maintain an active lifestyle.

___how to find ways to participate in physical activities on a regular basis.

___how to make conscious decisions regarding my physical activity participation and assume a mature role in managing my participation based on needs, personal interests, capabilities, and resources.

___how to demonstrate an understanding of how and why adult patterns of physical activity participation change throughout life and are capable of implementing meaningful strategies to deal with those changes (for example, time constraints due to work and/or family responsibilities)

___ how to evaluate commercials and advertisements that pertain to fitness and healthy living.

___how to create and implement a fitness program that includes all components of health-related fitness.

___how to design and implement a nutrition plan to maintain an appropriate energy balance for a healthy, active lifestyle.

___how to identify stress management strategies to reduce stress.

Standard #4—Exhibits responsible personal and social behavior that respects self and others.

In Standard # 4 I want to learn:

___how to identify barriers to my engagement in physical activity and learn to modify my physical activity patterns to increase my activity level.

___how to identify and critique body images in various forms of media that are unrealistic and can jeopardize my health.

___how to use proper etiquette while working with others in physical activity settings (for example disagreement in sport)

___how to use effective communication skills and strategies to promote team or group dynamics.

___ how to think critically and solve problems along and in a group within a physical activity or dance setting.

___how to apply best safety practices in physical activity settings.

___how to take leadership roles in physical activity settings.

Standard #5—Recognizes the value of physical activity for health, enjoyment, challenge, self- expression and/or social interaction.

In Standard #5 I want to learn:

___how to analyze health benefits of physical activities I like to do.

___how to choose an appropriate level of challenge to experience success in the types of activities I like to do.

___how to select physical activities or dance that meet my needs for self-expression and/or enjoyment.

___how to identify opportunities for social support in various physical activities or dance.

GAME CARD

Below is a list of possible things to learn this semester. We have taken out the description of the standards and put in the examples of things you might learn that help you to meet the individual standards. Please select your top 3–4 choices and put your GROUP # in the line provided.

Game directions. Your goal is to add to your game card EVERY group's top 3–4 learning interests. As fast as you can, you will work to talk to each group about what they want to learn and then put their group # on the appropriate line for their top 3–4 choices. In the end you should have all groups marked on the lines provided.

In Standard #1 I want to learn:

_____

Different skills that will allow me to participate in and enjoy different lifetime activities such as (tennis, self-defense, hiking, orienteering, golf etc.)

_____

Different skills that will allow me to participate in and enjoy different dance and rhythm activities such as (e.g., line dancing, jazz dance, hip hop, ballet, social dance etc.)

_____

Different skills that will allow me to participate in and enjoy different fitness activities such as (i.e., aerobics, Zumba, cardio kick boxing, circuit training, yoga, walking fitness, martial arts, etc.)

In Standard #2 I want to learn

_____

how to use complex movement concepts and principles to get better at the skills I need in sports or physical activities I like.

_____

how to develop the ability to learn, self-assess, and improve movement skills without help from others.

_____

how to develops an appropriate conditioning program for a self-selected game/ activity to engage in for life.

_____

how to develops realistic short-term and long-term physical fitness goals.

In Standard #3 I want to learn:

_____

about the significance of physical activity in the maintenance of a healthy lifestyle.

_____

how to develop the skills, knowledge, and interest to maintain an active lifestyle.

_____

how to find ways to participate in physical activities on a regular basis.

how to make conscious decisions regarding my physical activity participation and assume a mature role in managing my participation based on needs, personal interests, capabilities, and resources.

how to demonstrate an understanding of how and why adult patterns of physical activity participation change throughout life and are capable of implementing meaningful strategies to deal with those changes (for example, time constraints due to work and/or family responsibilities)

how to evaluate commercials and advertisements that pertain to fitness and healthy living.

how to create and implement a fitness program that includes all components of health-related fitness.

how to design and implement a nutrition plan to maintain an appropriate energy balance for a healthy, active lifestyle.

how to identify stress management strategies to reduce stress.

In Standard # 4 I want to learn:

how to identify barriers to my engagement in physical activity and learn to modify my physical activity patterns to increase my activity level.

how to identify and critique body images in various forms of media that are unrealistic and can jeopardize my health.

how to use proper etiquette while working with others in physical activity settings (for example disagreement in sport)

how to use effective communication skills and strategies to promote team or group dynamics.

how to think critically and solve problems along and in a group within a physical activity or dance setting.

how to apply best safety practices in physical activity settings.

how to take leadership roles in physical activity settings.

In Standard #5 I want to learn:

how to analyze health benefits of physical activities I like to do.

how to choose an appropriate level of challenge to experience success in the types of activities I like to do.

how to select physical activities or dance that meet my needs for self-expression and/or enjoyment.

how to identify opportunities for social support in various physical activities or dance.

Once these three lessons are taught, the professor and pre-service teachers analyze the data, looking for patterns that influence students' interest, motivation and learning in physical education. We also look for gaps in students learning of physical activity. Once this information is gathered and analyzed, we create and teach a variety of sample lessons designed to broaden students' perspectives of what is possible in physical education with respect to curriculum and pedagogy. Here we teach lessons around content the students have not experienced and we use multiple teaching styles so that students can experience a variety of ways to learn. Finally, we debrief with the high school students about what has facilitated and hindered their interest, motivation and learning with respect to what we have done and make decisions about how to move forward.

We take all the information we have gathered and use it to help us develop a "themed unit" (e.g., Helping students learn ways to increase physical activity outside of school) from which to create future content (see example of debriefing lesson below). The reason we moved to theme units as opposed to single content units such as volleyball, is because what fundamentally influenced students' interest, motivation and learning was having the opportunity to have a variety of physical activities. They consistently reported being bored when they played the same sport or physical activity over and over for an extended period of time.

Debriefing Guide: High School Student Debriefing Questions
1. In the time we have worked with you, which of the physical activities have most facilitated your interest? Why?
2. Which activities have least facilitated your interest? Why
3. In terms of what we have done thus far, what aspects of the class have motivated you to want to participate? Why?
4. What parts of the class have NOT motivated you to want to participate? Why?
5. In terms of your learning, what have we done thus far that has helped you learn best? Why
6. What have we done that has made it more difficult for you to learn? Why?
7. If you could give the college students 3 things that would make this class either more interesting, more motivating, or help you learn better what would they be?

Once the foundation is built, a one-time process, we move into the cyclical portion of SCIC. First comes planning.

Planning. Planning requires simultaneously matching young people's interests, motivation, and learning *with* teachers' knowledge of their content. Every time the pre-service teachers develop lesson plans, they need to identify how their lessons relate to student voice. That is, what did they learn from the building the foundation section that has influenced their planning. The content of the lessons must also be connected to the state standards in some capacity, but not reflect predesigned traditional curriculum. From planning we moved to responding to students.

Responding to Students. Responding to students allows the pre-service teachers to learn about teaching from the perspective of a teacher and an outside observer. In this process, they either teach or they observe and collect data on the people teaching. As the teacher, they teach; reflect on their teaching; receive observational data from their peers and analyze it; and reflect on their data analysis.

In the role of observer, the pre-service teachers collect data on different aspects of the class such as peer interactions, teacher behaviors (feedback, interactions), and body language of students. The observations center on factors that influence young people's interests, motivation, and learning of the content such as gender, skill level or body size. The observation data is useful in two ways. First, the observers really have to focus on what is happening with youth. They might watch exclusively the differences in how the teacher relates to girls or boys or to high skilled or low skilled students. They might observe how engaged girls are or how engaged boys are. It focuses their attention on one aspect of teaching and how that is influencing youth. Given that there are usefully 3–4 different people observing different aspects of the class, the teacher candidate receives information about what is going on while they are teaching. Usually the data reveal things that they missed while engaged in the process of teaching. It gives them a snapshot of what was going on in their class from the perspective of an outsider. From here we move to listening to respond.

Listening to Respond. In this phase, we debrief with the high school students (see debriefing sheet). The purpose of debriefing is two-fold. First, it creates a space for high school students to reflect on their experiences so that they can better understand what influences their interests, motivation, and learning. Second, it continues to center student voice to allow teacher candidates to better understand how their students are interpreting their curriculum and pedagogy. Finally, we analyze the responses.

Analyzing the Responses. In this phase, the pre-service teachers analyze the data gathered during the listening to respond phase as well as from their observation data and reflections from the responding to students phase. In this way, they utilize feedback from their experience as teachers and their students' experiences in the class. This analysis allows them to articulate changes they will make in their future planning and teaching, and gives them direction to the types of readings or materials they need in order to better facilitate their students' interests, motivation, and learning. Following this phase, we return to planning and begin the process over. The four-phase cyclical process of *Planning, Responding to Students, Listening to Respond*, and *Analyzing Responses* thus becomes student-centered inquiry *as* curriculum so that the basis of all content and pedagogical decisions arises from the reiteration of the four phases.

BENEFITS AND CHALLENGES OF STUDENT CENTERED INQUIRY AS CURRICULUM

Inquiry based field-experiences centered in student voice brings together the unique contexts that exist in specific classrooms (Cook-Sather, 2009a,b; Schultz, 2003; Short & Burke, 1996). When teacher educators create field-based experiences in which pre-service teachers must negotiate specific contextual knowledge, teaching and learning can no longer be directed from their own solitary values and beliefs (Joram & Gabriele, 1998; Oliver et al, 2015). *Student-Centered Inquiry as Curriculum* is an analytical scaffold that creates consequential changes in the pre-texts of pre-service teachers because the cacophony of voices and experiences makes solitary, long-held beliefs about teaching, learning, and young people impossible to hold on to (Oliver & Oesterreich, 2013). When pre-service teachers' pre-texts are placed in the contexts of trying to maintain a congruence between what they hear from student voices, their own experiences in schools, and their pretexts of teaching, learning, and youth, there is a collision between what they think they know and what they are experiencing that requires them to "rethink their assumptions about education and students" (Manor et al., 2010, p. 11). We use a SCIC approach in our teacher education programs because we are committed to challenging the status quo of teacher education and physical education and one way to do this is by challenging our pre-service teachers assumptions about teaching, learning, and youth.

Having used a SCIC approach in my secondary physical education methods course for nine years, I have had the opportunity to critically study the process of working with pre-service teachers and youth simultaneously. There are several benefits of using a SCIC approach in addition to challenging their assumptions about teaching and learning. First, it allows pre-service teachers to *experience* the process of co-creating a class environment based on what facilitates and hinders youths' interest, motivation and learning in physical education. Rather than telling them how to do it, they get to see and feel it for themselves. Second, it allows pre-service teachers to experience first-hand the time it takes to develop a class environment and the relationships that allow for student engagement and learning. Again, they get to experience how to negotiate with youth in order to create an environment that works for all members. Third, it allows pre-service teachers to collaboratively work to develop and implement PE curriculum across time. Rather than just read about it and create curriculum in a vacuum, they are actually doing it with youth and seeing the results of their work. This allows them to see the challenges and learn how to negotiate those challenges in the moment with others as opposed to having to do it alone. Finally, a SCIC process allows pre-service teachers to learn how to accommodate both skill level and interest differences that all classes exhibit. This is especially critical given that girls and low skilled boys are often marginalized in physical education classes.

While there are several benefits of using a SCIC approach with youth, there are also some challenges. One of the early challenges we faced before we structurally changed our teacher education curriculum was time to debrief with pre-service teachers after they worked with the youth and time for them to work in their groups. As such, we combined a 3 credit methods course with a 3 credit curriculum and assessment course to make a 6 credit secondary methods course. This allowed us to be able to work with youth in a PE setting daily for 75 minutes followed by another 75 minutes to debrief, analyze data, plan, and have time for group work across the semester. A SCIC is not nearly as useful and successful without this additional time together.

A second challenge that we have had to negotiate over the years is how to help pre-service teachers learn to manage the interpersonal dynamics that come from working in groups. While Kim was very cognizant of how she grouped her pre-service teachers, there can still be problems if the group members have diverse working habits. There is usually one group that struggles to work well together and often it takes much of the semester for them to figure it out and make it work. Being aware that this can cause problems can help teacher educators address some of these problems before they arise.

A final challenge to using a SCIC approach can occur when a PE class has a high number of students that have enjoyed traditional physical education that privilege team sport and competition. While the classes we have worked with over the last nine years have had only small numbers of kids that like traditional PE, teacher educators must work diligently with their pre-service teachers to not let the voices that mimic the status quo dominate. This is true in any situation, because it is far easier to hear the status quo than to hear resistance to that status quo. A SCIC approach allows the resistance to emerge, but we have to be mindful of not listening to that which is easier.

Overall, we have found that a SCIC approach to working with pre-service teachers as they work with youth better allows us to meet the needs of a diverse group of students, including girls and low skilled youth that have been historically marginalized. We are now using the SCIC approach in a variety of physical activity settings both in and out of schools and are finding some of the same benefits and challenges across culture and across settings (Luguetti & Oliver, 2017; Luguetti et al, 2017; Oliver et al, 2017).

REFERENCES

Collier, C. (2006). Models and curricula of physical education teacher education. In D. Kirk, D. Macdonald, & M. O'Sullivan (Eds.) *The handbook of physical education* (pp. 386–406). London, UK: SAGE Publications.

Cook-Sather, A. (2009a). 'I am not afraid to listen': Prospective teachers learning from students. *Theory Into Practice, 48*, 176–183. DOI: 10.1080/00405840902997261

Cook-Sather, A. (2009b). *Learning from student's perspectives: A sourcebook for effective teaching.* Boulder, CO: Paradigm.

Enright, E., & O'Sullivan M. (2012a). Physical education 'In all sorts of corners': Student activists transgressing formal physical education curricular boundaries. *Research Quarterly for Exercise and Sport, 83*, 255–267. DOI: 10.1080/02701367.2012.10599856

Fernandez-Balboa, J. M. (1997). Knowledge base in physical education teacher education: A proposal for a new Era. *Quest, 49*(2), 161–181.

Joram, E., & Gabriele, A. J. (1998). Pre-service teachers' prior beliefs: Transforming obstacles into opportunities. *Teaching and Teacher Education, 14*(2), 175–191.

Kirk, D. (2010a). *Physical education futures.* London, UK: Routledge.

Levine, A. (2006). *Educating school teachers.* Washington, DC: Education Schools Project.

Luguetti, C., & Oliver, K. L. (2017). 'Getting more comfortable in an uncomfortable space': Challenges in becoming an activist researcher in a socially vulnerable sport context. *Sport, Education and Society.* DOI: 10.1080/0271367.2016.1263719.

Luguetti, C., Oliver, K. L., Dantas, L. E. P. B. T., & Kirk, D. (2017). An activist approach to sport meets youth from socially vulnerable backgrounds: Possible learning aspirations. *Research Quarterly for Exercise and Sport.* DOI: 10.1080/02701367.2016.1263719

Manor, C. Block-Schulman, S., Flannery, K. & Felten, P. (2010). Foundations of student-faculty partnerships in the scholarship of teaching and learning. In C. Werder & M.M. Ortis (Eds.), *Engaging student voices in the study of teaching and learning* (pp. 3–15). Sterling, VA: Stylus.

McIntyre, D. J., Byrd, D. M., & Foxx, S. M. (1996). Field and laboratory experiences. In J. Sikula, T. J. Buttery, & E. Guyton (Eds.) *Handbook of research on teacher education: A project of the association of teacher educators* (pp. 171–193). New York, NY: Macmillian.

National Council for *Accreditation of Teacher Education. (2010). Transforming teacher education through clinical practice: A national strategy to prepare effective teachers: Report of the Blue Ribbon Panel on Clinical Preparation and Partnerships for Improved Student Learning.* Washington, DC: National Council for Accreditation of Teacher Education.

National Council on Teacher Quality. (2010). *Blueprint for change: National summary.* Washington, DC: National Council on Teacher Quality.

Oliver, K. L. (1999). Adolescent girls' body-narratives: Learning to desire and create a 'fashionable' image. *Teachers College Record, 101*(2), 220–246.

Oliver, K. L., & Hamzeh, M. (2010). 'The boys won't let us play': 5th grade *Mestizas* publicly challenge physical activity discourse at school. *Research Quarterly for Exercise and Sport, 81*, 39–51. DOI: 10.1080/02701367.2010.10599626.

Oliver, K. L., Hamzeh, M., & McCaughtry, N. (2009). 'Girly girls *can* play games/*las niñas pueden jugar tambien'*: Co-creating a curriculum of possibilities with 5th grade girls. *Journal of Teaching in Physical Education, 28*, 90–110.

Oliver, K. L., & Kirk, D. (2015). *Girls, physical education and gender: An activist perspective.* London, UK: Routledge Publishers.

Oliver, K. L., & Lalik, R. (2000). *Bodily knowledge: Learning about equity and justice with adolescent girls.* New York, NY: Peter Lang Publishing, Inc.

Oliver, K. L., & Lalik, R. (2004). Critical inquiry on the body in girls' physical education classes: A critical poststructural analysis. *Journal of Teaching in Physical Education 23*, 162–195.

Oliver, K. L. Luguetti, C., Aranda, R., Nunez-Enriquez, O., & Rodriguez, A. A. (2017). 'Where do I go from here?': Learning to become activist teachers through a community of practice. *Physical Education and Sport Pedagogy*, DOI: 10.1080/17408989.2017.1350263.

Oliver, K. L., & Oesterreich, H. A. (2013). Student-centered inquiry as curriculum as a model for field-based teacher education. *Journal of Curriculum Studies, 45*, 394–417.

Oliver, K. L. & Oesterreich, H. A. *with* Aranda, R., Archuleta,J., Blazer, C., De La Cruz, K., Martinez, D., McConnell, J., Osta, M., Parks, L., & Robinson, R. (2015). 'The sweetness of struggle': Innovation in PETE through student-centered inquiry as curriculum in a physical education methods course. *Physical Education and Sport Pedagogy 20*(1), 97–115. DOI: 10.1080/17408989.2013.803527

O'Sullivan, M., & MacPhail, A. (Eds.). (2010). *Young people's voices in physical education and youth sport.* London, UK: Routledge.

Schultz, K. (2003). *Listening: A framework for teaching Across differences.* New York, NY: Teachers College Press.

Short, K. G., & Burke, C. (1996). Examining our beliefs and practices through inquiry. *Language Arts, 73*(2), 97–104.

CPSIA information can be obtained
at www.ICGtesting.com
Printed in the USA
BVHW040536011019
559848BV00004B/22/P

9 781641 137195